W9-CNM-233

# NATURAL RESOURCE ECONOMICS

# NATURAL RESOURCE ECONOMICS

## Issues, Analysis, and Policy

CHARLES W. HOWE

Department of Economics
University of Colorado

JOHN WILEY & SONS

New York · Chichester · Brisbane · Toronto

Copyright © 1979, by John Wiley & Sons, Inc.

All rights reserved. Published simultaneously in Canada.

Reproduction or translation of any part of
this work beyond that permitted by Sections
107 and 108 of the 1976 United States Copyright
Act without the permission of the copyright
owner is unlawful. Requests for permission
or further information should be addressed to
the Permissions Department, John Wiley & Sons, Inc.

*Library of Congress Cataloging in Publication Data:*

Howe, Charles W
  Natural resource economics.

  Bibliography: p.
  Includes index.
  1. Natural resources.  I. Title.

HC55.H69     333     78-24174
ISBN 0-471-04527-6

Printed in the United States of America

10 9 8 7 6 5 4 3 2 1

# To ALLEN V. KNEESE

*expositor, policy analyst,*
*and foresighted research leader*

*with thanks for counsel,*
*trust, and friendship*

# Preface

Natural resources have attracted increasing attention in the 1970s as energy, food, water, and other resources have undergone a sequence of crises. There is greatly heightened concern about national and world capacities for producing sufficient reproducible resource commodities (e.g., products of agriculture, forestry, and water), and perhaps even greater concern over the implications of world and national dependence on finite stocks of nonrenewable resources (e.g., the fossil fuels and nonfuel minerals). These issues of resource availability have been associated more and more with environmental problems resulting from expanded energy use, the exploitation of more diffuse resources, deforestation, and certain agricultural practices. The accumulation of pollutants in the atmosphere, the soils, and in water bodies has become a global phenomenon, no longer limited to local or regional settings.

This book integrates the field of natural resource economics for the first time, exhibiting the common structure of many of the prominent natural resource management problems, whether they relate to renewable or nonrenewable resources, at the economywide level or within particular natural resource sectors. Throughout the book, the theoretical formulation of problems and the use of the tools of economic analysis to analyze those problems are accompanied by historical and contemporary real-world illustrations. Several extended case studies are included, and the policy implications of the analyses are clearly drawn. In accomplishing these objectives, the book utilizes the most up-to-date theoretical and empirical research results, not only from economics but from geology, hydrology, and the environmental sciences. This book seeks to establish this broader context within which natural resource issues can be understood and evaluated.

Markets continue to play important roles in the development and allocation over time of natural resources, both nationally and internationally. Therefore, an understanding of the functioning of markets and their strengths and weaknesses is important. These markets, along with government agencies, produce data from which we must infer the evolving natural resources situation and its implications for human welfare. Are resources growing scarcer? Is this important? Will past solutions continue to work? A data base of the available evidence on these issues is presented and analyzed.

The analytical framework first applied to macroeconomic growth is specialized to the analysis of the particular resource scarcity situations in several key natural resources sectors: energy, nonenergy minerals, forestry, fisheries, water resources, and preserved natural environments. The problems and policy issues of these sectors are described and analyzed in a dynamic management context.

The book concludes with a review of the factors that will be critical to our future natural resources situation, and seeks to derive from the earlier analysis a set of guidelines for the formulation of what is called a "responsible natural resources policy" that emphasizes intergenerational equity.

This book is intended for upper-division undergraduates and graduate students taking a first course in natural resource economics. Typical undergraduate economics majors with principles, intermediate theory, and quantitative methods courses behind them are ideally prepared to use these materials, but students from many disciplines with principles of economics and college mathematics will be sufficiently prepared. The course will attract students from geography, geology, political science, engineering, agriculture, ecology, forestry, and conservation. Masters candidates from these disciplines often take the course, especially when it can be applied toward graduate credit.

The book provides a full semester's work without outside supplementation. The bibliography provides a highly *selected* list of readings that can be used by the instructor to add emphasis to particular areas, but this is not at all necessary. The mode of presentation alternates among verbal exposition, graphical analysis, and simple mathematical models. Whenever mathematical tools are used, clear verbal summaries of results are provided for the nonmathematical reader. While a particular mathematical tool (e.g., the selective use of results from optional control theory) may be thought of as "advanced math," the application of a single basic theorem often permits the quick derivation of important results that would otherwise have to be derived through tedious, notationally burdensome approaches.

St. Paul
May 1978
                                                    Charles W. Howe

# Acknowledgments

Had it not been for a sabbatical leave, publication of this book would have been much delayed, so I thank the Department of Economics of the University of Colorado for granting the leave and the Department of Agricultural and Applied Economics of the University of Minnesota for providing an appointment as Hill Visiting Professor.

Among the many persons who have generously assisted the author, several have been particularly helpful. Dwight R. Lee, of the University of Colorado, shared with the author for several years the teaching of the basic course in natural resource economics at the University of Colorado, which led to the idea of this book. This collaboration has been a rich experience for me. V. Kerry Smith, of Resources for the Future, Inc., provided extensive and penetrating critiques of several versions of the manuscript, always suggesting alternative approaches and valuable literature (much of it his own writing) bearing on the subject. The entire undertaking would have been much more modest without this input. Lee R. Martin, of the Department of Agricultural and Applied Economics, University of Minnesota, generously read and reread several versions of the core chapters, always insisting on clarity of exposition and greater generality of the analytical framework. It was through extended conversations with him that much of the unity of the natural resources field became clear to me. Anthony C. Fisher, of Resources for the Future, Inc. and the University of California, Berkeley, provided many of the insights on which this book was constructed. His seminal paper "On Measures of Natural Resource Scarcity" (1979) profoundly affected the approach taken in this book.

Others who have been of great assistance are Harold J. Barnett of Washington University, whose earlier work constitutes a major building stone of current resource economics and who gave guidance to an early draft; Daniel W. Bromley, of the University of Wisconsin, who critiqued earlier outlines and pointed to important omissions (some of which remain); Gardner Brown, of the University of Washington, and Barry C.

ix

Field, of the University of Miami, whose joint work on indicators of scarcity contributed greatly to this book; Emery N. Castle, of Resources for the Future, Inc., who reviewed one draft; Marion Clawson, of Resources for the Future, Inc., who has shown many how to do effective applied research and who taught the author a lot about forestry; Ronald G. Cummings, of the University of New Mexico, whose exuberance over natural resource economics has been a stimulus to the author for a long time; K. William Easter, of the University of Minnesota, who coauthored an earlier book and provided stimulating discussions during this leave period; Robert H. Haveman, of the University of Wisconsin, with whom many beneficial discussions have been held; John V. Krutilla, of Resources for the Future, Inc., whose pioneering research in water and natural environments opened those important areas to economics; Richard B. Norgaard, of the University of California, Berkeley, who critiqued the first draft; Clifford S. Russell, of Resources for the Future, Inc., who provided detailed critique of the earlier chapters; Vernon W. Ruttan, of Minnesota, who demonstrated the importance of induced innovation to the author; and Anthony Scott, of the University of British Columbia, who provided many excellent suggestions for broadening the treatment to include institutional issues. John S. Howe, currently a graduate student at Purdue University, sought out much of the data presented in the book and acted as a student soundingboard for many of the ideas. Frederick H. Bell and Manuel H. Johnson, Jr., of Florida State University, provided their updated series of the Barnett and Morse data base. P. J. Wilkinson, former economics editor with John Wiley and Sons, Inc., was extremely helpful in the task of defining the audience to which the book should be directed and in keeping me in that track.

Not at all the least of the help was that of Frances Macy, in the Department of Economics at Colorado, who was of tremendous assistance in many ways but, of particular relevance, helped protect some of my time over the several years when the book was being conceived. She also typed part of the first draft. Linda L. Schwartz, of the Department of Agricultural and Applied Economics at Minnesota, completed the typing of the first draft and typed the entire final draft, in good humor and in keeping with the deadlines, and all for a visitor. To her, many thanks.

C.W.H.

# Table of Contents

*List of Figures*                                                      xvii
*List of Tables*                                                        xxv

1. **Overview of the Natural Resources Field**                          1

    1.1.  Characteristics and Definitions                               1
    1.2.  Major Natural Resource Issues                                 3
    1.3.  Historical Background                                         6
    1.4.  Reserves, Rates of Use, and Exploration                       7
    1.5.  Scarcity of Resources                                        10
    1.6.  Factors Mitigating Scarcity                                  11
    1.7.  The Long-Term Outlook                                        13
    1.8.  The Role of Economics in Natural Resources
          Policy Formulation and Management                            14

2. **Natural Resource Commodity Production and *in Situ*
   Stocks: A Conceptual Framework and Empirical Survey**              16

    2.1.  A Basic Model of Natural Resources Use                       17
    2.2.  The Nature of Natural Resource Stocks                        19
    2.3.  Motivations for Holding Reserves                             24
    2.4.  Interpreting Reserve-to-Use Ratios                           25
    2.5.  The Historical and Current Natural Resource
          Situation in the United States                              27

3. **Natural Resources Concern Is Not New**                           44

    3.1.  Historical Episodes of Natural Resources
          Concern                                                     44

3.2.  Natural Resources in Classical Economic
      Thought                                                    49
3.3.  The American Conservation Movement and
      Related Issues                                             52
3.4.  U.S. Government Agencies and Programs
      Involved in Natural Resources Management                   58


**4.  The Impacts of Natural Resource Availability on
     Economic Growth: Forms and Effects of Scarcity            61**

4.1.  A Model of Frontier and Simple Ricardian
      Economies                                                 62
4.2.  Special Examples of the Frontier and Simple
      Ricardian Economies                                       65
4.3.  A Malthusian Special Case                                 68
4.4.  A Simple Ricardian Economy With Technological
      Change                                                    69
4.5.  Natural Resource Stock Effects and the Concept
      of User Cost                                              71
4.6.  Stock Effects, User Cost, and Rents on *in situ*
      Natural Resources                                         75
4.7.  A Generalized Model of User Cost and Scarcity
      Rents                                                     79
4.8.  Further Analysis of Economic Growth Potential
      Under a Fixed Supply of Natural Resources                 82
4.9.  Summary                                                   87


**5.  Optimal Resource Use Over Time and Likely Market
     Behavior                                                  89**

5.1.  A Basic Model of Optimum Natural Resource
      Use Over Time                                             90
5.2.  The Pattern of Natural Resource Use Over Time
      Under a Competitive Market Structure                      94
5.3.  The Pattern of Natural Resource Use Under a
      Monopolistic Market Structure                             97
5.4.  Market Adjustment Processes                               98
5.5.  The Stability of Natural Resource Market
      Adjustment Processes                                     101

5.6.  A Review of Reasons for Market Failure to
      Achieve Optimum Patterns of Resource Use
      Over Time                                                     103
5.7.  Summary                                                       107


6.  **Empirical Indicators of Evolving Natural Resources
    Scarcity**                                                     **108**

6.1.  Further Observations on Prices as Indicators of
      Natural Resources Scarcity                                    111
6.2.  Relative Price Evidence                                       114
6.3.  Scarcity Rents: Prices of *in situ* Resources                118
6.4.  Unit Costs of Natural Resource Commodity
      Production                                                    119
6.5.  Evidence on Elasticities of Substitution of Other
      Inputs for Natural Resources                                 121
6.6.  The Commission on Population Growth and the
      American Future: Population, Resources, and
      Environment                                                  127
6.7.  Summary of the Evidence                                      127


7.  **Factors Mitigating Natural Resources Scarcity**             **129**

7.1.  The Salvation of Telluride: An Example of the
      Process of Adaptation                                        129
7.2.  Technological Innovation                                     130
7.3.  The Process of Natural Resource Discovery and
      Related Technological Changes                                132
7.4.  Technological Changes Increasing the Efficiency
      of Resource Recovery                                         134
7.5.  Technological Changes Facilitating Substitutions
      in Production Processes Away from Scarce
      Resources                                                    135
7.6.  Scale Economies                                              137
7.7.  Facilitating Substitutions in Consumption                   139
7.8.  Improved Transportation and Trade                           139
7.9.  Recycling                                                    140
7.10. Do We "Waste" Natural Resources?                             144
7.11. Will Mitigating Forces Continue in the Future?              147

8.  **Intertemporal Comparisons of Well-being: Efficiency, Equity, and Risk**                                             **149**

    8.1.  Criteria for Intertemporal Decision Making: Pareto Efficiency                                                   151
    8.2.  The Determination of "Present Values" of Benefits and Costs through Discounting                                 152
    8.3.  The "Social Time Preference" Approach to Discounting                                                            155
    8.4.  What Discounting Does *Not* Do                                                                                  158
    8.5.  Considerations of Risk and Uncertainty in Natural Resources Planning and Management                            160
    8.6.  Alternatives to the Intertemporal Discounting Type of Criterion for Natural Resources Planning                 165

9.  **The Management of Energy Resources**                                                                               **169**

    9.1.  Factors Leading to the 1973 Energy Crisis                                                                       170
    9.2.  An Economic Analysis of the Energy Crisis                                                                       173
    9.3.  Aftermath of the Energy Crisis                                                                                  177
    9.4.  International Comparison of Energy Use                                                                          181
    9.5.  The Outlook for New Supplies of Energy Commodities                                                              186
    9.6.  Nuclear Power: The Great Dilemma                                                                                196

10. **Mineral Availability and Exploration**                                                                             **203**

    10.1. Physical Characteristics of Mineral Resource Availability                                                       203
    10.2. The Effects of Exploration on the Socially Optimal Paths of Natural Resource Use, Price, and *in situ* Rents    208
    10.3. Dealing with the Risks of Exploration and Development from the Mining Firm's Viewpoint: Baysean Decision Strategies  212
    10.4. Exploration and Discovery from Society's Viewpoint                                                              218
    10.5. Summary and Outlook                                                                                            219

**11.　The Economics of Forest Management**　　　　　　　　**221**

　　11.1.　Background of U.S. Forestry　　　　　　　　　　221
　　11.2.　Timber Harvesting Practices: The Optimum
　　　　　Rotation　　　　　　　　　　　　　　　　　　225
　　11.3.　The Optimum Rotation: Mathematical Derivation　228
　　11.4.　Sensitivity Analysis of the Optimum Rotation　　230
　　11.5.　Multiple-Use Forestry Management　　　　　　　232
　　11.6.　Some Traditional Concepts in Forest
　　　　　Management　　　　　　　　　　　　　　　　235
　　11.7.　Unanswered Questions and Future
　　　　　Developments　　　　　　　　　　　　　　　237

**12.　Common Property Resources: Theory and Examples**　**241**

　　12.1.　The Analytics of the Static Common Property
　　　　　Problem　　　　　　　　　　　　　　　　　　243
　　12.2.　Congestion of Facilities as a Case of Common
　　　　　Property Resource Management　　　　　　　　245
　　12.3.　Environmental Pollution as a Case of Common
　　　　　Property Resource Management　　　　　　　　248
　　12.4.　Policy Tools for Improving the Management of
　　　　　Common Property Resources　　　　　　　　　249
　　12.5.　More on Congestion in Natural Resource
　　　　　Systems　　　　　　　　　　　　　　　　　　252

**13.　The Management of Fisheries: A Case of Renewable
　　　but Destructible Common Property Resources**　　　**256**

　　13.1.　Basic Biological Relationships　　　　　　　　258
　　13.2.　An Example of a Static Fisheries Management
　　　　　Model　　　　　　　　　　　　　　　　　　261
　　13.3.　Optimum Fisheries Management Over Time　　　263
　　13.4.　The Dynamic Behavior of a Competitively
　　　　　Exploited Fishery　　　　　　　　　　　　　267
　　13.5.　Regulation Alternatives for Fisheries
　　　　　Management　　　　　　　　　　　　　　　　270
　　13.6.　Summary　　　　　　　　　　　　　　　　274

**14.  Water Resource Systems**                                          **276**

    14.1.  Characteristics of Water Resource Systems         276
    14.2.  The Nature of Water System Developments           282
    14.3.  The Colorado River: A Brief Case Study            291
    14.4.  Economic Aspects of Groundwater Management        295
    14.5.  Water Quality Management                          302
    14.6.  Minimum Cost of Meeting Standards                 307
    14.7.  Two Case Studies of Water Quality Management      308
    14.8.  Some Characteristics of the Demand for Water      311


**15.  Natural Areas and Ecosystems as Natural Resources**               **316**

    15.1.  Economic Aspects of Unique Natural Areas          318
    15.2.  Measuring the Demand for Outdoor Recreation       321
    15.3.  A Suggested Benefit-Cost Exercise in Comparing
           Development with Preservation                     327
    15.4.  Closing Observations on the Natural
           Environment as Amenity and Constraint            328


**16.  Elements of a Responsible Natural Resources Policy**              **330**

    16.1.  Definition of a Responsible Natural Resources
           Policy                                            331
    16.2.  A Review of Critical Factors Conditioning Future
           Natural Resource Availability                     332
    16.3.  Guidelines for a Responsible Natural Resources
           Policy                                            335
    16.4.  Necessary Conditions for a Responsible
           Decision-making Process                           337


    **Bibliography**                                              **340**
    **Index**                                                     **345**

# Figures

2.1  U.S. Bureau of Mines/U.S. Geological Survey
mineral and coal resource and reserve categories          21

2.2  Availability diagram for uranium (expressed as
$U_3O_8$)                                                  23

2.3  U.S. population, 1900–1980; consumption of raw
materials, 1900–1969                                       27

2.4  Resource sectors: per capita consumption             28

2.5  Mineral sectors: per capita consumption              29

2.6  Production of raw materials in the United States:
1960–1969                                                  30

2.7  Annual visits to various types of recreation areas,
1920–1976                                                  31

2.8  Employment and output: resource industries as
percent of all industries                                 32

2.9  Estimated labor requirements: total agriculture
and agricultural sectors (at five-year intervals)         33

2.10  Employment: total mining and mining sectors (at
five-year intervals)                                       33

2.11  Resources, manufacturing, gross national
product: employment/output                                34

2.12  Resource sectors: employment/output                 34

2.13 Price indexes for raw materials, finished
commodities, and all wholesale commodities in
the United States: 1900–1969                               35

2.14 All extractive: net trade as percent of consumption
(1954 prices—gold and silver excluded)                    42

2.15 Agriculture: net trade as percent of consumption      42

2.16 Net trade: all minerals except gold and silver        42

2.17 Mineral fuels: net imports (five-year averages)       43

3.1 Depletion history of Lake Superior district iron
ore, showing overlapping stages of depletion of a
mining region                                              47

3.2 Ricardian increasing costs                             51

4.1 Input transfortation curves, GNP isoquants, and
the optimum expansion path of a simple Ricardian
economy                                                   64

4.2 Growth in a frontier economy                           65

4.3 Growth of GNP in a malthusian economy with a
fixed limit on the input of $R_0$                         68

4.4 Hypothetical costs of exploiting two deposits          77

4.5 The short-run supply curve                             77

4.6 The time paths of the rent on *in situ* resources and
optimum resource use                                      81

5.1 Characterization of the optimal rate of natural
resource commodity production at each instant $t$         93

5.2 Paths of socially optimum and competitively
determined natural resource commodity
production and *in situ* stocks                            96

5.3    Paths of natural resource commodity price and *in
       situ* scarcity rents along the socially optimum and
       competitive paths                                              96

5.4    Initial monopolistic and competitive production
       rates and prices for given $q(0)$ and $S(0)$                   98

5.5    A simple depiction of the natural resources
       commodity market and the *in situ* resources
       market                                                         99

5.6    The imposition of an effective price ceiling                   105

5.7    Unregulated and regulated results with constant
       *MC*: an example                                               106

6.1    Douglas fir stumpage price relative to Douglas fir
       lumber price                                                   113

6.2    Production and price history of mercury in the
       United States                                                 114

6.3a   Forestry products                                             116

6.3b   Agricultural products                                         116

6.3c   Metals                                                        116

6.3d   Fuels                                                         116

6.4    Differing degrees of substitutability between
       labor-capital and natural resources                           122

7.1    Average cost curves, Model *A*                                138

7.2    Optimal reuse ratio for paper residuals in the
       production of newsprint                                       141

8.1    Net benefit streams of three alternative policy
       changes or projects                                           153

8.2   Typical time pattern of construction costs, site
      opportunity costs, and benefits from a water
      project                                                   159

9.1   The postwar energy market                                174

9.2   The market for gasoline in 1973–1974                     176

9.3   Energy intensiveness for the United States              178

9.4   The 1967 energy intensiveness of consumer goods
      and services                                             179

9.5   The 1967 energy intensiveness of capital
      investments                                              180

9.6   The energy/GNP ratio for several countries over
      time, with hydroelectric power counted at 3
      kwht/kwhe                                                182

9.7   1973 per capita energy consumption rate versus
      per capita GNP                                           183

9.8   Past estimates and future projections of world
      ultimate oil reserves                                    188

9.9   Global proved reserves at year end—annual and
      cumulative crude oil production (MMbbls)                 189

9.10  Reserves proved annually in United States,
      world (MMbbls)                                           190

9.11  Potential oil-bearing areas and worldwide
      concentration of oil drilling                            191

9.12  History of exploratory drilling and discoveries of
      $8 per pound $U_3O_8$                                     197

9.13  Discovery rate compared to cumulative
      exploration                                              198

9.14   Cumulative production and cumulative
       discoveries                                                                        199

9.15   Possible cycle of production for $U_3O_8$                               199

10.1   Production history of the Comstock Lode in
       Nevada                                                                               205

10.2   Energy requirements for recovering abundant and
       scarce elements                                                                 207

10.3   Possible distributions of scarce and abundant
       minerals                                                                            208

10.4   Decision tree for test-drilling and development
       decisions                                                                           217

11.1   Determination of the optimum rotation                             227

11.2   Timber management costs and values per
       thousand board feet of timber sold: U.S. national
       forests, 1972 and 1973                                                       233

11.3   Distributions of numbers of trees and volumes of
       timber by age class in a fully regulated forest               236

11.4   Average stumpage prices for all timber sold, State
       of Washington, 1959–1976                                                 238

12.1   The static common property model                                   244

12.2   The congestion model                                                       247

12.3   The pollution model                                                           249

12.4   Determination of optimum and equilibrium traffic
       flows                                                                                 255

13.1   Age distribution of a fish population                               258

13.2   Size, biomass, and number as functions of
       year–class age                                                                   259

13.3    Idealized and achievable catch-effort relationships          259

13.4    The stock-growth relation                                    260

13.5    Constant stock catch-effort relation                         262

13.6    Possible time paths and equilibrium points for the
        number of firms and the fish stock in a
        competitive fishery                                          269

13.7    The effects of optimum taxes on catches                      273

14.1    The hydrograph of Oaks Creek, Susquehanna
        Basin                                                        277

14.2    Annual flow of the Colorado River at Lees Ferry
        and monthly flow of a desert stream                          278

14.3    The long-term average flow of the Colorado River
        at Lees Ferry, Arizona                                       279

14.4    Distribution of average annual runoff in the
        United States                                                283

14.5    Percentage of mean annual runoff equalled or
        exceeded in 19 of 20 years                                   284

14.6    River flows and withdrawal rates                             286

14.7    A Rippl diagram                                              287

14.8    Storage required in the Upper Missouri Basin                 288

14.9    Average and marginal costs of water supply at the
        storage site, Upper Missouri Basin                           290

14.10   The Colorado River Basin                                     292

14.11   Percentage of water pumped actually diverted
        from the river                                               300

14.12   A water body surrounded by pollutors and
        receptors                                                    303

14.13   Reaction functions for various levels of abatement:
        Wisconsin River                                                                      310

14.14   Demand function for water withdrawals: 1000
        tons per day ammonia plant                                                   314

15.1    Irreversibility of development of natural areas and
        the asymmetry of technological change                               317

15.2    Hypothetical demands for and costs of producing
        recreational services and gravel in Yosemite Park             318

15.3    A segment of a consumer's utility function
        depicting option demand                                                        319

15.4    Simulated demand function for big-game hunting         324

15.5    Shifting recreation demand curves                                   326

# Tables

1.1     Ratios of U.S. reserves to extraction rates     10

2.1     Relation between reserve-resource terminology and characteristics of natural stocks     20

2.2     Resource stock definitions relating to the reliability of geological knowledge     22

2.3     Date of exhaustion as a function of $T$ and $r$     26

2.4     World proved oil reserves year end, 1955, 1966, 1972     36

2.5     Production and proved reserves of oil and natural gas, United States, 1964–1973     37

2.6     United States and world reserves of selected nonfuel minerals, ca. 1968     38

4.1     Overall returns to scale     67

4.2     Percentage rates of GNP growth with technological change in the Cobb-Douglas model     71

4.3     Definitions of terms relating to natural resources scarcity     78

6.1     The linear relative price hypothesis: 1870–1972     115

6.2     Prices of minerals relative to labor, 1970 = 100     117

6.3   Countries exhibiting significant upward
      exponential trends in agricultural prices relative to
      the wholesale price index                                    118

6.4   Summary of Barnett and Morse's results                       120

6.5   Partial elasticities of substitution: U.S. agriculture       124

6.6   Partial elasticities of substitution, 1963                   124

6.7   Partial elasticities of substitution, 1967                   125

6.8   Partial elasticities in electric power generation            125

6.9   Partial elasticities of substitution among capital
      (K), labor (L), energy (E), and other intermediate
      materials (M): U.S. manufacturing 1947–1971                  126

7.1   Generation of solid wastes from five major sources
      in 1967                                                      142

7.2   Some reported compositions of mixed solid
      residuals collected by municipalities                        143

7.3   Annual domestic prompt and obsolete scrap
      consumption for selected commodities in the late
      1960s                                                        144

9.1   Total U.S. energy consumption (BTU and
      percentage by source)                                        169

9.2   Posted prices of Arabian crude oil                           170

9.3   World energy consumption and population,
      selected years, 1925–1972                                    171

9.4   World energy consumption, 1950–1973                          172

9.5   U.S. energy and oil consumption                              172

9.6   Production and proved reserves of oil and natural
      gas, United States, 1964–1973                                173

TABLE                                                                        xxvii

9.7     U.S. elasticities of demand for electricity                      175

9.8     Per capita energy consumption in the United
        States and Sweden in 1971                                        184

9.9     Energy use per dollar of value added in industry
        (kwh/$)                                                          185

9.10    Energy price comparisons: United States and
        Sweden (1974 unless otherwise indicated)                        186

9.11    Estimates of world ultimate reserves of crude oil
        from conventional sources                                       187

9.12    Shale oil resources of the world land areas                     192

9.13    Shale oil resources by country                                  192

9.14    World natural gas reserves (January 1, 1975)                    194

9.15    Ultimate U.S. uranium reserves and projected
        year of exhaustion                                              200

9.16    Dollar estimates of health effects                              202

10.1    Cutoff grade and crustal abundance for selected
        minerals                                                        204

10.2    Percentage distributions by weight and value of
        the U.S. use of the non-fossil non–renewable
        resources, 1975                                                 206

10.3    The joint probability distributions of mine
        characteristics and drilling results                           216

10.4    The posterior probabilities of mine characteristics,
        given the drilling results                                     216

11.1    Data on productive forest lands in the United
        States: 1970 by ownership                                      222

11.2    Degree of compatibility among various forest uses             224

11.3     Determination of the optimum rotation for
         Douglas fir                                                                       230

12.1     Inputs, outputs, and delay costs of a three-dam
         river system                                                                      254

14.1     Current annual consumptive rates of use of
         Colorado River water in the Lower Colorado Basin                                  293

14.2     Solution for the optimum rate of groundwater use
         in La Costa de Hermosillo                                                         299

14.3     Annual systemwide treatment costs of specified
         DO goals under alternative strategies: the
         Delaware River                                                                    309

14.4     Costs of alternative water quality management
         systems: the Wisconsin River                                                      310

14.5     Patterns of household water use from the Johns
         Hopkins Residential Water Use Research Project                                    312

14.6     Residential water use before and after metering:
         Boulder, Colorado                                                                 313

14.7     Marginal value of water as a function of water
         applied, by farm size, Tulare County, California                                 315

# NATURAL RESOURCE ECONOMICS

# Chapter 1

# OVERVIEW OF THE NATURAL RESOURCES FIELD

## 1.1. CHARACTERISTICS AND DEFINITIONS

Natural resources could refer to all the living and nonliving endowment of the earth, but traditional usage confines the term to naturally occurring resources and systems that are useful to humans or could be under plausible technological, economic, and social circumstances. Today, however, we must augment this definition to include environmental and ecological systems. The major classes of natural resources are agricultural land; forest land and its multiple products and services; natural land areas preserved for esthetic, recreational, or scientific purposes; the fresh and salt water fisheries; mineral resources that include the mineral fuels and nonfuels; the renewable nonmineral energy sources of solar, tidal, wind, and geothermal systems; water resources; and the waste-assimilative capacities of all parts of the environment. After removal from their natural settings, resources are often called natural resource commodities. From these definitions it becomes clear that what we perceive as natural resources depends on the conditions we have inherited from the past, present or foreseen technologies, economic conditions, and tastes. A century ago, the Mesabi Range was yet to be exploited, environmental problems were only local issues, aluminum was a mere curiosity, and uranium was unknown.

Natural resource uses include direct consumption such as fresh fish, water, outdoor recreation, and firewood; inputs into intermediate processing such as iron or copper ores into smelting; consumptive uses in intermediate processing such as fuels consumed in manufacturing and transport; and *in situ* uses like free-running rivers, parks, and wilderness areas. In some cases, these modes of utilization can be combined into multiple-purpose natural resource systems that utilize resources simultaneously to satisfy several needs. An example would be the management of forest lands to produce timber, to act as a water shed, and to provide recreation.

Natural resource supplies must be thought of both in terms of the stocks or inventories that are thought to exist at the moment (reserves) and the flow of useful natural resource commodities or services being produced from those stocks. The stocks or reserves indicate what is known to be available for use over future time, while the flow of commodities or services is indicative of current utility being realized. For *in situ* uses, the distinction is not so clear since the stock consists of the natural resource system itself (1000 acres of mature fir forest), while the flow of services may consist of interactions with other natural systems or humans (wildlife produced or recreation-days experienced).

Some natural resource stocks are renewable by natural or human-assisted processes while others are nonrenewable—an often-used dichotomy in classifying resources. Solar, wind, and tidal energy and farm land, forests, fisheries, air, and surface water exemplify the renewable resources, while the mineral ores and fossil fuels exemplify the nonrenewables. Renewability often depends on appropriate nondestructive methods of management, as with farm lands, fisheries, and waste disposal, since some changes in natural resource systems are irreversible.

What is understood as the relevant stock of a resource depends on available technology, costs, and social constraints. Aluminum contained in ores other than bauxite was not a useful resource until the needed recovery technology was developed. The production of many minerals from seawater is feasible but is currently ruled out by high costs in most cases. The exploitation of minerals adjacent to a city or the cutting of a scenic forest are often precluded by law or other forms of social pressure.

In the assessment of natural resource stocks, it is important that interactions with other systems and potentially irreversible changes be taken into account. When coal is stripmined, flows of groundwater may be interrupted and streams and wells may permanently go dry. Acid from sulphur exposed to rain and air may foul water supplies and kill plants and fish. Thus natural resources must be looked on as parts of larger systems.

## 1.2.  MAJOR NATURAL RESOURCE ISSUES

The major question posed by the world's natural resource situation un-questionably is *"How long and under what conditions can human life continue on earth with finite stocks of in situ resources, renewable but destructible resource populations, and limited environmental systems?"* The famous Club of Rome report, *The Limits to Growth,* posed the possibility of world social collapse so dramatically that popular concern was aroused on this matter. Some facts seem clear: that some currently vital resource stocks (such as mineral fuels) are finite; that rates of consumption of these stocks have accelerated in recent decades far beyond all historical rates; that some major renewable resource systems (e.g., marine fisheries, and some groundwater systems) are being destroyed; and that environmental capacities are being seriously exceeded. To illustrate, the arithmetic of resource exhaustion shows that when use of a resource grows at 5 percent per year, the rate of use will double in 14 years. If currently known reserves are 100 times current annual use, the reserves will be exhausted in 36 years. Even if a huge discovery doubled reserves to 200 times current use, the reserves would last for only 48 years. Thus it is not surprising that people should be concerned.

A second major issue is the *location* of known reserves. World petroleum reserves are huge and more is being discovered each year but those reserves are not located in the major consuming countries of the West. The same is true of bauxite, iron ore, chromium, and natural gas. What does this imply for the vulnerability of consuming countries to political pressures and exhorbitant price increases by groups of supplying countries?

A third issue is the historical *shift away from renewable resources* toward dependence on nonrenewable resources. Landes (1969, p. 41) has characterized the British industrial revolution as the substitution of mineral for vegetable or animal substances. For example, coal became important when charcoal supplies became increasingly costly, both in terms of proximity of forests and in terms of undesirable environmental effects. In the United States, agriculture has shifted from animal power to petroleum-driven machines, from natural fertilizers to those synthesized from natural gas. Consumer durables and commercial packaging shifted from patterns of reuse and repair to throwaway strategies. As nonrenewable natural resource stocks dwindle, can these patterns be reversed? Should they be reversed?

A fourth issue is the contemporary evaluation of *the wisdom of past patterns of resource utilization.* Without a doubt, there are examples of unwise, shortsighted, rapacious exploitation of natural resource systems along with their related social systems. The exploitation of coal in Appalachia is undoubtedly such an example, described with poignancy by Caudill in *Night Comes to the Cumberlands* (1963). However, the horrors of that region and era are not related to coal *per se,* but to the extreme negative social and environmental externalities resulting from what economists call market failure, from monopolistic exploitation, political corruption, and unanticipated technological change. This also provides an excellent example of the need to look at natural resource management in a larger systems context. Other examples that have been condemned by some environmentalists and historians are, on closer inspection, not so easy to judge. Was the cutting of eastern U.S. forests overly rapid? Was the timbering of Michigan's Upper Peninsula inappropriately or wastefully done? Did we use up the rich iron ores of the Mesabi Range too fast? Was the process of plowing, planting, and abandoning the plains lands shortsighted and unwise? When the relative factor proportions of that day and the importance of increasing the stock of man-made capital are recognized, the evaluation of these practices is no longer clear-cut.

A fifth issue closely related to the foregoing is whether or not we have correctly understood *the role and importance of natural resources and environmental services* as factors in our past economic growth. Most analyses of the causes of economic growth have placed great emphasis on the growth of technology and improvement of human capital, but few have adequately examined the role of raw material inputs and the increasing use of the environment for waste disposal. It appears possible that these inputs may have been more important than suspected and may *not* be freely available in the future.

A sixth issue is the growing dependence on *increasingly inferior reserves* of natural resources. The grades of all metallic ores currently in use are far below those exploited in the past. In the cases of many resource stocks, one finds a continuous spectrum of quality and quantity, implying greater reserves at the cost of exploiting poorer ores. Copper ores containing $3/10$ percent copper are currently being used, implying the need to move, process, and dispose of 333 tons of ore to get 1 ton of copper. Seawater contains incredible stores of minerals, but the energy requirements for recovery are, in most cases, prohibitive. Will *energy availability* permit the exploitation of these resources or must we forget them as usable reserves? And then, what of the environmental consequences of exploiting such resources? How do we dispose of 333 tons of copper-ore refuse after recovering the ton of copper, or of the ton of powdered shale after recovering the one barrel of shale oil? How is it possible to continue exploiting more diffuse resources without defiling our environment? Is it possible to avoid major changes in ecosystems as we push back the margins of agricultural land use, forest harvesting, fishing, and water development?

But the issue has become more complex than simply facing gradually declining qualities of resources. There is increasing geological evidence that many of the scarcer minerals exhibit large discontinuities in the way they appear in the earth's crust, that after the easily found high concentrations are exploited, the minerals may be found only in very diffuse and molecularly different forms requiring 1000 to 10,000 times as much energy to extract.

A seventh issue closely related to the previous two is the *evolution of limiting global environmental conditions.* The most widely discussed is the buildup of carbon dioxide in the upper atmosphere, largely as a result of fossil fuel combustion and deforestation. This may have major effects on the earth's temperature and climate. If science determines that it does, severe limits may be placed on economic activity. Other examples are found in the increasing pollution of oceans, crucial as carbon dioxide sinks and oxygen sources, and in the buildup of persistent toxins in the soil.

An eighth issue is *the role to be given to market processes* in determining how resources will be managed over time. Markets have historically played an important role in determining exploration activity and rates of use. It has been convincingly demonstrated that technological innovation has largely been induced by changing relative prices. Yet most countries, including the United States, today show a great ambivalence, professing the virtues of (modified) free enterprise while, through price controls and bureaucratic regulation, refusing to let the market work. Can market processes work in a socially responsible way in the natural resources area? What is the rationale of such processes? As we will see, there are major sources of bias in natural resource market processes, but what are the alternatives? Can public bureaucracies perform in socially superior ways?

What we understand about these eight issues will have profound implications for what we perceive to be socially responsible patterns of natural resources and environmental management. Does our comprehension of these issues imply that economic growth, population, and material standards of living must inevitably fall? As Barnett and Morse state in their classic work, *Scarcity and Growth* (1963),

> . . . if growth and welfare are inescapably subject to an economic law
> of diminishing returns, the necessary social policies and the moral and
> human implications are surely different than if they are not. Alterna-
> tively, if there is reason to believe that man's ingenuity and wisdom

offer opportunities to avoid natural resource scarcity and its effects, then the means for such escapes and their moral and human implications become the center of attention.

## 1.3.  HISTORICAL BACKGROUND

Concern with natural resource shortage is not at all new. The culturally rich Mesopotamian civilization between the Tigris and Euphrates Rivers crumbled because of the destruction of their irrigation canals and the buildup of salts in the valley soils. A major reason for the English attempt to hold their French territories following the Norman conquest of England was to maintain a supply of shipbuilding timber and masts that were becoming increasingly scarce in England. Following the industrial revolution in England, great concern was expressed in the 1860s by the eminent economist William Stanley Jevons that coal reserves would be exhausted or costs increase to a point where industry could no longer operate.

A famous case history of evolving resource scarcity and responses to it has been reported by W. Philip Gramm (1973). In ninth-century France, whale oil came to be substituted for wood for internal lighting purposes because of its clean burning properties. Under the pressure of the whalers, the whales apparently migrated toward the Arctic, making capture more difficult and costly. Innovation in shipbuilding and navigation helped to overcome these difficulties and made it possible later to extend whaling to the Indian Ocean. By the eighteenth century, the location of the whales and the increasing shortage of shipbuilding timber combined to transfer the whaling industry to the northeastern United States, but by 1800 it was becoming clear that depletion of whale stocks was taking place and that catches were becoming increasingly difficult. This was partly offset by further improvements in ship design and fishing and navigation techniques; but, in spite of these technological improvements, the price of whale oil increased 400 percent between 1820 and 1860.

The increased price induced various innovations, including the use of coal gasification for lighting in some European cities in the 1840s. The Civil War, with its destruction of whaling ships, caused prices to escalate even more, stimulating commercial interest in Drake's experiments with petroleum drilling as a source of possible substitutes. By 1863 there were approximately 300 experimental refineries in the United States producing various products, including kerosene. By 1867, kerosene had almost replaced whale oil and in 1870 the price of whale oil struck an historical low. While repetitions of such a sequence of events in response to current shortages cannot be relied upon to occur when needed, the whale oil story poignantly describes a process that has often been repeated.

The English classical economists of the eighteenth and nineteenth centuries were quite concerned with the effects of natural resource shortages on humans and their material well-being. Thomas Malthus, in 1798, wrote of the gloomy prospect of increasing population pressing on a fixed supply of agricultural land with resultant starvation as the ultimate population check. David Ricardo, in the 1820s, pointed to the diminishing quality of all natural resources as the cause of differential land rents and the ultimate check on economic and population growth.

In the United States, George Perkins Marsh published a landmark book in 1865, *Man and Nature*, pointing to the environmental damage being done and the ecological imbalances being created by man's increasingly intensive industrial and agricultural activities. This may have been the seed of one school of the conservation movement that was soon to follow. Conservation interests followed two paths represented by the writing of Marsh and the later actions of Gifford Pinchot, the former emphasizing the reestablishment of a human-nature balance while the latter emphasized technocratic efficiency in the husbanding of natural resources.

The United States had been a natural resource exporter until the 1920s. Following World War II, it became increasingly clear that the growing U.S. economy would have to depend increasingly on imports of raw materials and fuels. The first comprehensive national study of the evolving natural resource situation was carried out by the President's Materials Policy Commission (Paley Commission), which submitted its report *Resources for Freedom* in 1952, inquiring "into all major aspects of the problem of assuring an adequate supply of production materials for our long range needs. . . ." The themes of this report were that natural resources were vital to the U.S. economy, that this importance and problems of resource exploitation warranted a substantial role for government planning and management, and that growing natural resource scarcity made the welfare of future generations increasingly dependent on current prudent management. The recent developments in the energy area indicate that these caveats were timely, but it is less clear that government has played a helpful role since that time.

## 1.4. RESERVES, RATES OF USE, AND EXPLORATION

The term "reserves" sounds as if it should indicate definite quantities and qualities of resources *known* to exist. Yet, reserve data seem to change frequently and appear to be subject to great uncertainty. Why should there be so much uncertainty regarding reserves?

The first and simplest reason is the nonstandard use of terms such as resources, resource base, and reserves. (Currently accepted definitions for minerals will be given later.) A second reason is geological uncertainty: inventories by quantity, quality, and location are subject to margins of estimating error that differ by resource and location but that are often quite wide.

A third reason that is often ignored is that the very concept of socially relevant reserves depends heavily on technological and economic circumstances. This dependence is most easily seen in terms of the relation between *price* and the reserves that could be exploited at that price. The U.S. Bureau of Mines estimated in 1971 that at a uranium ($U_3O_8$) price of $8 per pound, 191,000 tons could be produced; at prices between $8 and $10 another 45,000 tons could be produced; from $10 to $30 another 285,000 tons become recoverable; and from $30 to $70 per pound, another 2.6 million tons would be economically recoverable (Bureau of Mines, 1971).

While reserves are most frequently mentioned in connection with the nonrenewable mineral resources, information on the stocks of the renewable resources is just as vital to their management. The population size and age distribution of a fish population are crucial to the reproductive capabilities of that population and constitute vital inputs into the determination of allowable fishing practices. The volume of usable standing timber in a forest and its rate of change are crucial to the determination of the best time to harvest the timber (the "optimal rotation").

Stocks of resources are supplemented by the discoveries resulting from exploration. Renewable resources have their own growth or replenishment processes, but even for them exploration for existing stocks has been an important source of new supplies. The processes of exploration are, therefore, intimately related to natural resources management.

Exploration produces information on resource stocks. Sometimes this information is precise with a high degree of certainty, but at other times the information is at best probabilistic in nature and subject to wide margins of error. If exploration were costless, it would be desirable to have all possible information on existing resource stocks. However, exploration is costly and the information it yields must be treated as a scarce input into the process of producing natural resource commodities. It would not be sensible from an economic viewpoint to obtain complete information, even if this permitted savings in production costs and reduced uncertainties about our endowments of resources. For example, it would not pay to determine the precise contours of a coal seam before bringing it into production, for the savings in production costs or the value of the coal saved would not offset the high costs of such precision. On a larger scale, it does not pay to eliminate all uncertainties of what the earth contains or to identify stocks that will not be exploited for many years.

Thus there exists an optimum program of exploration and an optimum array of known stocks of each natural resource. This is an important issue for many countries that invest large sums in exploration, sometimes in the hope of striking it rich, but often irrationally overinvesting in exploration for resources that could not be exploited even if known. Overexploration can also occur where public lands are open to mineral exploration by private parties, for the resources on those lands can be claimed only through the identification of exploitable deposits. Such resources are among the so-called common property resources, and there tends to be excessive and duplicative exploration and a build-up of excessive reserves under such circumstances.

The terminology relating to reserves has been most clearly defined and broadly accepted for mineral and coal resources because of the lead taken by the U.S. Bureau of Mines and the Geological Survey to standardize these terms. In defining terms, two characteristics of resource stocks are recognized: (1) the extent of geologic knowledge and (2) the economic feasibility of recovery. The most inclusive term is "resources," which refers to all deposits, whether geologically identified or simply speculated to exist and whether economically exploitable with present technology and market conditions or not. "Reserves" is a term restricted to deposits that have been geologically identified and are currently economically exploitable. For coal, a "recovery factor" is applied to the "reserve base" to allow for physical limitations on recovery.

Reserves thus can be augmented both by an increasing degree of geological certainty and by changes in the economic feasibility of recovery. Geologists are professionally concerned with the exploration activities that increase the reliability of our knowledge of deposits, while mining engineers concern themselves with improvements in recovery technology to bring costs down. Economists are concerned with the interplay of these factors with market conditions in determining current "reserves."

Data are often quoted on the ratios of reserves to rates of use as an index of the adequacy of reserves. Caution must be exercised in interpreting such ratios for two reasons: (1) reserves are always subject to a wide margin of error, and (2) rates of use may be increasing or decreasing from today's levels, implying a lesser or greater lifetime for existing

**Table 1.1.** Ratios of U.S. Reserves to Extraction Rates

|          | 1934     | 1974 |
|----------|----------|------|
| Copper   | 40       | 57   |
| Iron ore | 18       | 24   |
| Lead     | 15 to 20 | 87   |
| Crude oil| 15 to 20 | 11   |

Source: Cook, 1976. Copyright 1976 by the American Association for the advancement of Science.

stocks. For example, if today's reserves are 50 times today's rate of extraction, the reserves would last 50 years if the rate of extraction remained unchanged. If the rate of extraction were falling 0.5 percent per year, the reserves would last 58 years; but if the rate of extraction were growing at 2 percent (5 percent), the reserves would last only 35 years (25 years).

Ratios of U.S. reserves to extraction rates have not fallen for all commodities, as commonly supposed. Some have actually risen, as indicated in Table 1.1. Imports of these resources have been increasing over the 1934–1974 period, so that ratios of reserves to U.S. consumption in 1974 were 50, 14, 67, and 8 for the above resources.

## 1.5.  SCARCITY OF RESOURCES

Is natural resource scarcity increasing or decreasing? To answer the question requires a definition of scarcity. Economists would say that any commodity having a positive price in competitive markets is scarce. Fisher (1978) stated that an ideal index of scarcity should measure the direct and indirect sacrifices made to obtain a unit of the resource. Various indexes of scarcity has been suggested: (1) the price of a natural resource commodity, (2) the rental or royalty payment made for land containing resources, (3) the costs of physical extraction (not including royalty payments), and (4) measures that indicate how easily capital and labor can be substituted for natural resource inputs.

Barnett and Morse, in *Scarcity and Growth*, analyzed data that had been assembled by Potter and Christy (1962). Using data on the agriculture, minerals, forestry, fishing, and total extractive sectors for the period 1870–1957, they investigated the path of extraction or production costs, cost being expressed as labor plus capital per unit of natural resource commodity produced. They postulated three scarcity hypotheses: (1) that real unit production costs had increased over the period, (2) that the production costs of extractive commodities had increased relative to the production costs of all nonextractive commodities, and (3) that the real prices of extractive commodities had increased relative to the real prices of nonextractive commodities. On the basis of their data, Barnett and Morse *rejected* these hypotheses for all classes of extractive resources except forestry. That is, they found that real costs and prices had fallen from 1870 to 1957 with the exception of forestry.

V. Kerry Smith (1976) has updated the Barnett and Morse data to 1972 and has investigated the trends in relative prices for agricultural products, metals, fuels, and forestry products. Smith has found that there was a small but significant uptrend in the relative price of agricultural products, a strong but fluctuating upward movement in relative forestry prices, a significant downward trend in relative metals prices, and a downward but not significant trend in relative fuels prices. The upward movements in forestry and agricultural product prices seemed to abate later in the period, while the downward movements of metals and fuels prices also tended to abate.

While it thus appears that scarcity has been increasing for forestry products and perhaps agriculture, along with decreasing scarcity for metals and perhaps fuels, the data and analyses of the period since 1973 are not yet available. The structure of the world natural resources economy is undergoing rapid change, and the longer-term implications are still difficult to discern.

## 1.6. FACTORS MITIGATING SCARCITY

How can it be that a rapidly developing nation that has experienced strong economic and population growth has not, to date, experienced greater increases in natural resource scarcity? Many factors have been at work, some of which are listed below. Each factor is followed by specific examples, with more complex examples being developed at the end of the section.

*Technological Changes*

Those increasing the efficiency of resource use: greater smelting recovery of metals from ores and finer woodworking techniques to save wood.

Those increasing natural resource recovery, both through leaving less *in situ* and by facilitating use of lower grades: tertiary petroleum recovery, longwall coal mining, pelletizing of taconite iron ores.

Those that permit use of formerly unusable resources: aluminum from nonbauxite sources.

Those that permit new products to fulfill old functions: solid-state electronics for vacuum tube systems, communication conference networks for personal travel.

*Substitution of More Plentiful Resources for Less Plentiful*

Substitutions in production processes: aluminum for copper, prestressed concrete for structural steel, organic biocides for mercury compounds.

Substitutions in consumption: grains for meat, artificial fibers for natural fibers, plastics for leather.

*Trade*

General improvements in transport that make more remote resources economically competitive.

Utilization of international sources: bauxite from Jamaica, iron ore from Liberia.

*Discovery*

Extension of traditional exploration methods for discovery of new deposits.

Improvements in exploration techniques: geophysical and geochemical methods, satellite reconnaissance.

*Recycling*

Percentages of U.S. consumption derived from scrap: iron, 37 percent; lead, 37 percent; copper, 20 percent; aluminum, 10 percent; nickel, 35 percent; antimony, 60 percent.

An historical example will illustrate the way in which a sequence of responses often serves to avoid severe resource shortages. Gold was discovered near Telluride, Colorado, in 1885. High-grade ores had been exhausted by 1890 and miners had to turn to steam-driven equipment fired by wood. Timber became increasingly scarce, so coal was substituted for wood, but delivery by ox cart to the high altitude mines became increasingly costly, pushing many mines close to bankruptcy. Direct current electricity was available on a small scale but was costly and subject to heavy line losses. Lucius Nunn, then a local lawyer and businessman, had heard of alternating current and persuaded George Westinghouse in Pittsburgh to join a venture to provide alternating current for the mines. The venture was successful and Colorado mining received a new lease on life.

Nowhere has resource-saving technological improvement been better demonstrated than in electrical power production. From 1907 to 1957, reductions in energy required for coal mining, coal transport, electricity generation, and delivery of electric power resulted in more than a 10-fold increase in the consumer services provided by a ton of coal. This spectacular improvement resulted from a long sequence of frequent but unspectacular improvements and modifications. Has the trend come to an end? There is evidence that it has (Christensen and Green, 1976).

Resource saving or resource augmenting technological improvements are sometimes stimulated *indirectly* by changing economic, legal, or environmental conditions. Continuous copper smelting has been motivated by the need to reduce $SO_2$ emissions. Activated carbon has largely replaced mercury in gold recovery because of pollution control needs. France's early leadership in synthetic alkali production was a result of the loss of traditional Spanish sources during the Napoleonic Wars, and Germany developed the Haber nitrogen fixation process during World War I when Chilean nitrates were blockaded. The Japanese occupation of Malaysia shut off supplies of natural rubber and expedited the development of a U.S. synthetic rubber industry.

## 1.7. THE LONG-TERM OUTLOOK

Can these processes that have been so successful in alleviating natural resource constraints to date continue to keep the U.S. economy out of trouble? Can finite resources be made to provide acceptable living standards into the long-term future?

The historical record gives us reason to be optimistic that innovation of a resource-augmenting nature will continue. There is no known limit on possible improvements in technology, although the possibility of diminishing returns to research and development has been raised. Solow (1974) has proved theoretically that under relatively plausible conditions of aggregate production technology, a national economy having enough man-made capital and technology but facing a finite stock of necessary natural resource inputs can sustain a constant level of output of goods and services indefinitely through substitutions of man-made capital and labor for natural resources. Optimism is generated by the strong record of technological change and its responsiveness to changing market prices. These factors imply a powerful role for human technological inventiveness.

Several causes for pessimism also present themselves. There is a question of whether or not market economies will devote sufficient resources to research and development activities to maintain the past pace of technological progress. R & D activities, when successful, produce outputs that are *public goods* (i.e., knowledge that everyone can and should use without additional cost). Even with patent and copyright laws, the producer of R & D results cannot capture all the benefits they create. Thus, there may be an inadequate profit motive for R & D.

Another source of pessimism for democratic market economies is the frequently found unwillingness to face up to changing resource situations, not letting the market operate with sufficient freedom to reflect scarcity in prices. The failure of the United States to develop appropriate energy conservation measures is a major case in point.

Overall, it must be admitted that we cannot forecast the natural resources situation very far in the future, probably not beyond 20 or 30 years. But it is not required to lay plans now for all time. Plans can change as new information becomes available, but we must insure a *responsiveness* to new information. Rational public policy response and freedom for the market to price natural resource commodities in keeping with their real scarcity and to stimulate innovation and conservation can continue offsetting tendencies toward increasing resource scarcity in those countries not under population pressure. Also required, however, are world conditions that permit efficient use of world resources through dependable international trade.

## 1.8.  THE ROLE OF ECONOMICS IN NATURAL RESOURCES POLICY FORMULATION AND MANAGEMENT

The relevance of economics to the natural resources field hardly needs explanation, for economics is (in a broad sense) the study of the processes by which societies decide how to use their scarce resources. Some parts of economics treat questions of how societies *should* use their scarce resources, but we prefer to think of the challenge as one of generating good information for decision making, whether by members of Congress, the Secretary of Interior, or the individual citizen.

The subject matter treated by nearly every subdiscipline of economics relates to natural resources. The level of macroeconomic activity affects the demands for domestic and foreign natural resource commodities. The availability and costs of these resources can affect macroactivity levels (remember the post-oil-embargo recession). Trade balances are overwhelmingly determined by natural resource commodities, especially oil imports and agricultural exports. Regional growth and certainly local development are often highly dependent on a particular commodity (e.g., Southwestern irrigated agriculture, Rocky Mountain coal, Pacific Northwest lumbering, or coastal fisheries). The current array of problems over energy boom towns and the need to finance rapid infrastructure expansion are manifestations of the influence that natural resources can have.

Regarding the issue of whether economics is supposed to be *descriptive* of how things actually happen ("positive economics" in professional jargon) or whether it is supposed to design how things should be ("normative economics"), we prefer to think of economics as *analytical* in the sense that it is supposed to produce information on the *implications* of alternative policies, projects, or practices. Today, public decision making is explicitly multiobjective. Officially and unofficially, the nation seeks various objectives through choices about resource use: economic growth, environmental enhancement, equity in the distribution of economic well-being and power, a satisfactory degree of independence of foreign sources, and so on. A democratic, informed decision-making process must be informed about possible alternative resource-use policies and their implications. Thus natural resource economics is concerned with the design and evaluation (in terms of all national and regional objectives) of alternative natural resource policies.

Clearly economics cannot do the entire policy analysis job alone. First, the weights to be placed on different objectives are known only to the politician. Second, the analysis of the impacts of alternative policies on partially noneconomic objectives such as environmental quality, equity, or social stability requires inputs from other disciplines: sociology, law, engineering, hydrology, geology, and agriculture. Nonetheless, we are here to learn what economics can tell us about natural resource issues and to learn some of its methods of analysis.

# Chapter 2

# NATURAL RESOURCE COMMODITY PRODUCTION AND *IN SITU* STOCKS: A CONCEPTUAL AND EMPIRICAL SURVEY

Natural resources exist as stocks at every moment, augmented by discovery or growth, and diminished through extraction or natural processes such as death, predation, and decay. In many cases, the usefulness of these resources to society is found in the resource flow represented by extraction or harvest. Other natural resource systems, such as recreational lakes, wilderness areas, and beautiful landscapes, produce utility through the natural resource stocks. Some natural resource systems provide utility in both ways. This chapter suggests a simple macroeconomic model that will help us visualize the relationships among natural resource stocks, extraction, exploration, and the nation's capability for producing final goods and services. The model also identifies the important issue of allocating scarce capital and labor among the natural resources sector and the other sectors of the economy. The chapter then discusses the complex nature of natural resource stocks, introducing currently accepted concepts and terminology. Motivations for developing and holding *in situ* stocks are discussed, and the notion of optimum levels of natural resource stocks is illustrated. Reserve-to-use ratios, often quoted in the press as a measure of how secure we are, are inter-preted. Finally, the chapter ends with an important section giving a statistical picture of U.S. natural resource history.

## 2.1. A BASIC MODEL OF NATURAL RESOURCES USE

It is helpful to establish a conceptual framework for relating natural resource stocks, exploration, the production of natural resource com-modities, and the ultimate utilization of these commodities. The follow-ing simple model provides such a framework. The first relationship represents the production of the final goods and services—those utilized for consumption, government use, investment, or export purposes and whose aggregate value constitutes the gross national product (GNP):

$$(2.1.1) \qquad GNP(t) = f[L_0(t), K_0(t), R_0(t), t]$$

where the production function $f$ stands for the aggregate final goods and services production capability of the national economy, utilizing labor, $L_0(t)$, capital goods, $K_0(t)$, and the input of natural resource com-modities, $R_0(t)$. $t$ indicates calendar time and is included as a separate argument of $f$ to remind us that this relationship changes with time as technology or other factors change. The following things can reasonably be assumed about $f$:

1. There exist substitution possibilities among $L$, $K$, and $R$.
2. Any input is subject to diminishing returns when the other inputs are held constant.
3. Technological change can modify this relationship over time.

Undoubtedly, a country will tend to use more of their relatively plentiful inputs in the production process, so different input mixes will be ob-served over time and among countries.

A second relation in the model relates the level of consumption (including enjoyment of the services of the public sector) of both pro-duced goods and services and the natural amenities of the environment to other variables. Consumption is identified because it is a better index of contemporary economic welfare than GNP.

$$(2.1.2) \qquad \begin{aligned} C(t) &\equiv C_g(t) + A[S(t)] \\ &= [GNP(t) - I(t) - X(t)] + A[S(t)] \end{aligned}$$

$C_g(t)$ is simply the value of *produced* goods and services consumed, while $A[S(t)]$ stands for the value of satisfaction gained from activities such as outdoor recreation, sightseeing, observing lovely vistas, and environmental values generally. The second line first restates $C_g$ in terms of GNP and its other components, showing that greater values for investment, $I$, or exports, $X$, imply lower current consumption of produced goods and services. Next, $A[S(t)]$ is noted as some function of $S(t)$,the untapped volume of *in situ* natural resources. This relation identifies the tradeoff between services of the natural environment and the recovery of natural resources.

The next relation represents the production of natural resource commodities from *in situ* resources such as mined, cleaned coal from coal deposits; iron ore or taconite pellets from ore deposits; lumber from standing timber; landed fish from schools at sea; or a controlled, reliable water supply produced from natural sources through various control systems.

(2.1.3)                    $$R_0(t) = g[L_1(t), K_1(t), S(t), t]$$

$S(t)$ again represents the stock of natural resources present in period $t$. Note the following:

1.  The resource *in situ,* $S(t)$, may be quite different in physical composition from the natural resource commodity, $R_0$, and in practice, may be measured in different units, for example, the magnesium in sea water *versus* recovered magnesium salts or metal; oil shale *in situ* *versus* recovered oil; extracted and concentrated ores *versus* ores of varying quality *in situ*. However, we assume that $R_0(t)$ and $S(t)$ can be measured in common units for accounting purposes.

2.  The stock $S(t)$ also represents an index of the ease of recovery, in that the more stocks have been drawn down, the more difficult it often becomes to recover more of the resource, for example, deeper coal seams, more diffuse ore bodies, more scattered fish populations, or lower pressures in oil reservoirs.

3.  The available stock $S$ constitutes an upper limit on what can be produced.

4.  The labor and capital devoted to natural resource commodity production, $L_1(t)$ and $K_1(t)$, are not available for other uses.

Finally we turn to the processes by which stocks are augmented over time. In the case of minerals, the process is exploration and the refining of geological information to bring suspected deposits into the category of known reserves (more of this later). With renewable resources, stocks are expanded through natural processes like growth (fish, forests, crops), precipitation, wind, and solar radiation, sometimes assisted by human management inputs.

(2.1.4) $$H(t) = h[L_2(t), K_2(t), S(t), t]$$

This relationship will be interpreted in a variety of ways, depending on the natural resource system under consideration. For mineral exploration, $L_2$ and $K_2$ represent inputs to the exploration process and $S$ might stand for crustal abundance, while for forests, $L_2$ and $K_2$ represent management inputs (thinning, pest and fire control, reseeding) and $S$ represents the volume (and age) of the timber stand. This relationship usually will exhibit some random, probabilistic behavior typical of exploration or growth processes.

While a number of additional relationships would be needed to construct a complete model (in the sense of being able to compuze the paths of the variables over time), we conclude the model with the basic stock-flow accounting indentity:

(2.1.5) $$S(t) \equiv S(t-1) + H(t) - R_0(t)$$

which simply states that stocks at the end of period $t$ are composed of the stocks at the end of the previous period plus additions through discovery or growth less the amount of the *in situ* resource removed during the period. In terms of a continuous time model, (2.1.5) could be written:

(2.1.5a) $$S(t) = S(o) + \int_o^t [H(\eta) - R_0(\eta)]d\eta$$

A number of important choices that the economy must make can be identified in the model above: how to use available $L$ and $K$ among direct GNP production, intermediate production of natural resource commodities, and "exploration"; and the time path of use of *in situ* resources.

## 2.2. THE NATURE OF NATURAL RESOURCE STOCKS

We have spoken glibly of stocks as if all had a clear understanding of what was meant. In some cases it should be "obvious" what is meant. The stock of standing timber in Roosevelt National Forest is obviously a clear-cut concept (no pun intended)—or is it? How accurately can we

**Table 2.1.**   Relation between Reserve-Resource Terminology and Characteristics
of Natural Stocks

|  | *Characteristics* | | |
| --- | --- | --- | --- |
| *Terms* | *Occurrence* | *Economic* | *Technological* |
| Reserves | Known | Present cost level | Currently feasible |
| Resources | Known + unknown | Any cost level specified | Currently feasible and feasibility indicated in future |
| Resource base | Known + unknown | Irrelevant | Feasible + infeasible |

Source: Zwartendyk, 1972, p. 5.

estimate the cubic footage of timber, allowing for quality differences, damaged trees, blowdowns, areas too steep to harvest, and the variability of tree size? A major operating expense of the U.S. Forest Service is timber appraisal prior to timber auctions. The variability of the estimates is very high using practical appraisal methods.

The stock of fish in a lake can be estimated with amazing accuracy using statistical sampling techniques, as can stocks of demersal (bottom feeders) ocean fish. Estimates for pelagic (surface feeding) and anadromous fish are much less accurate.

Regarding minerals, most economic analyses and extrapolations of stocks have been based on an assumed smooth "tonnage-grade" curve, implying an ever-increasing volume of poorer-grade ores. Certainly not all minerals occur this way. Copper is found in three types of deposits: strata-bound, massive sulfide deposits, and porphyry deposits. More than half the world's copper (Cook, 1976) is currently produced from porphyry deposits. A tonnage-grade analysis of known North American porphyry deposits (Whitney, 1975) indicates that lower-grade deposits do not correspond to increasingly large additions of ore but the opposite, and analyses of the other types of deposits are consistent with the same relationship. Thus describing and extrapolating mineral deposits by volume and quality is not a simple business.

Not surprisingly, great confusion is found in the vocabulary of resource reserves. In the recent past, the term "proved reserves" meant different things: for metals, it referred to tons of ore within a certain grade range, 85 percent of which was estimated to be recoverable; for oil, it meant the quantities estimated to be recoverable; and for coal, it referred to estimated total coal in the ground regardless of recovery possibilities. Fortunately in recent years certain definitions have been adopted by most of the relevant U.S. resource agencies and are being increasingly followed by industry and other countries. For minerals, these definitions are given in Table 2.1. Note that the terms reserves, resources, and resource base are defined in terms of three dimensions: certainty of geological knowledge, economic feasibility of recovery, and technological feasibility of recovery. The first two dimensions are plotted in Figure 2.1 showing the relation between "reserves" and "resources" as functions of geological knowledge and economic feasibility. The economic classifications speak for themselves, but the geological classes require definitions. These are given in Table 2.2 on page 22.

To illustrate the use of this terminology and the changeable nature of our resource information, we paraphrase a U.S. Geological Survey news release of October 6, 1975:

The estimated coal resources of the U.S. total 3,968 billion tons, an increase of 23% over previous estimates. The revised estimate has

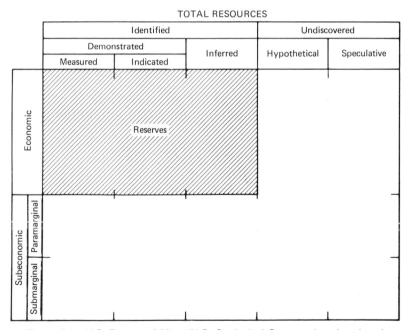

**Figure 2.1** U.S. Bureau of Mines/U.S. Geological Survey mineral and coal resource and reserve categories. Source: Dept. of Interior news release, "New Mineral and Coal Resource Terminology Adopted," May 26, 1976.

**Table 2.2.**   Resource Stock Definitions Relating to the Reliability of Geological
Knowledge

---

*Identified Resources:* specific bodies of mineral-bearing material whose location, quality, and quantity are known from geologic evidence, supported by engineering measurements.

*Measured Resources:* material for which quantity and quality estimates are within a margin of error of less than 20 percent, from geologically well-known sample sites.

*Indicated Resources:* material for which quantity and quality have been estimated partly from sample analyses and partly from reasonable geologic projections.

*Inferred Resources:* material in unexplored extensions of demonstrated resources based on geological projections.

*Undiscovered Resources:* unspecified bodies of mineral-bearing material surmised to exist on the basis of broad geologic knowledge and theory.

*Hypothetical Resources:* undiscovered materials reasonably expected to exist in a known mining district under known geologic conditions.

*Speculative Resources:* undiscovered materials that may occur either in known types of deposits in favorable geologic settings where no discoveries have been made, or in yet unknown types of deposits that remain to be recognized.

---

been made possible by increased geologic mapping, exploration, and study by Federal and State agencies and private industry. Resources of 1,731 billion tons are identified from detailed mapping and exploration, while 2,237 billion tons are believed to be present in unmapped and unexplored areas and in deeper parts of known basins.

Natural resource economists have long pointed to the price-cost-quantity relationship of reserves, typified by the following U.S. Bureau of Mines price-reserves diagram for uranium oxide, shown as Figure 2.2. One readily observes the increase of reserves as price increases. However, the degree of certainty about the existence and conditions of recovery is a dimension typically estimated by geologists but often ignored by economists. It is not clear, for example, whether all tonnages in Figure 2.2 have the same degree of certainty attached to them.

We must think of Figure 2.1 as a snapshot of a dynamic process, or we may experience what must have been the professional embarrassment of Pennsylvania State Geologist Wrigley after forecasting in 1874 that the U.S. had enough petroleum to keep its kerosene lamps burning for only four years. Increased geologic information and improved economic circumstances (higher natural resource commodity prices and lower production costs) act to move resources out of the southeastern area of Figure 2.1 towards the "reserves" area.

With this background, it will be easier to discuss reserves, resources, and related issues like the important question of whether or not we will run out of resources. In the case of minerals, the extensive crustal abundance almost guarantees being able to discover more of the resource. The ultimate issue is economic. Exhaustion is, in nearly all cases, an economic phenomenon.

To link our new definitions to the model in Section 2.1., the stock $S(t)$ in (2.1.3) can best be thought of as the "identified resources" of Figure 2.1 rather than reserves, for we are vitally interested in the trend of natural resource recovery costs over time as poorer-quality resources must be tapped. The history of exploration, discovery, resource-related technological improvement, and price trends can be thought of as movements of stocks into "reserves" from outside.

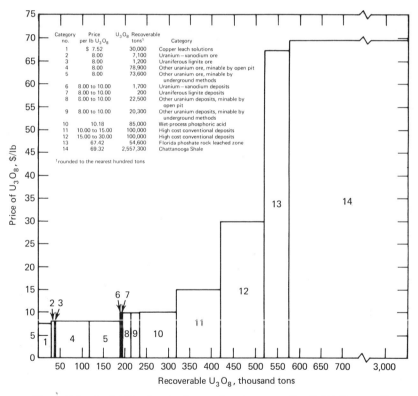

**Figure 2.2** Availability diagram for uranium (expressed as $U_3O_8$). Source: C. L. Bieniewski, F. H. Persse, and E. F. Brauch, U.S. Bureau of Mines Information Circular 8501, *Availability of Uranium at Various Prices from Resources in the United States,* Washington, GPO, 1971, p. 14.

## 2.3.  MOTIVATIONS FOR HOLDING RESERVES

Reserves are a form of inventory. If needed resources could be acquired immediately upon demand without price or cost penalties, there would be no motivation for holding inventories, whether of minerals or retail goods by a local store. However, time lags exist between ordering and receipt of materials. There may be uncertainty about what will be received after the order is placed, and there are fixed costs involved in placing an order.

While these terms are more akin to retail store inventory problems, each of the assertions above applies to reserves of natural resources. Exploration (and development) take time. One cannot wait until the *in situ* resource is needed to start exploring for it. Once exploration is started, it remains uncertain what will be found. If a dry hole is struck or the resources identified are subeconomic, it is necessary to have reserves on hand to avoid disrupting production. Some types of exploration are not economically carried on at a small scale. Large-scale exploration plus the geology of the occurrence of some minerals imply that discoveries are likely to represent large additions to reserves. This "lumpiness" of additions to reserves implies that inventories of *in situ* resources must be carried.

If we add to these reasons the decreasing quality of a natural resource deposit that is usually experienced as the deposit is worked, we see that rational minimum cost production requires having access to reserves. A deposit is usually not fully exhausted but is closed down when extraction costs rise to the level associated with opening new deposits. This is a rational and desirable policy, especially if the unrecovered resources remain accessible to future recovery.

Just as there is a notion of the optimum inventory to be carried, there exists a finite optimum level of reserves at each point in time. Let us argue by analogy by considering a simple inventory policy for a firm facing uncertain demand for a perishable product. Let $f(x)$ be the probability distribution (density function) of the quantity demanded during one period, $x$, assuming price to be fixed; $\pi_1$ the gross profit per unit sold; $c$ the unit purchase price of the perishable commodity; and $S$ the number of units in the firm's inventory which, presumably, cannot be augmented until the next period. Profit per period for this firm is given by

$$(2.3.1) \qquad \pi\,(x,S) = \begin{cases} \pi_1 \cdot x - c \cdot s \text{ for } x \leqslant S \\ \pi_1 \cdot S - c \cdot S \text{ for } x > S \end{cases}$$

The expression for "expected" or average profits per period for a given value of $S$ is easily arrived at by weighting (integrating) the two segments of this profit function by the density function. The optimum inventory, $S^*$, to be ordered at the beginning of each period can then be found by calculus and is characterized by the condition:

(2.3.2) $$\text{(Probability that } x \leqslant S^*) = \frac{\pi_1 - c}{\pi_1}$$

From this expression we quickly note that, as $c$ falls, the optimum inventory rises; but only as $c$ becomes zero does it pay to carry enough inventory to guarantee that all demands will be met.

Thus, only if reserves were costless to discover and hold would it be rational to try to identify all possible reserves. Since exploration and holding costs are positive, it is always rational to settle for less than full information about our resource stocks, that is, it would be highly irrational to identify today sufficient reserves to last forever.

## 2.4. INTERPRETING RESERVE-TO-USE RATIOS

In Chapter 1 we cited some reserve/use ratios over time for different natural resources. A popular use of such ratios is to prove either that we are running out or that we are safe. But one *caveat* has been learned: the reserve concept being used may be quite unclear, so the ratio itself must be unclear.

A second difficulty in interpretation stems from the fact that the rate of use is usually changing over time, either growing or falling. In this case, what is the meaning of the ratio of reserves to *today's* rate of use? It will not tell us when we will run out, even if reserves are assumed not to change. Let us look at this assertion mathematically to see why.

Let $S(0)$ be today's reserves and let $R_0(0)$ be today's rate of extraction of the *in situ* resource. Suppose the rate of extraction is growing at a constant rate $r$ (like 4 percent annual growth in consumption). We can write this relation as

(2.4.1) $$R_0(t) = R_0(0) \cdot e^{rt}$$

Today's reserve/use ratio is given by

(2.4.2) $$\frac{S(0)}{R_0(0)} = Y \text{ years}$$

If reserves are not augmented and if we keep extracting the resource at the rate of $R(0)$ units per year, we will run out of reserves in $Y$ years but if $R_0$ is *changing* over time, when will we really run out?

*Cumulative* extraction of the resource to a point of time $T$ years in the future is given by the following integral:

(2.4.3)
$$\bar{R}_0\ (T) = \int_0^T \dot{R}_0(t)dt = \int_0^T R_0(0)e^{rt}\ dt$$

$$= \frac{R_0(0)}{r}\ (e^{rT} - 1)$$

We want to know the value of $T$ at which cumulative use will add up to $S(0)$, given the current reserve/use ratio, $Y$. Observing from (2.4.2) that $S(0) = R_0(0) \cdot Y$, we have to solve the following equality for $T$:

(2.4.4)
$$R_0(0) \cdot Y = \frac{R_0(0)}{r}\ (e^{rT} - 1)$$

implying

(2.4.5)
$$T = \frac{\ln(rY+1)}{r}\ \text{for} \begin{cases} r \neq 0 \\ ry + 1 > 0 \end{cases}$$

That is, if today's reserve/use ratio is $Y$ and the extraction rate is changing at a rate of $r$, this formula will give us the future date at which the reserves will be exhausted. Table 2.3 provides illustrative figures which show how we must interpret the reserve/use ratio. Thus, if $r > 0$,

**Table 2.3.**  Date of Exhaustion As a Function of $Y$ and $r$

| $r$ | $Y$ | $T$ |
|---|---|---|
| −0.005 | 100 | 139 |
| 0.00 | 100 | 100 |
| 0.05 | 100 | 36 |
| 0.10 | 100 | 24 |
| 0.15 | 100 | 18 |
| −0.005 | 50 | 58 |
| 0.00 | 50 | 50 |
| 0.05 | 50 | 25 |
| 0.10 | 50 | 18 |
| 0.15 | 50 | 14 |

Y overstates the "time to exhaustion" and if $r < 0$, Y understates it. Naturally, it is extremely unlikely that reserves will not be augmented in response to continuing use.

## 2.5. THE HISTORICAL AND CURRENT NATURAL RESOURCE SITUATION IN THE UNITED STATES

Reciting statistics is never very exciting, especially when it is offered as general background information. However, some knowledge of the

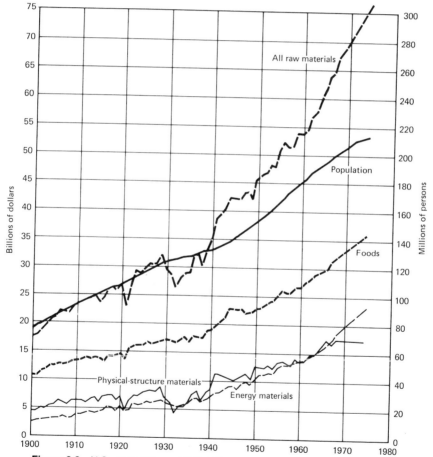

**Figure 2.3** U.S. population, 1900–1980 consumption of raw materials, 1900–1969 (consumption measured in constant 1967 dollars). Source: Spencer 1972, Chart 4, p. 12.

natural resource characteristics of the U.S. economy is necessary to any person concerned with policy issues. Thus, we present some fundamental statistics that all readers should have in mind, at least in outline form. There will be occasions later in the book to refer to some of these data.

Figure 2.3 relates raw material consumption to population. Raw materials are here defined as the products of the primary stages of production, semifabricated products—what we have called natural resource

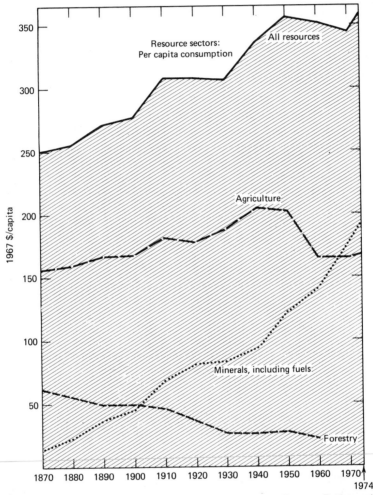

**Figure 2.4** Resource sectors: per capita consumption. Source: Potter and Christy (1962), with permission of The Johns Hopkins University Press, publisher.

commodities. Thus iron ore is included but not pig iron; sawlogs and pulpwood are included, but not lumber and woodpulp. First note that total raw material consumption has grown significantly faster than population, especially since the early 1930s. One can observe the sensitivity of raw material use to general economic conditions by observing the dips corresponding to important recessions, such as 1921, 1929–1932, 1938, 1949, and 1957. This has been less prominent in recent recessions.

Figure 2.4 shows on a relative scale the growth of per capita consumption of all primary resources. One notes a slight but persistent growth in total resources and agricultural products, a dramatic increase in minerals (which include fuels), and a dramatic decrease to about 1930 in forest products. These latter two series are not unrelated, since mineral fuels and construction materials have been strongly substituted for forest products. Figure 2.5 provides a breakdown of the minerals categories, vividly illustrating the increased per capita use of fuels and metals. Figure 2.6 illustrates production of the major raw material categories. Quite naturally, these patterns closely follow the consumption patterns shown in Figure 2.3 as long as domestic supplies were the most easily developed. After 1920, the United States generally ceased

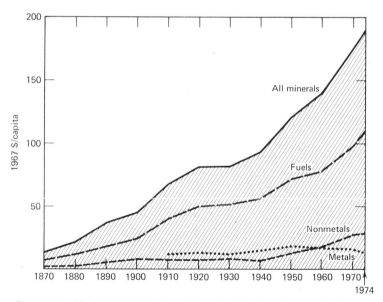

**Figure 2.5** Mineral sectors: per capita consumption. Source: Potter and Christy (1962), with permission of The Johns Hopkins University Press, publisher.

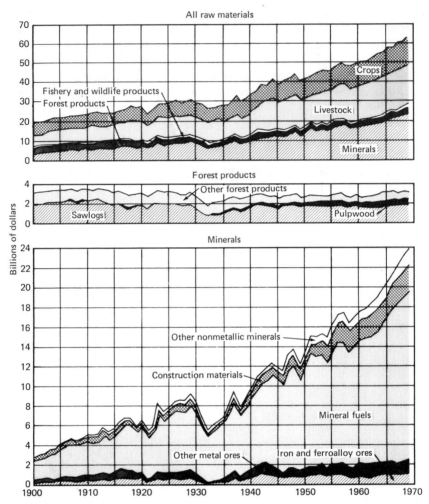

**Figure 2.6** Production of raw materials in the United States: 1900–1969 (production measured in constant 1967 dollars). Source: Spencer, Chart 5, p. 15.

being a net exporter of primary commodities, and consumption and production patterns began to diverge. Again, the growth of mineral production, especially mineral fuels, stands out in these growth patterns. Mineral fuels appear to have peaked in 1972 because of the peaking of oil and gas production in that year. Coal production will be increasing rapidly in the late 1970s and 1980s. Figure 2.7 provides historical data on a different "natural resource" service—outdoor recreation.

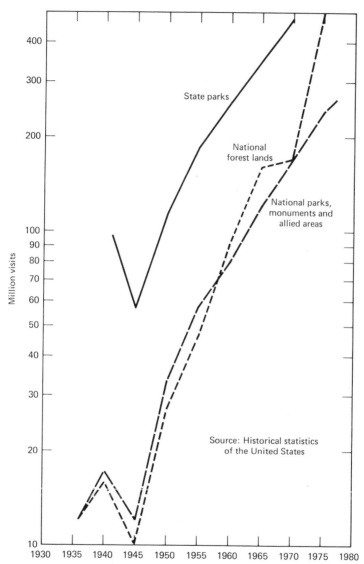

**Figure 2.7** Annual visits to various types of recreation areas, 1920–1976.
Source: *Historical Statistics of the United States.*

This tremendous growth in outdoor recreation of all types is quite important for natural resources policy, for many of the same areas that produce natural resource commodities are also best at producing recreational services. Often, these uses conflict, so the tradeoffs must be carefully evaluated. We now look at data that show the relative importance of the primary natural resource industries in the U.S. economy. Figure 2.8 shows the dramatic fall in the relative importance of these industries from 1870 to the present. Naturally, absolute levels of physical output were increasing, but the rates of increase were lower than for other components of GNP (e.g., manufacturing) and relative prices were falling. It appears that employment has followed a similar path. While the percentage of resource industries in total employment seems to have fallen from 1880 on, the patterns within the resource industries themselves were not uniform. Figures 2.9 and 2.10 contrast the patterns within agriculture to those within the mineral industries.

What has been happening to productivity in the natural resources industries? This requires a definition of productivity, for one must ask "Productivity of what?" Output per unit of labor is the usual standard of comparison, even though such a measure ignores the other inputs that are vital to the production process—capital and land. It must be em-

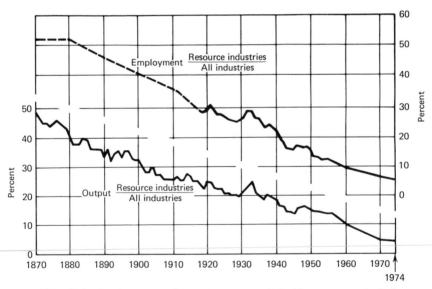

**Figure 2.8** Employment and output: resources industries as percent of all industries. Source: Potter and Christy, Chart 42, 1962, with permission of The Johns Hopkins University Press, publisher.

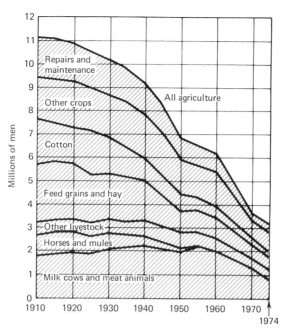

**Figure 2.9** Estimated labor requirements: total agriculture and agricultural sectors. Source: Potter and Christy, Chart 43, 1962, with permission of The Johns Hopkins University Press, publisher.

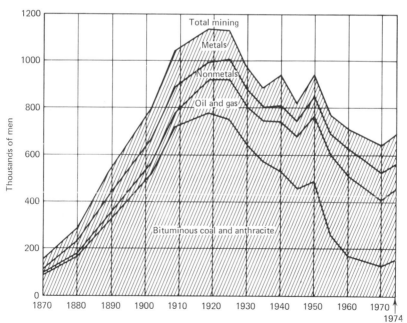

**Figure 2.10** Employment: total mining and mining sectors. Source: Potter and Christy, Chart 44, 1962, with permission of The Johns Hopkins University Press, publisher.

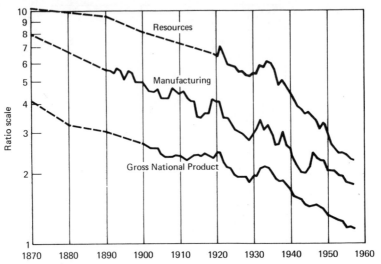

**Figure 2.11** Resources, manufacturing, Gross National Product: employment/output. Source: Potter and Christy, Chart 46, 1962, with permission of The Johns Hopkins University Press, publisher.

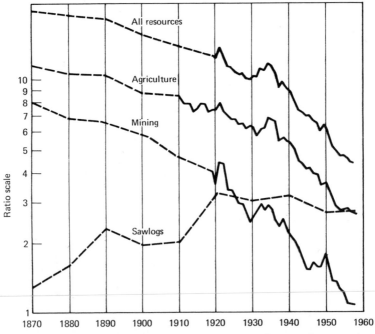

**Figure 2.12** Resource sectors: employment/output. Source: Potter and Christy, Chart 45, 1962, with permission of The Johns Hopkins University Press, publisher.

phasized that output per worker or its inverse, work-time per unit of output, is not a measure of the economic cost of production since it does ignore the other inputs. Figures 2.11 and 2.12 give the time paths of employment divided by output, the reciprocal of "productivity." It seems clear that the resource industries compare favorably with manufacturing, all sectors except forestry showing rates of decrease greater than that for manufacturing. We will be seeing more of these figures in Chapter 6 when measures of scarcity are discussed.

The movement of natural resource commodity *relative prices* over time is of great interest since this movement may be a useful indicator of the scarcity of natural resource commodities in comparison to other economic resources. At least if the competitive structure of the natural resource industries, government natural resource programs like farm price supports and tariff protection, and other conditions of natural resource ownership have not changed a lot, then relative price movements will be good indicators of changing scarcity. Figure 2.13

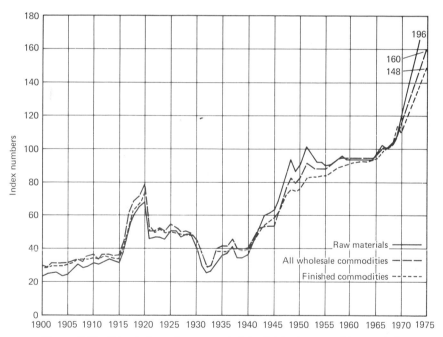

**Figure 2.13**   Price indexes for raw materials, finished commodities, and all wholesale commodities in the United States: 1900–1969 (index numbers: 1967 = 100). Source: Spencer, Chart 7.

**Table 2.4.**  World Proved Oil Reserves Year End, 1955, 1966, 1972

|  | 1955 | | 1966 | | 1972 | |
|---|---|---|---|---|---|---|
|  | Billion Barrels | Percent | Billion Barrels | Percent | Billion Barrels | Percent |
| United States | 35.4 | 18.2 | 39.8 | 10.2 | 43.1 | 6.4 |
| Middle East North Africa | 126.2 | 64.8 | 263.0 | 67.2 | 433.7 | 64.5 |
| Other non-Communist countries | 22.5 | 11.5 | 54.9 | 14.0 | 97.9 | 14.6 |
| Communist countries | 10.8 | 5.5 | 33.8 | 8.6 | 98.0 | 14.6 |
| Total | 194.9 | 100.0 | 391.5 | 100.0 | 672.7 | 100.0 |

Source: Darmstadter and Landsberg, 1975, Table 9. Reprinted by permission of *Daedalus*, Journal of the American Academy of Arts and Sciences, Boston.

shows the movements of price indexes for all finished commodities, all wholesale commodities, and all raw materials. One most readily notes the long-term upward trend in all prices, the greater volatility of raw materials prices, and the great surge in raw materials prices since 1971. The greater volatility of raw materials prices has long been observed in world natural resource commodity markets, not just in the United States, and has been the source of many problems for the Third World countries that supply an important portion of our natural resources.

While there was no significant deviation of natural resource commodity price trends from the general trend from 1900 (and earlier) to 1971, the surge starting in 1972 may indicate a unique change in scarcity relationships. The time span is too short to tell for sure, but the formation and stability of the Organization of Petroleum Exporting Countries (OPEC) for oil and the changing location of natural resource reserves indicate a changing distribution of market power if not a change in worldwide reserve/use ratios.

Let us turn our attention to the United States and world natural resource reserve positions and the international trade patterns emerging from them. Table 2.4 gives the distribution of oil reserves in 1955, 1966, and 1972. While the decreasing percentage of world oil reserves held by the United States is obvious, it is interesting that the reserves were absolutely bigger in 1972 than in 1955 or 1966. Naturally, that says nothing about the average costs of recovery. Table 2.5 shows the recent history of U.S. production and reserves for oil and natural gas. The Alaskan North Slope reserves clearly accounted for the reserve increase between 1966 and 1972 noted in Table 2.4. U.S. imports of petroleum have surged in recent years, continuing to grow in spite of the massive price increase imposed by OPEC in 1973. In 1955, U.S. imports as a percent of consumption were 10 percent; by 1965 they had jumped to 20 percent; and by 1973, 36 percent. At present, they are over 40 percent.

Table 2.6 provides data on the extent and locations of reserves of non-fuel minerals around 1968. The data are old and of questionable reliability, but they suffice to tell us that the United States doesn't any longer hold very substantial portions of world reserves. If iron, aluminum, copper, and sulfur are selected as the "most important" natural resource commodities because of their industrial roles and phosphorus and potassium are selected because of their agricultural roles, the United States holds relatively small endowments of all but sulfur and phosphorus. It is also interesting how frequently the U.S.S.R. appears among the three principal locations. They also have huge fossil fuel reserves of all types. The international trade position of the United

**Table 2.5.** Production and Proved Reserves of Oil and Natural Gas, United States, 1964–73

| | Oil (Billion Barrels)[a] | | | Natural Gas (Trillion Cubic Feet) | | |
|---|---|---|---|---|---|---|
| | Proved Reserves[b] | | | Proved Reserves[b] | | |
| | At End of Year | Change During Year | Production | At End of Year | Change During Year | Production |
| 1964 | 38.74 | 0.09 | 3.18 | 281.3 | 5.1 | 15.3 |
| 1965 | 39.38 | 0.64 | 3.24 | 286.5 | 5.2 | 16.3 |
| 1966 | 39.78 | 0.41 | 3.45 | 289.3 | 2.8 | 17.5 |
| 1967 | 39.99 | 0.21 | 3.68 | 292.9 | 3.6 | 18.4 |
| 1968 | 39.31 | −0.69 | 3.83 | 287.3 | −5.6 | 19.4 |
| 1969 | 37.78 | −1.53 | 3.93 | 275.1 | −12.2 | 20.7 |
| 1970 | 37.10 (46.70) | −0.68 (8.93) | 4.07 | 264.8 (290.7) | −10.3 (15.6) | 22.0 |
| 1971 | 35.77 (45.37) | −1.34 (−1.34) | 4.00 | 252.9 (278.8) | −11.9 (−11.9) | 22.1 |
| 1972 | 33.53 (43.13) | −2.24 (−2.24) | 4.04 | 240.2 (266.1) | −12.7 (−12.7) | 22.5 |
| 1973 | 32.15 (41.75) | −1.37 (−1.37) | 3.93 | 224.1 (250.0) | −16.1 (−16.1) | 22.6 |

[a]Including natural-gas liquids.
[b]Figures in parentheses refer to a measure of proved reserves, or change therein, which includes reserves ascribed to the Alaskan North Slope. North Slope proved oil reserves are carried at 9.6 billion barrels, natural gas, at 22.9 trillion cubic feet.

Source: Darmstadter and Landsberg, 1975, Table 7. Reprinted by permission of *Daedalus*, Journal of the American Academy of Arts and Sciences, Boston.

**Table 2.6.** U.S. and World Reserves of Selected Nonfuel Minerals, ca. 1968

| Mineral | Unit^a | Reserves, by Location | | | | |
| --- | --- | --- | --- | --- | --- | --- |
| | | U.S. | Percent of World | Rest of World | World | Three Principal Locations |
| Iron | Bil. tons | 2 | 2 | 95 | 97 | U.S.S.R. 31<br>So. America 18<br>Canada 12 |
| Aluminum (bauxite) | Mil. tons | 9 | 0.7 | 1,159 | 1,168 | Australia 400<br>Guinea 240<br>Jamaica 120 |
| Copper | Mil. tons | 86 | 11 | 222 | 808 | United States 86<br>Chile 59<br>U.S.S.R. 39 |
| Lead | Mil. tons | 35 | 37 | 60 | 95 | United States 35<br>Canada 12<br>Australia 10 |
| Zinc | Mil. tons | 34 | 27 | 90 | 124 | United States 34<br>Canada 25<br>East/West Europe, ea. 14 |
| Manganese | Mil. tons | 68 (see basis) | 9 | 729 | 797 | Rep. of S. Africa 300<br>U.S.S.R. 200<br>Gabon 96 |
| Chromite | Mil. tons | 2 | 0.3 | 773 | 775 | Rep. of S. Africa 575<br>Rhodesia 175<br>U.S.S.R. 15 |

| | Unit | | | | | | |
|---|---|---|---|---|---|---|---|
| Nickel | Mil. tons | 0.2 | 0.3 | 73.3 | 73.5 | Cuba | 18.0 |
| | | | | | | New Caledonia | 16.5 |
| | | | | | | Canada/U.S.S.R., ea. | 10.0 |
| Tungsten | Thous. tons | 95 | 6.7 | 1,317 | 1,412 | China (mainland) | 1,050 |
| | | | | | | United States | 95 |
| | | | | | | So. Korea | 51 |
| Molybdenum | Thous. tons | 3,150 | 58 | 2,265 | 5,414 | United States | 3,150 |
| | | | | | | U.S.S.R. | 1,000 |
| | | | | | | Chile | 875 |
| Vanadium | Thous. tons | 115 | 1.1 | 10,000 | 10,115 | U.S.S.R. | 6,000 |
| | | | | | | Rep. of S. Africa | 2,000 |
| | | | | | | Australia | 1,500 |
| Cobalt | Thous. tons | 28 | 1.1 | 2,377 | 2,405 | Zaire | 750 |
| | | | | | | New Caledonia | 440 |
| | | | | | | Zambia | 383 |
| Tin | Thous. tons | 58 (see basis) | 1.2 | 4,851 | 4,909 | Thailand | 1,570 |
| | | | | | | Malaysia | 672 |
| | | | | | | Indonesia | 616 |
| Magnesium | Mil. tons | 15 | 0.6 | 2,565 | 2,580 | China (mainland) | 1,370 |
| | | | | | | No. Korea | 820 |
| | | | | | | New Zealand | 165 |
| Titanium | Mil. tons | 25 | 17 | 122 | 147 | Norway | 30 |
| | | | | | | U.S./Canada, ea. | 25 |
| | | | | | | U.S.S.R. | 25 |
| Sulfur | Mil. tons | 342 | 12 | 2,425 | 2,767 | Near East & So. Asia | 1,226 |
| | | | | | | East. Europe | 437 |
| | | | | | | United States | 342 |

continued

| Mineral | Unit[a] | Reserves, by Location | | | | |
|---|---|---|---|---|---|---|
| | | U.S. | Percent of World | Rest of World | World | Three Principal Locations |
| Phosphorus | Bil. tons | 6.8 | 31 | 15 | 21.8 | Morocco 3.2<br>United States 6.8<br>U.S.S.R. 2.6 |
| Potassium | Bil. tons | 0.8 | 0.7 | 109 | 110 | U.S.S.R./Canada, ea. 41.5<br>E. Germany 8.3<br>W. Germany 7.9 |
| Nitrogen | Mil. tons | In limitless supply from atmosphere, provided energy for recovery is available. | | | | |

[a] All tons are short tons.

Source: U.S. Bureau of Mines, *Mineral Facts and Problems, 1970*. Terminology is that used by Bureau of Mines. The term "known and potential reserves" presumably refers to total resources. Meaning of terms used, in context of narrative, is not in all instances unequivocal. The basis of measurement or estimate for each mineral is as follows:

Iron — Reserves in terms of recoverable iron (Fe). Potential ore easily twice as large.

Aluminum (bauxite) — Reserves of bauxite, including inferred, in Al equivalent. Potential bauxite resources (Al equivalent) ore estimated at an additional 2.1 billion tons.

Copper — Principal commercial copper reserves in Cu content.

Lead — Measured, indicated and inferred reserves of lead in ore.

Vanadium — Reserves of contained vanadium, U.S. vanadium resources estimated at an additional 3.5 million tons.

Cobalt — Principal known reserves. U.S. resources estimated at an additional 100,000 tons. Resources elsewhere, different types of minerals and deposits many times larger than reserves.

Tin — U.S. figure refers to resources. Reserves alone are only about 6,000 tons. World reserves could be as high as 7.8 million tons, with some price increase, inclusion of other countries, and offshore sources.

Magnesium — Limited to reserves of magnesite, in magnesium equivalent. Dolomite, seawater, and well and lake brines, the sources of most of the world's magnesium and magnesium compounds, are virtually unlimited, given energy.

| | |
|---|---|
| Zinc | Measured, indicated and inferred reserves of zinc in ore. |
| Manganese | U.S. deposits are low-grade resources, not reserves. Rest-of-world figure refers to principal reserves. All data in contained Mn. Excludes potential from sea-bottom nodules. |
| Chromite | Principal and potential reserves of chromite ore, in terms of Cr content. |
| Nickel | U.S.: measured, indicated and inferred reserves of nickel in ore. World reserve estimates probably low. Considerable potential reserves throughout the world, of currently uncertain status. |
| Tungsten | Reserves of contained tungsten. U.S. estimate based on price of $63 per short-ton-unit (20 lbs.) of $WO_3$. At current price of $43, reserves would be only 83,000 tons. At prices up to $80: 150,000 tons additional U.S. resources estimated at 155,000 tons. |
| Molybdenum | Molybdenum contained in ores. Substantial amounts of sub-marginal grade ores are presumed to exist throughout the world. |
| Titanium | Reserves of ilmenite and rutile, in titanium equivalent. Additional resources of both with an estimated titanium content of 200–300 million tons are judged to exist, about half of which are located in the U.S. and Canada. |
| Sulfur | Includes native; by-product from petroleum, natural gas, sulfide ore smelting; Frasch sulfur, and pyrites. |
| Phosphorus | U.S. figure consists of 1.0 billion tons "known" and 5.8 billion tons "potential" reserves. Rest of world and world figures are "known and potential reserves." All data in phosphorus content (P). |
| Potassium | U.S. figure: Known plus inferred. Rest-of-world and world: indicated reserves. All figures in K content. Ultimately sea water and other sources could provide virtually unlimited supply. |
| Nitrogen | In limitless supply from atmosphere, provided energy for recovery is available. |

Source: U.S. Commission on Population Growth and the American Future, 1972, Table 2.

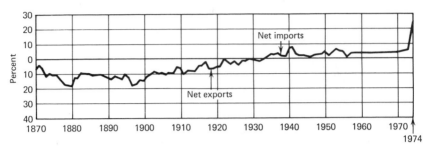

**Figure 2.14** All extractive: net trade as percent of consumption (1954 prices—gold and silver excluded). Source: Potter and Christy, Chart 34, 1962, with permission of The Johns Hopkins University Press, publisher.

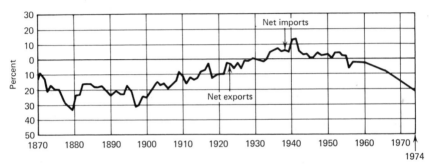

**Figure 2.15** Agriculture: net trade as percent of consumption. Source: Potter and Christy, Chart 36, 1962, with permission of The Johns Hopkins University Press, publisher.

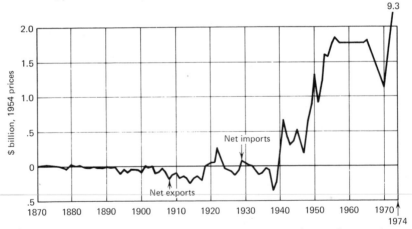

**Figure 2.16** Net trade: all minerals except gold and silver. Source: Potter and Christy, Chart 35, 1962, with permission of The Johns Hopkins University Press, publisher.

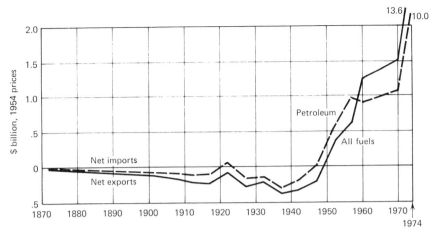

**Figure 2.17** Mineral fuels: net imports (five-year averages). Source: Potter and Christy, Chart 39, 1962, with permission of The Johns Hopkins University Press, publisher.

States in natural resource commodities is briefly summarized in Figures 2.14 to 2.17. The surge in net imports since 1970 is striking and would have been even more disruptive of trade and capital flows had it not been for the surge in U.S. agricultural exports.

# Chapter 3

# NATURAL RESOURCES CONCERN IS NOT NEW

In this chapter we seek to place the current concerns about natural resource shortages in a better time perspective by citing a few instances of similar past concerns. This is not to lull us into thinking that these historical problems were solved, but to begin exhibiting the processes by which humans and their economic systems have been able to adapt. Following these episodes, we review the thinking of a few eminent economists concerning natural resource issues. Some facets of the conservation movement are then considered and related to the history of natural resource policy development in the United States.

## 3.1. HISTORICAL EPISODES OF NATURAL RESOURCES CONCERN

Medieval England was well forested and certainly faced no shortages of timber.[1] However, by the time of Elizabeth I's reign and the ascendancy of British seapower, problems of timber supply were being recorded. Three competing forces were growing rapidly: the demands for timber for shipbuilding, the demands for charcoal in the rapidly expanding iron industry, and the demands for cleared land for crops and pasture.

The early processes of iron making consumed great quantities of charcoal in a simple forging process in which a relatively small quantity of crushed ore, mixed with limestone and a type of clay, was sur-

---

[1]The organization of the English timber case follows closely a paper researched and written by Michael Kelley for Economics 451 under Professor Barry Poulson, May 1977.

rounded with charcoal and heated, followed by hammering. This was repeated several times before a workable bloom of iron was produced.[2] Timber destruction led to a government inquiry in 1548 that reported such a shortage of wood that the Channel ports were said to be threatened with a lack of fuel. A writer of 1607 is quoted on the devastation of the welds of Sussex, Surrey, and Kent where the great beech and oak groves were being rapidly reduced.[3] The iron industry was so dependent on good stands of timber that such stands were likely to attract foundries, a fact said to lead to timber destruction just to keep ironworks away.

Shipbuilding also required great quantities of high-quality timber, including increasingly scarce English oak. This required increasing imports of planking from the Baltic and the substitution of inferior grades. Masts required nearly perfect trees, necessitating not only a careful search but very careful techniques of felling. The search extended quite early to the New World.[4]

As early as 1558, these conflicting demands led to restrictions that prohibited the use of trees for fuel within 14 miles of the coast or navigable rivers. Nef (1966) notes that the timber shortage during the Elizabethan era increasingly pushed manufacturers to attempt coal substitutions. Timber prices were rapidly rising and beginning to slow the expansion of iron output, actually bringing it to a standstill before the English Civil War. Production of lead, copper, tin, and seasalt was also being interfered with. However, the process of substitution had begun, and coal was being used for calcining ores prior to smelting, working with lead, making steel, and producing wire. The breakthrough in being able to use coal (as coke) for smelting was apparently achieved by Darby in 1709, but earlier successes in using coal had been recorded. Wilkerson's launching of an iron boat in 1787 began another process that ultimately reduced demands for timber.

Thus coal became the base of English industry and the Industrial Revolution, both for smelting and, later, to fire the many steam boilers that powered the increasing mechanization of all branches of industry. Should England have done things differently? Should the forests have been protected to a greater extent? While iron making and environment undoubtedly suffered in the seventeenth century, England gained ad-

[2]T. S. Ashton, *Iron and Steel in the Industrial Revolution*, Manchester: The University Press, 1924.
[3]P. Mantoux, *The Industrial Revolution in the Eighteenth Century*, London: Jonathon Cape, 1961.
[4]R. G. Albion, *Forests and Sea Power*, Cambridge, Mass.: Harvard University Press, 1926.

vantages over the continental countries through early experimentation with coal. It is certainly not obvious that the sequence of events could have been changed to significant advantage.

Timber had been a renewable resource, but coal was not. How long could British industry thrive on that fixed supply? William Stanley Jevons' publication of *The Coal Question: An Inquiry Concerning the Progress of the Nation and the Probable Exhaustion of Our Coal Mines* in 1865 brought this to broad public attention. The main idea was much like Malthus' population theory, with industry in lieu of population and coal in lieu of food.

> We are growing rich and numerous upon a source of wealth of which the fertility does not yet apparently decrease with our demands upon it. . . .
>
> But then I must point out the painful fact that such a state of growth will before long render our consumption of coal comparable with the total supply. In the increasing depth and difficulty of mining we shall meet that vague but inevitable boundary that will stop our progress. . . .
>
> . . . A farm, however far pushed, will under proper cultivation continue to yield forever a constant crop. But in a mine there is no reproduction and the produce once pushed to the utmost will soon begin to fail and sink to zero.[5]

Keynes evaluated Jevons' arguments as overstrained and exaggerated, tracing them to a "certain hoarding instinct, a readiness to be alarmed and excited by the idea of the exhaustion of resources, . . . ." However, the arguments assume a contemporary ring simply by substituting petroleum for coal. Hutchinson[6] felt that "For 1865 it (the book) shows a clairvoyant understanding of the fleeting temporary nature of British industry's supremacy as the workshop of the world. . . ." What length of time is best described as "fleeting temporary" is not stated.

Humorously, Keynes tells us that Jevons held quite similar ideas regarding an approaching shortage of paper, acting on his fears by laying in such large stores of writing and packing paper that 50 years after his death his children still had not used up the stock.[7]

Chapter 1 has already recited the scenario that has come to be known as "the whale oil crisis." Gramm's recital of that scenario beautifully illustrates not only an interesting history but the broad systems context within which changing natural resource scarcities must be con-

---

[5]Quoted from "Keynes on Jevons" in Spiegel, 1952, p. 494.
[6]T. W. Hutchinson, *A Review of Economic Doctrines: 1870–1929*, Oxford: The Clarendon Press, 1953.
[7]Keynes in Spiegel, 1952, p. 497.

sidered. The range of technologies that proved directly relevant to alleviating the shortage of fuels for interior lighting is startling and contains technologies that would never be picked as relevant if only a "whale oil shortage" were mentioned: improved shipbuilding, improved navigation techniques, a change in industry location to secure better inputs, coal gasification, and petroleum drilling and refining. It appeared that petroleum and its kerosene derivative had put the "whale oil crisis" to rest forever. But what of petroleum?

As noted in Chapter 1, by 1874 Pennsylvania's state geologist (Pennsylvania being the site of nearly all producing wells) estimated that the United States had enough petroleum to keep its kerosene lamps burning for only four years! By the turn of the century, some adventuresome explorers began to look west of the Mississippi for oil. The U.S. Geological Survey discouraged such exploration because of the unlikely geological conditions and Standard Oil's experts kept that company out of the West. The year 1900, however, brought the Spindletop strike near Beaumont, Texas, and by 1901 one independent well was producing more petroleum than the rest of the United States.

Another commodity of concern has been iron ore. The data in Chapter 2 clearly showed that the United States has only a small fraction of known world reserves. The rich deposits in the Lake Superior iron district have nearly been exhausted, the time pattern of exploitation being shown in Figure 3.1. These deposits had very sharp physical boundaries corresponding to the economic mining limits. Cook (1976) notes that the upgrading of low-grade ores first added substantial quantities to possi-

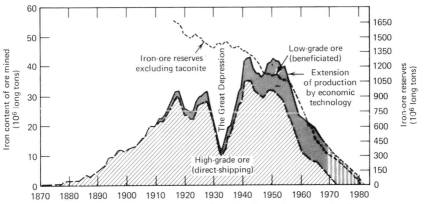

**Figure 3.1** Depletion history of Lake Superior district iron ore, showing overlapping stages of depletion of a mining region. Five-year running averages of iron content plotted at midpoints of five-year periods. Source: Cook, 1976, Figure 3, p. 680. Copyright 1976 by the American Association for the Advancement of Science.

ble production. This was followed by a major breakthrough that made it possible to utilize taconite from the region, a formerly worthless iron-bearing rock. This has vastly extended U.S. reserves. Of course, large reserves exist elsewhere (e.g., Jamaica and Mauritania) if they remain available to the United States on reasonable terms.

After World War II, there was concern about the adequacy of our natural resource base to continue supporting economic growth and high standards of living, stemming partly from the vast use of resources during the war. This led President Truman in January 1951 to appoint The President's Materials Policy Commission under the chairmanship of William S. Paley (thus popularly referred to as the Paley Commission) to study "the broader and longer range aspects of the nation's materials problem." This landmark report concluded in a cautious, even some-what pessimistic vein, recommending an important policy role for government and cautioning that the future would face materials-related difficulties. To paraphrase from the report entitled Resources for Freedom:[8]

> . . . In this Commission's view, today's threat is that this downward trend in real costs may be stopped or reversed tomorrow, if indeed this has not already happened. . . .
> . . . Our strongest weapons for fighting the threat of rising real costs have been energy and technology, but this raises serious future problems. . . .
> How well supplied are we with energy and technology to support the burdens of the future? The simple answer is: not well enough. Petroleum and gas will experience strong upward pressures on costs. Coal is not the ideal fuel, and hydroelectric sites are limited. . . .
> . . . Most Americans have been nurtured on the romantic notion that technology will always come to the rescue whenever the need arises. Isolated solutions to particular materials problems, no matter how dramatic, are no substitute for the broad frontal attack which technology needs to make on the materials problem as a whole.
> . . . There are formidible blocks to technological progress, including monopolistic restraints by industry and labor. Technological progress depends on scientifically trained personnel and basic knowledge, the development of which has been neglected.
> Less developed countries have resources but prefer to build industry than to develop these products of a "colonial" era. . . . Political instability and investor fear of expropriation hinder the flow of capital to these areas. At home, "buy American" legislation and tariffs further clog the channels of free world trade.

[8]From Chapters 4 and 5.

> ... Overcoming these barriers and offering positive spurs for developing and applying energy and technology... will never be achieved at random: only a consistent policy toward materials can hope to bring them about.
> ... It is the Commission's belief that the bulk of the task of insuring adequate future supplies can best be carried out by private business under the competitive market structure, operating within broad policy outlines which it is the responsibility of Government to provide....
> The tests to be applied to Government policy making are complex. How will a policy affect national security? What weights should be given the claims of the future against the present? How will a measure affect friendly nations? Will national benefits outweight costs, and who will enjoy the benefits and who will bear the costs?

It is difficult to imagine a more appropriate statement of today's concerns than these phrases from the Paley Commission report of 25 years ago. It is a bit frightening to realize that no significant policy changes occurred in response to the report.


## 3.2. NATURAL RESOURCES IN CLASSICAL ECONOMIC THOUGHT

We have seen that natural resource adequacy is not a new concern in the world. Neither is it a new topic for economists. This section provides a quick sketch of the thinking of a few eminent economists in history who have tried to identify and analyze basic natural resource problems. In so doing, they have left us with concepts or modes of analysis still relevant to our concerns.

Thomas Robert Malthus lived from 1766 to 1834 and published his famous book, *An Essay on Population*, in 1798. His basic proposition was that there is a very strong tendency for population to increase faster than the food supply, largely because of the fixity of land.

> ... When acre has been added to acre till all the fertile land is occupied, the yearly increase of food must depend upon the melioration of the land already in possession. This is a fund which, from the nature of all soils, instead of increasing, must be gradually diminishing. But population, could it be supplied with food, would go on with unexhausted vigour.... (Everyman's Library, No. 692, p. 8)

Malthus spoke of the possibilities of improvements in agricultural production and even of moral restraint resulting in a stoppage of population growth short of the margin of starvation, vice, and misery, but he felt such an outcome unlikely: "That population does invariably increase where there are the means of subsistence, the history of every people that ever existed will abundantly prove." He overlooked the possibilities of increasing the ratio of capital to labor so as to offset the increasing ratio of labor to land.

William Godwin (*Of Population*, London, 1820) much more optimistically (in fact, overoptimistically) perceived the potentials of emerging technology when he stated:

> Of all the sciences, ... chemistry is that which has advanced the most rapidly.... Whatever man can decompose, man will be able to compound.... Thus, it appears that, wherever earth and water and the other original chemical substances may be found, there human art may hereafter produce nourishment: and thus we are presented with a real infinite series of increase of the means of subsistence, to match Mr. Malthus' geometrical ratio for the multiplication of mankind.[9]

Thus, quite early we had a prediction of continued pressure on the means of subsistence as well as a glimpse of the potential of technology in alleviating that pressure.

David Ricardo (1772–1823) was taken into the British Stock Exchange business of his father at age 14. Here he acquired not only a fortune but the admiration of his competitors. By age 25 he had begun to devote himself to studies in mathematics, chemistry, and mineralogy. His contributions to economics included an elaboration of the labor theory of value, the principle of comparative advantage in international trade, a theory of the incidence of taxes, and his interpretation of rent as a return to differential soil qualities. The latter was an important insight into the way in which natural resources (including land) are used and served to explain the progressively increasing scarcity of resources as lands of decreasing quality are brought under cultivation or as mines of decreasing richness are opened. If we think of agricultural land, the Ricardian concept could be pictured as in Figure 3.2, where the quantity of land annually cultivated is shown on the $x$ axis and the labor-capital input required to produce a unit of output is shown on the $y$ axis. The different segments of the curve represent lands of decreasing quality. If lands up to $L_0$ were cultivated, those of superior quality would command a rent because of their ability to produce output at lower cost. The aggregate annual rent accruing to the lands up to $L_0$ are shaded in the figure. For such a relationship to exist, it must be that the various qualities of land are known and that they are used in order of quality—that is, the best first. Ricardo asserted that the same type of relationship also

---

[9]Quote from Rosenberg (1972), p. 146.

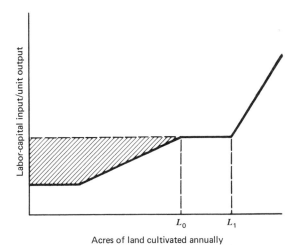

**Figure 3.2** Ricardian increasing costs.

applied to mining, but this application of the theory was not elaborated on, nor was the effect of exhaustion discussed.

While the Ricardian relation between the extent of resource exploitation and the marginal productivity of the resource can be expected to hold after an equilibrium is reached within a given geographical area, an historical growth process involving geographical extension of the populated and cultivated area may not exhibit this relation at all. In the United States, settlement was long confined to the eastern seaboard and piedmont, settlers occupying the rocky, low productivity lands of the Blue Ridge and Appalachian Mountains, while the lush farmlands of the Midwest lay beyond. Henry C. Carey (1793–1879) pointed to this as a reason for expecting *increasing* productivity at the margin as expansion occurs.[10] Naturally this would be a temporary phenomenon.

John Stuart Mill (1806–1873) elaborated on the Malthusian and Ricardian principles by noting the practically unlimited extension of the margin of productivity, both in terms of geographical extent and intensity of cultivation. Furthermore, the power of population to expand to the margin of subsistence is usually not exercised: "In proportion as mankind rises above the condition of the beast, population is restrained by the fear of want rather than by want itself. (*Principles of Political Economy*, London: Longmans, Green, 1929, p. 158). He also recognized the potential role of technology and improved institutions in warding off

[10]Henry C. Carey, *The Harmony of Interests: Agricultural, Manufacturing, and Commercial,* Philadelphia: H. C. Baird and Co., 8th Ed., 1883.

the Malthusian margin. In a discussion of mining, however, he noted the unhappy effects of progressive exhaustion of the richer deposits, making a sustained yield at constant cost impossible. While ... "all natural agents which are limited in quantity ... yield to any additional demands on progressively harder terms ... this law may, however, be suspended or temporarily controlled by whatever adds to the general power of mankind over nature, and especially by any extension of their knowledge ... of the properties and powers of natural agents" (*Principles*, p. 188).

Thus, J. S. Mill provided a more optimistic analysis of the natural resources situation, holding out distinct hope that knowledge and technology could keep the Malthusian margin at a good remove. He was, however, even more perceptive than that, for he had concerns with the quality of life as affected by land and natural resource availability: "A population may be too crowded, though all be amply supplied with food and raiment. A world from which solitude is extirpated is a very poor ideal" (p. 750). As Barnett and Morse interpret (1963, pp. 70–71): "He was asking others to share his confidence in the evolutionary direction of the world (while) coupling a concern for the quality of human living with the classical concern over diminishing returns."

Alfred Marshall (1842–1924) was the founder of the Cambridge school of neoclassical economics, best known for his *Principles of Economics*, 1890. His great achievement was the development of partial-equilibrium marginal economics. Spiegel (1952, p. 718) asserts that "Since the publication of this work (*Principles*), no other original book in economics has encompassed the entire theoretical thought of the time." He added a pessimistic note to the analysis of technological change by asserting that improvements in production techniques must themselves, like ordinary production operations, show diminishing returns.

## 3.3. THE AMERICAN CONSERVATION MOVEMENT AND RELATED ISSUES

What is *conservation*? This term is bandied about much like Motherhood, to be called into use whenever useful on any side of an argument: "Build the dam because that will *conserve* water and prevent its waste in spring floods" or "It is only by *not* building the dam that the natural beauties of the valley can be *conserved*."[11]

---

[11]Quoted from an excellent essay, "What Is Conservation?" in *Three Studies in Mineral Economics* by Orris C. Herfindahl, Washington, D.C.: Resources for the Future, Inc., 1961. Reprinted with permission.

Gifford Pinchot, a young Connecticut forester, trained in Germany and largely responsible for the establishment of scientific forestry in the United States, as well as for the federal agencies managing the national forest lands, is often identified as the founder of the American Conservation Movement. He stated, in a famous dictum, that "Conservation is the use of natural resources for the greatest good of the greatest number for the longest time," a statement of very little help to the harried natural resources official and sufficiently contradictory to drive any logician mad. Another famous dictum of this gentleman was that "conservation implies both the development and protection of resources...." While Mr. Pinchot may well have had in mind the improved management (development) of forests while protecting them from fire, pestilence, and unwise private exploitation, the dictum is contradictory when applied to other natural resource systems. The "development" of Glen Canyon on the Colorado River meant the construction of Glen Canyon dam, but it meant the destruction of much that was beautiful and unique in the Canyon.

The continuing confusion over the use of the term reflects the historical and contemporary conflicts among various interest groups within the conservation movement, that is, groups directly interested in natural resources but defining best use in different ways. A dominant conflict is that between "development" and "preservation." While these terms sound antithetical, they both can fit into a consistent program of resource management. Development can mean scientific management of a resource system to put it onto a sustained yield basis, so that continuation of its output is guaranteed on a reliable and highly productive basis,—that is, the system is "preserved." However, preservation *usually* means little or no interference with the natural system, leaving the entire natural system intact for human direct present or future enjoyment. This conflict between development and preservation as forms of "conservation" finally tore apart the American Conservation Movement of Theodore Roosevelt's era.

This conflict underlies much of the history of U.S. natural resources policy: pressures for and against the establishment of the "forest preserves" (national forests); pressures for and against various types of forest management; for and against public access to federal lands for mining, homesteading, grazing, and timbering. The great historical controversy over the Adirondack State Park lands in New York State, over the Hetch-Hetchy Reservoir in a beautiful Sierra Mountain Valley to provide water for San Francisco, and the contemporary fights over wilderness areas and wild and scenic rivers illustrate this continuing conflict. For many years, nature preservation groups criticized the National Park Service for permitting too much development and commercialization in national parks. Currently, the Park Service is setting aside as wilderness parts of many national parks and is, naturally, being criticized by various groups for doing so.

But stating development versus preservation conflicts in this simple way deflects attention from various forms of reasonable compromise. Tradeoffs between the production of traditional natural resource commodities and preservation of natural conditions exist in practically every project. In Hell's Canyon (Idaho), if the High Mountain Sheep Dam would inundate too much of the canyon, a lower dam at an alternative location might be built. When preservation and development are mutually exclusive, we can still look at the larger system or region, pursuing development at some points and preserving others. These broader possibilities are also part of "conservation" policy.

Woven among the development and preservation schools of thought is another perhaps not totally separate issue: the question of the pattern of natural resource use over time. Clearly, both development and preservation interest groups are concerned with the time path of resource use but it stands out as an important issue that warrants separate consideration. In fact, Scott, in his well-known book *Natural Resources: The Economics of Conservation* (1972, p. 30), gives this definition:

> Conservation is a public policy which seeks to increase future usable supplies of a natural resource by present actions.

Herfindahl[12] also concludes that "It is preferable, in my opinion, to preserve common usage and to agree that a conservative act is one which saves something for future use. . . ." Much of this school of conservationist concern arises from doubts about the ways in which we are allocating resources over time, especially doubts about the free market results.

George Perkins Marsh and his 1865 book, *Man and Nature,* were major influences on early U.S. conservation thought, leading to concern about ecological balance and human impact on nature. Marsh was an imaginative and influential person, a founder of the Smithsonian Institution, and his book sought to display the character and extent of the changes in physical conditions that humans had brought about. It pointed out the necessity of caution in considering large operations that can interfere with natural balances in the global system. (How omniscient this seems to an age concerned with $CO_2$, particulate matter, and hydrocarbon gas buildup in the upper atmosphere!) The book emphasized the complexity and dynamic nature of many natural systems,

[12]Ibid., p. 6.

observations that tended to complicate or even obscure what the classical economists had meant by natural resource scarcity. Humans' dependence on natural resources was pictured as more than food production and minerals, but as a mutual dependence and interaction involving both material and intangible goods and services.

> ... But man is everywhere a disturbing agent. ... These intentional changes and substitutions constitute, indeed, great revolutions; but vast as is their magnitude and importance, they are, as we shall see, insignificant in comparison with the contingent and unsought results which have flowed from them. (*Man and Nature*, p. 35).

These thoughts became an important part of the later conservation movement, especially the preservationist school.

An important contemporary development in conservation planning following in the Marsh tradition is what might be called "scientific preservation," an attempt to meld a scientific approach with a preservationist inclination in order to approach the controversies of preservation versus development through careful observation and quantification rather than through emotional appeals. An early example of this type of work is found in Clawson and Knetsch's work on the prediction and valuation of outdoor recreation (1966). It was their objective to bring recreation into the realm of quantifiable economic benefits, and subsequent developments have largely succeeded in this task. Reasonable valuation and prediction techniques exist, and a service once considered intangible and beyond economic measurement has become a fairly standard part of economic benefit/cost analyses.

Two less developed areas are the valuation of water and air qualities. Many studies have attempted to quantify the damages from air and water pollution (conversely, the benefits from environmental quality improvement). It seems likely that in densely populated areas or areas of unusual recreational value where damages, risks, or marginal costs of abatement are high, careful benefit studies will continue to be made and utilized in the standard setting process. The studies of Lave and Seskin (1977) relating air quality to human morbidity and mortality represent some of the best work to date. Their highly policy-relevant results show a strong relation between average long-term levels of particulates and sulfur dioxide and human sickness and mortality. While no attempt has been made fully to quantify these impacts in dollar terms, decision makers are provided a highly relevant type of information.

Other examples of "scientific preservation" are found in attempts to quantify esthetics. Dr. Luna Leopold of the U.S. Geological Survey has developed several quantitative procedures for evaluating natural areas and the impacts of development on environment. In Geological Survey Circular 620 (1969), Leopold develops a "uniqueness index" for riverscapes to permit nonmonetary quantitative comparisons of esthetic factors among rivers. In 1971, Leopold published "A Procedure for Evaluating Environmental Impact" (USGS Circular 645), which proposed a large evaluation matrix, the columns of which represent actions comprising the parts of project development (burning, paving, highways, blasting, feed lots, etc.) and the rows of which represent conditions of the environment (e.g., soil conditions, land forms, water conditions, flora and fauna, cultural factors, etc.). The cells of the matrix are to be filled with two numbers, one indicating the positive or negative magnitude of the impact (0 to ± 10), the other indicating the importance of the impact (0 to 10). The result is a summary display of a great deal of information and judgment.

The development or "scientific management" school arose from the perceived potential for applying the expanding sciences to the management of natural resource systems. As Hays (1959, p. 2) notes:

> The new realms of science and technology ... filled conservation leaders with intense optimism. They emphasized expansion, not retrenchment; possibilities, not limitations. ...
> ... they bitterly opposed those who sought to withdraw resources from commercial development. They displayed that deep sense of hope which pervaded all those at the turn of the century for whom science and technology were revealing visions of an abundant future.

Pinchot was the outstanding leader of this school. In 1898, Pinchot became Chief of the Division of Forestry (then in the Department of Interior and later transferred to Agriculture) and infused the service with a new sense of mission. He was a close advisor of President Theodore Roosevelt, under whom the National Forest system was increased from 46.4 million acres in 41 reserves to 150.8 million acres in 159 national forests.

Pinchot's opposition to "preservationists" was, however, profound for he felt the reserves should be developed for commercial use. In 1903, he told the Society of American Foresters:

> The object of our forest policy is not to preserve the forests because they are beautiful ... or because they are refuges for the wild creatures of the wilderness ... but the making of prosperous homes. ... Every other consideration comes as secondary. (Hays, pp. 41, 42)

Many other expressions of this philosophy can be found in the same era. Lord Kelvin, in response to a question concerning the impact of hydroelectric power facilities at Niagara Falls on the natural beauty of the Falls, is asserted to have said:

> What has that got to do with it? I consider it almost an international crime that so much energy has been allowed to go to waste. (Hayes, p. 127)

Charles Macdonald, President of the American Society of Civil Engineers in 1908, said that archeologists had complained that irrigation works on the Nile would inundate important ruins, but

> engineers will naturally consign all such archaic questions to the oblivion of the past and concern themselves with that which confers the greatest good upon the greatest number (*Proceedings*, ASCE, August 1908),

another use of Pinchot's famous dictum.

This does not mean that the preservationist school was without influence. Hayes (p. 264) concludes that the campaign to establish the forest reserves originated in the efforts of wilderness groups, eastern arborculturists and botanists to perpetuate areas of natural beauty and save trees for the future, in collaboration with western water users concerned with watershed protection.

The scientific conservation movement was an elitist movement, intending to utilize technical and scientific methods to decide and administer natural resource policy through highly centralized government agencies. Interestingly, large-scale private developments like the railroads, the timber companies, and the cattle companies that were decried as monopolistic often were better equipped and motivated to carry out good conservation practice than were the smaller homesteaders and sheepherders.

Three additional issues were raised during this early period and persist in natural resource policy debates today: the concept of efficiency, the issue of maximum recovery, and the use of the best resources first. Efficiency concepts used by the scientific conservationists were drawn from the sciences and engineering and not at all from economics. "Sustained yield forestry" was a physical concept, not even related in practice to the "maximum sustainable yield" concept. Lacking an economic framework for analysis, they had concern about the low recovery factors in forestry, oil, and coal, without any consideration of how much was economically recoverable. There was also concern about the fairness of always using the best deposits or stands first, that is, concern for intergenerational fairness. There were even proposals to require use of a cross section of resource qualities, so that some of the "good" resources would be left for the future. Economic analysis would have enlightened those debates.

## 3.4.  U.S. GOVERNMENT AGENCIES AND PROGRAMS INVOLVED IN NATURAL RESOURCES MANAGEMENT

Federal government participation in the management of natural resources began quite early and has expanded continuously to the present. In 1808, Secretary of the Treasury Albert Gallatin prepared his classic "Report on the Extent and Condition of the Highways and Canals," in which he inventoried the roads and canals that had been built by the states and private interests, including the methods of financing and extent of debts incurred. More relevant to our immediate interests, he recommended federal participation in the provision of the means of interstate transport and set forth the outlines of how feasibility studies on such projects might be carried out.

The U.S. Army Corps of Engineers received its first mandate to clear the interior rivers for navigation and to assist in harbor development in 1824. This began the evolution of the nonmilitary functions of the Corps of Engineers that remained confined to waterway transportation until flood control was recognized as a responsibility and, much more recently, water supply, water quality, and other social objectives were accepted as program objectives.

In 1881, the U.S. Geological Survey (Department of the Interior) was established with John Wesley Powell as director. The Survey was charged with the compilation of scientific data on the resources of the public lands and scientific studies related thereto. Its Geological and Water Resources Divisions continue to compile data on these physical resource systems, increasingly emphasizing the results of interactions among resources, environment, and man. Powell, a one-armed veteran of the Civil War, was famous for his explorations of the Colorado River in 1869 and 1871, during which he passed through the unexplored rapids of the uncontrolled Colorado River strapped to a chair fixed to the prow of a long boat. His classic "Report on the Lands of the Arid Region of the United States" covering the Great Basin between the Rockies and the Sierras provided the first accurate picture of that vast region. It pointed out the opportunities and limitations of agriculture in the region and the needs for irrigation, an issue Powell continued to promote. In 1902, the year of his death, the Reclamation Act brought the federal government into the irrigation business in the west.

The Reclamation Service, later called the Bureau of Reclamation (Department of the Interior), was charged with the development of water supply for irrigation and related drainage activities. The role of farming in the opening of the West and the importance of the family farm were explicitly noted in the Act. Since that time, the multiple purposes of modern water management (irrigation, municipal and industrial water supply, flood control, hydroelectric generation, and water quality) have been adopted by the Bureau of Reclamation. Water development by the Bureau and Corps of Engineers has become controversial because of economic, environmental, and equity conflicts. A hot current issue is the enforcement of the so-called "160 acre limitation" under the Reclamation Act that was intended to encourage family farming by limiting federally subsidized water to 160 acres per owner or 320 acres per farm couple.

The U.S. Forest Service (Department of Agriculture) was established by the Forest Reserve Act of 1891 and was first directed by Gifford Pinchot in the supervision of the newly established forest reserves. These federal holdings were rapidly expanded under Theodore Roosevelt. The Forest Service has adopted a multiple-use, multiple-objective philosophy of management under the Multiple Use-Sustained Yield Act of 1960. Praise for its management of many intensively used recreational areas has mingled with criticism of its timber management policies.

The General Mining Act of 1871 opened the federal lands to mineral prospecting and establishment of title to proven claims. This law stands largely unmodified to this day. The Forest Reserve Act, the Homestead Acts, and the setting up of the National Parks (the latter under the U.S. Park Service, Department of the Interior) left a large set of fragmented federal land holdings that was overseen by the General Land Office, now the Bureau of Land Management (Department of Interior). This Bureau has charge over the vast marginal grazing lands of the west, some of the largest holdings of mature and virgin timber (in the Northwest), and vast holdings of coal and oil shale.

The Soil Conservation Service (Department of Agriculture) has a large program of small water project development and soil conservation practices throughout the country.

In addition to agencies mentioned above, the newly formed Department of Energy has regulatory and research responsibilities over fossil and nuclear fuels, and the development of energy alternatives. Two independent executive agencies, the Council on Environmental Quality and the Environmental Protection Agency, oversee environmental standards and programs for their achievement. The current environmental management program of the federal government has correctly been referred to as the largest public works program in history.

Other agencies involved in resources management include the Fish and Wildlife Service and Bureau of Mines (Department of the Interior); the Economic Development Administration and the National Oceanic and Atmospheric Administration (Department of Commerce), the latter containing the National Weather Service, the Environmental Data Service (earth satellite data programs), and the National Marine Fisheries Service; and various state agencies.

# Chapter 4

# THE IMPACTS OF NATURAL RESOURCE AVAILABILITY ON ECONOMIC GROWTH: FORMS AND EFFECTS OF SCARCITY

This chapter illustrates the basic ways in which the conditions of natural resources availability affect the growth potential of an economy. We show how different conditions of availability of natural resources restrict the economy's growth potential in quantitatively different but qualitatively similar ways. This is equivalent to saying that the "scarcity" of natural resources can be present in different physical forms, all of which constrain the production potential of the economic system. Scarcity thus is not a simple notion, quickly explained and straightforwardly measured over time. Barnett and Morse observed the complexity of the issue (1963, p. 49):

> In economic terms, the belief seems to be that natural resources are scarce; that the scarcity increases with the passage of time; and that resource scarcity and its aggravation impair levels of living and economic growth.... But in our view—contrary to much of the opinion

surveyed—these propositions are neither self-evident nor easy to formulate in meaningful terms.[1]

To understand natural resource scarcity, we must understand the natural resource, reserves, the production technologies, and resource allocative mechanisms of the economic system. Depending on the degree of detail of our inquiries, it may be necessary to know the structure of demands for final goods and services since these can influence the mix of goods made and technologies used. To state this in simpler terms, scarcity must be defined and measured in a general equilibrium context. To what extent is this possible?

We feel that an understanding of the role of natural resources and the different forms of scarcity can be developed through a sequence of relatively simple macroeconomic models, each of which incorporates particular conditions of natural resource availability and certain assumptions about technological change. The implications of those conditions for the economy's continued production performance are then investigated. As these models are developed, we want to observe at least three things for each: (1) which factors clearly affect the changes in national output and national output per capita, (2) in what sense do limits to growth exist, and (3) what evidence of natural resource shortage would we be able to observe in each case?

## 4.1.  A MODEL OF FRONTIER AND SIMPLE RICARDIAN ECONOMIES

Here we further develop the model of Chapter 2 to investigate the effects of the conditions of natural resource availability on the level of GNP and its growth over time. A *frontier economy* is defined as one with very plentiful supplies of natural resources relative to capital and labor. Unlimited natural resources imply that the conditions or costs of natural resource availability are constant over time and unaffected by either contemporary rates of use or cumulative use over time. A *simple Ricardian economy* is one in which the unit cost of natural resource commodity production increases as the rate of production is increased, much like bringing increasingly inferior agricultural land into production as required output is increased. The basic relationships of the model are given below.

(4.1.1) $$\text{GNP}(t) = f[L_0(t),\ R_0(t)]$$

[1]Used with permission of the Johns Hopkins University Press, publisher.

(4.1.2) $$R_0(t) = g[L_1(t)]$$

(4.1.3) $$L_0(t) + L_1(t) = L(t)$$

The first relationship again represents the production of final goods and services, using a composite labor-capital input, $L_0(t)$, and natural resource commodities, $R_0(t)$. The latter are intermediate goods produced according to the technology (or production function) $g(\cdot)$ and also using the composite labor-capital input in the amount $L_1(t)$. We note that $g(\cdot)$ logically can exhibit increasing, constant, or decreasing returns to scale but that "stock effects" are absent, that is, cumulative subtractions from or additions to the stock of *in situ* natural resources are assumed *not* to affect natural resource commodity production. Equation 4.1.3 simply states that the total amount of labor capital used must equal the amount available in each period, $L(t)$. The growth in this variable is assumed to be exogenously determined.

There is now a tradeoff between how much of $L(t)$ is applied directly to GNP production and how much is committed to natural resource commodity production, $R_0(t)$. This tradeoff is derived by substituting (4.1.3) into (4.1.2):

(4.1.4) $$R_0(t) = g[L(t) - L_0(t)]$$

If $R_0$ and $L_0$ values are plotted from this relation, a set of transformation or production possibilities curves is derived as shown in Figure 4.1. The shape of these curves—whether they are concave, convex, or linear—and the manner in which they shift outward as $L(t)$ grows depends on the returns to scale inherent in the natural resource commodity production function $g(\cdot)$.

If the family of GNP isoquants is superimposed on the figure, it is possible to identify the $L_0$ and $R_0$ values that would maximize GNP at each point in time, like $L_0^*(1)$ and $R_0^*(1)$. As $L(t)$ grows, the transformation curve shifts outward and the points of tangency with GNP isoquants trace out the expansion path of the economy.

A *frontier economy* of superabundant natural resources can be defined as one for which the natural resource commodity production function, $g(\cdot)$, exhibits constant returns to scale. Resources are so readily available that natural resource commodity production can always be expanded in proportion to the labor-capital input. The GNP level is limited at any time not by a natural resource shortage in any physical sense but because some of the labor-capital input must be used to gather or otherwise prepare the resources for use in producing final goods and services. Labor capital and not natural resources limit GNP. For this use, the transformation curves of Figure 4.1 would be straight lines and would shift outward in equal parallel steps as $L(t)$ grows. Such a pattern of growth is exhibited in Figure 4.2.

A *simple Ricardian economy* is one in which $g(\cdot)$ exhibits decreasing returns to scale in each period. In this case, not only must some of the limited $L$ be committed to the production of $R_0$, but $L_1$ must be increased more than in proportion to increases of $R_0$. This creates an additional drag on GNP growth. The $R_0$–$L_0$ transformation curves shift outward in an asymmetric way with equal increments of $L_0$ corresponding to diminishing increments of $R_0$. This was illustrated in Figure 4.1.

What indicators of changing natural resource scarcity might be observed in a frontier or simple Ricardian economy? In any economy seeking to maximize GNP through the use of two scarce factors, $R_0$ and $L_0$, the relative values of the factors will be determined by the rate at which they can be substituted for one another in the production of GNP since this is the only use for the factors. This rate of substitution is given by

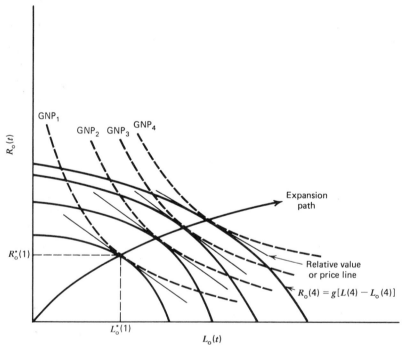

**Figure 4.1** Input transformation curves, GNP isoquants, and the optimum expansion path of a simple Ricardian economy.

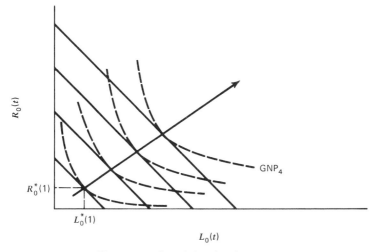

**Figure 4.2** Growth in a frontier economy.

the *slope* of GNP isoquant at the point of tangency, $(R_0^*, L_0^*)$. This slope is identical to that of the tangent line at $(R_0^*, L_0^*)$. The changing slopes of these tangent lines as the economy moves out its growth path measure the changing relative values of the two factors. If the tangent lines swing out in a counterclockwise pattern, $R_0$ is becoming relatively more scarce and valuable. If the lines swing out in a clockwise pattern, $R_0$ is becoming relatively more plentiful and less valuable. Figure 4.1 exhibited a pattern of increasing scarcity and unit values while Figure 4.2 exhibited constant relative scarcity and value.

In the *frontier economy*, the isoquant slopes will be constant along the expansion path, implying that the relative prices of $R_0$ and $L_0$ will not change over time. This result seems plausible since the conditions of natural resource availability, by definition, are not changing. In the *simple Ricardian economy*, the relative price of $R_0$ must rise as growth occurs, since the transformation of $L_0$ into $R_0$ is becoming less efficient as $R_0$ output is expanded. Figure 4.1 also illustrates the plausible result that the ratio of inputs in GNP production, $R_0/L_0$, decreases along the expansion path.

## 4.2. SPECIAL EXAMPLES OF THE FRONTIER AND SIMPLE RICARDIAN ECONOMIES

This example will permit us to derive sharper results by giving specific mathematical form to the GNP and natural resource commodity production functions. In particular, they are assumed to be "power" functions, that is the well-known Cobb-Douglas function:[2]

(4.2.1) $$\text{GNP} = b_0 L_0{}^{b_1} R_0{}^{b_2}$$

(4.2.2) $$R_0 = a_0 L_1{}^{a_1} = a_0 (L - L_0)^{a_1}$$

Using these particular functional forms could be defended by referring to the large number of empirical studies in which the function has been found to fit data on GNP and aggregate inputs quite well. For the Cobb-Douglas function, returns to scale are given by the sum of the exponents. If (4.2.2) is substituted into (4.2.1), GNP can be expressed as a function of $L$ and $L_0$:

(4.2.3) $$\text{GNP} = b_0 a_0{}^{b_2} L_0{}^{b_1} (L - L_0)^{b_2 a_1}$$

The $L_0$ values that will carry this economy along the maximal growth path of Figure 4.1 can be found by maximizing (4.2.3).[3] The resulting optimum $L_0^*$ is:

(4.2.4) $$L_0^* = \frac{b_1}{b_1 + b_2 a_1} L$$

When $L_0^*$ is substituted back into (4.2.3), the maximum GNP value for any given $L$ is found to be:

(4.2.5) $$\text{GNP}^* = K L^{b_1 + b_2 a_1}$$

where $K$ stands for a term involving the parameters of the two production functions.

This result immediately establishes two points for the Cobb-Douglas case: (1) the growth of $L$ determines the growth path of GNP; (2) overall returns to scale, $\rho$, are given by $(b_1 + b_2 a_1)$, a term involving the exponents of *both* production functions. Table 4.1 provides numerical illustrations of how returns to scale in the GNP production func-

[2]Some economists reserve the name "Cobb-Douglas" for a power function in which the exponents sum to 1, but the two terms will be used interchangeably in this book.
[3]The maximization is carried out by differentiating (4.2.3) with respect to $L_0$, setting the derivative function equal to zero, and solving the resulting equation. The second derivative conditions for a maximum will be met if $b_1 + b_2 \leq 1$ and $a_1 \leq 1$, very reasonable conditions for any aggregate production technology.

**Table 4.1.**  Overall Returns to Scale

| Case No. | $b_1$ | $b_2$ | $a_1$ | $\rho = b_1 + b_2 a_1$ | |
|----------|-------|-------|-------|------------------------|---|
| 1 | 0.6 | 0.4 | 1.0 | 1.0 | Constant returns |
| 2 | 0.6 | 0.4 | 0.5 | 0.8 | Decreasing returns |
| 3 | 0.6 | 0.4 | 1.5 | 1.2 | Increasing returns |
| 4 | 0.6 | 0.2 | 1.0 | 0.8 | Decreasing returns |
| 5 | 0.6 | 0.3 | 2.0 | 1.2 | Increasing returns |
| 6 | 0.6 | 0.6 | 0.5 | 0.9 | Decreasing returns |

tion $(b_1 + b_2)$ combine with returns to scale in natural resource commodity production $(a_1)$ to determine overall returns to scale, $\rho = b_1 + b_2 a_1$. The table shows that decreasing returns to scale in natural resource commodity production $(a_1 < 1)$ can offset constant or even increasing returns in GNP production, while increasing returns $(a_1 > 1)$ can compensate for decreasing returns in GNP production.

If we assume that population is proportional to the labor-capital stock, $L = \ell P$, the path of GNP per capita can very easily be computed:

$$(4.2.6) \qquad \frac{\text{GNP}}{P} = \ell K L^{(b_1 + b_2 a_1 - 1)}.$$

Thus, GNP per capita will rise, remain constant, or fall over time as $L$ grows, depending on the value of $\rho$. For the frontier economy $(a_1 = 1)$, the trend in per capita GNP will depend solely on the returns to scale in the GNP production function. Any hope for constant or increasing per capita GNP in the simple Ricardian economy depends on increasing returns to scale in GNP production.

What will happen to the relative scarcity and value of $R_0$ over time in this Cobb-Douglas economy? To determine the common slope of the $R_0 - L_0$ transformation function, the GNP isoquant, and the tangent line (see Figure 4.1), we can take the derivative of the $R_0 - L_0$ transformation curve of (4.2.2), arriving at

$$(4.2.7) \qquad \frac{dR_0}{dL_0} = \frac{-a_0 a_1}{(L - L_0)^{1-a_1}}$$

It is clear from this expression that in the frontier economy $(a_1 = 1)$ the slope will remain constant, while in the simple Ricardian economy $(a_1 < 1)$ the tangent line will shift outward with a slope of decreasing steepness.

## 4.3.  A MALTHUSIAN SPECIAL CASE

Malthus was concerned with the fixity of arable land and its ultimate impact on food production relative to population. While the absolute fixity of any resource seems implausible, this special case is worth brief pursuit. The situation is pictured in Figure 4.3. This economy begins its growth under frontier conditions at $[R_0^*(1), L_0^*(1)]$ and continues along this growth path to the point $[R_0^*(4), L_0^*(4)]$ where some type of absolute limit is reached on the amount of $R_0$ that can be produced. From this point on, all growth in $L$ is committed directly to GNP production and the growth path becomes the horizontal line emanating from $R_0^*(4)$.

What will happen to GNP and GNP per capita in this case? Clearly, after $R_0^*(4)$ is reached, it is no longer possible to increase the inputs in the same proportion. If constant or decreasing returns to scale in the GNP production function hold, GNP cannot increase in proportion to $L_0$ and GNP per capita must continuously fall, although total GNP will continue rising. If the GNP production function exhibits increasing returns to scale, it is *possible* that GNP could continue rising more than in proportion to $L$ for some time. However, the $L_0/R_0$ ratio would continue rising so that, under any plausible technology, GNP per capita would eventually fall and the Malthusian margin of subsistence would be approached.

A Cobb-Douglas example will illustrate the process. Let $\hat{R}_0$ =

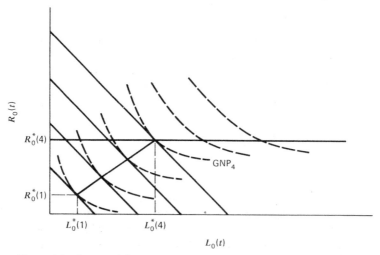

**Figure 4.3**  Growth of GNP in a Malthusian economy with a fixed limit on the input of $R_0$.

$a_0 \hat{L}_1{}^{a_1}$ represent the maximum $R_0$ output rate and the related labor-capital input rate. Once $\hat{R}_0$ has been reached, GNP can be written as

(4.3.1) $$\text{GNP}(t) = b_0[L(t) - \hat{L}_1]^{b_1} \hat{R}_0{}^{b_2}$$

GNP per capita can be written

(4.3.2) $$\frac{\text{GNP}(t)}{P(t)} = \frac{\ell b_0[L(t) - \hat{L}]^{b_1} R_0{}^{b_2}}{L(t)} = k \, \frac{[L(t) - \hat{L}_1]^{b_1}}{L(t)}$$

Since $b_1 < 1$ under any plausible technology, GNP per capita must fall as $L(t)$ grows.

## 4.4.   A SIMPLE RICARDIAN ECONOMY WITH TECHNOLOGICAL CHANGE

Technological change has been excluded from our models thus far so we could observe the effects of other factors at work. However, technological change is too important to be ignored very long. Abramovitz and Denison have shown that over 50 percent of the real U.S. economic growth since 1860 has been attributable to organizational, educational, and technological improvements. Thus we modify the earlier model by incorporating calendar time $t$ in the two production functions, representing technological change as a function of time. In addition, we will assume that (optimized) $L_0$ is a constant fraction of $L$.[4]

(4.4.1) $$\text{GNP} = f(L_0, R_0, t)$$

(4.4.2) $$R_0 = g(L_1, t)$$

(4.4.3) $$L_0 = k \, L$$

All of the variables are now to be thought of as functions of time. What can be said about the rate of change of GNP over time? Differentiating (4.4.1) and (4.4.2) with respect to time[5] we get

---

[4]As we have seen, in the Cobb-Douglas model the optimized $L_0^*$ is a constant fraction of $L$. This need not be true with other production functions but is assumed here to facilitate exposition.

[5]To indicate time derivatives, we use the "dot" notation (e.g., GNP). Differentiating with respect to time involves the repeated application of the chain rule.

$$(4.4.4) \qquad \dot{\text{GNP}} = \frac{\partial f}{\partial L_0} k\dot{L} + \frac{\partial f}{\partial R_0} \dot{R}_0 + \frac{\partial f}{\partial t}$$

$$(4.4.5) \qquad \dot{R}_0 = \frac{\partial g}{\partial L_1} (1 - k)\dot{L} + \frac{\partial g}{\partial t}$$

The first equation says that the time rate of change of GNP is equal to the rate of change of GNP with respect to $L_0$ times the time rate of change of $L_0$, plus the rate of change of GNP with respect to $R_0$ times the time rate of change of $R_0$, plus the time rate of change of GNP attributable to technological change in the GNP production process. Similarly, the second equation states that the time rate of change in the output rate of natural resource commodities equals the rate of change of $R_0$ with respect to $L_1$ times $L_1$'s time rate of change, plus the autonomous rate of change in $R_0$ due to technological improvements in those production processes. It must be remembered (in spite of our simplified notations) that the partial derivatives like $\partial f/\partial L_0$ and $\partial g/\partial L_1$ remain functions of all the original arguments of the functions.

If we substitute (4.4.5) into (4.4.4), we get an explanation of the rate of GNP growth in terms of labor-capital applications and rates of technological change in the two production functions:

$$(4.4.6) \quad \dot{\text{GNP}} = \frac{\partial f}{\partial L_0} k\dot{L} + \frac{\partial f}{\partial R_0} \cdot \frac{\partial g}{\partial L_1} (1 - k)\dot{L} + \frac{\partial f}{\partial t} + \frac{\partial f}{\partial R_0} \cdot \frac{\partial g}{\partial t}$$

The first term shows the direct effect of growing $L_0$ on GNP. The second term shows the indirect effect of the growth of $L$ as it increases $R_0$ and hence increases GNP. The last two terms are the direct and indirect technological change effects.

To be more specific, let's turn again to the Cobb-Douglas forms for $f$ and $g$, writing the model

$$(4.4.7) \qquad \text{GNP}(t) = b(t) L_0^{b_1} R_0^{b_2}$$

$$(4.4.8) \qquad R_0(t) = a(t) L_1^{a_1}$$

where $L_0 = k L$ and $L_1 = (1 - k) L$ and where it is assumed that technological change takes the form of changing $b(t)$ and $a(t)$. For this case, it is possible to derive the optimized percentage rate of growth of GNP.

$$(4.4.9) \qquad \frac{\dot{\text{GNP}}}{\text{GNP}} = \frac{\dot{b}(t)}{b(t)} + b_2 \frac{\dot{a}(t)}{a(t)} + (b_1 + a_1 b_2) \frac{\dot{L}}{L}$$

This tells us that the percentage rate of growth of GNP relates directly to the percentage rates of technological improvement in the GNP and $R$ production processes and to the percentage rate of growth of $L$. The overall returns-to-scale parameter, $\rho$, reappears as the coefficient of $\dot{L}/L$.

There will be some positive percentage rate of GNP growth as long as $\dot{L}/L$ is positive, provided technological change isn't negative. To determine whether or not GNP *per capita* is growing over time, it is necessary to compare GNP/GNP to the population growth rate which is, under an earlier assumption, the same as $\dot{L}/L$.[6] A glance at (4.4.9) tells us that there are many ways in which the GNP growth rate can exceed the population growth rate, including various combinations of technological change and scale economies. Table 4.2 illustrates various combinations of values.

What will be happening to the relative values of labor-capital, $L$, and natural resource commodities, $R_0$, in the Cobb-Douglas economy? Our economic intuition (perhaps aided a bit by some mathematics[7]) would probably tell us the following:

1.  In a frontier situation with $a_1 = 1$, the existence of positive technological change in the production of $R_0$ would cause its relative value to fall over time, while no technological advance would leave relative values unchanged.

2.  In a Ricardian situation with $a_1 < 1$, the absence of technological change into the production of $R_0$ would imply a rising scarcity and unit value of $R_0$, but sufficiently strong technological advance could offset the Ricardian tendency toward falling efficiency in the production of $R_0$, keeping the relative scarcity of $R_0$ constant or even falling.

## 4.5. NATURAL RESOURCE STOCK EFFECTS AND THE CONCEPT OF USER COST

The preceding models have exhibited three ways in which the conditions of natural resource availability can place a drag on economic growth, thus making natural resource commodities scarce:

[6]It was assumed that $L = \ell P$, so that $\dot{L} = \ell \dot{P}$ and $\dot{L}/L = \ell \dot{P}/\ell P = \dot{P}/P$.
[7]Using the formula for the slope of the $R_0 - L_0$ transformation curve (4.2.7), taking its logarithm and differentiating, one can show that the percentage rate of change of the absolute value of this slope is

$$\frac{\dot{a}}{a} - (1 - a_1)\frac{\dot{L}}{L}$$

**Table 4.2.**   Percentage Rates of GNP Growth with Technological Change in the Cobb-Douglas Model

$$\frac{\dot{b}}{b} = 0.02, \frac{\dot{a}}{a} = 0.01, \frac{\dot{L}}{L} = 0.02$$

| $b_1$ | $b_2$ | $a_1$ | $\rho$ | $\dfrac{\dot{GNP}}{GNP}$ |
|-------|-------|-------|--------|------------------|
| 0.6 | 0.4 | 1.0 | 1.0 | 0.044 |
| 0.6 | 0.4 | 0.5 | 0.8 | 0.040 |
| 0.6 | 0.4 | 1.5 | 1.2 | 0.048 |
| 0.4 | 0.6 | 1.0 | 1.0 | 0.046 |
| 0.4 | 0.6 | 0.5 | 0.7 | 0.040 |

1. Through the necessity of using scarce labor capital in the production of natural resource commodities.
2. Through a Malthusian limit on natural resource commodity production, whatever the reason.
3. Through increasing costs of natural resource commodity production (decreasing returns to scale) as the scale of production is expanded.

The possibility that the size of the remaining *stock* (or reserves) of natural resources might affect the costs of natural resource commodity production has not been considered other than by way of brief introduction in Chapter 2. It seems reasonable that stocks should affect natural resource commodity production costs, for as depletion of reserves proceeds, poorer quality deposits are generally utilized. Conversely, if new discoveries lead to expanded reserves, it is conceivable that production costs might fall.

A feature of the preceding models with no stock effects is that producing another unit of $R_0$ output in any one year had no effect on potential $R_0$ production in other years. In such a case, maximizing GNP on a year-by-year basis makes perfect sense. Naturally, we have abstracted from the process of capital accumulation (i.e., investment in man-made equipment), but if the objective were to increase such investment, it still could be done most easily out of an annually maximized GNP.

The real world *does* exhibit stock effects in natural resource commodity production, thereby introducing some of society's most perplexing technical and moral problems. Stock effects can take two forms: (1) an increase of extraction costs as depletion proceeds, and (2) a reduction in future use due to a finite limit to the total quantity of the *in situ* resource. While finite limits are often mentioned in casual discussions, the first type of stock effect is the most generally applicable, for there are nearly always ways of producing more of the resource if costs are not limited.

Stock effects can be exhibited in our model in the following fashion:

(4.5.1) $$GNP(t) = f[L_0(t), R_0(t)]$$

(4.5.2) $$R_0(t) = g[L_1(t), S(t)]$$

(4.5.3) $$S(t) = S(0) - \sum_{\tau=1}^{t-1} R_0(\tau)$$

Little has changed except that the current stock or reserves, $S(t)$, appears in the natural resource commodity production function, while (4.5.3) defines $S(t)$ in terms of a beginning stock, $S(0)$, and cumulated use.

Equation 4.5.3 raises an interesting issue of the units in which natural resource commodities and reserves are stated. The *in situ* resource may be an ore, with 20 percent iron content, while the natural resource commodity may be taconite, with a 75 percent iron content of a different chemical makeup. However, this problem of units can always be skirted by agreeing to measure both the *in situ* resource and the natural resource commodity in units of the same basic resource (e.g., tons of iron). This convention may lead to other problems, for one unit produced may require the effective removal of more than one unit from stocks. For example, one ton of taconite containing 0.75 tons of recoverable iron may require the processing of ores containing 0.9 tons of iron of which 0.15 ton is left in unrecoverable form in the tailings. Similar relations exist between board feet of saw logs produced (the natural resource commodity) and board feet of standing timber removed (the *in situ* resource), or between tons of fish caught (the natural resource commodity) and total stock depletions that include fish killed or maimed and not recovered.

These examples show that our simple accounting identity (4.5.3) may obscure some conceptual difficulties. Nonetheless, this simple accounting device suffices to capture the essential features of intertemporal interdependence.

Stock effects clearly connect the decisions made in one period with the production potentials of following periods: the more *in situ* resources used today *ceteris paribus*, the higher will be tomorrow's recovery costs. The perception of such a pattern of increasing costs may then

affect the behavior of private or public agents who make natural resource commodity production decisions.

Even if this type of depletion effect is not present because of the
uniformity of known reserves, resources used up today will simply not
be available for use in future periods. Naturally, recycling possibilities
exist for some natural commodities, requiring some qualification of this
simple picture.

The introduction of depletion effects greatly increases the complexity of the analysis. It is no longer true that maximizing GNP each year is
the best policy to follow. Thus, if we wish to ask what pattern of natural
resource use over time is "best," we must define "best" as some function of the values of GNP over time. If our aim is to develop a descriptive
model of how an actual system would use natural resources over time,
we must characterize both the perceptions of reserves and the
motivations of the different agents making natural resource use decisions over time.

To clarify the nature of these intertemporal interdependencies, we
will develop the simplest possible version of the model of (4.5.1 to 4.5.3).
Let time be divided into only two periods: now and the future. Let GNP
production depend on the labor-capital input, the amount of natural
resources used, $R(t)$, and the stock present at the beginning of each
period, $S(t)$, the latter to reflect the stock effects. The initial *in situ* stock,
$S(1)$, and the amount of labor-capital, $L(t)$ are given. Thus we can write

(4.5.4)          $$GNP(1) = f_1[L(1),\ R(1),\ S(1)]$$
$$GNP(2) = f_2[L(2),\ R(2),\ S(2)]$$

Deferring to Chapter 8 the discussion of appropriate intertemporal
criteria for social decision making, we simply assume that this two-
period economy would choose to maximize the present value of present
and future GNP. The decision problem then is to

(4.4.5)     maximize $\{\phi[R(1), R(2), S(2)] = f_1[L(1), R(1), S(1)]$
$$+\ \delta \cdot f_2[L(2), R(2), S(2)]\}$$
subject to: $R(2) = S(1) - R(1)$
$$S(2) = S(1) - R(1)$$

where $\delta$ is the social weight to be given to future GNP. The tradeoff
between GNP today and in the future is obvious: the more natural
resources we use today, the fewer will be available for use in the future
and the more severe will be the effects of depleted stocks on future costs
of production.

One can use the Lagrange technique for solving this simple problem, which produces the following necessary condition for an optimum intertemporal allocation of our natural resource:

$$(4.5.6) \qquad \frac{\partial f_1}{\partial R(1)} = \delta \left[ \frac{\partial f_2}{\partial R(2)} + \frac{\partial f_2}{\partial S(2)} \right]$$

This tells us that the socially optimum amount of $R^*(1)$ equates the marginal increase in today's GNP to the present value of the marginal sacrifices being imposed on the future. These future sacrifices take the forms of future production precluded through resource exhaustion, $\partial f_2/ \partial R(2)$, and increased future production costs caused by stock depletions, that is, decreased efficiency of future production ($\partial f_2/\partial S_2$).

The present value of the sacrifices being imposed on the future has come to be called the "*user cost*" of natural resource use in natural resource economics' jargon. For the marginal unit of *in situ* resource being used today it is nothing more than the *marginal intertemporal opportunity cost* of the natural resources being used.

User cost is an important natural resource concept for several practical reasons. First, it is central to defining any concept of social optimality in the intertemporal use of resources—a fact we have just exhibited. Second, we have an interest in analyzing the extent to which our existing institutions for natural resource decision making adequately take user cost into account. When people question the adequacy of existing market arrangements for the intertemporal allocation of natural resources, they are basically raising questions of the appropriate definition and consideration of user cost.

The next section further develops the concept of user cost and relates it to the equally important concept of *rent* on *in situ* natural resources.

## 4.6.  STOCK EFFECTS, USER COST, AND RENTS ON *IN SITU* NATURAL RESOURCES

Let us consider the relationship between user cost and rents on *in situ* resources. "Rent" is a widely used but confusing term in economics jargon. One usually thinks of rent as a periodic payment for the use of a capital asset, such as the rent paid for the occupancy of a house or farmland. Such payments will generally contain two components: payments to cover the owner's cost of upkeep and management and a premium reflecting the market's willingness to pay for the uniqueness of the site.

Take the simple example of an urban house of a typical sort, costing $50,000 to construct. If equally desirable urban houses could be reproduced without limit (like automobiles, but with the supply curve being infinitely elastic at $50,000), the market price of a new urban house would be $50,000. This price would cover the wages of management of the housing developer as well as his or her out-of-pocket costs, but it would not include any positive land price under our assumption of unlimited reproducibility. If developers generally tried to raise prices above $50,000, other developers would find it temporarily profitable to come into the housing business, pushing the price back down. If houses typically last 40 years and 5 percent of their construction cost must be expended on upkeep per year, then the annual "rental" on an urban house would be 7.5 percent of its construction cost or $3750. This payment would represent simply the coverage of construction and upkeep costs but no payment for site uniqueness.

Now increase realism a bit by assuming that there exists a limited number of "superior" sites that are differentiated from the endless supply of other sites by proximity to the work center of the city. These sites permit their occupants to save $1000 per year on necessary travel costs. If the typical consumer's discount rate is 10 percent per year, houses in these superior sites would tend to sell for a premium of $10,000—the capitalized value of an infinite sequence of $1000 savings. These plots of land would have a rent of $1000 per year, attributable to the permanent uniqueness of their location. Rents arising from permanently unique characteristics of assets are called *Ricardian* or uniqueness rents.

The concept of Ricardian rent is also applicable to exhaustible resources such as ores or mineral fuels under a special set of circumstances. In such cases, rent as a payment for uniqueness stems not from a permanent characteristic like "closeness to the work center" but from differences in the one-time recovery costs of various resource deposits. Like land, reserves of nonland natural resources are often nonhomogeneous in terms of concentration or costs of recovery. Thus one can intuit that if demand is strong eough to require the simultaneous exploitation of more than one quality of deposit, Ricardian rents like those arising on land would be generated.

But why would deposits of differing qualities be brought into use simultaneously? It is obvious that any entrepreneur interested in maximizing the present value of his or her mining enterprise will exploit the best (least costly) deposits first and turn to inferior deposits only after the superior deposits are exhausted. Rational simultaneous ex-

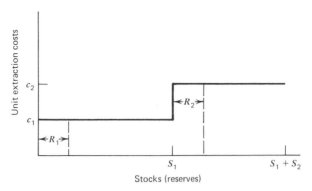

**Figure 4.4** Hypothetical costs of exploiting two deposits.

ploitation of differing grades can occur only if the costs of production from any one deposit increase with the current rate of production. A limiting case of this is found where some physical limit on the rate of production exists. Figure 4.4 illustrates that case. $S_1$ and $S_2$ represent two known deposits with unit extraction costs $c_1$ and $c_2$. However, because of some physical feature such as limited access to the deposits, the rates of production per period are limited to $R_1$ on the first deposit and $R_2$ on the second deposit. Thus while the long-run supply curve consists of the segments in Figure 4.4, the short-run supply curve consists of the sequence of segments shown in Figure 4.5. If the demand per period is given by the curve $D_1$, only the superior deposit will be worked until the stock $S_1$ is exhausted. But if $D_2$ obtains, then both deposits will be worked simultaneously and Ricardian rents will accrue to the units extracted from the first deposit.

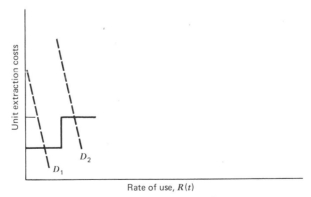

**Figure 4.5** The short-run supply curve.

If only a few deposits were known worldwide (like the diamond "pipes" of southern Africa), such a situation might continue over a long period. In other cases, its continuation seems implausible. The owners of the deposit $S_1$ (Figure 4.4) have every motivation to expand their production capacity to a point where they can supply a larger share of the market. Indeed, if $S_1$ is competitively owned by many owners, capacity would be expanded until all current output is being supplied from the lower cost deposits and price has fallen to $c_1$. However, if deposits of different average quality exist, each deposit exhibiting increasing marginal cost beyond some rate of output, and if demand is then strong enough to call inferior deposits into production, output from superior deposits can continue to generate Ricardian rents.

Stock effects lead to intertemporal interdependence of decisions, and we have seen how the optimal pattern of use of *in situ* resources over time requires recognition of user cost (i.e., the present value of future sacrifices implied by current resource use). When user cost is positive, we would expect that the parties who face the prospect of experiencing these sacrifices would be willing to enter the market for deposits of *in situ* resources to buy and hold these deposits as long as the going price for *in situ* resources is less than the present value of the future sacrifices to be avoided, provided that all of the sacrifices to be avoided are of a private and not a public goods nature. Under conditions of well-informed, competitive markets, today's market price for currently marginal ("just producible") *in situ* resources will equal the user cost associated with their use. This price could be called a *"scarcity rent"* representing the price a producer of natural resource commodities has to pay for currently "just producible" marginal *in situ* resources. Anyone choosing to buy superior resources would, naturally, have to pay an

**Table 4.3.**   Definitions of Terms Relating to Natural Resources Scarcity

---

*Stock Effects:* the physical effects on future conditions of natural resource availability, including changed extraction costs and changed limits on the total stock available, caused by today's resource extraction.

*User Cost:* the present value of all future sacrifices (including foregone use, higher extraction costs, increased environmental costs) associated with the use of a particular unit of an *in situ* resource.

*Scarcity Rent:* the user cost of the marginal unit being extracted at any point of time and, under appropriate market conditions, the market value of these marginal *in situ* resources.

*Ricardian Rent:* the excess of the market value of supramarginal units of *in situ* resources over current scarcity rents.

---

additional Ricardian rent equal to the production cost saving on such resources.

Several definitions have been introduced in this section and these can be confusing, not only to the reader seeing them for the first time but to economists whose terminology is not standardized in this field. Thus Table 4.3 presents the definitions that will continue to be used in this book.

## 4.7. A GENERALIZED MODEL OF USER COST AND SCARCITY RENTS

The concept of user cost was developed in the last section in the context of a simple two-period model in which one had to know only one value for the user cost—that obtaining in the first period. Reality exhibits an infinite sequence of todays and tomorrows. Since user cost is the present value of the sacrifices placed on the future, we might expect it to change over time, as the severity of depletion increases. We will see that user cost is, generally, a continuous function of time. We will now develop a simple model which will permit us to generalize the two-period model of (4.5.4) to an indefinite time horizon. As a result, we will be able to observe the time pattern of user costs and scarcity rents on *in situ* resources. To keep things as simple as possible, we assume that GNP is a function of the rate of natural resource use and the natural resource stock, incorporating the changing value of $L(t)$ in the argument $t$.

$$(4.7.1) \qquad GNP(t) = f[S(t), R(t), t]$$

where time is considered to be continuous.[8] The stock accounting relationship for this model is

$$(4.7.2) \qquad S(t) = S(o) - \int_0^t R(\tau)d\tau$$

the integral representing accumulated usage. It follows from (4.7.2) or intuition that the time rate of change of $S(t)$ is

$$(4.7.3) \qquad \dot{S}(t) = -R(t)$$

Society's problem of optimum intertemporal resource use can now be stated as choosing the entire time path $R(t) \geq 0$ in order to

[8]Assumed conditions on the parital derivatives of $f$ are that $f_S > 0$, $f_R > 0$, and $f_{RS} > 0$.

(4.7.4)                    $\text{maximize} \int_0^\infty f[S(t), R(t), t]e^{-rt} \, dt$

$$\text{subject to: } \dot{S}(t) = -R(t)$$
$$S(t) > 0$$

where $e^{-rt}$ represents the continuous time discount factor. This statement of the problem looks simple enough, but we must have techniques for solving it. Fortunately, the modern generalization of the classical calculus of variations known as *optimal control theory* makes it possible to derive the *necessary conditions* for $R^*(t)$ just as one does in a standard calculus maximization problem. This theory tells us to form an auxiliary function, $H$, and to maximize it with respect to $R(t)$ as in ordinary calculus.

(4.7.5)                    $H = f[S(t), R(t), t] - q(t)R(t)$

In this expression $q(t)$ acts like a Lagrange multiplier on the constraint linking $R(t)$ and $S(t)$.[9] If we interpret $q(t)$ as the marginal *user cost* associated with the rate of resource use $R(t)$, the maximization of (4.7.5) as a necessary condition for $R^*(t)$ makes intuitive sense: at every point in time, $t$, $R^*(t)$ must maximize the difference between current GNP resulting from the use of $R$ and the user cost associated with that use. Differentiating $H$ with respect to $R(t)$ and setting the result equal to zero yields:

(4.7.6)                    $\dfrac{\partial f[S(t), R(t), t]}{\partial R(t)} = q(t)$

That is, the contemporary marginal product of $R$ (in terms of current GNP) should always be equated to the marginal user cost. Assuming competitive, well-informed markets, we can also interpret (4.7.6) as saying that the value of marginal product of $R$ should always be equated to the contemporary scarcity rental rate on *in situ* resources.

While this characterizes $R^*(t)$ generally, it doesn't tell us anything directly about the path of $R^*(t)$ over time. If we can characterize the time

---

[9]For a general exposition of optimal control theory, see Michael D. Intriligator, *Mathematical Optimization and Economic Theory*, Englewood Cliffs, N.J.: Prentice-Hall, Inc. 1971, Chapter 11, or K. J. Arrow and M. Kurz, *Public Investment, the Rate of Return, and Optimal Fiscal Policy*, Baltimore: The Johns Hopkins Press, 1970, Chapter 2.

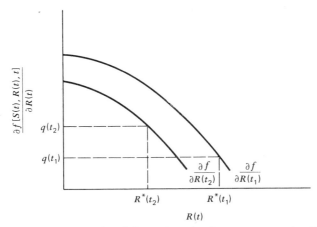

**Figure 4.6** The time paths of the rent on *in situ* resources and optimum resource use.

path of $q(t)$, our knowledge of the shape of $\partial f/\partial R(t)$ will permit us to trace out the path of $R(t)$ as shown in Figure 4.6.

The optimality condition (4.7.6) characterizes the optimal *flow* of resources from *in situ* status to intermediate good (natural resource commodity) status. The time path of scarcity rents, $q(t)$, must relate to the optimum stocks of *in situ* resources that society should hold since $q(t)$ is the price of marginal *in situ* resources. The size of the stocks carried forward, $S(t)$ will affect $q(t)$ and vice versa. Holding an *in situ* stock involves sacrificing the current uses to which it might be put, so the holding of stocks must be justified by some kind of reward or return. Within the context of our simple model, holding a unit in stock for a short interval can produce two forms of reward: an increase in value if $q(t)$ rises over the interval (reflecting higher-valued uses in the future); and a reduction in future recovery-production costs as a result of having a larger, higher quality stock. If *in situ* resources have a unit value $q(t)$ today, the rate of return on this value generated by these two forms of reward should be as great as society could obtain from alternative investments. Stated mathematically, this gives us the following characterization of optimal *in situ* stocks and their price, $q(t)$, over time:[10]

$$(4.7.7) \qquad \frac{\dot{q}(t) + \dfrac{\partial f}{\partial S(t)}}{q(t)} = r$$

[10]This result can also be directly derived from optimum control theory.

where $r$ is the appropriate opportunity cost of capital, that is, the discount rate used in (4.7.4). From (4.7.7) we can conclude the following about optimum stocks:

1.  If $\dfrac{\partial f}{\partial S(t)} = 0$, that is, if reduced stocks do not affect production costs,

then *in situ* scarcity rents must arise at a rate equal to the discount rate.

2.  If $\dfrac{\partial f}{\partial S(t)} > 0$, *in situ* scarcity rents will rise more slowly than $r$.

This tells us a great deal about the behavior of *in situ* scarcity rents, $q(t)$, as an indicator of *in situ* scarcity under optimum management: finite stocks would cause rents to rise at a rate $r$, but stock effects of the type $\partial f/\partial S(t) > 0$ would diminish this rate of rent increase. It is perhaps possible but implausible that the value of $\partial f/\partial S(t)$ could be so large that $\dot{q}(t)$ would be negative. These possibilities will be further investigated in Chapter 5.

## 4.8. FURTHER ANALYSIS OF ECONOMIC GROWTH POTENTIAL UNDER A FIXED SUPPLY OF NATURAL RESOURCES

The models presented to date have abstracted from a very important element in the total economic growth picture: man-made capital and its role in production. This section once again introduces capital into a setting of no technological change to investigate very long-term production potentials with a finite resource stock. It is also assumed that the natural resource input, $R(t)$, is "essential" to production, so that it is not possible to substitute *completely* other inputs for natural resources.

One can imagine several scenarios of resource use in keeping with a finite stock:

1.  That the resources would be used up quickly in a period of rapid growth and high living, followed by a collapse of the system because of the essential nature of the resources.
2.  That the resources would be used very slowly, resulting in low output levels and standards of living but lasting a long time.
3.  That natural resources are used rapidly to develop production capacity for renewable inputs that can then be substituted in large measure for further use of the nonrenewable natural resource, making continued production possible for a long time span.

4. That natural resources are "conserved" and used very slowly, only to be made obsolete by technological breakthrough.

5. That technological change and the substitution of renewable inputs for natural resources are sufficient to keep GNP growing indefinitely, but the environmental effects become so detrimental that welfare may not be improved.

These possibilities suggest a number of characteristics of the economy that are likely to be vital in determining the long-term path of economic and environmental well-being: (1) the ease with which renewable inputs can be substituted for natural resources, (2) the strength of time preference that is actually applied in the decisions being made (i.e., the effective discount rate), and (3) the social utility function that indicates society's well-being as a function of GNP or the consumption level. These characteristics are all incorporated in the analysis of Dasgupta and Heal (1974), who ask *whether or not aggregate output must inevitably decline to zero* in the face of finite "essential" resource stocks with a constant population, and in the absence of technological change. They are not claiming that these are realistic conditions, of course, but these pessimistic conditions provide the basis for a conservative analysis of long-run production possibilities.

Very interestingly, the answer to their question turns out to be "no," although that answer is not applicable to all situations. Let us see how they incorporate this issue in a model, then interpret some of their results. They assume a production function for final goods and services $F[K(t), R(t)]$ where $K(t)$ is the man-made capital stock at time $t$ and $R(t)$ is the rate of use of natural resources, the finite stock of which is $S(0)$. It is assumed that an optimum natural resource use path is that which maximizes

(4.8.1) $\quad \phi = \int\limits_0^\infty U[C(t)]e^{-rt}\, dt$

$\qquad$ subject to: (a) $\dot{K}(t) = F[K(t), R(t)] - C(t)$

$\qquad\qquad\qquad$ (b) $\int\limits_0^\infty R(t)dt \leqslant S(0)$

$\qquad\qquad\qquad$ (c) $C(t), K(t), R(t) \geqslant 0$

$U[C(t)]$ is a social utility function with consumption as its argument. The objective function represents the present value of utility over an infinite horizon when the social discount rate is $r$. Since investment, $\dot{K}(t)$, and consumption constitute the possible uses of the output of final goods and services, they are related to each other and to the level of output by the constraint (a). Constraint (b), of course, simply says that cumulative natural resource use over the infinite planning horizon cannot exceed the stock, $S_0$, while (c) requires the variables to remain nonnegative.

Dasgupta and Heal derive their interesting results from this simple model through the application of optimal control theory. We interpret some of those results without presenting them in mathematical form.

1. If the production function $F$ is such that the marginal productivity of the natural resource input increases without bound when $R(t)$ approaches zero, then $R^*(t) > 0$ for all $t > 0$.

This says that the socially optimum path of natural resource use is one calling for some positive rate of continued use *forever*, provided the marginal product of the $R(t)$ input increases without bound whenever $R(t)$ approaches zero. The best-known example of such a production function is (once again) the Cobb-Douglas function,[11] for which each input is clearly "essential," and for which

(4.8.2) $$MP_R \equiv \frac{\partial F}{\partial R(t)} = \frac{b_0 b_2 K^{b_1}}{R^{1-b_2}}$$

As $R$ approaches zero, $K$ remaining positive, this expression clearly increases without bound. Many people feel that this is a very unrealistic or impossible condition to be met in reality, so they tend to discount the relevance of this result. The reader should also note that only certain patterns of natural resource use can remain positive forever and still sum to a finite quantity (so they meet constraint 4.8.1b). One example would be $R(t) = S(0) \, ae^{-at}$, the definite integral of which is $S(0)$.

2. If the production function $F$ is such that the marginal productivity of the natural resources input approaches a finite limit as $R(t)$ approaches zero, then either
   (a) $R^*(t) > 0$ for all $t$, or
   (b) there exists a finite point in time, $T$, such that $R^*(t) > 0$ for $t \leq T$ and $R^*(t) = 0$ for $t > T$.

This result tells us that even if the marginal productivity of $R(t)$ remains finite (an assumption which may be more realistic), $R^*(t)$ can remain positive forever; otherwise it will initially be positive, dropping to zero at some time $T$ and staying at zero. An example of a production function with this marginal product characteristic is the "constant elasticity of

---

[11] $F[K(t), R(t)] = b_0 K(t)^{b_1} R(t)^{b_2}$.

substitution" production function with parameter $\sigma$ in the interval $0 \leq \sigma < 1$.[12]

These results characterize $R^*(t)$ to some extent, but they tell us nothing about $C^*(t)$, the aggregate consumption path corresponding to $R^*(t)$. Dasgupta and Heal derive the following result:

3. If the production function $F$ is a CES production function with $0 \leq \sigma < 1$, then depending on the discount rate and additional characteristics of $F$, it is possible that
   (a) $C^*(t)$ will grow without bound over time, or
   (b) $C^*(t)$ will approach zero over time.

This establishes the *logical possibility* that aggregate consumption could grow without bound even in the face of a finite stock of an essential resource and in the absence of technological change.

Solow (1974) has taken a different approach to the issue by asking, "With a finite non-renewable stock of 'essential' natural resources, what is the highest level of consumption which can be maintained forever?" Note the difference in the criterion used: there is no utility function and no discounting of the future, simply an intertemporal egalitarian objective often referred to as the Rawlsian or max-min criterion (John Rawls, 1971). This criterion will be more fully discussed in Chapter 7. Solow assumes a Cobb-Douglas aggregate production function

(4.8.3) $$Q = kL^g R^h K^{1-g-h}$$

having labor, natural resources, and capital as its arguments, with $R$ constituting an essential input. If (4.8.3) is divided by $L$, one gets

(4.8.4) $$\frac{Q}{L} = k\left(\frac{R}{L}\right)^h \left(\frac{K}{L}\right)^{1-g-h}$$

making it clear that with a fixed amount of capital per worker ($K/L$), output per worker must fall to zero if resources per worker fall to zero. The only way to maintain a positive level of $Q/L$ is to permit $K/L$ to increase without bound to offset $R/L$ falling toward zero. However, economic growth theory has proved that if $L$ grows exponentially, there is

[12]The CES production function is given by $F(K,R) = [\beta K^{(\sigma-1)/\sigma} + (1-\beta)R^{(\sigma-1)/\sigma}]^{\sigma/(\sigma-1)}$. The parameter $\sigma$ is, for this function, the "elasticity of substitution," measuring the ease or difficulty of substituting one input for the other. Only if $0 \leq \sigma < 1$ is the $R$ input "essential."

an upper bound to the amount of capital per worker ($K/L$) that can be accumulated. But just above we noted that $K/L$ must tend toward infinity if $Q/L$ is to be maintained. Thus:

4. If the aggregate production function is Cobb-Douglas and the labor force grows exponentially, then output per worker must fall to zero over time.

This reinforces our intuitive feeling that continued exponential population growth ultimately must confront a Malthusian limit. This result does not depend on the "corner" properties of the Cobb-Douglas function.

Solow's further analysis continues under the assumption of a constant labor force, and his main conclusion is the following:

5. With the Cobb-Douglas production function, a *positive* level of aggregate consumption that can be maintained *forever* does exist. This level is a concave, unbounded function of the initial capital stock.

Any level of consumption can be maintained forever if the initial capital stock is big enough. The implied pattern of natural resource use is tending toward zero, with an offsetting increase in the capital input. "In particular, earlier generations are entitled to draw down the pool [of resources] (optimally, of course!) so long as they add (optimally, of course!) to the stock of reproducible capital." (Solow, 1974, p. 41).

What is concluded from all of this regarding long-term prospects for the human race? The Dasgupta, Heal, and Solow results were arrived at from a conservative viewpoint in the sense that no technological improvement was assumed. On the other hand, the assumption of stationary population and particular forms for the production function may have been optimistic. Following the optimum policy derived from the utilitarian criterion (4.8.1) under an assumed CES production function, there is a logical possibility of aggregate consumption growing forever. If, however, a Cobb-Douglas function best represents aggregate production possibilities, "optimal aggregate consumption" as they define it must fall to zero. If the criterion is changed to Solow's Rawlsian criterion, then following the optimum natural resource use path can sustain aggregate consumption at some positive level forever, but the level will be high or low, depending on the initial capital stock.

Do such findings have any policy relevance? They certainly tell us that, under quite conservative assumptions, it is *not logically impossible* to maintain aggregate consumption forever, or perhaps even to have it grow forever. However, the results nearly all depend heavily on the properties of the production function at its "corners," that is, at extreme values of its arguments. Empirical production functions (see Chapter 6) frequently indicate that Cobb-Douglas or CES functions fit actual data well, but the functions are always estimated from nonextreme observations. Furthermore, the results assume an adherence to an optimum natural resource-use path. If we could estimate such a path, would our institutions lead us along it or not? Recent experiences with national energy use and water use under emergency conditions lead one to be pessimistic. The policymaker had best not count on these results.

## 4.9. SUMMARY

This has been a difficult chapter but it is central to all further consideration of natural resources. Its purpose has been to identify ways in which the conditions of natural resource availability can affect the growth potential of the economy. The strategy has been to introduce one feature of resource availability at a time into an appropriately simple macroeconomic model to permit the derivation of the implications of that feature for long-run economic growth. Simultaneously, we have identified at least two indicators of natural resource scarcity, the relative price of natural resource commodities and the scarcity rent on *in situ* resources, and have learned about their behavior in relation to known conditions of physical scarcity and technology.

Natural resource scarcity can make itself felt through absolute limits on available stocks or through the costs of recovering natural resource commodities. A "frontier economy" of unlimited natural resources still faces growth limits imposed by the scarcity of its labor-capital input, but the relative value of natural resource commodities and labor capital would not change over time. A "simple Ricardian economy" faces similar limits, but the relative value of natural resource commodities will rise over time as the marginal cost of recovering larger quantities of natural resource commodities rises. Returns to scale in such an economic system depend on the technologies of both natural resource commodity production and final goods and services production. Malthusian limits to natural resource commodity production serve to slow growth and to cause per capita output to fall, but such limits seem unlikely.

Technological change opens many new possibilities for aggregate and per capita economic growth. The aggregate growth rate becomes a function of the growth rate of the labor-capital input and the rates of technological improvement in natural resource commodity production and GNP production.

Natural resource "stock effects" can be expected to be operational in the real world and they imply intertemporal interdependence in the management of natural resources. No longer will year-by-year maximization of output be appropriate. Current natural resource commodity production now has associated with it not only extraction costs but a "user cost" consisting of the present value of the sacrifices imposed on the future by current use of *in situ* resources. In a competitive, well-informed economy, a market value of *in situ* resources at the current margin of exploitation called "scarcity rent" will be established. Rent on *in situ* resources is often mentioned as a measure of natural resource scarcity, but it has been shown that the rate of increase of rents will be affected by the impact of changing *in situ* stock levels on extraction costs. In the absence of such effects, rents always increase with increasing scarcity at a rate equal to the discount rate.

Finally, a review of some major theoretical studies of very long-term growth potentials with limited stocks of "essential" natural resources showed it to be logically possible (under some not-unreasonable conditions of production) to continue positive output forever and, under some conditions, even to have the output level increase without bound. While these conclusions free us from the *certainty* of a Malthusian fate, they provide few grounds for relaxing our current concerns.

# Chapter 5

# OPTIMAL RESOURCE USE OVER TIME AND LIKELY MARKET BEHAVIOR

Chapter 4 identified various ways in which the conditions of natural resource availability could affect the economic growth path of a national economy. The models used were highly aggregated as growth models typically must be. This chapter looks in greater detail at the natural resource commodity producing sector of the economy in order to (1) further clarify the idea of a socially optimum pattern of natural resource use over time, (2) to ask the extent to which well-informed, reasonably competitive markets are likely to approximate such a pattern of resource use, and (3) to determine from these inquiries the likely relationships of natural resource commodity prices, production costs, and *in situ* scarcity rents to physical concepts of scarcity.

The characterization of a socially optimum pattern of resource use, while of necessity quite abstract, provides a benchmark against which the performance of different market structures can be judged. Since the onset of increasing energy prices and accompanying worries about the international availability of other nonrenewable resources, many doubts have been expressed about the likelihood that free enterprise, within a market setting, will establish a socially responsible pattern of use of nonrenewable resources. References are made to the myopia of the market and the greediness of private enterprise, but the accusations are often contradictory. If decisions are short sighted and resources are being used up overly rapidly, why, on March 23, 1977, did the Secretary of Interior feel impelled to warn companies holding federal oil and gas leases to show cause why they weren't producing or face the possibility of losing their leases? Prior to that, on February 3, 1977, the *Wall Street Journal* ran a front-page article entitled "The Waiting Game: Sizeable Gas Reserves Untapped as Producers Await Profitable Prices."

We must distinguish between short-run decisions and the long run. It is logically possible that the long-run trend might represent overly rapid use of resources, accompanied by an undesirable degree of withholding of supplies during unusual short-term conditions. The occurrences referred to by the Secretary and in the *WSJ* occurred at a time when it seemed likely that price controls on gas might be dropped or price ceilings sharply raised. Under such expectations, firms might withhold supplies over a short period.

For the most part, we are interested in the long term, and we want to inquire how markets can be expected to work in allocating natural resources over time, that is, how a realistic market-determined pattern of natural resource use is likely to compare with a theoretically derived optimum pattern. These markets will also produce data that we can observe, data on natural resource commodity prices, *in situ* scarcity rents, extraction costs, quantities produced, and quantities estimated to be in reserve. What can we learn from these data about the effectiveness of our actual market processes? Can we detect from them when our national or world economies are getting into trouble re resources? Thus we ask about the usefulness of some of these variables as indicators or indexes of scarcity.

## 5.1.  A BASIC MODEL OF OPTIMUM NATURAL RESOURCE USE OVER TIME

A model of the natural resource commodity sector must reflect conditions of demand for natural resource commodities, the technology for producing natural resource commodities, the effects of the existing stocks of *in situ* resources on production costs, and the rules or procedures that govern the decisions made by the sector over time. Such a model could be a *positive* model that describes actual observed behavior or it could be a *normative* model permitting the derivation of rules concerning how the sector *should be* run according to some specified criterion. The model developed below is a normative model that will permit us to derive rules characterizing optimum behavior from a societywide economic viewpoint. We then ask to what extent the existing socioeconomic system is likely to behave in this way.

The relationships of the model are given below.

(5.1.1)          $R_0(t) = g[L(t), S(t), t]$

$p(t) = D[R_0(t), t]$

$$SB(t) = \int_0^{R_0(t)} D[\eta(t), t]d\eta + A[S(t)]$$

The first relation is the natural resource commodity production function we have worked with before, with $L(t)$ being the rate of input of the composite capital-labor input, $S(t)$ entering as an argument of the function to reflect "stock effects" on current production, and $t$ indicating the possibility of technological improvement over time. The second relation is the demand function for natural resource commodities with $t$ acting as a surrogate for factors that may shift the demand function over time. The last relation simply indicates that the social benefits associated with a rate of natural resource commodity utilization of $R_0(t)$ are represented by the area under the natural resource commodity demand curve up to the output rate $R_0(t)$, plus the value of environmental services related to the undisturbed stock, $S(t)$.

The costs *directly* associated with the production rate $R_0(t)$ are composed of the opportunity costs of the capital-labor input and the loss of environmental services that will be assumed to be related to the remaining undisturbed stock of *in situ* resources. The costs *indirectly* associated with $R_0(t)$ are those imposed on the future as a result of using up some of the commodity stock. If we let $w$ represent the unit opportunity cost of the capital-labor input,[1] the problem of optimizing the natural resource commodity sector can be written as:

(5.1.2)    $\displaystyle \text{maximize}_{L(t)} \int_0^{\infty} \left[ \int_0^{R_0(t)} D(\eta, t)d\eta + A(S(t)) - wL(t) \right] e^{-rt} dt$

subject to $S(t) = S(0) - \int_0^t R_0(\tau) d\tau$

$S(t) \geq 0$

Equation 5.1.2 is once again a problem in optimum control theory, with the instrument or decision variable being $L(t)$ and the state variable being $S(t)$. The function specifying the rate of change of $S(t)$ is simply

[1]While a constant unit opportunity cost may seem overly simplified, it must be remembered that the natural resource sectors of the industrialized countries comprise no more than 5 to 15 percent of the employment or value added of such countries.

(5.1.3) $$S(t) = -R_0(t)$$

This relation, combined with the given initial stock, $S(0)$, and the non-negativity constraint on $S(t)$, serves to impose a finite stock constraint, too.

As noted in the preceding chapter, a necessary condition for the derivation of the optimum function $L^*(t)$ is that $L^*(t)$ maximize the so-called Hamiltonian function that can be interpreted as the rate of net social benefits at the instant $t$:

(5.1.4) $$H = \int_0^{R_0(t)} D(\eta, t) \, d\eta + A(S(t)) - wL(t) - q(t)R_0(t)$$

In this expression, the first two terms represent the direct and environmental benefit rate, the third term the opportunity cost of the labor-capital inputs, and the last the sacrifices imposed on future periods. $q(t)$ is the Lagrange multiplier or costate variable corresponding to the constraint (5.1.3). Differentiating $H$ with respect to $L(t)$ yields:

(5.1.5) $$\frac{\partial H}{\partial L(t)} =$$

$$D[R_0(t), t] \frac{\partial R_0(t)}{\partial L(t)} + \frac{dA[S(t)]}{dS(t)} \cdot \frac{dS(t)}{dR_0(t)} \cdot \frac{\partial R_0(t)}{\partial L(t)} - w - q(t) \frac{\partial R_0(t)}{\partial L(t)}$$

Setting this equal to zero, we get the following *Basic Condition 1* on price, cost, and rents, since $D[R_0(t), t]$ is simply the price at time $t$ when the output and utilization rate is $R_0(t)$:

(5.1.6)   Basic Condition 1: $$p(t) = \frac{dA[S(t)]}{dS(t)} + \frac{w}{\dfrac{\partial R_0(t)}{\partial L(t)}} + q(t)$$

This condition states that, under an optimum program of resource utilization, the marginal social value of natural commodities (represented by price) at any time $t$ must equal the marginal loss of environmental services plus marginal production cost[2] plus the user cost or scarcity rent on the *in situ* resources being used up. This is very similar to the simple static efficiency conditions for the production of a commodity that has

---

[2]The expression $w/[\partial R_0(t)/\partial L(t)]$ represents the marginal cost of output since $w$ is the cost of the last unit of $L$ used while $\partial R_0(t)/\partial L(t)$ is the number of units produced by that last unit. It must be remembered that $\partial R_0(t)/\partial L(t)$ remains an increasing function of $S(t)$.

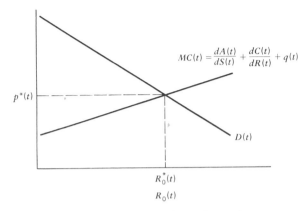

**Figure 5.1**  Characterization of the optimal rate of natural resource commodity production at each instant $t$.

no stock effects, that is, that production should be extended to a rate for which price equals marginal cost. In our case, however, marginal cost includes production, environmental, and intertemporal costs as shown in Figure 5.1.

Basic Relation 1 provides a basis for analyzing the optimal paths of $p(t)$, marginal environmental and production costs, and scarcity rent over time. While one can imagine the procedures for estimating the benefits from environmental services, $A[S(t)]$ and marginal production costs, it is much less clear how $q(t)$ can be expected to move, so we consider that issue next.

The movement of scarcity rents on *in situ* resources was rationalized at some length in Section 4.7. As we saw there, the application of optimal control theory to our optimization problem (5.1.2) also yields the following fundamental relation that we label Basic Condition 2:[3]

(5.1.7)   Basic Condition 2:   $\dot{q}(t) + [p(t) - q(t)] \dfrac{\partial R_0(t)}{\partial S(t)} + \dfrac{dA}{dS(t)} = r \cdot q(t)$

On the left-hand side of the equation, we observe the three types of benefits society enjoys from carrying forward an additional unit of *in situ* resource: (1) the increase in its value, (2) the reduction in future production costs of natural resource commodities, and (3) the value of additional environmental services. Basic Condition 2 tells us that when

[3]Basic Condition 2 can also be derived by placing the optimized values of the variables back into (5.1.2), equating that value to $q(t) \cdot S(t)$, the imputed value of the *in situ* stocks, and differentiating with respect to time.

the optimum size stock is being carried forward, the sum of these three types of benefits associated with the last unit included in the stock carried forward should yield the socially required rate of return, $r$, on the value $q(t)$. That is, $r$ is the social rate of discount and thus the minimum acceptable rate of return on any publically undertaken investment.

Basic Condition 2 is thus a condition characterizing *optimal stocks* of *in situ* resources while Basic Condition 1 characterizes the *optimal production rate* of natural resource commodities and hence the optimum rate of use of the stock. This stock-flow relationship is vital to our understanding of the necessary conditions for optimality *and* to our later discussions of the performance of planning or market mechanisms for *effecting* these conditions.

With decreasing stocks of resources over time, one would expect $q(t)$ to be positive, at least when abstracting from the effects of factors left out of our model such as shifts in the demand function or large discoveries of new stocks. Basic Condition 2 shows, however, that $\dot{q}(t)$ can be negative if the stock and environmental effects are strong enough. Obviously, if there are no such effects, optimum scarcity rents should be rising at a rate equal to the social rate of discount.

Basic Condition 2 is a generalization of a classic theorem first derived by Harold Hotelling (1931), which asserted that the socially optimum percentage rate of change of the rental rate (or net margin as it was often called) had to equal the rate of interest. That formulation of the problem was, however, incomplete for it omitted "stock effects" and environmental effects.

## 5.2.  THE PATTERN OF NATURAL RESOURCE USE OVER TIME UNDER A COMPETITIVE MARKET STRUCTURE

The point now is to characterize the path of natural resource commodity production that would be likely under well-informed, highly competitive markets. This can be done by amending the economic planning model of the preceding section. A competitive market for an ordinary product is known to "equate supply and demand"; that is, a quantity of output is determined at which marginal benefits (values along the demand curve) equal marginal costs (values along the supply curve). If we assume that the technologies of the many identical firms can be represented by the aggregate production function of (5.1.1), then that same model can be used to characterize the production pattern likely to come out of a competitive market process, with two likely exceptions: (1) the market rate of discount used by firms, $\hat{r}$, may differ from that chosen by the public sector for its planning; (2) individual firms are likely to ignore the value of environmental services related to the stock of *in situ* resources. Given the "common property" nature of environmental amenities (see Chapter 12) and waste disposal services, firms are likely to ignore these values unless they are reflected in effluent taxes or extraction taxes that the firms have to pay. The formulation of the competitive determination of the path of resource use can thus be posed as in (5.1.2) with the omission of the $A[S(t)]$ term and by substituting $\hat{r}$ for $r$. Basic Conditions 1 and 2 corresponding to this formulation of the problem are:

(5.2.1)   Basic Condition $\hat{1}$: $\hat{p}(t) = \dfrac{w}{\dfrac{\partial R_0(t)}{\partial L(t)}} + \hat{q}(t)$

(5.2.2)   Basic Condition $\hat{2}$: $\dot{\hat{q}}(t) + [\hat{p}(t) - \hat{q}(t)]\dfrac{\partial R_0(t)}{\partial \hat{S}(t)} = \hat{r} \cdot \hat{q}(t)$

Imagine starting two sets of time paths of production $R_0(t)$, stocks $S(t)$, extraction costs, price $p(t)$, and *in situ* scarcity rents $q(t)$ from a given initial set of values for $S(t)$ and $q(t)$, the first set evolving according to (5.1.6) and (5.1.7) and the second evolving according to (5.2.1) and (5.2.2). What differences would we expect to see over time?

Comparing (5.2.1) and (5.1.6), we see that the natural resource commodity price $\hat{p}(t)$ would be lower than $p(t)$ because the market is ignoring environmental costs. A lower price implies a higher initial rate of production and a more rapid initial depletion of stocks. Will this continue?

If we compare (5.2.2) with (5.1.7), we note that three factors differ: (1) the $p(t) - q(t)$ difference initially is smaller; (2) the $dA/dS(t)$ term is omitted; and (3) $\hat{r} > r$ is substituted on the right-hand side. What do these changes imply for $\dot{\hat{q}}(t)$ in relation to $\dot{q}(t)$? Since private discount rates will be at least as high as social discount rates, the right-hand side value almost surely will be higher initially. If environmental services are important and significantly affected by decreases in $S(t)$, it is obvious from comparing (5.2.2) and (5.1.7) that initially $\dot{\hat{q}}(t) > \dot{q}(t)$: *in situ* rents will have to increase more rapidly than they would under a socially optimum pattern of resource use. This is not surprising, since stocks are being drawn down more rapidly.

In summary, from a starting point with given stocks, $S(t)$, the competitive market price, $\hat{p}$ will be lower, the rate of production of natural resource commodities and extraction of *in situ* resources will be higher, and the rate of increase of *in situ* scarcity rents will be higher than the socially optimum values.

This situation cannot persist indefinitely, however, since higher production rates and lower stocks will mean higher marginal extraction costs, and $\hat{\hat{q}}(t) > \hat{q}(t)$ means that rents rise more rapidly. Eventually, the time must come when the competitively determined price, $\hat{p}(t)$, is likely to rise above and the production rate, $\hat{R}_0(t)$, fall below what they would have been under the socially optimum program of use.[4] The relationships of these time paths are shown in Figures 5.2. and 5.3.

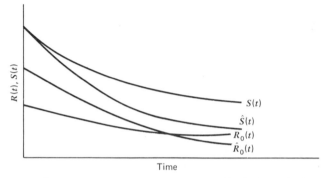

**Figure 5.2**  Paths of socially optimum and competitively determined natural resource commodity production and *in situ* stocks.

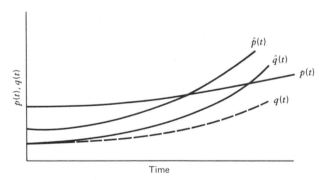

**Figure 5.3**  Paths of natural resource commodity price and *in situ* scarcity rents along the socially optimum and competitive paths.

It is clear that, in the near-term future, the competitively determined output rate will exceed the socially optimum rate, while prices, and rents will be lower. In the longer-term future, the situation will be reversed.

[4]This is a plausible scenario but difficult to prove unless some stringent assumptions are made.

## 5.3. THE PATTERN OF NATURAL RESOURCE USE UNDER A MONOPOLISTIC MARKET STRUCTURE

It is enlightening to take a brief look at the likely performance of the market structure furthest from perfect competition, that is, a monopoly of the natural resource commodity market by one firm. The differences from the formulation of the social optimization problem (5.1.2) are that the monopolist seeks to maximize the present value of profits, probably ignoring the foregone value of environmental services, and using a rate of discount higher than the social discount rate. We thus formulate the likely behavior of the monopolist as trying to:

(5.3.1)
$$\underset{L(t)}{\text{maximize}} \int_0^\infty [R_0(t) \cdot D(R_0(t),t) - wL(t)]e^{-\bar{r}t}\,dt$$

$$\text{subject to: } S(t) = S(0) - \int_0^t R_0(\tau)d\tau \text{ and } S(t) \geq 0.$$

Following the same rules for maximization as before, the basic conditions under a monopoly turn out to be as follows:

(5.3.2) Basic Condition 1: $MR(t) = \dfrac{w}{\dfrac{\partial R_0(t)}{\partial L(t)}} + \tilde{q}(t)$

(5.3.3) Basic Condition 2: $\dot{\tilde{q}}(t) + [MR(t) - \tilde{q}(t)]\dfrac{\partial R_0(t)}{\partial S(t)} = \bar{r} \cdot \tilde{q}(t)$

Here, $MR(t)$ stands for marginal revenue associated with the rate of output $R_0(t)$. Given a demand function with a finite elasticity, $MR(t)$ always lies below $p(t)$ at each quantity $R_0(t)$. Let us again imagine the evolution of $MR(t)$, $\tilde{p}(t)$, $\tilde{q}(t)$, $R_0(t)$, and $\dot{S}(t)$ from an initial set of values. Our understanding of the beginning position will be assisted by Figure 5.4 on page 98.

We see that, for the same $q(o)$ and $S(o)$, the monopolist would produce a smaller output than a competitive market and price would be higher. Thus it appears that the monopolist, even while ignoring environmental costs and possibly using a high discount rate, starts out by being "more conservative" of *in situ* resources than the competitive market. Depending on the elasticity of demand for $R_0$ and the value of environmental services, the monopolist might start out close to the socially optimum rate of output. On the basis of this observation, it has

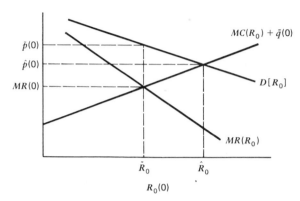

**Figure 5.4**   Initial monopolistic and competitive production rates and prices for given $q(o)$ and $S(o)$.

been said (somewhat naively) that "the monopolist is the conservationist's best friend."

Basic Condition 2 indicates, however, that because of the small initial value of $[MR(t) - q(t)]$, $\check{q}(t)$ is likely to be higher than in the competitive case. The path of $\check{q}(t)$ is likely to climb above that of $\hat{q}(t)$ and of the optimum $q(t)$. Should the rate of production, $R_0(t)$, remain below the socially optimum rate, there appears to be no corrective mechanism which would correct the condition over time. Monopoly might thereby *remain overly conservative* indefinitely, while in the competitive market case, excessive early rates of production at least lead to falling rates later on because of rising extraction costs and rising *in situ* rents.[5]

## 5.4.  MARKET ADJUSTMENT PROCESSES

Two markets play a role in shaping the time pattern of resource use under market arrangements: the market for natural resource commodities, $R_0$, and the market for *in situ* resources. We have seen that competitive markets, while likely to ignore environmental costs and therefore to establish an overly rapid rate of resource use, bring about the relationship (5.2.1), which we rewrite as:

$$(5.4.1) \qquad\qquad \check{p}(t) - \acute{m}c(t) = \hat{q}(t)$$

[5]It can be shown in the very special case of a constant elasticity demand function for natural resource commodities and zero extraction costs, that the monopolistic and competitive patterns of production would coincide.

Clearly, $\dot{p}(t)$ is set in the market for natural resource commodities, while $q(t)$ is set in the market for *in situ* resources. We can think of these two markets at a point in time being represented by the functions in Figures 5.5*a* and (*b*), although the market for *nonhomogeneous in situ* resources could not be so simply depicted.

These two markets will have, at least in part, the same participants, because many natural resource commodity producers will not want or be able to buy their *in situ* resources on a continuous basis just as they are needed. There may also be speculators who deal only in the *in situ* resources with no intention of ever producing them but only hoping to make a capital gain. We'll see that their role in natural resources markets is, in theory and practice, rather limited.

Looking back at (5.4.1), we can imagine the adjustments that would be motivated by any failure of the equality to hold. For example, suppose $p - mc > q$. Then producers would be motivated to increase production, using their own *in situ* stocks or purchasing stocks in the *in situ* market at the price $q$. The increase in output of natural resource commodities would have two effects: $p$ would fall and $mc$ might rise. The purchase of additional *in situ* stocks for immediate exploitation would drive up their price, $q$. All these changes would tend to reestablish the equality (5.4.1). Similarly, if $p - mc < q$, producers would reduce the output of natural resource commodities and reduce their purchases of *in situ* resources, $p$ would rise, $mc$ might fall, and $q$ would fall, again tending to reestablish the equality.

A market can be established for *in situ* resources only if the holders of *in situ* resources can reap some reward from holding them. We have already seen from (5.2.3) that there are two forms of reward from holding: an increase in price, $\dot{q}$, and the benefit from lower future production

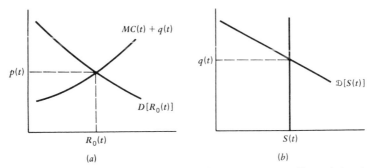

**Figure 5.5**  A simple depiction of the natural resources commodity market and the *in situ* resources market.

costs. Whether or not *in situ* owners can, in fact, secure these gains for themselves depends on (1) the institutional arrangements for ownership of *in situ* resources and (2) the physical route by which *in situ* retention reduces future production costs.

In the first case, if ownership of *in situ* resources is not clearly defined, owners who clearly perceive the benefits of holding *in situ* resources will not be able to guarantee that the resources held will be theirs to claim in the future. An example would be the oil driller who knows the advantage of slower oil pool exploitation, both physically and marketwise, but who also knows that any quantities he attempts to save will be pumped out by others. Another example from the renewable resource field would be the fisherman who perceives that the stock of fish should not be further reduced, because further production will drive down current market prices of fish and will impair future fishing. However, if he abstains from further fishing, others are likely to enter and take what he gave up, while he suffers the future costs just the same. Thus, in the absence of clearly defined and enforceable rights in the *in situ* stock, no market can be established, and the *effective* (motivational) *in situ* price will be zero. This obviously will lead to overly rapid exploitation of the *in situ* stocks, especially under perfect competition.

To illustrate the second point, the physical system through which the cost advantages of a larger stock are experienced will again determine whether or not producers who hold stocks will take these advantages into account. You will recall the second basic condition under competition (5.2.2). Substituting from Basic Condition 1, $p = mc + q$, we can rewrite Basic Condition 2 as:

$$(5.4.2) \qquad \dot{q}(t) + \dot{m}c(t) \cdot \frac{\partial \hat{R}_0(t)}{\partial S(t)} = \hat{r} \cdot \hat{q}(t)$$

This states that the advantages a producer-holder of resources gains from the increase in *in situ* prices, $q$, and from the reductions in future extraction costs must be as great as the best alternative returns on current *in situ* value, $\hat{r}\hat{q}$. How can such cost advantages be experienced? If they are purely internal to the firms' operations, there is no problem. If each mine reduces its own future costs by not digging so deeply today, the mine management will give full cognizance to such savings. However, if the cost savings are spread over many firms or operations through the medium of a common physical system, the individual firm is not irrational to give them very little weight. Examples would be found in the exploitation of common oil pools and fisheries. Once again, even under perfect competition, benefits from holding resources may be ignored by the individual operator, resulting in overly rapid exploitation.

In summary, we have described the roles of the natural resources commodity market and the market for *in situ* resources. The creation and appropriate functioning of an *in situ* market is absolutely essential if market processes are to approximate socially optimum time patterns of resource use. While the logic of the mutual adjustment processes in the two markets has been demonstrated, it has also been noted that lack of definition of property rights in *in situ* resources can prevent the establishment of any market in such resources. Furthermore, even when property rights are well defined in the *in situ* resource itself, the physical resource system may spread the cost advantages from one operator's holding actions over so many others that such advantages will, in practice, be ignored. Thus, potentially important problems loom with market processes of intertemporal resource allocation.

## 5.5. THE STABILITY OF NATURAL RESOURCE MARKET ADJUSTMENT PROCESSES

Figure 2.13 in Chapter 2 showed that natural resource commodity prices have historically had a tendency to be more volatile than the general price level. The issue discussed here is the stability of the adjustment process described in the preceding section.

Consider again the case where $p - mc > q$, that is, where the rate of natural resource commodity production is too low (if we ignore environmental effects). The adjustments that would be motivated would involve $R_0$ increasing, $p$ falling, $mc$ possibly rising, and the demand for *in situ* resources rising. The resulting increase in $q$ helps to reestablish Basic Condition 1, but its secondary effects depend on the kind of expectations that this price change creates. If the trend of expected *in situ* prices is shifted above that indicated by Basic Condition 2, further *in situ* resources will be held off the market, preventing the expansion of $R_0$ and intensifying the increase in $q$. Similarly if $p - mc < q$, a condition of excess current production, the rate of demand for *in situ* resources for immediate conversion would decline, and $q$ would fall. If this price movement sets up an expectation of $q$ below that of Basic Condition 2, more *in situ* resources will be thrown on the market intensifying the decrease in $q$ and facilitating the continued production of excessive $R_0$. Again, if expectations in the *in situ* market are highly sensitive to current price adjustments, the *in situ* market may be *destabilizing* in its net effect.

What is the role of the speculator in this process? The speculator attempts to make a profit by identifying situations where his or her best estimate of future market conditions differ from the dominant expectations. In doing so, he or she also allows producers who must carry working inventories of raw materials (*in situ* resources) to *hedge* (i.e., to enter into contracts for future sales at prices fixed today, thereby reducing their risk of adverse price changes).

Speculators and hedgers, however, really need organized futures markets to permit efficient communication and contract agreements to be made. In the absence of organized futures markets transactions costs will be high, competition will be weak, and speculators will largely be limited to "one side of the market." Suppose speculators come to believe that future *in situ* prices will rise more rapidly than others expect. They can then buy today at prices ($q$) that reflect the common expectation. If their forecasts of future prices are correct, they can later sell their *in situ* resources at prices that will yield them a rate of return in excess of other investments. Their actions will have caused *in situ* prices to rise more rapidly than otherwise, bringing them more closely into alignment with their (hopefully correct) expectations. However, should the speculators believe that future prices will be lower than others expect, there is no way in which they can profit from this expectation unless they can themselves locate a party wanting to buy at some future time at prices reflecting market expectations. High transactions costs will preclude such private searches in most cases. As a result, the speculators' only action is inaction, that is, staying out of the market. Thus, the effectiveness of speculation is asymmetric in the absence of futures markets. The absence of hedging opportunities on the part of risk averse producers may also depress near term *in situ* prices, unduly increasing near-term production rates.

There is also a question regarding speculator behavior in *in situ* markets when cost-related stock effects are important (i.e., $\partial R_0 / \partial S(t) > 0$). *In situ* market equilibrium conditions were given by (5.4.2), which indicated that $\dot{\hat{q}} < \hat{r}\hat{q}$ under such circumstances, that is, that *in situ* price rewards from holding will be less than the rate of return on alternative investments because the holder also reaps the production cost advantages stemming from larger stocks. It is not clear that speculators who are not producers will be able to secure these benefits. If they buy into a common pool resource like oil, the cost advantages of larger stocks would accrue largely to others. If they buy mines and hold them unworked so the production costs of those mines become lower than those in mines being worked, it is possible that these mines could be sold later at prices fully reflecting not only the generally higher *in situ* prices, $q(t)$, but also their production cost advantage. However, such transactions would be very resource specific, and transactions costs would again be high.

In summary, markets for *in situ* resources may be destabilizing in their effects on adjustments in natural resource commodity markets. The role of speculation, an activity that generally assists in organizing orderly markets over time, appears to be limited by the absence of organized futures markets and by difficulties that nonproducers face in capturing future cost savings stemming from larger stocks.

## 5.6.  A REVIEW OF REASONS FOR MARKET FAILURE TO ACHIEVE OPTIMUM PATTERNS OF RESOURCE USE OVER TIME

Our analysis has now uncovered a number of reasons why even well-informed competitive markets may fail to allocate resources in the socially most desirable way over time. We have noted the following factors:

1.  Private markets are likely to overlook the values of environmental services related to stocks of *in situ* resources.
2.  Private interest rates are likely to be higher than appropriate social rates of discount.
3.  Common access to *in situ* resources may preclude the establishment of markets for these resources.
4.  Future production cost savings related to carrying stocks of *in situ* resources may be spread among many producers in common pool resources, causing producers to ignore or undervalue such savings.
5.  Monopoly will generally result in quite a different time pattern of resource use than a competitive market, but this pattern may be closer to the optimum pattern than the competitive one.

Additional factors at work in the real world that can interfere with optimum allocation are noted below.

1. Different rates of income taxation. If a uniform rate were applied to all incomes earned in all periods, there would be no change in the competitive time pattern. The introduction of a lower *capital gains rate* would undoubtedly stimulate some artificial bookkeeping practices between *in situ* holding operations and production operations, but such a tax could be structured to stimulate *in situ* holding of resources. Depletion allowances, on the other hand, will lead to more rapid production

since actual production is required to take advantage of the tax break. Oil and gas producing companies have argued that exploration would be stimulated by depletion allowances, but there is no empirical evidence that this has happened. If reserves were expanded as a result, $q(t)$ would fall and current production would rise.

2. Leasing policies for reserves on government lands contain features which can distort the path of resource use. As noted earlier, the Secretary of Interior has applied pressure to the holders of federal gas and coal leases to increase production rates. New offshore oil leases and new coal leases require production within certain time periods. Now if the government were able and motivated to calculate an optimum path of resource production and if the production requirements placed on leases were tools for executing this optimum path, such constraints would be warranted. It isn't clear, however, that the government's effective time horizon is any longer or any more responsive to future conditions than that of private enterprise—large amounts of rhetoric notwithstanding. There undoubtedly exist great pressures to keep current natural resource commodity prices low, especially for energy commodities. The next election is always just around the corner. At the same time, private enterprise has exhibited a willingness to assume relatively long time horizons for planning and investment. Forestry products firms are engaged in planting forests that will not be harvestable for 60 to 75 years. Many of the federal coal leases that have attracted so much criticism were signed in the early 1950s and have been held without development ever since. While some characterize this as "trying to corner the energy market," it is precisely the pattern of behavior that our model of socially rational resource allocation would predict. Thus, while it can't be proved that either private firms or government are closer to the social optimum, it isn't at all clear that the intertemporal decisions of the private sector are worse or more shortsighted than those that the federal government would impose.

3. Price regulations. Price regulations have been invoked during periods of crisis and in regulating situations of natural monopoly such as public utilities. The effects of these regulations have been widely debated. While the informal "jawboning" attempts of the Kennedy administration in the early 1960s are rather generally acknowledged to have helped hold prices down under increasing inflationary pressures, the price regulations in the early 1970s are seen as seriously distorting the relative price structure and, at best, slightly delaying general inflationary effects.

Here our concern is with price controls on specific natural resource commodities, a regulatory field in which the United States has much experience. It is widely acknowledged that the federal price ceilings on natural gas for interstate delivery have distorted gas production and sales away from interstate distribution and into the unregulated intrastate markets where prices have been as much as three times higher. These price ceilings also have discouraged exploration for gas. The price controls on "old oil" may not have such serious effects on the supply side to date, but they have certainly prevented the price of petroleum products from reflecting their current scarcity value.

What general propositions can be stated regarding the effects of price controls on the patterns of exploitation of non-renewable natural resources? The most extensive studies of this question have been Lee's theoretical analyses (1978) and Sheerin's numerical analyses (1977). Assuming a competitive market structure with extraction being subject to constant marginal costs, marginal costs that increase with the extraction rate within each period, and marginal costs that increase with cumulative extraction, they systematically compare the price-quantity paths that would result from unregulated competition to the results from imposing various regimes of price control. The imposition of a price control is exhibited in Figure 5.6 in which $\bar{p}$ is the price ceiling. Remember from Section 5.1 that a socially optimal pattern of resource use is characterized by the margin between price and marginal extraction cost rising at the discount rate, with price hitting its maximum value (if such exists) just as the resource is exhausted. Very similar features characterize the behavior of the competitive market subject to a price control, that the price-quantity path adjusts so that the net margin can still grow at the discount rate to the time of exhaustion when price reaches its allowed maximum value. We present the results of one simple case.

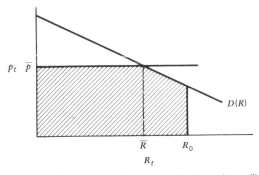

**Figure 5.6**  The imposition of an effective price ceiling.

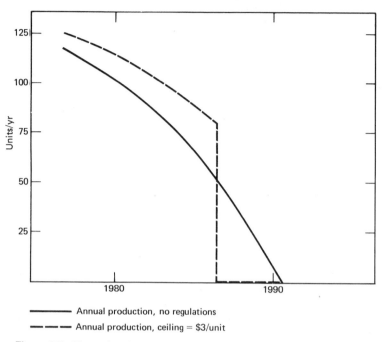

**Figure 5.7**  Unregulated and regulated results with constant MC: an example.
Source: Sheerin, Figure IX, p. 99.

**Constant Marginal Extraction Costs with $\bar{p}$ Below the Price Intercept.**   It can be shown that competitive production under such a price ceiling and the unregulated path of production compare as shown in Figure 5.7. The net effect is to keep quantity higher and price lower than it would be in the absence of regulation, leading to the quicker exhaustion of the resource. Prices remain below $\bar{p}$ until the moment of exhaustion. Intuitively, the increased rates of extraction occur because the opportunity cost of present production in terms of foregone future market values has been reduced.

These results are highly dependent on the *permanent* nature of the price ceiling. If a price ceiling is only temporarily imposed, production in the short term may be induced to fall sharply (possibly to zero). This can be seen in the extreme case in which the price ceiling is so low that the present value of the expected $(p - mc)$ margin upon termination of the price controls exceeds the current margin. A rational producer would stop production until the price ceiling is lifted. This probably underlies some of the short-term production withholding behavior in oil and gas that was so sharply criticized in 1975–1976.

## 5.7. SUMMARY

This chapter started by more sharply defining what an economist would mean by "optimum resource use over time." This led to Basic Conditions 1 and 2, necessary optimum conditions on the rate of production of natural resource commodities and on *in situ* resource stocks. These conditions were derived again for competitive market conditions and monopolistic market conditions so that inherent tendencies of market processes of natural resource allocation over time to deviate from the economic optimum could be detected. Section 5.6 noted eight major reasons why markets could be expected to deviate from the optimum pattern.

With this understanding of resource use optimality over time and with insights into likely patterns of market behavior, in the next chapter we briefly discuss natural resource commodity prices, production costs, and *in situ* prices as indicators of the evolving natural resource scarcity situation. The empirical evidence available on these potentially useful indexes is then presented.

# Chapter 6

# EMPIRICAL INDICATORS OF EVOLVING NATURAL RESOURCES SCARCITY

Fisher (1978) has given a very apt characterization of what is wanted from a measure of resource scarcity:

> ... it should summarize the sacrifices, direct and indirect, made to obtain a unit of the resource.

We will be asking to what extent prices, costs, and rents, as determined in real markets, have this characteristic. Note that we are *not* asking about the optimality of market determined patterns of resource use, but rather about the usefulness of various observable indicators as signals of natural resource troubles.

The strategy adopted now is to describe four basic cases in which the evolution of resource scarcity is obvious. An intuitive analysis of price, cost, and *in situ* rent movements will be made. Then the competitive market time paths of these variables will be deduced with the help of our Basic Conditions $\hat{1}$ and $\hat{2}$ [(5.2.1) and (5.2.2)] to see how the indicated movements agree with our intuitive analyses and the physical description of the situation. That is, we ask how the real world variables are likely to move over time and to what extent those movements reflect the evolving scarcity situation.

*Case 1:* an infinite stock of a homogeneous (and thus constant production cost) resource. This is the "frontier economy" once again in which resources are scarce only to the extent they require scarce labor-capital for their recovery. Intuition tells us there can be no *increase* in scarcity and there would be no scarcity rents. Whether or not environmental losses would occur in this case is not entirely clear, but "infinite resource stocks" suggest not. One would, therefore, expect price to equal unit production cost.

Basic Condition $\hat{1}$ tells us that, under such circumstances, the price of natural resource commodities would remain proportional to the price of labor capital, $w$, because $\partial R_0/\partial L$ is constant in a frontier economy. That is, the relative scarcities of labor-capital and natural resource commodities would remain constant, as would $p(t)$. If technological improvement in the production of natural resource commodities occurs, $p(t)$ would fall over time, both absolutely and relative to $w$, correctly reflecting the decreasing scarcity of natural resource commodities. Scarcity rents would remain at zero, correctly reflecting the nonscarce nature of *in situ* resources.

A well-informed, competitive economy could be expected to operate in just this fashion. The environmental and intertemporal externalities that frequently lead to market failure are not present.

*Case 2:* an infinite stock of *in situ* resource exhibiting smoothly increasing recovery costs with cumulative use. This is clearly a case where scarcity by any reasonable definition is increasing. An intuitive analysis of this situation suggests that environmental impacts might be increasing, scarcity rents would be positive (not because of the limitations of a finite stock but because today's use of *in situ* resources increases tomorrow's costs), and price should be increasing.

A glance at Basic Condition $\hat{1}$ verifies that the increasing production costs (and increasingly severe environmental costs to whatever extent they are borne by firms) should contribute to a rising price. The time path of scarcity rents is, however, less clear as Basic Condition $\hat{2}$ shows. It tells us that the more severe the stock effects on recovery costs, the less the required rate of increase of scarcity rents ($\dot{q}/q$) would have to be to justify holding *in situ* resources. Thus, under competitive conditions, positive scarcity rents would exist but they *might* be falling over time as firms take their rewards for holding resources *in situ* partly in the forms of reduced future production costs. Overall, the price of natural resource commodities, $p(t)$, probably would be rising but it is not impossible that it might fall under some unusual conditions.

This case requires a careful distinction between the social optimality conditions and what one is likely to observe in the real world. If Basic Condition 1 is to hold in a competitive economy, the private producer would have to take cognizance not only of his production costs, but of the environmental and user costs related to the use of *in situ* resources. Since environmental amenities have a largely public goods nature, it is likely that private firms would understate or ignore the effects of their actions on such amenities unless environmental standards or taxes were being enforced. User costs would be reflected in private decisions if *in situ* resources are appropriately priced by the market. However, private decisions in the market for *in situ* resources are likely to ignore the environmental benefits from *in situ* resources and heavily discount the stock effects of resource use. Basic Condition 2 then suggests that price increases in *in situ* resources may take place at too fast a rate relative to the optimum rate.

What can we conclude regarding the *likely* movements of natural resource commodity price, production cost, and prices of *in situ* resources in this case of obvious increasing scarcity? *In situ* prices will be moving up, probably faster than under optimum resource management. Production costs, by definition, are rising. Natural resource commodity price will be rising, but is likely not to reflect the environmental sacrifices associated with resource use.

*Case 3:* a finite, homogeneous stock. This is a case of increasing scarcity, not because of increasing production costs but because increasingly valuable future uses of resources are being precluded. If the market for *in situ* resources is working, their price should be increasing. The severity of environmental effects is probably rising.

Under optimum management, Basic Condition 2 tells us that *in situ* prices should be rising unless environmental effects are very severe. It then follows from Basic Condition 1 that commodity price, $p(t)$, should also be rising. In the real world, environmental effects and the value of future production are again likely to be heavily discounted by private decision makers, so the increase in scarcity rents is likely to be positive and too high. As a result, price will rise in spite of constant production costs and ignored environmental impacts. We conclude that price and rent move in the right direction while cost is misleading since it fails to rise.

*Case 4:* a finite stock with increasing extraction cost. Here we clearly have increasing scarcity. Intuition indicates that all indicators ought to be moving upward.

Under optimum management, increasing extraction costs and the recognition of increasing environmental costs should push price upward. The behavior of rents is less clear, for strong stock and environmental effects reduce the required increase in *in situ* values. It is conceivable that optimum *in situ* rents would fall.

In the real world, stock and environmental effects are likely to be understated, implying a positive and excessively high rate of increase of rent (Basic Condition 2). This implies that both cost and rent components of price (Basic Condition 1) will be increasing over time, causing price to increase even when environmental effects are ignored. It seems likely that all three indicators will be moving in the right direction, if not at optimal rates.

What can we conclude from these cases regarding natural resource commodity price, production cost, and *in situ* rents as indexes of scarcity? To what extent do they capture "the sacrifices involved in obtaining a unit of the resource"? We must remember that there are two resources: natural resource commodities and *in situ* resources. Under a program of socially optimal resource use, $p(t)$ and $q(t)$ would measure the relevant sacrifices being made for natural resource commodities and *in situ* resources, respectively. The holding of the basic optimality conditions (5.1.6) and (5.1.7) guarantee that. It is also clear that production costs alone do not fully capture the relevant sacrifices.

Even under optimum management, the *movements* in the indicators can be deceptive. In the three cases investigated where "increasing scarcity" was built into the scenario through increasing production costs and/or finite stocks, it was seen that both $p(t)$ and $q(t)$ might *fall*. Thus their movements could be interpreted as signalling *decreasing* scarcity in situations where everyone would agree that *increasing* scarcity was present. The absence of production cost *movements* can also fail to reflect increasing scarcity that is due to limited stocks.

In practice, the actual *values* of $p(t)$ and $q(t)$ are likely *not* to capture the full sacrifices involved for many reasons. Nonetheless, it seems *likely* that in most practical cases of increasing scarcity, all three indicators would be *moving* in the right direction.

## 6.1. FURTHER OBSERVATIONS ON PRICES AS INDICATORS OF NATURAL RESOURCES SCARCITY

An obvious but very important point is that changing scarcity as measured by changing relative prices is an economic and not physical concept. Brown and Field (1978) note the case of the passenger pigeon in the United States that was first commercially harvested in the 1840s and that became extinct in the 1890s. Apparently market prices showed little tendency to increase right to the time of extinction. The failure of prices to rise can be explained in terms of the *common property nature of the birds,* the existence of nearly perfect substitutes in consumption, and improvements in harvesting technology. Nonetheless, anyone valuing the perpetuation of the pigeon and counting on price increases to signal reduction of the stock would have been seriously misled.

A second issue that is important in interpreting price movements is the vertical level of processing at which natural resources scarcity is to be measured. This is critical since it delimits substitution possibilities. For example, if iron ore mining is taken as the industry, certain capital and labor substitutions versus *in situ* iron are available: more complete recovery of ore, beneficiating of lower grade ore thus allowing more complete recovery of iron from the ore, etc. On the other hand, if steel is considered the industry, then a whole range of additional technologies intervene, in each of which capital or labor can be substituted for iron or iron ore: pelletizing, transport, blast furnaces, and steel conversion and shaping. Thus it's a different ball game to talk about the elasticity of substitution of capital-labor for natural resources in steelmaking than to talk about substitution in iron mining.

The level of processing also affects what we *mean* by "increasing scarcity." Suppose scarcity rents on iron ore deposits are going up, recovery cost is going up, and the real price of iron ore (at the surface) is rising. At the same time, transport, smelting, and conversion techniques are either improving or are such as to allow capital-labor to be substituted for iron ore. As a result, steel prices are falling. Since steel (let us assume) is the first level of product to be directly usable by consumers, do we have "increasing scarcity" in any meaningful sense? Presumably "yes" for iron ore and "no" for steel, but the former may have little social significance.

A similar situation is nicely illustrated by Brown and Field in Figure 6.1 showing the changing relationship from 1910 to 1970 of Douglas fir stumpage price to lumber prices. Stumpage refers to a volume of timber present in standing trees. Its price is represented by what is paid the landowner for the privilege of cutting the timber or the price established in auctions of standing timber on public lands. This price represents a willingness to pay beyond harvest costs and is thus the rent on the *in situ* resource. When the trees are harvested, they are felled, trimmed, perhaps cut in several sections, and hauled to a sawmill. These sawlogs have a price, although many sawmills do their own harvesting so that explicit prices are not always developed. The product of the sawmill is lumber for which prices always exist. Brown and Fields' data thus exhibit the changing relation between the price of a *natural resource commodity lumber* and the rent on *the resource while still in situ*: the latter is rising relative to the former.

A third issue affecting the usefulness of observed prices as indexes of scarcity is that of *changing* market or regulatory structures over time that can cause market prices of natural resource commodities or *in situ* natural resources to change for reasons other than changing scarcity. Herfindahl (1959), in his well-known study of copper costs and prices,

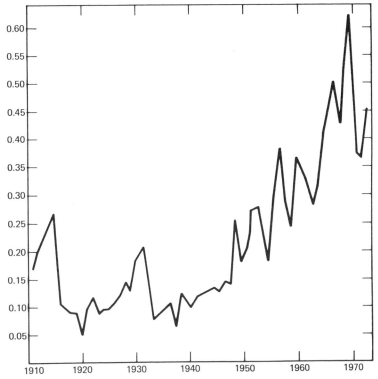

**Figure 6.1**   Douglas fir stumpage price relative to Douglas fir lumber price.
Source: Brown and Field, 1979, p. 28, with permission of the authors.

stated the problem very clearly as it related to changes in the market
structure (pp. 236–38):

> ... But if changes in the price of copper relative to other prices are
> to indicate changes in cost, there must be a tendency for price to equal
> cost (including necessary return on investments) over the long run.
> The force that could have produced a strong tendency for price to be
> brought to cost is competition. ...
>
> The price of copper during certain collusive episodes has not been
> included in the record. ... The London price has been substituted for
> the U.S. price from 1870–83, since during a part of this period Calumet
> and Hecla was responsible for raising the U.S. price above the foreign
> price behind a tariff wall. The years 1888–90 have been excluded be-
> cause of the attempted Secretan corner of the supply of copper. Be-
> cause of restriction of supply by the Amalgamated Copper Company
> and some co-operating firms, 1899–1901 have been excluded. The very
> disturbed period following World War I, 1919–22, the period when the
> Copper Export Association was operating, has been excluded. ...

Changing government regulations may have had noticeable impacts on prices that were unrelated to changing scarcity. The federal regulation of gas prices starting in 1954 and the more recent price ceilings on domestically produced petroleum are examples, as would be the establishment of the 27½ percent depletion allowance on petroleum in 1926, the initiation of agricultural price supports in 1929, and acreage controls in the postwar period.

## 6.2.   RELATIVE PRICE EVIDENCE

We have hypothesized that a meaningful increase in natural resource scarcity would be evidenced by a long-run upward trend in the real (corrected for inflation in the general price level) prices of natural resource commodities. An interesting partial case is provided by mercury, for it is clearly a resource close to exhaustion in the United States. The price history of mercury is shown in Figure 6.2. The price trend appears to have risen since 1900 at an exponential rate of approximately 3.5 percent. The falling price can probably be attributed to improved technology and economies of scale, while it seems clear that the rising price phase is attributable to increasing recovery costs and increasing scarcity rents. The absence of good production cost data makes it difficult to estimate the magnitude of the scarcity rent itself over time.

Economic theory doesn't tell us the appropriate form of the price

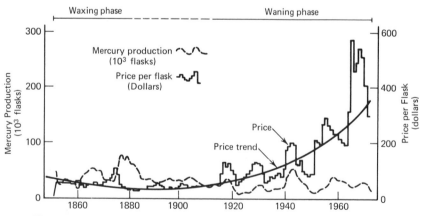

**Figure 6.2**  Production and price history of mercury in the United States. Source: Cook, *Science*, 1976, p. 681. Copyright 1976 by the American Association for the Advancement of Science.

**Table 6.1.** The Linear Relative Price Hypothesis: 1870–1972

| Commodity Group | Value of $c_0$ | Value of[a] $c_1$ |
|---|---|---|
| Agricultural products | 25.0 | 0.046 (3.907) |
| Metals | 1633.4 | −4.349 (−4.998) |
| Fuels | 11853.3 | −10.447 (−0.934) |
| Forestry products | 5020.6 | 20.878 (5.816) |

[a]Numbers in parentheses are the values of the $t$ statistic. A significant difference from zero is indicated by values in excess of 1.65 in absolute value.

trend function, but the simplest form for the increasing scarcity hypothesis would be:

$$(6.2.1) \qquad \dot{p}_{R_0}(t) = c_0 + c_1 t + \epsilon_t$$

where $\dot{p}_{R_0}(t)$ is the price of some particular natural resource commodity or a price index of a group of NR commodities relative to the general price level. Using U.S. data compiled by Robert Manthy (School of Forestry, Michigan State University) for the period 1870 to 1972, V. Kerry Smith (1976) estimated the parameters of the function (6.2.1) with the results given in Table 6.1. These findings indicate a significant upward trend for agricultural products and forestry products, and a significant downward trend for metals. One may question the hypothesis of the same linear trend over such a long period, and tests run by Smith indeed indicated different periods when the price trends appeared to be changing. The relative price regressions were run and rerun using increasingly long periods of observation that started in 1870 and ended in each of the years through 1972. The changing values of the regression coefficients show us what we would have observed as the linear trend in relative price as viewed backward (to 1870) from year $t$. The results are shown in Figures 6.3a–d.

Forestry and agricultural products have shown an uptrend over nearly the entire period, but the average increase has been falling. The

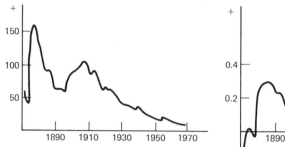

Figure 6.3a   Forestry products. Source:
V. Kerry Smith, 1976.

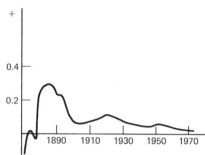

Figure 6.3b   Agricultural products.
Source: V. Kerry Smith, 1976.

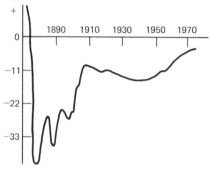

Figure 6.3c   Metals. Source: V. Kerry
Smith, 1976.

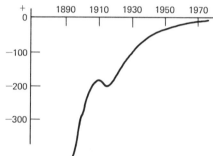

Figure 6.3d   Fuels. Source: V. Kerry
Smith, 1976.

period through, say, 1930 appears to have been one of much stronger
upward pressure on relative prices than the later period.

Metals and fuels exhibit an opposite pattern, with strong downward
trends in earlier periods (especially to 1910), but with the trends becoming small in recent years.

These results agree only in part with the well-known earlier conclusions of Barnett and Morse (1963), which were that the increasing relative price hypothesis had to be rejected for agricultural and mineral
products as groups, but could not be rejected for forestry products. The
differences regarding agriculture probably stem from different deflators
(wholesale prices for monthly, nonextractive products for Barnett and
Morse) for the relative price and quantity weights from different years.

Nordhaus (1974) has calculated the price of various mineral resource
commodities relative to that of labor for various years from 1900 to 1970.
These ratios may be thought of as approximations to the $p_{R_0}/p_L$ ratio

introduced in Chapter 4 that was expected to rise during periods of increasing natural resource scarcity. They are presented in Table 6.2. Certainly through 1970 there appears to be no sign of increasing scarcity within the minerals group according to this measure. Iron rose a bit in 1960 but fell in 1970. Additional data complied by Brown and Field (1976, pp. 15–19) on metals prices relative to wage rates show very similar results.

Barnett, in a recent paper (1979), analyzed international data on relative prices of natural resource commodities. The most extensive data were agricultural prices relative to general wholesale prices for 53 time series involving 31 countries in the two periods, 1950–1962 and 1961–1972. An exponential trend of the form $\dot{p} = c_0 e^{c_1 t}$ was fitted in each case. Out of the 53 trends fitted, 23 supported the increasing scarcity hypothesis, as shown in Table 6.3. The fact that 15 countries showed significant upward trends in the 1961–1972 period compared with 8 in the 1950–1962 period may also be significant, although 5 countries that appeared in the earlier period failed to repeat in the second.

Where does the relative price evidence point overall? V. K. Smith and Barnett (1976 and 1974) have found significant evidence of increasing relative prices for agricultural commodities and forestry products in recent decades, although the earlier Barnett-Morse study (1963) had rejected the hypothesis of rising agricultural prices. Metals and minerals generally appear to have fallen, but at lower rates in recent decades. Fuels in particular had a long history of falling relative prices, but this, too, appears to have been tapering off in recent decades. The dramatic price increases that started in 1973 result directly from cartel action,

**Table 6.2.** Prices of Minerals Relative to Labor, 1970 = 100

|              | *1900* | *1920* | *1940* | *1950* | *1960* | *1970* |
|--------------|--------|--------|--------|--------|--------|--------|
| Coal         | 459    | 451    | 189    | 208    | 111    | 100    |
| Copper       | 785    | 226    | 121    | 99     | 82     | 100    |
| Iron         | 620    | 287    | 144    | 112    | 120    | 100    |
| Phosphorus   | —      | —      | —      | 130    | 120    | 100    |
| Molybdenum   | —      | —      | —      | 142    | 108    | 100    |
| Lead         | 788    | 388    | 204    | 228    | 114    | 100    |
| Zinc         | 794    | 400    | 272    | 256    | 125    | 100    |
| Sulphur      | —      | —      | —      | 215    | 145    | 100    |
| Aluminum     | 3150   | 859    | 287    | 166    | 134    | 100    |
| Gold         | —      | —      | 595    | 258    | 143    | 100    |
| Crude petrol.| 1034   | 726    | 198    | 213    | 135    | 100    |

Source: Nordhaus, 1974, Table 2. Values are price per ton of mineral divided by hourly wage rate in manufacturing.

**Table 6.3.**    Countries Exhibiting Significant Upward
Exponential Trends in Agricultural Prices
Relative to the Wholesale Price Index

| Country | 1950–1962 | 1961–1972 |
|---|---|---|
| Germany | X | |
| Italy | X | |
| Spain | X | X |
| Sweden | X | |
| Yugoslavia | X | |
| Mexico | X | X |
| Argentina | X | |
| Japan | X | X |
| Costa Rica | | X |
| Chile | | X |
| Ecuador | | X |
| India | | X |
| Iran | | X |
| Korea | | X |
| Philippines | | X |
| Belgium | | X |
| France | | X |
| Greece | | X |
| Netherlands | | X |
| United Kingdom | | X |
| | 8 | 15 |

Source: Barnett, 1979, p. 17.

although free market prices probably would have increased. Thus, the evidence indicates that significant upward trends are developing in agriculture, forestry, and fuels, while metals have not yet changed from their long-term downward trend.

## 6.3.    SCARCITY RENTS: PRICES OF *IN SITU* RESOURCES

Prices of the *in situ* resources can change relative to the price of the natural resource commodity produced from them as we have seen in the basic price-cost-rent relation (5.2.2). A changing pattern was exhibited in Figure 6.1, showing the long term increase in the Douglas fir stumpage price relative to Douglas fir lumber price.

Basic Condition $\hat{2}$ has indicated that scarcity rents can fall over time if stock effects are strong enough. This possibility is partly explained by Basic Condition $\hat{1}$ that tells us if $p(t)$ can not increase much because of very elastic demand, then increasing production costs will rise relative to price, squeezing rents on *in situ* resources toward zero.[1] This makes sense in situations where the high elasticity of demand is attributable to the presence of a close substitute commodity made from other *in situ* resources. The future sacrifices implied by present use become very small since the cost differential between currently tapped resources and the substitute becomes very small.

As noted in Chapter 5, two practical circumstances may prevent scarcity rents from adequately reflecting scarcity. One is the absence of organized futures markets that may discourage the holding of reserves by reducing liquidity and increasing the cost of risk bearing to those inclined to hold reserves. Another is the common-property nature of some resources that can preclude the capture of the benefits of efficient holding of reserves for the future.

To what extent can scarcity rents even be observed? Much of the information on land rents and royalties is proprietary and not available for study. Even if it were available, many of the actual payments are likely to represent Ricardian rents for differentials in quality of deposits for there are many regulations aimed at fostering production from sub-marginal deposits. The current price regulations for "stripper"[2] oil wells versus other "old" oil wells are an example, for they permit oil from reworked stripper wells to be sold at world prices, while oil produced by much more efficient wells is held to a much lower historical figure. The prorating scheme of the Texas Railroad Commission that for years was aimed at keeping prices high by reducing output kept wells of many different costs in operation.

Thus, unfortunately, data on *in situ* rents are both hard to find and difficult to interpret.

## 6.4. UNIT COSTS OF NATURAL RESOURCE COMMODITY PRODUCTION

The model of Section 1 told us rather plainly that production costs of natural resource commodities might fail to signal increasing scarcity since they omit any scarcity rents on the *in situ* resource and all residual

---

[1]This case was analyzed by Fisher (1979).

[2]"Once a stripper, always a stripper" is a maxim in the trade. A stripper is a low-yield, high-cost well producing 10 or less barrels per day, usually in the last stages of exhaustion. Encouraging production from such wells while discouraging production from more efficient wells is absurd. If a stripper is improved and comes to yield, say, 50 barrels per day, it is still classed as a stripper for pricing purposes—hence the maxim.

costs to the environment. However, under a wide range of situations, these three components of total social cost can be expected to move together. Barnett and Morse (1963) argued that the labor-capital cost per unit of natural resource commodity output ($L_1/R_0$ in our earlier notation) was the only measure that would incorporate the effects of all relevant forms of technological change and the only measure that could not be distorted by changing government regulations and market structures over time. This latter point favors their view.

Barnett and Morse formulated two unit cost hypotheses: (1) the "strong scarcity hypothesis" that real unit costs of extractive outputs had been increasing; and (2) the "weak scarcity hypothesis" that the real unit costs of such outputs had been increasing relative to the real unit costs of nonextractive outputs. They gathered data on labor and capital inputs into agriculture and minerals for the period 1870 to 1957. For forestry and fisheries, they had to settle for the use of labor inputs only, an unfortunate shortcoming since there has been a large degree of substitution of capital for labor in those sectors. The labor-output ratio then fails to incorporate a significant element of real extraction cost. However, their findings on forestry and fisheries were corroborated to some extent by price and import data.

The Barnett and Morse results are given in Table 6.4 with the exception of fisheries where they felt the data too weak to support conclusions. "Extractive sectors" is simply the aggregation of data on agriculture, forestry, minerals, and fisheries. Only with forestry did they feel the data were consistent with increasing costs. For the other sectors, they solidly rejected both the strong and the weak increasing unit cost

**Table 6.4.**    Summary of Barnett and Morse's Results

|  | Strong Unit Cost Hypothesis | Weak Unit Cost Hypothesis |
|---|---|---|
| Late 1800s to 1920s: | | |
| Extractive sectors | Rejected | Rejected |
| Agriculture | Rejected | Rejected |
| Minerals | Rejected | Rejected |
| Forestry | Not rejected | Not rejected |
| 1920s to 1957: | | |
| Extractive sectors | Rejected | Rejected |
| Agriculture | Rejected | Rejected |
| Minerals | Rejected | Rejected |
| Forestry | Not rejected | Not rejected |

hypotheses. Bell and Johnson[3] have updated the Barnett–Morse labor, capital, and output series through 1972. These series seem consistent with the trends observed in the earlier period, although the downward trend of minerals seems to have slackened. There is one contradiction with the relative price data: agricultural costs seem to have kept falling while Smith's data on agricultural relative prices indicated a long-term increase. This divergence of evidence is not readily explainable, but is consistent with a long-term uptrend in agricultural land values.

While unit production cost data represent only partial coverage of relevant costs, this evidence should not be ignored in a world where evidence on the evolving resource situation is scarce.

## 6.5. EVIDENCE ON ELASTICITIES OF SUBSTITUTION OF OTHER INPUTS FOR NATURAL RESOURCES

Common sense tells us that capital and labor can be substituted for natural resources in many production processes. Rosenberg showed that American woodworking technology, while quite advanced, was very wasteful of wood compared with contemporary nineteenth–century English technology. English saws were made of better steel and were thinner, producing less sawdust. The fuel efficiency of steam engines increased as insulation, higher pressures, higher temperatures, and more complex controls came into use. In agriculture, intensity of cultivation can be substituted for land, although one of the principal inputs of intensive cultivation is fertilizer, another natural resource commodity input. Water input can be saved in agriculture, home, and industry through increased labor inputs in controlling applications and through more capital in the forms of better transport systems, sprinkling systems, and recycling systems. In the aggregate, such opportunities may represent the potential for very large savings of natural resource inputs.

At the theoretical level, the work of Dasgupta, Heal, and Solow cited in Chapter 4 indicated the importance of substitution possibilities to the long-term sustainability of aggregate output in the face of limited resources. Thus, while measures of substitutability do not constitute measures of resource scarcity per se, they do reflect one of our major capabilities for adapting to resource scarcity.

Since economics uses the production function to represent the efficient production technologies available to an economy or a sector within

---

[3]Frederick H. Bell and Manuel H. Johnson, Jr. at Florida State University, in correspondence with the author and others.

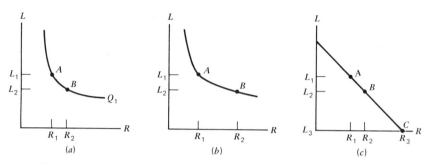

**Figure 6.4** Differing degrees of substitutability between labor-capital and natural resources.

an economy, it is natural that some characteristic of the production function be used to summarize available substitution possibilities. The elasticity of substitution, designated $\sigma$, is the most commonly used measure. Consider a two-input production function using combined labor-capital and natural resources, $f(L, R)$. Three differently shaped isoquants representing different substitution possibilities are shown in Figure 6.4. In part $(a)$, the isoquant shows little opportunity for substitution. If we take a given change of the slope of the isoquant, say from $A$ to $B$, the change in factor proportions is very small. Since the slope of the isoquant is known as the marginal rate of substitution,[4] we can say that as the marginal rate of substitution changes along the isoquant, factor proportions change very little. One simple way of specifying the factor proportions would be the ratio $L/R$. Part $(b)$ illustrates a case where the same change in the marginal rate of substitution as in $(a)$ corresponds to a much larger change in $L/R$. Part $(c)$ illustrates a case where the marginal rate of substitution is constant and where either input can be completely eliminated through sufficient use of the other. These differing degrees of substitutability can be captured by the elasticity of substitution, $\sigma$, which is defined in the following way:

$$(6.5.1) \qquad \sigma \equiv \frac{d\left(\dfrac{L}{R}\right)\Big/\left(\dfrac{L}{R}\right)}{d\left(\dfrac{\partial f/\partial R}{\partial f/\partial L}\right)\Big/\left(\dfrac{\partial f/\partial R}{\partial f/\partial L}\right)}$$

[4]Since an isoquant represents all the $(L, R)$ combinations capable of producing the same level of output, we can write
$$dY = \frac{\partial f}{\partial L} \, dL + \frac{\partial f}{\partial R} \cdot dR = 0$$
as a characterization of an isoquant. This can be quickly transformed into
$$\frac{dL}{dR} = - \frac{\partial f/\partial R}{\partial f/\partial L}$$
showing the slope to be minus one times the ratio of the marginal products.

that is, the ratio of the percentage change in the factor ratio to the percentage change in the marginal rate of substitution. Given a selected value of the denominator, the elasticity depends on the percentage change in $(L/R)$: if it is large, $\sigma$ is large, etc. In Figure 6.4, $(a)$ illustrates a very small $\sigma$, $(b)$ a larger value, and in $(c)$ $\sigma$ is infinite since the denominator is zero.

A production function having three inputs, such as $f(K, L, R)$, can be described in terms of three *partial elasticities* of substitution, $\sigma_{12}$, $\sigma_{13}$, $\sigma_{23}$, which characterize the ease of substitution between two inputs given the value of the third. In this case, however, inputs can be *complements* as well as *substitutes*, that is, some pairs of inputs may increase together along an isoquant as the third input is reduced. $\sigma_{ij}$ takes on negative values if inputs $i$ and $j$ are complements.

Several mathematical forms of production functions are used in empirical studies, but the most common are the Cobb-Douglas, the constant elasticity of substitution function, and the very general translog function. The Cobb-Douglas is characterized by $\sigma = 1$ and the CES by a constant elasticity, while the translog function has an elasticity that can change with the parameters and arguments of the function.

Experience and intuition indicate that partial elasticities can be expected to change sign (i.e., factors shift from a substitute to complementary relationship) if relative factor prices change radically. An example is found in various capital-energy-labor applications. Historically, when energy was cheap, capital and energy were being substituted for increasingly costly labor. More recently, as energy prices have escalated, capital has increasingly been applied to the saving of energy. One would obviously observe different partial elasticities of substitution during these two time periods.

Another matter to be kept in mind is the vertical level of production and aggregation at which $\sigma$ is being estimated. Most of the empirical studies cited below have dealt with the manufacturing sector with natural resource commodities as one input. Substituting capital and labor for natural resource commodities in manufacturing differs from substituting capital and labor for *in situ* resources in the production of natural resource commodities.

What can we expect to learn, then, from estimates of substitution elasticities? Simply that if substitution away from *in situ* resources and natural resource commodities is easy ($\sigma_{ij} > 1$), adjustments of the economy to changing resource scarcities will be much easier than if substitution is difficult ($\sigma_{ij} < 1$). No estimates have been made at the level of aggregation of the Dasgupta-Heal-Solow-type growth model, but values of lower levels of aggregation would certainly influence the aggregate elasticity and be positively correlated with it.

**Table 6.5.**  Partial Elasticities of Substitution: U.S. Agriculture

|  | Fertilizer | Machinery | Labor |
|---|---|---|---|
| Land | 2.99 | 1.22 | 0.20 |
| Fertilizer | — | −0.67 | −1.62 |
| Machinery | | — | 0.85 |

Source: Binswanger, 1974, Table 2.

Binswanger (1974) has estimated the partial elasticities of substitution among inputs in U.S. agriculture, his data consisting of cross sections of state data for 1949, 1954, 1959, and 1964. His results are in Table 6.5. Fertilizer is a natural resource commodity while land is *in situ*. The high elasticity between land and fertilizer is not unexpected, especially since the data cover a period when acreage restrictions were used as a production control, motivating very heavy fertilizer applications. Machinery also appears to substitute readily for land in terms of the intensity of cultivation. The complementarities ($\sigma_{ij} < 0$) between fertilizer, machinery, and labor indicate a need to be used in relatively fixed proportions, probably reflecting the directions of technological change of this period. It thus appears that the only easy substitution away from natural resources in U.S. agriculture is machinery for land, the latter being a renewable resource in relatively abundant supply.

Humphrey and Moroney (1975) examined the partial elasticities of substitution between labor, capital, and natural resource commodities for two-digit manufacturing industries. The natural resource commodity input used in their production function and cost function approaches was the sum of values of 12 renewable natural resource commodities

**Table 6.6.**  Partial Elasticities of Substitution, 1963

|  | $\sigma_{KR}$ | $\sigma_{LR}$ |
|---|---|---|
| Food and beverages | 0.64* | 0.64* |
| Textiles and apparel | 0.17 | 0.47 |
| Lumber and products | 1.12* | 0.61 |
| Pulp and paper | −0.68* | 4.49* |
| Stone, clay, and glass | −0.58 | 0.06 |
| Primary metals | 1.84 | 5.92* |

Note: *indicates statistical significance.

Source: Humphrey and Moroney, Table 6.

Table 6.7. Partial Elasticities of
Substitution, 1967

|  | $\sigma_{KR}$ | $\sigma_{LR}$ |
|---|---|---|
| Steel | 3.0 | 4.5 |
| Aluminum | 3.4 | 3.0 |
| Copper | 9.4 | 15.1 |
| Pulp and paper | 6.0 | 1.9 |

Source: Brown and Field, 1979, Table 4.

(e.g., farm dairy products, meat, cotton, vegetables, forestry, and fishery products, etc.) and seven nonrenewable natural resource commodities (iron and ferroalloy ores, copper ore, nonferrous metal ores, coal, crude petroleum and gas, stone and clay, chemical and fertilizer mineral mining). Data from 1963 for 235 four-digit industries were grouped into 12 two-digit industries, but 6 industries exhibiting a very low level of natural resource commodity inputs did not yield meaningful results. The results are presented in Table 6.6. With the exceptions of primary metals and lumber, substitution possibilities appear limited. It is interesting that the exceptions occur with the use of *in situ* resources or, at least, resources farther down the production chain.

Brown and Field (1976) estimated partial elasticities for the steel, aluminum, copper, and pulp and paper industries for 1967 with the results shown in Table 6.7. The results on primary metals agree with the Humphrey-Moroney results, including the extraordinarily high values for $\sigma_{LR}$. The pulp-and-paper-sector results are not consistent between the studies.

Substitution possibilities against energy are of great contemporary

Table 6.8. Partial Elasticities in
Electric Power
Generation

|  | Capital–Fuel | Labor–Fuel |
|---|---|---|
| 1955 I[a] | 0.22 | 0.65 |
| 1955 II | 0.20 | 0.57 |
| 1970 | 0.22 | 0.17 |

[a]1955 II groups various firms into holding companies.

Source: Christensen and Greene, 1976, Table 6.

interest and importance. In a sharply focused study of thermal-electric power generation using cross sections of data from firms, Christensen and Greene found quite limited substitution possibilities as indicated in Table 6.8.

Substitution possibilities among capital, labor, energy, and other intermediate materials in the (aggregate) U.S. manufacturing sector have been evaluated by Berndt and Wood (1975). Intermediate materials are mostly nonenergy natural resource commodities. For the period 1947–1971, they found the various partial elasticities to be quite stable. Approximately average values are given in Table 6.9. The estimates seem plausible with the exception of the high degree of *complementarity* indicated for capital and energy. There are too many everyday examples of the substitution of capital for energy to permit us to interpret this result as saying that no substitution possibilities exist. Instead, we must interpret this parameter as descriptive of that segment of the production function that was in use during a cheap energy era. We also note substitution possibilities between capital and the "other materials" category, although the elasticity is modest.

Our interpretation of the Berndt-Wood result is reinforced by a more recent study of Griffin and Gregory (1976) that utilized intercountry data. Their contention was that the range of relative price variation would be much greater than in time series of one country and that the data would represent a more complete degree of adaptation to these persistent price differences. Their data were collected on the manufacturing sectors of nine industrialized countries for the years 1955, 1960, 1965, and 1969. Their results were $\sigma_{KE} = 1.05$ and $\sigma_{LE} = 0.85$. Thus it seems that when significant and persistent energy price differentials exist, very significant substitution possibilities between capital and labor do exist and are exploited.

**Table 6.9.**  Partial Elasticities of Substitution Among Capital (K), Labor (L), Energy (E), and Other Intermediate Materials (M): U.S. Manufacturing 1947–1971

| $\sigma_{KE}$ | $\sigma_{LE}$ | $\sigma_{KM}$ | $\sigma_{LM}$ | $\sigma_{EM}$ |
|---|---|---|---|---|
| −3.2 | 0.64 | 0.55 | 0.57 | 0.76 |

Source: Berndt and Wood, 1975, Table 4.

## 6.6.    THE COMMISSION ON POPULATION GROWTH AND THE AMERICAN FUTURE: POPULATION, RESOURCES, AND ENVIRONMENT

Ridker (1972) supervised a large-scale study titled as above for the Commission on Population Growth. Using an input-output model approach to future NR demands and pollution loads in the United States, Ridker came to the following principal conclusions for the intermediate term to 2000.

1. The United States is not likely to experience truly serious shortages of raw materials during the next 30 to 50 years because of population and economic growth. A serious shortage was defined as one involving a relative price increase of more than 50 percent for a number of significant natural resources.
2. The U.S. economy will become increasingly dependent on mineral, fuel, and other raw material imports.
3. Policies to clean up the environment will not be excessively expensive, constituting about 2 to 2½ percent of GNP through the year 2000.

These conclusions were drawn before OPEC raised petroleum prices and were based on the following assumptions (among others): that labor productivity would keep increasing as in the postwar period; that "best practice" in various industries today would become the average practice by the end of the century; that the trend toward services and away from goods would continue; that environmental constraints would not slow power plant development, nuclear or otherwise; and that the world trading and investing system would be maintained, including absence of OPEC "monopolistic control over a large fraction of the world's petroleum supplies." These conditions are fairly stringent, and some have obviously been breached. One can probably speculate that an updating of this analysis would produce "guarded optimism" for the intermediate term.


## 6.7.    SUMMARY OF THE EVIDENCE

This chapter opened with Fisher's definition that a measure of natural resource scarcity "should summarize the sacrifices, direct and indirect, made to obtain a unit of the resource." It is necessary to differentiate between resources *in situ* and natural resource commodities since various technologies intervene between the two. It was concluded that changes in the real price of natural resource commodities under realistic circumstances would probably correctly signal the direction of changing scarcity even though the price might not capture the total sacrifices correctly. Scarcity rentals on *in situ* resources can be affected by so many factors that they could, in theory, be falling in situations where all would agree that scarcity was increasing. Nonetheless, in most practical situations, scarcity rents can be expected to indicate the correct direction of change. Even natural resource commodity production costs, while failing to capture environmental and intertemporal costs, will move in the right direction in a majority of cases.

The empirical evidence through 1972 indicates that only forest products were growing decidedly more scarce by all measures. Minerals, including fuels, exhibited downward trends in relative prices and costs, but these trends were weak at the end of the period. Some price changes since 1972 are clearly due to changes in market structure rather than changes in scarcity alone. Substitution possibilities of other inputs for natural resources—a factor known to be important in the long term—have been shown to be significant.

# Chapter 7

# FACTORS MITIGATING NATURAL RESOURCES SCARCITY

The conditions of natural resource availability affect the productive potential of an economy in various ways as was shown in Chapter 4. We have also seen that technological change in the direct production of GNP and in the production of natural resource commodities could overcome any inherent tendencies of natural resource costs to rise. The evidence in Chapter 5 indicated rather clearly that natural resource scarcity was not a serious problem in the United States from 1870 through 1972, with the exceptions of rising costs of forest products and environmental degradation.

The United States and all industrialized nations have thus benefited from many factors acting in concert to keep natural resource scarcity in retreat. This chapter discusses several of the major scarcity-mitigating factors and then asks whether or not these factors are likely to remain operational in the future.

## 7.1. THE SALVATION OF TELLURIDE: AN EXAMPLE OF THE PROCESS OF ADAPTATION[1]

Telluride, Colorado, is now known for wonderful skiing, but until recently it was a sleepy, isolated mountain town living on memories of

[1]This story has been summarized from an article by Louis Newell, "Lucius Nunn, AC Electricity Saved Colorado Mining in 1890's," appearing in the *Denver Post,* Oct. 5, 1975.

earlier mining prosperity. Gold was discovered near Telluride in 1885, but by 1890 all of the accessible, high-grade ores had been taken. Mines had to be sunk deeper or new ones opened at higher altitudes. This required steam power for drills, hoists, and ore mills and the power was provided by wood-fueled boilers. However, all nearby timber had been cut, so the increasing cost of securing wood made coal more attractive, even though it had to be hauled 60 miles from the railroad by ox cart or mule. At timberline, coal rose to $50 per ton. By 1890, many mines were facing bankruptcy because of the soaring fuel costs.

Lucius Nunn, a local lawyer and stockholder in the Gold King Mine, which was on the verge of failure, thought it possible to save the mines by converting to electricity, a form of power not unknown in the town. A small direct-current system provided costly electricity (two bulbs used at night cost $4 per month, with a day's wage being $3) for some homes and businesses, and large line losses precluded transmission as far as the mines. Nunn had heard of alternating current and traveled back to Pittsburgh where he convinced George Westinghouse to join in a venture for the generation of AC power and its transmission to the Gold King Mine. None of the locals thought it would work and, indeed, there were mighty displays of sparks throughout the system. However, the system was successful, cutting the mine's monthly power bill from $2500 to $500, and was extended to other mines. Nunn went on to form several of the largest western power companies.

This colorful episode illustrates the sequential substitution of one input for another, and the vital interjection of a new technology.

## 7.2. TECHNOLOGICAL INNOVATION

An important part of the historical process of innovation can be seen and understood as response to natural resource scarcity in some form. As Rosenberg stated (1972, pp. 20–23):

> ... But from the perspective of the economic historian surveying the historical experience of the wealth—and poverty—of nations, the production and use of technological knowledge must be seen against the backdrop of specific societies with different cultural heritages and values, different human capital and intellectual equipment, and confronting an environment with a very specific collection of resources.... Although we may usefully *conceive* of technological change ... in an abstract way, it does not *occur* in the abstract but rather in very specific historical contexts. It occurs, that is, as a successful solution to a particular problem thrown up in a particular resource con-

text.... Moreover, the *kind* of solution which any society can produce... will turn on the level of knowledge and expertise which is available to it....

Regarding the U.S. response to resource challenges, J. Milton Mackie (quoted in Rosenberg, p. 30) stated in a magazine article in 1854:

> The genius of this new country is necessarily mechanical. Our greatest thinkers are not in the library, nor the capitol, but in the machine shop. The American people is intent on studying, not the beautiful records of a past civilization, not the hieroglyphic monuments of ancient genius, but how best to subdue and till the soil of its boundless territories; how to build roads and ships; how to apply the powers of nature to the work of manufacturing its rich materials into forms of utility and enjoyment. The youth of this country are learning the sciences, not as theories, but with reference to their application to the arts. Our education is no genial culture of letters, but simply learning the use of tools.

A substantial body of recent research emphasizes the endogenous nature of technological change itself and presents impressive evidence of the influence on the direction of technological change of input prices. In Hayami and Ruttan's study of international agricultural development (1971), the enormous differences observed in land/labor ratios could not be explained by the ordinary process of factor substitution. As noted in a later paper,[2]

> ... in the early 1960's, the U.S. had a land/labor ratio of 141 hectares per worker while Japan's ratio was 1.74 hectares per worker. The U.S. ratio exceeded the Japanese ratio by a factor of 81. However, Japan's land/labor price ratio exceeded the U.S. ratio by a factor of less than 30 during the same period. To explain the difference in factor ratios by factor price effects, the elasticity of substitution between the two factors would have to be 3 or more....
>
> The single most important conclusion that emerges out of the several tests of the induced technical change hypothesis is the powerful role of economic forces in inducing technical change. In view of the great differences in the physical, cultural and economic environments in the historical cases against which the tests were conducted and the different methodologies employed in the tests, this conclusion must be regarded as remarkably robust.
>
> One clear implication of the tests of the theory of induced innova-

---

[2]Vernon W. Ruttan, Hans P. Binswanger, and Yujiro Hayami, "Induced Innovation in Agriculture," 5th World Congress of the International Economic Association, Tokyo, August 1977.

tion is to reinforce the significance of the neoclassical concern with efficiency in resource allocation as central to the process of economic development. The effectiveness with which research resources have been allocated to release the constraints on growth imposed by resource endowments has been strongly influenced by the efficiency of market mechanism in interpreting the factor price implications of relative resource endowments.

The pervasive role of economic forces in research resource allocation places a major burden on the efficiency of the pricing system. Our analysis suggests that if price relationships are distorted through either market imperfections or public intervention in market processes, the innovative behavior will be biased. . . .

Griliches demonstrated the importance of demand in determining the diffusion of hybrid corn, while Schmookler concluded that in railroads, petroleum, paper, and agricultural equipment, the rate of return to inventive activity was of far greater importance than advances in the state of knowledge in explaining technical change. The demonstration of a dynamic, induced innovation process is certainly an optimistic factor in the natural resources outlook. It also has important implications for the role of markets and prices.

## 7.3.  THE PROCESS OF NATURAL RESOURCE DISCOVERY AND RELATED TECHNOLOGICAL CHANGES

Discovery of new reserves (in the broadest interpretation of the word) has been a crucially important factor in the growth and industrialization of the world. The success of exploration efforts in the transition from the U.S. frontier economy is nowhere better seen than in the statistics of petroleum discovery. We recall the 1874 warning by the Pennsylvania State Geologist that the United States had petroleum reserves sufficient to satisfy its kerosene needs for only four years. In 1920, the U.S. Geological Survey reported that recoverable reserves were no more than seven billion barrels. Within three to five years, according to the report, petroleum production would peak and reserves would be exhausted by 1934. In 1934, proved reserves had increased to 12 billion barrels. By the mid-1960s, the five billion barrels produced between 1859 and 1920 were being produced every 20 months.[3]

This and similar successful epochs of discovery did not, however,

[3]Data from Lansberg and Schurr, *Energy in the United States,* New York: Random House, 1968, p. 98.

occur with a static exploration technology. Great strides have been made in increasing the effectiveness of locating and quantifying deposits of both renewable and nonrenewable resources. Among the major technological improvements in resource discovery and assessment would be the following:[4]

1.  *Aerial Photography.* Provides a complete, detailed record of terrain for recognizing surface and subterranean features. Can be used as base maps or sequenced into stereoscopic photomosaics. Main uses include:
    (a)  Field geology.
    (b)  Soil mapping.
    (c)  Forest surveys.
    (d)  Grassland and vegetation surveys.
    (e)  Land use surveys.
    Panchromatic, infrared, spectral, and exotic image photography are some of the specialized, highly sensitive techniques that have been developed. Recent years have seen the extensive development of satellite photography.

2.  *Geologic Survey Techniques.* These techniques are vital to the engineer in evaluating construction and road sites, to the prospector seeking minerals, to the agronomist seeking particular soil types, and to the demographic planner in seeking settlement areas. Among modern techniques are:
    (a)  Geophysical methods: electrical, gravimetric, magnetic, and seismic.
    (b)  Geochemical methods: especially important for the rare metals that occur in deposits too small to be detectable by geophysical means.

3.  *Soil Mapping.* Extremely important for agricultural planning. Aerial photography has proved invaluable in this work.

4.  *Forest Surveys.* The rational management of forest resources requires data on the location, composition, condition, and growth rates of the forest. Acquisition of such data requires use of aerial photography, statistical sampling, and other forms of field investigations.

5.  *Hydrologic Evaluation of Surface and Groundwater Resources.* It generally requires a long period of record to accurately evaluate surface

---

[4]A useful reference with case study materials is the publication *Physical Resource Investigations for Economic Development: A Casebook of OAS Field Experience in Latin America,* Washington, D.C.: Organization of American States, 1969.

flows, and assessment of groundwater is always difficult. Great improvements have been made through the following techniques:

(a) Aerial and satellite photography for both surface and groundwater.
(b) Statistically efficient gage network design procedures.
(c) Statistical procedures for the transfer of hydrologic models from one drainage basin to others.
(d) Models of groundwater flow through different media.

6. *Vegetation Surveys.* Such surveys are undertaken for two purposes:

(a) To evaluate the inherent value of the vegetative cover itself for grazing, wildlife, forestry, or watershed purposes.
(b) As an indicator of other characteristics of the environment. Vegetation types can indicate soil types, water conditions, geological discontinuities and even mineral deposits.

7. *Plate Tectonic Theory.* Recent advances in understanding the shifting and bending of the surface plates of the earth have furthered our understanding of the processes by which mineral deposits are created. This promises to be of great use in the future.

## 7.4. TECHNOLOGICAL CHANGES INCREASING THE EFFICIENCY OF RESOURCE RECOVERY

Included in this category would be the reprocessing of mine tailings, the increased use of scrap materials from timber cutting, and increases in the recovery rate from petroleum pools (still averaging only 35 percent for the United States). The technique of underground coal mining known as the "long-wall" technique has not only speeded the mining process but avoids the necessity of leaving large columns of coal to support the mine roofs as with the "room and pillar" technique.

Groundwater pumping techniques advanced after World War II, making it economically feasible for the first time to pump groundwater on a large scale for irrigation. Water is now pumped from depths as great as 1000 feet for irrigation, but increasing energy costs are making this costly. Much of the groundwater being tapped in the United States is from nonrecharging acquifers, so it represents a nonrenewable resource just like iron ore. The great Ogallala aquifer stretching from Nebraska through parts of Colorado, Kansas, Oklahoma, New Mexico, and Texas is the prime example. The problems arising from the unregulated use of this resource is analyzed further in Chapter 14.

New techniques are being developed to facilitate the use of lower-grade resources. An example of a technology with great potential is the flocculation-flotation process for beneficiating nonmagnetic iron ore.[5] While the currently refinable iron-ore reserves of this country are being rapidly drawn down (see Fig. 3.1), the Lake Superior iron ore district contains over 20 billion tons of nonmagnetic iron ore that requires beneficiation to make a usable concentrate. Unique problems exist in dealing with the nonmagnetic ores, but processes are being improved to make these ores more exploitable. The *in situ* leaching of uranium oxide from deposits too deep and low grade for mining has also been successfully undertaken. Much earlier in the 1920s, improvements in sulphate pulping technology made it possible to utilize the fast-growing southern pine for paper making.

## 7.5. TECHNOLOGICAL CHANGES FACILITATING SUBSTITUTIONS IN PRODUCTION PROCESSES AWAY FROM SCARCE RESOURCES

Illustrations in this category can be drawn from wood use technologies, the broad shift in this century from reliance on renewable resources to reliance on nonrenewables, the historical shift from charcoal to coal in iron and steelmaking, various metallic substitutions, and improvements in irrigated agriculture.

Rosenberg (1972 and 1974) has documented the patterns of change in wood using technologies in this country. American technology was appropriate for the frontier. Circular saws had thick blades and widely spaced teeth that produced large amounts of sawdust and required copious quantities of power, but they required less care and maintenance—a nice substitution of cheap wood for expensive labor. Fireplaces were large in order to use large logs, economizing on wood cutting labor. House building was largely of wood on wooden frames, reducing the labor input. Even roads and canal locks were built of wood. The railroads were built on steep gradients and sharp curves, increasing fuel consumption but reducing capital and labor inputs. Locomotives used wood for fuel and were quite inefficient.

However, these patterns changed—sometimes dramatically—as the difficulty of procuring wood increased. Fireplaces were replaced with Franklin stoves or pot-bellied stoves. Houses more frequently were built partly of stone or brick. The plank roads of Pennsylvania and the log

[5]From Joe B. Rosenbaum, "Minerals Extraction and Processing: New Developments," *Science*, V. 191, N. 4228, February 1976, pp. 720–23.

roads of the Rocky Mountains disappeared or fell into disrepair. As a national energy source, wood declined from 91 percent in 1850 to 21 percent in 1900, and to 2.5 percent in 1955. Locomotives were almost totally wood fueled until the Civil War, but by 1880 20 times more coal than wood was being used.

One of the most striking classes of technical change in this century has been the shift from renewable to nonrenewable resources. While this might be thought of in a physical sense as substituting limited (finite) resources for unlimited resources, the shift was induced by relative prices. The relative prices of many nonrenewables fell rapidly after World War II because of improved extraction techniques, the availability of pipeline transport, the application of new knowledge in the field of organic chemistry, and the like. Tractors fueled by petroleum have completely replaced horses and mules. Natural manures have been replaced by chemical fertilizers, plastics have replaced wood and rubber in many uses, synthetic fibers have surpassed wool and cotton in U.S. usage, and (again) petroleum, natural gas, and coal have replaced wood as a fuel. It now appears that some of these shifts may be reversed in the future with solar energy, fuel from grains, natural manures, and energy tree farms becoming more attractive once again.

The much earlier English shift from charcoal to coal presents a striking example of induced innovation, for the need to find a substitute fuel struck long before metallurgy was a science. Such breakthroughs occurred through the seemingly inefficient process of large numbers of iron workers experimenting until some improved process was uncovered nearly by chance. Many well-known iron masters had unsuccessfully tried to use coal until Darby finally succeeded in 1709 by using coke.

In later metallurgical developments, we have seen the substitution of stronger steels, of aluminum for copper, and of light exotic metals for stainless steel. Today, further ways are being sought to substitute glass wave guides for copper and aluminum transmission lines; copper, aluminum, and lead for silver and tin; and sodium and other metals for mercury.

Irrigated agriculture, where subjected to an increasing scarcity of water, has shown remarkable innovation in substituting capital for water, starting with improvements in the lining of canals to avoid seepage losses and extending to the design of better water control devices such as flow gages and instrumented underground drip irrigation systems. A major difficulty in the adoption of these techniques is that the price of irrigation water is usually not allowed to indicate its scarcity, thus much of irrigated agriculture has no motivation to seek ways of saving water.

Many examples can be found in the field of electronics, not simply in improving traditional tasks but in extending its range of application. Pierce[6] has compiled the following list of activities that would be impossible or very difficult without electronics: telegraphy; telephone; radio, sound movies, TV, radar and air-sea traffic control; electric power system control; modern medical diagnosis; synthesized sound; hand calculators; automated process control; seismography; research activities in many fields.

Increasingly, commercial activities such as banking, retail sales, editing and publishing, and automobile engines depend on electronics for further improvement. This electronics revolution is characterized by great savings in *both* energy and materials. The production of many electronic devices has proven to be subject to great economies of mass production, and the resulting low prices have stimulated broad adaptation. A major characteristic of many applications of electronics is that they improve productivity in the *service sectors* of the economy, sectors experiencing increasing demands but exhibiting lags in productivity.

There is evidence of *exponential growth* in productivity in electronics. In the telephone industry, the number of calls per employee per day has risen at a 2.5 percent per year rate since 1920 (Pierce, p. 1092). In integrated circuits, a silicon chip in 1959 contained one component of a circuit. By 1964, a chip contained 10 components, by 1970 the number had increased to 1000, and by 1976 to over 30,000. Theoretical considerations indicate that physical limits have not been approached, and Noyce (*Science*, 18 March 1977, p. 1103) states that "If the present rate of increase of complexity were to continue, integrated circuits with $10^9$ elements would be available in 20 years."

## 7.6.  SCALE ECONOMIES

Ruttan has characterized scale economies as a disequilibrium state resulting from technological change. Technological change, partly induced by changing factor prices, has made larger units economical, but it takes time to embody the new technologies in existing plants. One would,

[6]John R. Pierce, "Electronics: Past, Present, and Future," *Science*, V. 195, N. 4283, 18 March 1977, pp. 1092–1095. This entire issue of *Science* is devoted to developments in electronics.

therefore, expect the scale economies that are implicit in the state of technology at any point in time to be gradually exploited until no further scale economies remain. In a dynamic setting, however, technological change is a continuing process across numerous sectors, so one would expect always to find some unexploited scale economies.

Christensen and Greene (1976) have studied the nature of the post-World War II technology change in electric power generation. By fitting cost functions to operating data from major firms, they found that (1) in 1955, most major firms had substantial scale economies still to be exploited; (2) by 1970, these scale economies had been almost fully exploited; and (3) most of the very substantial reduction in average cost per kilowatt-hour over the 1955–1970 period was attributable to technological changes that effectively shifted the firm's average cost curve downward, rather than extending the range of scale economies. These results are illustrated in Figure 7.1. The small amount of evidence available since 1970 indicates, however, that this downward shift in costs has stopped. This major industry may have exploited all improvements available in the boiler-turbine-generator technology and further improvement may depend on totally new systems.

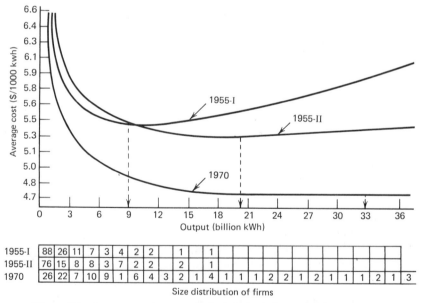

**Figure 7.1** Average cost curves (dotted arrow indicates minimum average cost). Source: Christensen and Greene, 1976, Figure 2, by permission of the University of Chicago.

## 7.7. FACILITATING SUBSTITUTIONS IN CONSUMPTION

Changes in consumption patterns can be important in alleviating natural resource shortages. One example would be veneering techniques and the development of plywood that permitted poorer grades of wood to be substituted for increasingly scarce hard woods and increasingly costly lumber.

The substitution of grains for meat, while not of impressive magnitude at present, represents a great reduction of demands against agricultural resources. Similarly, public transportation systems can provide services at much lower energy and environmental costs than private cars when population densities and land use patterns are appropriate.

Water-saving models of appliances can be used in the home (e.g., toilets, dishwashers, washing machines, showerheads, faucets), often at no increased cost. Their introduction where appropriate is partly dependent on education and partly on appropriate pricing of water.

A set of possibilities that has been less thoroughly analyzed is increasing the *durability* of so-called consumer durables. So far in this century, the change has been in the other direction, substituting more frequent replacements (and thus natural resource inputs) for maintenance and repair. Of course, the utility of variety from more frequent replacements is significant to some consumers. A contention that we produce insufficiently durable hard goods would have to rest on the inappropriateness of existing prices as indicators of scarcity, a topic that will be further discussed below in the section on recycling.

## 7.8. IMPROVED TRANSPORTATION AND TRADE

Improving transportation has historically been an important factor in expanding our reserves. This is essentially what happened in the case of whaling, in the logging of the forests of the Upper Midwest and Northwest, and in the opening of the Great Plains to crop farming. Improvements in shipping have facilitated international trade in natural resource commodities, too, such as processing Jamaican bauxite in Ghana, with the resulting alumina being shipped to other parts of the world. The worldwide shipments of oil, grains, and meat are obvious major trade patterns in nonrenewable and renewable resources. The data in Chapter 2 clearly show the shifting locus of nonrenewable reserves and the increasing role of U.S. mineral imports and agricultural exports.

Herfindahl, in *Natural Resource Information for Economic Development* (1969, especially Chapters 6 and 8), makes it very clear that transportation is not only a major determinant of the extent of (economic) reserves, but also a major determinant of the amount of exploration activity that is worth undertaking. This seems an obvious point, but many countries have spent large sums on exploration in regions so remote or difficult of access that even the most valuable resources could not economically be exploited.

## 7.9. RECYCLING

A great interest has arisen in the possibilities of recycling—interest, that is, on the parts of environmental groups but with a conspicuous absence of commercial interest. There is a general feeling that the U.S. economy recycles too small a portion of the materials left by production and consumption, and examples are cited of newspapers being used for food wrapping, bottles being collected and reused, and so on, in other countries around the world.

Indeed, one can think of cogent reasons why the market process under current institutional arrangements can be expected to recycle too little. While a competitive system with no externalities might be expected to motivate an optimal reuse ratio, existing systems have the following defects:

1.  The costs of disposal of residual materials are usually not fully borne by the party generating them. Some residuals are simply dumped on the countryside, but even materials "properly disposed of" through sanitary landfills or incineration impose external costs and may be financially subsidized.
2.  The use of virgin raw materials is frequently subsidized relative to recycled materials. The Environmental Protection Agency estimated that, in 1974, the sum of virgin material subsidies from depletion allowances, transportation rate differentials on common carriers, and other tax benefits amounted to 11 percent of price for aluminum, 10 percent for paper, and 7 percent for iron.

Yet it is not easy to specify how much should be recycled. As an example, the chain of raw materials, production, consumption, and recycling activities in paper making involve the following costs:[7] production of

[7]From Walter O. Spofford, Jr., "Solid Residuals Management: Some Economic Considerations," *Natural Resources Journal*, 1971, pp. 561–589.

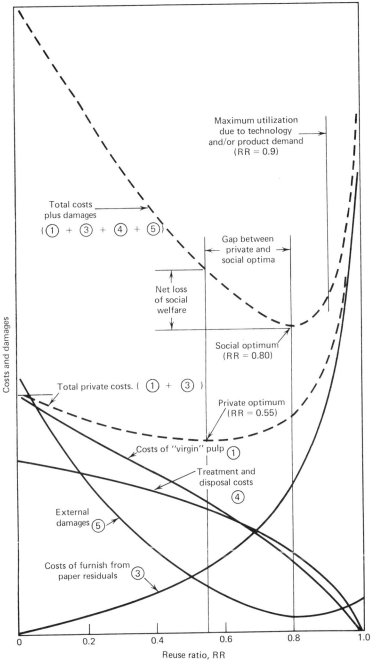

**Figure 7.2** Optimal reuse ratio for paper residuals in the production of newsprint. Source: Walter O. Spofford, Jr., Figure 4, reprinted with permission from The Natural Resources Journal, 1971, published by the University of New Mexico School of Law, Albuquerque, N.M.

**Table 7.1.** Generation of Solid Wastes from Five Major Sources in 1967

| Source | Solid Wastes Generated | |
| --- | --- | --- |
| | Lb/Cap./Day | Million Tons/Yr |
| Urban | | |
| Domestic | 3.5 | 128 |
| Municipal | 1.2 | 44 |
| Commercial | 2.3 | 84 |
| Subtotal | 7.0 | 256 |
| Industrial | 3.0 | 110 |
| Agricultural | | |
| Vegetation | 15.0 | 552 |
| Animal | 43.0 | 1,563 |
| Subtotal | 58.0 | 2,115 |
| Mineral | 30.8 | 1,126 |
| Federal | 1.2 | 43 |
| Total | 100.0 | 3,650 |

Source: Quimby, Thomas, H.E., "Some Economic and Ecological Considerations Involving Waste Newspapers," Resources for the Future Reprint No. 108, April 1973. Reprinted with permission.

pulp from pulpwood, including the costs of the latter; paper manufacturing; public and private paper residuals recovery activities; paper residuals collection, treatment, and waste disposal; and remaining external damages from disposal of waste. An optimum recycling ratio (recycled raw materials inputs recycled and virgin raw material inputs) for a particular type of material would be one minimizing the sum of these costs. Spofford has made an illustrative calculation of this ratio for paper residuals as inputs into newsprintmaking under somewhat average conditions, shown in Figure 7.2. Naturally, the optimal ratio would vary from area to area, depending on collection costs, the severity of externalities, and the level of disposal costs. Note the deviation of the socially optimum reuse ratio of 80 percent from the calculated private optimum of 55 percent.

Bower and his associates[8] estimated annual solid residuals management costs for the New York region for the year 2000 to be $300

[8] *Waste Management: Generation and Disposal of Solid, Liquid, and Gaseous Wastes in the New York Region*, prepared by Blair T. Bower and Associates for the Regional Plan Association, Inc., 230 W. 41st Street, New York, N.Y. 10036, March 1968.

million with a 20 percent reuse ratio for paper and $210 million for an 80 percent reuse ratio. In addition, incineration would add 1020 tons of particulates per day to the atmosphere for 20 percent paper reuse and 680 tons per day for 80 percent reuse. These figures do not net out the extra costs of collecting and processing the extra 60 percent of the residual paper, but the $90 million per year plus environmental benefits indicates that cost studies of increased recycling should be made.

The market can work to increase recycling. Increased costs of energy have greatly increased the demand for insulation of homes and other buildings. Used newspapers can be processed into insulating material, so this shift in demand for insulation has been partly transformed into a shift in the derived demand for used newspapers. In 1977–1978, the buying price for used newsprint has soared from less than $5 per ton to $50 per ton.

Large quantities of solid wastes are generated. Tables 7.1 and 7.2

**Table 7.2.** Some Reported Compositions of Mixed Solid Residuals Collected by Municipalities

| | Percentages by Weight | | | |
|---|---|---|---|---|
| Residual | A | B | C | D |
| Newspapers | 10.33 | | | |
| Corrugated containers | 23.92 | | | |
| Other paper | 21.76 | | | |
| Total paper products | 56.01 | 58.0 | 17.5 | 40–54 |
| Yard and garden waste | 7.56 | 8.4 | 13.5 | 3–80 |
| Wood and Christmas trees | 2.52 | 1.4 | 0.9 | 3–70 |
| Dirt and debris | 3.36 | 3.4 | 0.3 | 1–50 |
| Plastics, rubber, leather | 4.34 | 3.3 | 2.3 | 1–20 |
| Glass and ceramics | 8.50 | 8.1 | 17.9 | 8–11 |
| Food wastes | 9.24 | 6.1 | 32.6 | 10–26 |
| Rags and miscellaneous | 0.94 | 3.1 | 0.5 | 1–20 |
| Metals | 7.53 | 8.2 | 14.5 | 8–11 |
| Total | 100.00 | 100.00 | 100.00 | 100.00 |

Column A: Summary of a tabulation of typical refuse analysis, American Public Works Association, *Municipal Refuse Disposal*, Chicago, 1966.

Column B: A sample of municipal refuse taken and measured at the Alexandria, Virginia incinerator in May 1968, A. C. Achinger and L. E. Daniels, *An Evaluation of Seven Incinerators*, Environmental Protection Agency, 1971.

Column C: Annual average composition of domestic refuse collected in Flint, Michigan, based on samples taken in June and January, U.S. Department of Health, Education and Welfare, Cincinnati, *Solid Waste Disposal Study, Genessee, Michigan*, 1969, p. IV-7.

Column D: Typical percentage ranges of the components of municipal solid wastes, H. Lanier Hickman, "Characteristics of Municipal Solid Wastes," *Scrap Age*, February 1969.

Source: Quimby, 1973, Table 3. Reprinted with permission.

**Table 7.3.**  Annual Domestic Prompt and Obsolete Scrap Consumption for Selected Commodities in the Late 1960s

| Material | Year | Total Annual Material Consumption (000 Tons) | Prompt and Obsolete Scrap Recycled (000 Tons) | Recycling as Percent of Consumption |
|---|---|---|---|---|
| Newsprint | 1967 | 9,108 | 2,005 | 22.0 |
| Other paper and board | 1967 | 44,002 | 8,119 | 18.0 |
| Total paper and board | 1967 | 53,110 | 10,124 | 19.0 |
| Ferrous metals | 1967 | 105,900 | 33,100 | 31.2 |
| Nonferrous metals | 1967 | 9,775 | 3,006 | 30.8 |
| Glass | 1967 | 12,820 | 600 | 4.2 |
| Textiles | 1968 | 5,672 | 246 | 4.3 |
| Rubber | 1969 | 3,943 | 1,032 | 26.2 |
| Total | | 191,220 | 48,108 | 25.2 |

Source: Quimby, 1973, Table 1. Reprinted with permission.

provide information on generation and composition of solid residuals while Table 7.3 provides some ideas on actual recycling ratios.

In summary, while recycling has not played a major role in the U.S. economy with the possible exception of World War II, there appear to be strong arguments for *more* recycling. How much must be studied further.


## 7.10.  DO WE "WASTE" NATURAL RESOURCES?

There has long been a feeling that the United States has been profligate in its use of natural resources. An Englishman, J. Richards, in his book of 1872 on woodworking machines, said (quoted by Rosenberg, 1973, p. 113):

> Lumber manufacture, from the log to the finished state, is, in America, characterized by a waste that can truly be called criminal.

Contemporary comparisons of energy use have led to similar statements that the United States uses twice as much energy as other industrialized nations with equivalent GNP per capita (see Figure 9.7). Does this graph indicate that the United States is, in fact, "wasting" half the energy it is using? Apparently this is a common interpretation. In the heat of the 1973 energy crisis, an article entitled "Simple Energy Waste Lies Beneath America's Energy Crisis," appeared in many newspapers.[9] It said in part:

[9]By Tim O'Vrien and distributed by the L.A. Times-Washington Post News Service.

... however, one variable remains almost an afterthought: simple waste. Extravagance. Inefficiency. Squandering. Unnecessary guzzling of what fuel there is.

...

... a researcher in the Interior Department's Office of Energy Conservation says that "If this were a dictatorship and we could somehow control how people waste energy, we could save from two to three million barrels of oil a day."

...

The [Treasury Department] study found that through eight relatively easy, uncostly and quick conservation measures, about 2 million barrels of oil a day could be saved. The eight measures are: reducing speed limits to 50 mph; increasing commercial aircraft load factors from 50 to 70 percent; setting home thermostats 2 degrees lower; conservation measures in industry; cease hot water laundering of clothes; mandatory 6 months car tune-ups; conservation measures in commercial buildings; and increasing car pools.

Do you find this a convincing argument that waste is pervasive? What economic factors are involved and in what sense do they point to "waste"? We had better define this term, taking care not to label resource uses we simply don't like as "waste." One may not like a neighbor's practice of driving a block to see a friend, but this dislike doesn't prove that waste exists—just a clash in values. What of the eight "costless" steps to conservation? Reduced speed limits impose inconvenience on some. Increasing airline load factors decreases the number and convenience of flights and increases the frequency of overbooking. Lower thermostats will make some uncomfortable and cold water laundering of clothes will have negative comfort, esthetic, and sanitation effects. Twice yearly car tuneups would be costly to those who now find one a year with a bit more gas consumption more economical. And car pools are known to be very unpopular. Certainly it cannot be claimed that these costs in the aggregate would be negligible. Why did the Interior Department researcher stop at recommendations that would save only three million barrels per day? Why not 10, 20, or 30 million? Clearly, the researcher perceived an increasing rate of foregong benefits as consumption was further reduced, making it increasingly unclear that a net gain to society would result.

The economist would define *waste* in the use of *any* scarce resource as a situation in which the costs incurred directly and indirectly in reducing the level of use are less than the social value of the resource saved. Do such situations exist and, if so, are they of significant proportions and persistent over time? Undoubtedly some persistent occurrences of waste can be found. As an example, Russell, Arey, and Kates (1970) studied the effects of the 1962–1966 New England drought on three

Massachusetts communities: Braintree, Pittsfield, and Fitchburg. Losses and extra costs caused by the drought such as emergency supplies, replacement costs of trees and shrubs lost, incomes lost because of businesses closed down (e.g., car washes, laundries, and some manufacturing plants), and drought-related industrial expenditures were estimated to be about $5 per capita per year in Braintree and Pittsfield, and $11 in Fitchburg. However, a more careful look at industrialized Fitchburg indicated that many of the industrial expenditures were on in-plant water system improvements that would have had a high rate of return even if no drought had occurred.

How could this have occurred? How could "water waste" have persisted so long? Undoubtedly, water usually was never short and accounted for a very small part of the firms' total costs. Other issues typically commanded management's attention, simply because improving internal water use patterns could have made at best a small improvement in profit even though producing an attractive rate of return on the necessary investment. Suddenly, the formerly unimportant water savings became critical to continued physical operation and management terminated this real waste.

There is little doubt (but few supporting figures) that, after the energy crisis of 1973 when firms found themselves without gasoline and oil in the usual quantities and projected the possibilities of continuing energy shortages into the future, searches for energy-saving opportunities were made. Overnight, a cadre of "energy consultants" appeared and the Office of Energy Policy estimated that industry could save 40 percent of its plant fuel "through almost zero-cost kinds of things." Certainly some opportunities existed.

In spite of such recommendations, consumers continue to exceed 55 mph, wash clothes in hot water, and avoid car pools, and airlines only gingerly move to increase load factors. Can these decisions represent waste in the economic sense? After all, each consumer at least foggily compares benefits and costs at the margin when driving, washing clothes, or choosing an airline. If these decisions are privately rational, how can they represent waste from a social point of view?

Three factors cause a deviation of the private optimum from the socially optimum pattern of resource use: prices that confront the consumer are incorrect, negative externalities of resource use exist, and national security is involved. Federal regulations on the pricing of petroleum currently require an averaging of the costs of imports, of domestic "old oil" and domestic "new oil." Since domestic production costs are below the price of imports, this average is below the price imports, even though imports clearly represent the marginal supply unit. Consumers thus are confronted with the average rather than the marginal cost of oil.

Furthermore, the costs of pollution from private energy consumption are only partly borne by the consumer, while the consumer feels that national security risk considerations are beyond his or her responsibility and control.

Thus, prices seriously fail to reflect social marginal costs, private decisions are not socially efficient, and "waste" is permitted to occur—not because consumers are shortsighted dolts, but largely because public regulatory policies are inefficient.

## 7.11.   WILL MITIGATING FACTORS CONTINUE IN THE FUTURE?

The mitigating factors just discussed have played a crucial role in overcoming what would have been serious growth inhibiting effects over the past century. While human society may have the capability of indefinite survival without the ameliorating effects of technological change, life will be much more pleasant with its help. Can we expect these things to continue?

There is no known theoretical limit to technological discovery and innovation, but our institutional arrangements might not provide the motivation or the opportunities. Alfred Marshall, the great turn-of-the-century English economist (said to be the last economist capable of comprehending and contributing to all parts of the discipline) expressed concern that research and related technological innovation might be subject to long-term diminishing returns. Looking for empirical evidence indicative of future possibilities, one can find discouraging and encouraging examples.

Consider electric power generation, a case of impressive technological advance since the turn of the century. A long sequence of minor improvements leading to increases in pressure, temperature, and economies of large-scale production lowered the coal requirement of a kilowatt-hour of energy from 7 pounds in 1900 to about 0.9 pounds in 1960. Other complementary technologies relating to the provision of fuels and distribution of power have further expanded the effectiveness of the fossil fuel inputs. This progress continued at least until 1970. An optimistic feature of this success story was that it was based on the cumulative effects of many small improvements, not on chance breakthroughs or massive research and development (R&D) thrusts. However, Christensen and Greene (1976) showed that scale economies in this technology appear to have been exhausted.

In the civil works field (dams, tunnels, highways, buildings, etc.), pure construction scale economies appear to have been exhausted but technological change continues to improve the quality of the product (e.g., the strength of concrete and dams) and the capability of difficult tasks (e.g., construction in remote canyons).[10]

Much of past technological change has come in thousands of small steps, none startling in itself. In metallurgy over the centuries, thousands of interested artisans or firms were able to experiment through trial and error, insuring a broad social advance in these technologies even though many individuals must have failed to design viable changes. Are the types of future technological change that will be needed to avoid severe natural resource constraints on continuing activity subject to the same type of broad frontal attack, or have we advanced to the need for such esoteric technologies that only a few collectivities can pursue them and with a much higher risk of failure?

The evidence on this point is mixed. If we think of fusion power or other nuclear technologies, the research costs are so great that only the largest corporations or governments can afford the costs and the risks of failure. On the other hand, energy alternatives to fusion such as solar or self-sufficient microutility units seem to be subject to the traditional research and development approach.

What are the prospects that other new fields like electronics will open up and that progress in established fields will continue? Wise prediction is impossible, but appropriate policies can *at least* create an atmosphere conducive to the programs of research and development which are necessary for continuation of these favorable conditions. In R&D, we encounter a basic problem.

R&D activities are highly uncertain, that is, the relation of inputs to output is difficult to predict. While experience tells us overall that investments in R&D pay off well, this need not be true for any one firm. This inherent riskiness at the level of the firm tends to depress investment in these activities below what is socially desirable. Furthermore, the outputs of R&D—new knowledge—are not fully capturable by the party or firm undertaking the activity. Much of the new knowledge will get out and be used by society without payment. Even if a complex patent system could require licensing so that users would pay the originator, this would be undesirable because of the *public goods* nature of knowledge: its use by additional parties costs nothing and in no way decreases its usefulness to others.

There are these inherent reasons why private decisions will underinvest in R&D activities. Long term economic policy must compensate for this.

[10]R. Kraynick (unpublished Ph.D. dissertation, University of Colorado, 1975) has documented the exhaustion of scale economies in earthmoving, tunneling, and cement pouring.

# Chapter 8

# INTERTEMPORAL COMPARISONS OF WELL-BEING: EFFICIENCY, EQUITY, AND RISK

We have seen that stock effects are present in nearly all natural resource systems. As soon as this is admitted, decisions regarding natural resource use at different points of time become interdependent and simple-minded decisions independently made period by period can no longer be optimal from a social viewpoint. A central question then becomes, "What criterion or objective function should be adopted for the calculation of optimal resource use patterns over time?"

Chapter 4 rather glibly adopted the discounting of GNP at an unexplained discount rate, while Chapter 5, facing the same issue at the level of the natural resources sector, adopted the discounting of sector net benefits, again at some unexplained rate of discount. What are the origins of these discounting practices and are they consistent with a responsible concern for the future?

First, however, what form should "concern for the future" take? The endowment the present generation turns over to the future has many components: the physical infrastructure of buildings, roads, communications systems, housing stock, industrial equipment, and the like; stocks of known *in situ* natural resources, including natural areas; conditions of the global and ambient environments; size of human population; quality of human capital; states of scientific and technological knowledge; and states of the arts and culture. Each of these will be of value to future generations and the composition of the overall endowment can be greatly affected by our current policies and practices.

It used to be said that concern for the future was not a problem, for each generation was always richer than preceding generations. This generally has been true of Western countries since the Industrial Revolution, but it certainly has not been true in other regions and eras. The rich Babylonian civilization declined after the destruction of its vast water and irrigation systems by the Mongols. Persian, Turkish, and Greek civilizations passed through cycles of prosperity and decline resulting from changes in their resource bases, social organization, and external conquest. European population was decimated by the Black Plague and required two centuries to recover. Ancient Egypt and African kingdoms south of the Sahara Desert achieved levels of wealth and culture that disappeared and have not been equalled until modern times.

The tenuousness of the prosperity of ancient and medieval societies may suggest caution for the present generation, for we are experiencing new pressures on the resource base, the ambient and global environments, and the political and social environment. No longer can we absolve ourselves of responsibility for the future by asserting that the future will be richer than the present.

On the other hand, could it be that our patterns of living today, profligate though they appear to many, may be serving the interests of the future better than we appreciate? High standards of material well-being promote investment, education, better health, mobility, broader perspectives on world problems, technological innovation, and scientific research. What additional steps should we be taking to favor the future?

There is no question that a reduction in the input of energy and material resources would be beneficial if it could be achieved without a reduction in real investment. That is, reductions in consumption today, provided they do not cause reductions in the stocks of human and physical capital to be passed on to future generations, would favor the future by leaving more of everything.

Where income levels are very low, attempts to reduce consumption might well lead to social stagnation and the cessation of investments of all types. Secondary effects of reducing consumption depend on the forms of the political and economic systems and the mechanisms for social decision making. Even in advanced economies, reductions in consumption could cause recession and consequent reductions in desirable forms of capital formation. One need not advocate the immiseration of the current generation to point out that consumption accounts for 60 to 70 percent of GNP in an advanced Western country, accounting directly and indirectly for a very large part of resource and environmental depletion. If the components of GNP were labeled meaningfully, it would be noted that military uses of resources and workers comprise a very significant portion of total consumption.

These comments on consumption suggest that changes in life-styles within the high-income countries could greatly affect and enhance the legacy we leave for the future. Economic analysis can help us understand the implications of changes in life-styles and the likelihood of achieving such ends through economic forces. But economics cannot provide all the answers and may well overlook some highly beneficial changes in social institutions and policies. Like all sciences, economics can best analyze processes of smooth change, of gradual shifts in prices, incomes, tastes, and laws. Economic theory is largely based on continuity assumptions neatly summarized in the motto appearing on the title page of Alfred Marshall's famous *Principles of Economics: natura non facit saltum*—nature takes no leaps. But failure to consider large, discrete changes in social and economic organization may justify E. F. Schumacher's charge that much of economics is concerned with optimizing the arrangement of deck chairs on the Titanic.

This chapter considers the intertemporal equity and efficiency implications of some of the standard methods of analysis or evaluation used by public sector agencies in the planning and justification of their programs. Since some of these practices are faulty from the theoretical and/or practical viewpoints, some alternatives to current practice will also be considered.

## 8.1.  CRITERIA FOR INTERTEMPORAL DECISION MAKING: PARETO EFFICIENCY

"Intertemporal decisions" as we use it here refers to resource allocations that have long-term implications for benefits and costs. This introduces the passage of time as a crucial feature of such decisions, with the consequent problems of the comparability of values over time, predicting future conditions and tastes, facing risks that increase with futurity, and so on. Natural resource policy decisions are typically of this type.

The simplest criterion for assisting in intertemporal decision making and the evaluation of alternative policies or projects would be *intertemporal Pareto efficiency*. A policy or a pattern of resource use over time is said to be Pareto efficient if and only if it is not possible to increase the utility of the affected parties at any point in time without decreasing utilities at other points in time. This concept sounds fairly elementary but leaves one wondering whether or not it may be too simple ever to be applied. Most policy changes or projects could not be compared using this criterion since they typically *do* involve decreasing utilites at some points in time in order to increase utilities at other times.[1]

However, the concept of intertemporal Pareto efficiency provides a benchmark for considering other criteria and, interestingly, can actually be used in judging some policies. An example of a Pareto inefficient allocation of resources is found in the current helium storage program of the U.S. Bureau of Mines. While the entire scenario is too lengthy to relate[2], the situation in brief is this: helium has various uses in low temperature systems and could play an increasingly important role in several prospective technologies like fusion power generation and cryogenic (very low temperature) power transmission. Helium occurs in natural gas and is separated from natural gas in private gasfield liquification plants that formerly sold their helium to the federal government under a program aimed at saving helium for the future since the helium-rich natural gases are limited. The separation plants were built to extract several other useful rare gases simultaneously. The federal government decided to stop buying helium, partly because the amount in storage had grown greatly relative to use rates and partly because of prospective financial liabilities arising out of a lawsuit over royalty payments. Since the private companies are also involved with these prospective liabilities, no one is willing to store the helium that is still being separated, even though it could be stored at essentially zero cost. The gas is being vented to the atmosphere.[3] While future demands are uncertain, there is a possibility that helium will be extremely valuable in the future. Provision for this contingency could be made today at essentially zero cost. Failure to store this gas is clearly a Pareto inefficient policy.

## 8.2.  THE DETERMINATION OF "PRESENT VALUES" OF BENEFITS AND COSTS THROUGH DISCOUNTING

A change in a government regulation or the undertaking of some physical or social project generally generates a stream of positive effects (benefits) over time and a stream of negative effects (costs) over time. The difference between the benefit rate and the cost rate at any point in time

---

[1]Intertemporal Pareto efficiency can be made to incorporate the static concept that no individual can be made better off without making someone else worse off.

[2]See *Helium: A Public Policy Problem*, National Academy of Sciences, Washington, D.C., 1978.

[3]A humorous final barb is that the noise from venting at one plant was so great that nearby cattle herds were going berserk, and noise baffles had to be constructed!

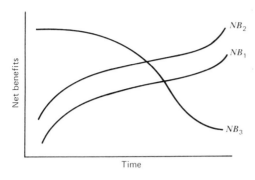

**Figure 8.1** Net benefit streams of three alternative policy changes or projects.

is called the *net benefit* rate. Three time traces of net benefits of three alternative policy changes or projects are plotted in Figure 8.1. There is no difficulty in comparing the desirabilities of net benefit streams $NB_1$ and $NB_2$, for $NB_2$ clearly *dominates* $NB_1$: it is better at every point in time, so is clearly better overall. $NB_1$ is Pareto inefficient. But how do we compare $NB_2$ and $NB_3$? Can we come to any clear conclusion regarding their relative desirabilities?[4]

If a policy maker is to decide between $NB_2$ and $NB_3$, there must exist some set of explicit or implicit weights that permit the comparison of net benefits at different time points. Viewed in terms of discrete time intervals (years), these weights could be used to "sum up" the net benefit streams of the policies or projects being compared, as shown in (8.2.1):

$$(8.2.1) \qquad PVNB_2 = w_0 NB_{2,0} + w_1 NB_{2,1} + \ldots + w_N NB_{2,N}$$
$$PVNB_3 = w_0 NB_{3,0} + w_1 NB_{3,1} + \ldots + w_N NB_{3,N}$$

Such weighted sums are called "present values," and it can be seen that the ratio of the weights of any two periods shows the relative values of net benefits accruing in those periods [e.g., $(w_N/w_2)$]. In general, the weights could vary in any way chosen as reasonable by the policy maker, decreasing or increasing, according to some specific formula or not. $PVNB_2$ and $PVNB_3$ can then be compared, the larger presumably indicating the superior project.

In practice, these weights are set according to a regular geometric pattern such that

$$(8.2.2) \qquad w_t = \frac{1}{(1 + r)^t}$$

---

[4]All this subsumes an ability to quantify all relevant benefits and costs at each point in time.

where $r$ is called the *discount rate* and is usually treated as a constant. For example, if $r = 0.1$ (i.e., 10 percent), the set of weights would be (1, 0.91, 0.83, 0.75, . . .). The implied tradeoff between net benefits in year $n_1$ and year $n_2$ would be given by the ratio of their weights, $w_{n_1}/w_{n_2} = 1/(1 + r)^{n_1} \div 1/(1 + r)^{n_2} = (1 + r)^{n_2 - n_1}$.

The comparison of present values arrived at through such a discounting process permits the comparison of complicated time streams of net benefits and permits a decision to be made between the projects producing streams $NB_2$ and $NB_3$. The decision obviously will be influenced by the choice of the discount rate $r$, so there must be a clear-cut rationale for the choice of $r$.

The historical rationale for the discount rate for public sector programs has been the achievement of economic efficiency over time in the allocation of resources between the private and public sectors. In brief, the argument has been that an efficient private sector—public sector allocation of resources will be achieved if the marginal rates of return on resource uses are equal in the two sectors. The rate of return on a private sector investment (e.g., a new factory or machine) can be defined as the rate of discount that makes the present value equal zero, that is:

$$(8.2.3) \qquad (B_0 - C_0) + \frac{(B_1 - C_1)}{(1 + r)} + \ldots + \frac{(B_N - C_N)}{(1 + r)^N} = 0$$

When investment rules in the private sector specify a required rate of return as calculated above as a criterion for undertaking the investment, this required rate can be taken as the marginal rate of return on investments in the private sector.

The meaning of the marginal rate of return on current consumption uses of resources in the private sector is less obvious but can be inferred from interest rates consumers are willing to pay to expedite consumption. A family having no debt but a home mortgage at 9 percent is willing to forego future consumption through interest payments to acquire the services of the house today. The consumer using extended credit card borrowing may be paying 18 percent. A family with sufficient income that they choose to save and invest in securities yielding 6 percent also exhibits a "rate of return on consumption" at the margin. These inferred rates are an expression of what economists call the *time preference* of the individuals involved.

When the public sector finances its programs through borrowing and taxation of the private sector, the rates of return on precluded investments and the inferred rates of time preference on precluded consumption can be taken as the *opportunity cost* of the redirected resources. The economic efficiency argument is that they should earn a rate of return in public sector uses at least equal to their rate of return in their private uses. This can be guaranteed by establishing the following public sector investment rule:

> undertake only those programs or projects that exhibit a positive present value of net benefits (8.2.1), using an appropriately weighted private sector opportunity cost rate as the discount rate.

Thus carried out, discounting presumably not only allows the comparison of complicated net benefit streams, but assures an efficient allocation of resources between private and public sectors.

## 8.3. THE "SOCIAL TIME PREFERENCE" APPROACH TO DISCOUNTING

Discounting, whatever the rate selected, implies a particular scheme of weighting for future events. If the discount rate is taken as the opportunity cost of capital as described in the previous section, it could be quite large, implying a heavy discounting of the future, perhaps inappropriately heavy if the public sector is expected to guard the interests of future generations. It would not be irrational for a consumer-voter or a businessperson-voter to say, "Yes, I pay 15 percent on consumer loans to expand my consumption and I require a 25 percent rate of return to justify investments in my business, but I expect government to place much greater weight than that on the future." This is a frequently heard opinion, that the public sector has a particular responsibility to look out for the future and to give greater weight to future events than would be implied by using a private sector discount rate. The discount rate used in evaluating public programs is then looked on as a parameter to be selected as part of the social decision-making process—the so-called rate of *social time preference*.

If this approach is adopted, economic efficiency considerations can still be incorporated into the calculation of present values. Consider a simplified public project with unlimited life, an initial capital cost of $C$, and constant benefits per year of $B$. If the resources represented by $C$ would have earned a rate of return (in the broad sense described earlier) of $r$ indefinitely, and if $\rho$ represents the desired rate of social time preference, we can calculate the present value of net benefits as follows:

$$(8.3.1) \quad PVNB = \frac{B - rC}{(1+\rho)} + \frac{B - rC}{(1+\rho)^2} + \ldots + \frac{B - rC}{(1+\rho)^i} + \ldots$$

$$= \frac{B - rC}{(1+\rho)} \left[ 1 + \frac{1}{(1+\rho)} + \frac{1}{(1+\rho)^2} + \ldots \right]$$

$$= \frac{B}{\rho} - \frac{rC}{\rho}$$

In this formulation,[5] the annual cost is $rC$, expressed in terms of the private rate of return foregone or the private rate of time preference, but the weights given to these costs (and the benefits) are calculated according to the rate of social time preference, $\rho$. Equation 8.3.1 can be interpreted as follows: society gets an infinite sequence of annual benefits $B$ but is required forever to give up the use of resources with a market value $C$ on which the annual private return would have been $rC$. An equivalent interpretation of the cost term, which yields further insight is this: the market has valued the resources involved in the project at $C$ dollars by using the private discount rate, $r$, to capitalize the benefit stream that would have been generated if the resources had been kept in the private sector. Assuming $r > \rho$, the market has undervalued these resources, so the nominal costs must be increased by the factor $r/\rho$.

Those favoring the social time preference approach have concluded that the private market or opportunity cost rate is undesirably high, that is, that $\rho < r$. A famous economic theorist, Frank Ramsey, argued in 1928 that discounting was unfair and A. C. Pigou, the famous welfare economist, thought its utilization to be attributable only to the myopia of the current generation. Further reasons that have been given for adopting a social discount rate less than $r$ would include the following:

1.  Future generations are not present to protect their interests. The bequest motivations of the current generation may imply concern for the next generation or two, but that is not a long enough time horizon. These factors call for heavier public weights on future events.

2.  Market rates of interest do not measure even private time preferences, for the typical consumer is myopic and pays little attention to interest rates as long as monthly payments can be met. Consumers have little experience with transactions in which interest is really a major factor, such as home or auto purchases. Their own feeling for

[5]The limit of an infinite geometric series $(1 + a + a^2 + a^3 + \ldots)$ where $a < 1$ is $1/(1 - a)$.

intertemporal tradeoffs is, as a result, nonexistent or formed in ignorance.

3.  There are so many different rates of return and interest with large differences between borrowing and lending rates even for the same individual that it is difficult to know which rates to average in calculating an appropriate opportunity cost rate.

4.  Market rates of interest and returns on private investments contain, on the average, a risk premium to cover the market uncertainties surrounding private investments. For a number of reasons (to be discussed in Section 8.5), such risks are likely to be less important for the public sector and the risk premium should not be incorporated in the public discount rate.

So, a social time preference approach to the determination of an appropriate public discount rate seems to have several strong arguments in its favor. But one must ask how the rate of social time preference is to be determined. If individuals have little feeling for intertemporal tradeoffs as asserted in (2) above, how can they as voters, members of Congress, or in other official capacities be any better prepared to select $\rho$?

Marglin has suggested a consistent method for societal determination of the social rate of time preference. Suppose that society decides on a desired rate of economic (GNP) growth, $g(t)$. Given the economy's structure (including the extent of central control), some rates of investment $I[g(t)]$ will be associated with the desired growth rate through the multiplier-accelerator mechanism. If we assume that an efficient program of investment will be selected so that marginal rates of return will be equated among various projects or programs, then the rate of investment $I$ implies a common marginal rate of return, $r\{I[g(t)]\}$. This would then be the appropriate social rate of discount, constituting a cutoff rate of return on investment for all sectors. An iterative policy-making process can be imagined that would converge on a $g(t)$ with associated $I$ and $r$, representing the optimal balancing of current and future consumption.

While such a process seems quite abstract, GNP growth goals are set by the federal government, with budgetary and monetary policy being shaped toward that goal. Large econometric models of the Brookings or Wharton School variety are used to determine what levels of investment in the various sectors (plus government surplus or deficit) would accomplish that growth. Estimating marginal rates of return corresponding to the various sector levels of investment would be subject to substantial uncertainty.

A more concrete suggestion by Maass and Major is that implicit discount rates and other values can be inferred from past public sector decisions to undertake certain programs and not to undertake others. The plausibility of this approach is low because of the typical dearth of information and appropriate analyses available to harassed decision makers. Most project analyses are compressed into a few tables and a benefit/cost ratio, with little if any explanation of alternatives or non-quantified effects. Thus it seems unlikely that the legislator's selection of projects really reflects his or her perception of society's willingness to trade current for future net benefits.

Where does this leave us in selecting an appropriate discount rate for public sector programs? The federal government in the United States currently follows a practice of averaging interest rates on certain classes of government bonds of far-off maturity.[6] The resultant rate, now 6⅜ percent per annum, is below market rates and represents a risk-free return. Some argue that even that rate is too high, but, on balance, it seems as appropriate as any other figure.

## 8.4.  WHAT DISCOUNTING DOES *NOT* DO

We have seen that the adoption of lower discount rates is one way of placing greater weight on the future, and that this can be done without sacrificing economic efficiency in the allocation of resources over time or between public and private sectors. We have noted, too, that adopting a social rate of discount lower than the private rate will require adjustments to be made to cost figures (see 8.3.1) so it is not simply a matter of grabbing a low random number. It is important to emphasize that selecting an appropriate discount rate is only one part of good program or project evaluation. Therefore, several important *caveats* must be emphasized:

1.  Adopting a reasonable social rate of discount cannot offset the effects of biased estimates of benefits and costs. Guarding the interests of the future is as much a matter of good benefit and cost stream estimation as it is of using a lower discount rate. As an example, consider the usual time patterns of benefits, $B$, and construction and maintenance costs, $C_c$ of a large water project as shown in Figure 8.2. When only $B$ and $C_c$ were included in the analysis, a lower dis-

---

[6]The U.S. Treasury Department makes the computation once each year and transmits it to the Water Resources Council, an independent executive coordinating agency.

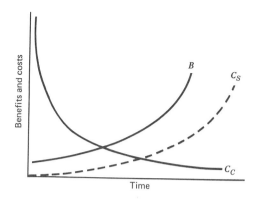

**Figure 8.2** Typical time pattern of construction costs, site opportunity costs, and benefits from a water project.

count rate was sure to increase *PVNB* and make the project more acceptable. Today, however, with little natural river left undeveloped, the site opportunity costs $C_S$, can be expected to rise in the future. When $C_S$ is added to the analysis, it is no longer clear that a lower discount rate will favor such traditional projects.

2. Using a low social rate of discount does not guarantee that more traditional public works projects will pass the *PVNB* > 0 test if appropriate adjustments to capital costs are made. For example, an agency interested in building a dam finds the market price of land in the reservoir area to be $1000 per acre. If the agency is permitted to adopt a 5 percent discount rate while market rates are 10 percent, project benefits farther in the future *will* receive more weight, but the cost of land used by the project must be increased to $2000 per acre since $(r/\rho) = 2$ as in (8.3.1). If the agency uses a 3 percent rate, land value must be increased to $3333 per acre.

3. Using a low social rate of discount will not guarantee that the total rate of investment in long-lived projects will increase. At the individual project level, the reason was given in (2) above. At the macro level, low public discount rates will not affect market rates of interest unless accompanied by changes in monetary policy. If market interest rates are forced down, the rate of saving may fall. Even if justified public sector investment increases, it may come at the cost of foregone private investment.

4. Discounting can lend to the economic attractiveness of some policies or actions that are not socially acceptable on various noneconomic grounds. Clark[7] has shown, for example, that discounting can lead

[7]Colin W. Clark, "The Economics of Overexploitation," *Science*, Vol. 181, 17 Aug. 1973, pp. 630–634.

to the economic desirability of the overexploitation and ultimate destruction of a fishery if the discount rate is sufficiently above the natural reproduction rate of the fish stock. Such policies are no longer tolerated on scientific and environmental grounds.

5. Discounting can lead to inconsistencies in the patterns of natural resources use that would be chosen by different generations. If one generation discounts the utilities of successive generations at increasingly heavy rates, each generation will find that the optimal resource use plan laid down for it by the previous generation calls for it to consume more of remaining resources than it cares to. Resource use plans will need to be revised each generation.[8]

These points have been made to emphasize that discounting at appropriately chosen rates is an aid in the social decision process which aids in designing efficient policies and that it is not inherently unfair to the future. On the other hand, discounting even at a "responsible" social rate cannot make up for other types of distortions which often plague public program evaluations.

## 8.5. CONSIDERATIONS OF RISK AND UNCERTAINTY IN NATURAL RESOURCES PLANNING AND MANAGEMENT

The need to face uncertainties is a burden on society. While one can speculate about the potentially beneficial roles of uncertainty (so that we don't know our ultimate fates, so that optimistic expectations are not suppresed, etc.), people generally desire to escape uncertainty in the economic dimensions of their lives. This is manifested in the many forms of insurance, in the cartelization of markets to avoid price wars, and in the higher expected rates of return that are necessary to induce investment in risky enterprise.

A distinction is frequently made between risk and uncertainty: the former represents a situation in which the success of a project or pro-

---

[8]Assume that each generation considers the utilities of subsequent generations by applying a discount factor of $b_2$ to the next generation's utility and $b_3$ ($< b_2$) to the generation second removed in the future. The present value of utility to be maximized by the first generation is $U(X_1) + b_2 U(X_2) + b_2 b_3 U(X_3)$, subject to $X_1 + X_2 + X_3 = X$. The marginal condition characterizing the optimal allocation of $X$ between the second and third generation is that $U'(X_2) = b_3 U'(X_3)$. When the second generation faces its own decision problem, it can maximize $U(X_2) + b_2 U(X_3)$ subject to $X_2 + X_3 = X - X_1^*$, the marginal condition being $U'(X_2) = b_2 U'(X_3)$. This results in a feasible but different pattern. This problem was first raised by Strotz in 1956.

gram depends on a random event or sequence of events for which the probabilities are known, while the latter represents a situation with unknown probabilities. Natural resources management involves both. Planning a dam for water supply and flood control on a river with a long record of flows can, at least on the hydrologic side, be handled as decision making under risk since the probability distribution of flows is pretty well known. On the other hand, the social and economic consequences of the dam—factors on which its success or failure rest—may be subject to a wide range of uncertainty for which no historical record exists. Thus, all decision situations contain some elements of uncertainty.

Natural resources management decisions are likely to have long-lived effects: *in situ* resources become exhausted, natural environments and ecosystems are affected, and waste disposal in the environment may build up stocks of residual materials that break down or dissipate only slowly. The longer the time horizon, the greater the degree of uncertainty that must be faced. A generally "conservative" approach to decision making thus seems warranted.

Some of the changes involved in natural resources management may be irreversible. When our knowledge of the factors determining the social utility of these changes is subject to great uncertainty, we face the possibility of not being able to "undo" a bad decision. Fisher and Krutilla (1974) use the example of the Everglades, a unique ecological system increasingly valued for scientific and recreational purposes. If agricultural developments in that region are allowed to change the groundwater flows sustaining the Everglades, irreversible changes are likely to occur. If, at a later date, it becomes clear that the value of the Everglades in their undisturbed form has come to exceed the value of the related agricultural production, it may not be possible to revert to the earlier state. All posterity will have to live with the results of the earlier decision.

Thus uncertainty and irreversibility dictate caution and conservatism in natural resource decisions. This conclusion is reinforced if information can be gained (i.e., risk or uncertainty reduced) by deferring decisions. Arrow and Fisher have called the utility gained from deferring irreversible decision "quasi-option value." Consider their simple example: a project is being considered that can be either fully or partially constructed in period 1 and, in the latter case, can be completed in period 2. Let $w_1$ and $w_2$ be the fractions of the project constructed in periods 1 and 2, $B_1$ the first period benefits from full construction, while the benefits from full construction in the second period are a random variable, $B_2$, which assumes a value $\alpha < 0$ with probability $p$ and a value

$\beta > 0$ with probability $(1 - p)$, such that the expected value, $E(B_2)$, is greater than zero. If the decision maker must commit himself or herself to a complete two-period construction strategy now, the relevant objective function would be:

$$(8.5.1) \qquad\qquad E(B) = w_1 B_1 + E(B_2)$$

To maximize $E(B)$, the decision maker would set $w_1 = 1$ if $B_1 > 0$, or $w_1 = 0$ if $B_1 < 0$, and would set $w_2 = 1 - w_1$. That is, the optimal decision rule is

$$(8.5.2) \qquad\qquad w_1^* = \begin{cases} 1 \text{ if } B_1 > 0 \\ 0 \text{ if } B_1 \leq 0 \end{cases}$$

$$w_2^* = 1 - w_1^*$$

Suppose, however, that the value of $B_2$ will become known at the beginning of period 2 and that the decision regarding completion of the project can be deferred until that time. Clearly, if any part of the project remains to be built and if $B_2 = \alpha < 0$, construction will not be completed in the second period. The appropriate objective function is then

$$(8.5.3) \qquad \begin{aligned} \hat{E}(B) &= w_1 B_1 + p w_1 \alpha + (1 - p)\beta \\ &= w_1(B_1 + p\alpha) + (1 - p)\beta. \end{aligned}$$

It is clear that maximizing $\hat{E}(B)$ implies the following decision rule:

$$(8.5.4) \qquad\qquad w_1^* = \begin{cases} 1 \text{ if } B_1 + p\alpha > 0 \\ 0 \text{ if } B_1 + p\alpha \leq 0 \end{cases}$$

$$w_2^* = \begin{cases} 1 - w_1^* \text{ if } B_2 = \beta \\ 0 \qquad\quad \text{ if } B_2 = \alpha \end{cases}$$

The second decision rule is *more conservative* than the first, since it requires that $B_1 > -p\alpha$ before $w_1$ is set equal to 1, while the earlier rule simply required that $B_1 > 0$ before $w_1$ was set equal to 1. *The ability to gain information by waiting has resulted in a more conservative decision rule* for project development.

**The Social Discount Rate and Risk.**   The preceding paragraphs have given various reasons why natural resource policy and project decision rules should be conservative in the face of uncertainties and irreversibilities. Earlier we had noted that one way that has been used to reflect uncertainty is to add a risk premium to the discount rate, thus giving less weight to the increasingly uncertain benefits and costs in future periods. It is known that private business investment decisions are made in this way, with higher discount rates or higher internal rates of return being required of riskier projects.

To what extent should the public sector include a risk premium in the social rate of discount? This has been a matter of long and furious debate but it has been nicely presented by James (1975) and need only be summarized here. The public sector has available to it two devices for reducing the cost of risk bearing: risk pooling and risk spreading. The first occurs when a large number of independent projects are undertaken by an agency with the capability of pooling the benefits and costs of all projects into one pot or account. As the number of independent projects increases, the mean or expected value of net benefits of the pool rises more rapidly than the dispersion of the return. This is easily seen if, for simplicity, we consider a set of identical but independent projects, the typical (random) return from each being $X$ with the same probability distributions. The characteristics of the pooled returns are then:

(8.5.5)
$$Y = X_1 + X_2 + \ldots X_n$$
$$E(Y) = E(X_1) + \ldots + E(X_n) = nE(X)$$
$$\sigma_Y^2 = \sigma_{X_1}^2 + \sigma_{X_2}^2 + \ldots + \sigma_{X_n}^2 = n\sigma_X^2$$
$$\sigma_Y = \sqrt{n}\, \sigma_X$$

The mean return, $E(Y)$, thus increases more rapidly than the standard deviation, $\sigma_Y$, as the number of pooled projects is increased. If the attractiveness of the pool to society is a function of the relative sizes of $E(Y)$ and $\sigma_Y$, say $E(Y)/\sigma_Y$, then the pool can be made acceptable when individual projects are not.

Risk spreading refers to spreading the risky net benefits of a single project over a large number of individuals. We can say that the scale of the project (meaning the range of net benefits) for the individual is thereby decreased. If the individual's utility function for income is concave (diminishing marginal utility of income), the burden of risk bearing will fall more rapidly than the expected income from the individual's share of the project. If the number of individuals grows large, the aggregate cost of risk bearing approaches zero in such a situation.

The critical question is the extent to which benefits and costs from public sector programs actually get pooled or spread. Certainly *many* public projects benefit primarily local groups or activities: irrigation projects, flood control projects, and probably navigation projects. Some of the benefits and costs get passed on indirectly through the market process. Nonetheless, it seems likely that a major part of the potential benefits and, in many cases, a significant part of the actual costs remain within a relatively small area, rather than being distributed throughout the economy. The implication is that the public sector should use discount rates with some risk premium in them, perhaps less than market risk premiums since government generally places bounds on the risks born by project participants, especially on the low side through "bailing out" faulty projects.

The risk spreading arguments also fail to apply to projects whose outputs have the nature of "public goods," that is, where one party's use doesn't diminish the amount available to other users. Since many public projects produce some public goods (e.g., flood control, environmental improvement, preservation of esthetic features, etc.), a risk premium seems called for. Some other types of risk simply cannot be insured. The risks of irreversible change in the global environment are of this type, for example, the buildup of carbon dioxide, the accumulation of nuclear wastes and oceanic pollution, and the extinction of ecological diversity.

The ultimate effects of these changes simply are not known at present, but they could be disastrous in magnitude. The risks are of a greater order of magnitude than the risks that were involved in the earlier evolution of technology. At the same time, the common property nature of the environmental media makes worldwide control almost impossible. The point is that current and projected natural resource uses and related technologies imply growing uncertainties for future generations. If, in the past, it had proved impossible to repair Appalachia after the rape of strip mining or to resettle the Dust Bowl, at least there were other regions to absorb migration and support life, but the greenhouse effect of $CO_2$ or the effects of killing oxygen-generating zooplankton in the oceans through pollution cannot be escaped.

A similar type of risk is created for future generations if we increase future dependence on the successful evolution of particular technologies. As noted earlier, the nature of some of the technological improvements needed for massive substitution of capital for natural resources that are frequently mentioned as panaceas for natural resource shortages (e.g., fusion) are quite different from the technological improvements that have served us so well in the past. Relying on such breakthroughs imposes risks on the future.

## 8.6. ALTERNATIVES TO THE INTERTEMPORAL DISCOUNTING TYPE OF CRITERION FOR NATURAL RESOURCES PLANNING

Preceding sections have indicated some of the difficulties involved in making welfare comparisons over long periods of time. The meaning and empirical determination of an appropriate discount rate, the possibility of changes in the rate among generations, and the question of the comparability of utility among persons have been raised as technical difficulties. Of course, tastes may change and technology may modify the situation of future generations in unforeseen ways, clouding the appropriate forms of future utility functions, as well as the values of their arguments.

These difficulties raise the question of the extent to which the utilitarian approach of maximizing the present value of some index of welfare (such as measurable consumption) can be utilized for normative purposes covering the long time periods we encounter in dealing with natural resources. This is not to question the usefulness of the partial-equilibrium evaluations we make of public projects (e.g., benefit-cost analyses), for most projects are relatively short lived and of small scale. Yet can we apply the same techniques to long-term natural resources and environmental issues? It seems appropriate to consider possible alternatives or modifications to the utilitarian type of criterion.

Daly (1976) has reopened the issue of the Ultimate End to be served by human economic activity by pointing out that placing priorities on various goals (e.g., economic growth, environmental quality, income distribution, etc.) presumes an ordering principle or "Ultimate End." The discipline of economics, however, in attempting to follow the presumably value-free methods of physical science, has come to avoid debate about the Ultimate End by accepting contemporary personal tastes to be the ultimate benchmark for assessing priorities. According to Daly, this refusal to reason about the Ultimate End may very well mean that our individual and collective goals are incoherent and that the high level of rationality that we attempt to achieve by applying economic analysis to the design and management of programs in pursuit of those goals has very little significance.

Regarding the nature of the Ultimate End, Daly concludes that, at a minimum, "it presupposes a respect for and continuation of Creation and the evolutionary process through which God has bestowed upon us the gift of self-conscious life.... This minimum answer begs many important questions: Survival and evolution in what direction? To what extent should evolution be influenced by man...? For now, however, the only point is that survival must rank very high in the end-means hierarchy. . . ."

This line of reasoning provides a broader philosophical base for a set of concerns that have been raised in the natural resources literature for at least 25 years: long-term ecological consequences, irreversible changes in ecosystems and environment, the maintenance of flexibility, and the observance of relevant policy "safety margins." These concerns have usually been raised in urging modifications to or constraints on a simple utilitarian criterion for social decision making.

S. V. Ciriacy-Wantrup, one of the great pioneers in the natural resources economics field with his *Resource Conservation: Economics and Policies* (1952, 1963), was concerned with the decrease in diversity of natural systems around us. His concerns sprang from esthetic and scientific grounds. He recommended "a safe minimum standard of conservation" for all renewable resources characterized by a critical zone. This safe minimum standard is achieved by avoiding the critical zone, that is, those physical conditions of the resource system which, once attained, culminate in the destruction of the system. Naturally, guaranteeing achievement of a safe minimum standard of conservation may involve certain costs that are accepted as the cost of guaranteeing the survival of the system.

Examples of safe minimum standards for particular renewable NR systems would include the following: (1) for soil conservation, a maximum rate of erosion per year; (2) for forestry, a maximum rate of destruction from natural elements or a minimum degree of diversity in tree and brush types; (3) for grasslands, a minimum residual of viable plants for revival of the turf; and (4) for animal species, a minimum breeding stock to guarantee survival.

Many national economic systems have, through motivation provided by economic conditions, exceeded safe minimum standards in their practices. Other areas, typically frontier areas, permit or encourage destructive exploitation of renewable resource systems. To such areas, the enforcement of safe minimum standards would entail a short-term cost.

The concept of safe minimum reserve is applied by Krutilla and Fisher to both the protection of genetic information and the preservation of cultural arts and crafts. The extinction of a species or even a variety of animals or plants represents, at least under current scientific capabilities, an irretrievable loss of genetic information and diversity. Similarly, if arts and crafts are allowed to die, the key to the skills may be forever lost.

We have seen in Chapter 4 that Solow investigated the possibility of maintaining a uniform level of aggregate consumption indefinitely in the face of finite natural resources. Solow accepted this criterion of maximizing the intertemporally uniform level of consumption because of an uneasiness over the justification of discounting future values and the impossibility of defining utilitarian optimality under a zero discount rate.

The resultant level of consumption established by Solow is not unlike the *steady-state economy* that Daly concluded had to be accepted as a social goal. Daly described the steady-state economy as one having:

1.  A constant human population.
2.  A constant man-made capital stock.
3.  A relation between population and capital, making possible an acceptably high standard of living that would be sustainable into the indefinite future.
4.  A minimum throughput of materials and energy.

In such an economy, while population and capital would be stable, technology, wisdom, goodness, genetic characteristics, distribution of wealth, output mix, and the like, could continue to change. Thus, the level of aggregate consumption could continue to increase in such a state.

Solow's criterion was expressly adapted from Rawl's *intra*generational maximin criterion for social justice. While there are difficulties in attempting to adapt the concept to intertemporal judgments, the concept itself has aroused sufficient interest among many disciplines to warrant definition and brief discussion here.

Rawls asserts that the only way in which a society can develop reasonable principles of justice (including economic justice) is to start from "the original position" in which all members of society can view that society but are deprived of all knowledge of their particular place in that society, their social status, their share in society's wealth, their aims and interests, and their psychological makeup. This places all persons on an equal plane as "free and equal moral persons." They are then called on to make up the rules for that society. On various grounds, including risk-averting behavior, Rawls concludes that two principles would be unanimously voted from the original position:

1.  All persons would be extended the maximum freedoms compatible with the extension of identical freedoms to all others.
2.  Social and economic inequalities would be justified only if they

serve to bring about the greatest improvement of the least advantaged members of society and are attached to positions open to all.

With regard to economic well-being, item 2 is equivalent to saying that society designs rules and a distribution of well-being that will $\max\{\min(U_1, U_2, \ldots, U_N)\}$, where $U_i$ is the level of well-being of the $i$th individual.

Rawls himself stated that the maximin criterion "is intended to hold only within generations"; but he did discuss possible adaptations to an intergenerational context. The basic problem is the asymmetry of intergenerational exchange possibilities: an earlier generation can decide to pass a certain inheritance on to later generations, but the later generations cannot share their assets with the earlier. If the original position, now defined as an intergenerational pool deprived of the knowledge noted above, occurred at a point where the society already had accumulated substantial wealth but faced decline because of exhausting natural resources, it would be physically possible to carry out a maximin policy by conserving natural resources, cutting near-term consumption, and passing along appropriate stocks of capital to generations that otherwise would experience lower standards of living. Such a situation would be much like Daly's steady state. On the other hand, if the original position occurred early in the economic development of the society when later generations would be expected to be wealthier, the imposition of the maximin criterion would imply holding later generations to the unduly low initial levels of consumption. Solow found that the uniform sustainable level of consumption was an increasing function of the initial stock of capital as our reasoning here suggests, but he also concluded that the maximin criterion "seems to give foolishly conservative (intertemporal) injunctions when there is stationary population and unlimited technical progress."

# Chapter 9

# THE MANAGEMENT OF ENERGY RESOURCES

The United States has always used large quantities of energy in its production processes and in its consumption of goods. In early years, the plentiful supply of wood provided cheap fuel for home and commerce, and coal was sufficiently plentiful to be easily substituted for wood as wood supplies close to points of demand became depleted. As noted earlier, kerosene quickly took over from whale oil for lighting, with petroleum becoming increasingly important as the automobile came upon the scene. The changing composition of U.S. energy sources in recent decades is shown in Table 9.1.

The United States was shocked in 1973 by the OPEC (Organization of Petroleum Exporting Countries) oil embargo and a very sudden increase in oil prices by OPEC. Since OPEC represented the sources of

**Table 9.1.** Total U.S. Energy Consumption (BTU and Percentage by Source)

| Year | Total Consumption ($10^{15}$ BTU) | Coal (%) | Petroleum (%) | N Gas (%) | Hydro-nuclear (%) |
|------|------|------|------|------|------|
| 1920 | 19.7 | 78 | 14 | 4 | 4 |
| 1930 | 22.3 | 61 | 27 | 9 | 4 |
| 1940 | 23.9 | 52 | 32 | 11 | 4 |
| 1950 | 34.2 | 38 | 39 | 18 | 5 |
| 1960 | 45.0 | 23 | 45 | 28 | 4 |
| 1970 | 68.8 | 20 | 43 | 33 | 4 |
| 1973 | 71.4 | 18 | 46 | 31 | 5 |

**Table 9.2.**   Posted Prices of
Arabian Crude Oil

| | |
|---|---|
| 1960–1970 | $ 1.80 per barrel |
| February 1971 | 2.18 |
| January 1973 | 2.59 |
| October 1973 | 5.11 |
| January 1974 | 11.65 |

supply that had sufficient reserves and production capacity to meet the surging demands of the United States, Western Europe, and Japan, it could make its price increases stick in the international market. The posted prices of Saudi Arabian light crude are given in Table 9.2.

## 9.1.   FACTORS LEADING TO THE 1973 ENERGY CRISIS[1]

The main factors leading up to the 1973 "crisis" were the tremendous growth in world energy demands, the rising share supplied by petroleum, and the increasing world role of imports from the Persian Gulf region. In the U.S., additional factors were the environmental constraints on the use of coal, lags in the completion of nuclear plants, and long delays in granting of oil and gas leases by the U.S. government.

World demands for energy had been increasing rapidly as shown in Table 9.3. Rates of growth are seen to be much higher in later years. In the early 1970s, there was a simultaneous economic boom in Western Europe, Japan, and North America. By 1973, real GNP growth rates were 5.4 percent for Western Europe, 10.4 percent for Japan, and 5.9 percent for the U.S. All through the industrialized world, basic materials industries were operating closer to full capacity than at any time since World War II.

The sharp increase in the relative importance of petroleum and natural gas that was observed in the United States also held for world patterns of energy use, as shown in Table 9.4. The United States was less vulnerable to an oil embargo than either Western Europe or Japan, since oil imports accounted for only 14 percent of U.S. energy consumption in 1974, while for Japan they comprised 73 percent and for Western Europe 59 percent. However, U.S. demand had been surging, the growth being covered totally by imports from the Persian Gulf. Canada and Venezuela, the traditional sources of U.S. imports, had only a lim-

---

[1]For an excellent treatment, see Darmstadter and Landsberg, 1975.

**Table 9.3.** World Energy Consumption and Population, Selected Years, 1925–1972

| | Total Energy Consumption [a] | | | Energy Consumption [a] per Capita (10⁶ Btu) |
|---|---|---|---|---|
| | $10^{12}$ Btu | 10⁶ Barrels/Day Oil Equivalent | Population (Million) | |
| 1925 | 44.249 | 21.6 | 1890 | 23.4 |
| 1950 | 76,823 | 37.5 | 2504 | 30.7 |
| 1960 | 124,046 | 60.5 | 2990 | 41.5 |
| 1970 | 214,496 | 104.7 | 3609 | 59.4 |
| 1972 | 237,166 | 115.7 | 3747 | 63.3 |
| | Average Annual Percentage Rate of Change | | | |
| 1925–50 | | 2.2 | 1.1 | 1.1 |
| 1950–60 | | 4.9 | 1.8 | 3.1 |
| 1960–72 | | 5.5 | 1.9 | 3.5 |

[a]One barrel of crude oil has a heat content of about 5.6 million Btu. Therefore, 1 million barrels a day equals approximately 2,044 trillion ($=10^{12}$) Btu per year. Oil consumption is sometimes also expressed in metric tons per year and energy consumption in metric tons oil-equivalent per year. Since 1 ton of crude oil is equal to about 7.3 barrels, 1 million barrels a day equals approximately 50 million tons a year. From the foregoing approximate calorific equivalents, we can then derive an additional one: 1 million tons of oil equals approximately 41 trillion Btu.

Source: Darmstadter and Landsberg, 1975, Table 1. Reprinted by permission of *Daedalus, Journal of the American Academy of Arts and Sciences, Boston.*

ited potential for increased production and their governments were adopting domestic conservation policies.

These trends were well established before 1970, but a sense of complacency apparently was created by the continuation of traditionally accepted use-to-reserve ratios on a world basis, by a general failure to

**Table 9.4.** World Energy Consumption, 1950–1973

| | 1950 | 1960 | 1970 | 1973 |
|---|---|---|---|---|
| Total ($10^{15}$ BTU) | 76.8 | 124.0 | 214.5 | 250.4 |
| Coal (%) | 56 | 44 | 31 | 29 |
| Oil (%) | 29 | 36 | 45 | 49 |
| Natural Gas (%) | 9 | 14 | 18 | 19 |

Source: *World Energy Suppliers,* U.N., 1976.

predict the increase in demands that occurred after 1970, and by a continued fall in the real price of energy. Among the factors accounting for the predictive errors were the ending of improvements in the fuel efficiency of electric power generation, a reduction in the fuel efficiency of new automobiles, and increasingly stringent environmental constraints on fuels. For the United States, the underprediction of oil imports was partly due to the collapse of oil import controls and an unanticipated decline in domestic exploratory and developmental activity. The pattern of U.S. energy use for 1960–1975 is shown in Table 9.5. In the late 1960s and early 1970s, oil was rapidly replacing coal as power plant fuel. It jumped from a 6 percent share in power plant fuels in the mid 1960s to 16 percent in 1972, substituting for coal and supplying all new plants. Much of this substitution was induced by environmental problems associated with the mining and burning of coal.

The demand for gasoline surged in the late 1960s, total use growing at nearly 6 percent. Causes included not only an increasing number of cars, but increased weight, popularity of air conditioning, and pollution control systems that reduced efficiency.

Natural gas production, a close substitute for oil, flattened out in the early 1970s, largely because of the price regulations imposed by the Federal Power Commission. Oil production from the Continental Shelf had slowed in the aftermath of the Santa Barbara well blowout and procedures for producing Alaskan oil proved to be slow and complicated. Nuclear plants, too, were being constructed at rates lower than anticipated because of design problems and environmental opposition.

Additions to reserves for oil and gas began falling short of production rates, partly as a result of the increasing attractiveness of foreign oil investments for American companies.

All of these events, which are summarized in Table 9.6, put the United States in an increasingly vulnerable position and increased the bargaining power of the Middle Eastern countries.

**Table 9.5.** U.S. Energy and Oil Consumption

|  | 1960 | 1970 | 1975 |
|---|---|---|---|
|  | ($10^6$ barrels per day) | | |
| Energy consumption (oil equivalent) | 19.5 | 29.7 | 30.6 |
| Oil consumption | 9.7 | 13.9 | 15.4 |
| Oil imports | 1.9 | 3.5 | 6.0 |

**Table 9.6.**   Production and Proved Reserves of Oil and Natural Gas, United States, 1964–1973

| | Oil (Billion Barrels) [a] | | | Natural Gas (Trillion Cubic Feet) | | |
|---|---|---|---|---|---|---|
| | Proved Reserves [b] | | | Proved Reserves [b] | | |
| | At End of Year | Change During Year | Production | At End of Year | Change During Year | Production |
| 1964 | 38.74 | 0.09 | 3.18 | 281.3 | 5.1 | 15.3 |
| 1965 | 39.38 | 0.64 | 3.24 | 286.5 | 5.2 | 16.3 |
| 1966 | 39.78 | 0.41 | 3.45 | 289.3 | 2.8 | 17.5 |
| 1967 | 39.99 | 0.21 | 3.68 | 292.9 | 3.6 | 18.4 |
| 1968 | 39.31 | −0.69 | 3.83 | 287.3 | −5.6 | 19.4 |
| 1969 | 37.78 | −1.53 | 3.93 | 275.1 | −12.2 | 20.7 |
| 1970 | 37.10 (46.70) | −0.68 (8.93) | 4.07 | 264.8 (290.7) | −10.3 (15.6) | 22.0 |
| 1971 | 35.77 (45.37) | −1.34 (−1.34) | 4.00 | 252.9 (278.8) | −11.9 (−11.9) | 22.1 |
| 1972 | 33.53 (43.13) | −2.24 (−2.24) | 4.04 | 240.2 (266.1) | −12.7 (−12.7) | 22.5 |
| 1973 | 32.15 (41.75) | −1.37 (−1.37) | 3.93 | 224.1 (250.0) | −16.1 (−16.1) | 22.6 |

[a]Including natural-gas liquids.
[b]Figures in parentheses refer to a measure of proved reserves, or change therein, which includes proved reserves ascribed to the Alaskan North Slope. North Slope proved oil reserves are carried at 9.6 billion barrels, natural gas, at 22.9 trillion cubic feet.

Source: Darmstadter and Landsberg, 1975, Table 7. Reprinted by permission of *Daedalus,* Journal of the American Academy of Arts and Sciences, Boston.

## 9.2.   AN ECONOMIC ANALYSIS OF THE ENERGY CRISIS

From 1889 to 1971, U.S. oil production increased 87 times, while the current price of oil rose from $0.77 per barrel to $3.39 per barrel. However, since the general price level increased six times in the same period, the *real* price per barrel fell 30 percent from $0.77 to $0.54. From 1950 to 1970, average energy prices in real terms fell 20 percent. The shifts in the demand and supply functions are pictured in Figure 9.1. Demand shifted in response to population and income increases and changing industrial technology. Supply shifted to the right, mostly as a result of technological improvements in exploration, production, and transportation, although other factors related to the status of the oil companies in the Middle East may have played a role in this shift. The result was a 20 percent fall in the real price of oil.

   The United States is frequently criticized both at home and abroad for being wasteful of energy, but it is clear that the energy use patterns

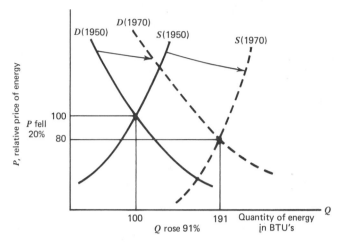

**Figure 9.1** The postwar energy market. Source: G. Horwich, "Energy: The View From the Market" in *Focus on Economic Issues,* Indiana Council for Economic Education, Purdue University, Spring 1977, Figure 1.

established in the post-war period were heavily influenced by falling real energy prices.

The increase in oil prices noted in Table 9.2 resulted not from a sudden change in physical supply conditions but as a result of the successful imposition of OPEC's monopolistic market powers, which can be pictured as a sudden leftward shift in the supply curve in Figure 9.1. Certainly the magnitude of this shift was much greater than could have been caused by changes in the two real cost components of the supply curve: production costs and scarcity rents on the *in situ* resource. Middle Eastern production costs have remained constant in the 10 to 40¢ per barrel range. The scarcity rent might be expected to increase because of the surging demands and resulting increases in the expected rate of price increase. It may well be that in the postwar period appropriate scarcity values of the *in situ* resource were not reflected in the supply curves of the large oil producing companies because of the uncertainty of their tenure in the Middle East. Nonetheless, the effective cartel action of OPEC in shifting the supply curve far to the left certainly exceeded any shift that would otherwise have been caused by increasing scarcity values.

The steep rise in price that OPEC was able to dictate depended also on the inelasticity of the demand curve for oil. We know that the short-run elasticity of demand for energy generally is low because most energy is used as an intermediate input to production and consumption processes. These processes use capital equipment (heat driven chemical processes, petroleum refineries, space heating systems, automobiles, appliances, etc.), which can be adapted or replaced only slowly over time in response to changing energy prices.

Several studies have estimated the price elasticities of energy demands. Griffen and Gregory (1976), using pooled cross-sectional data from the manufacturing industries of nine countries, have estimated the *long-run* real price elasticity by manufacturing to be −0.8. Bernt and Wood (1975) estimated the *short-run* manufacturing elasticity for the U.S. to be −0.45. This significantly greater long-run elasticity is what one expects.

Chapman, Tyrrell, and Mount (1972) have estimated price and "income" elasticities for electricity demand for different sectors of the United States using observations across states for the period 1946–1971. Their results are shown in Table 9.7. The demand for a *particular* form of energy (electricity) that has substitutes (natural gas, petroleum, and to a lesser extent coal) is expected to be more price elastic than for all energy commodities taken as a group. Contrary to common belief, the demands for electricity appear to be quite elastic. Naturally, demand diverted away from electricity by increased prices will, in part, "spill over" into the markets for its substitutes, shifting their demand functions and pushing up their prices. Indirect evidence for the effect is seen in the natural gas price cross-elasticities in Table 9.7.

What then was the U.S. response to increased world prices of petroleum? It was to suspend the market mechanism by imposing or maintaining price ceilings on petroleum products and natural gas. The ceiling on gasoline that had been imposed in 1971 as part of the general price controls to reduce inflation began to fall progressively below the market equilibrium price, and shortages began appearing in the summer of 1972 and 1973—just as we would predict from the demand and supply

Table 9.7. U.S. Elasticities of Demand for Electricity

| | Price Elasticity | "Income" Elasticity | Cross Elasticity wrt Natural Gas |
|---|---|---|---|
| Residential | −1.3 | +0.3 | +0.15 |
| Commercial | −1.5 | +0.9 | +0.15 |
| Industrial | −1.7 | +0.5 | +0.15 |

Source: Chapman, Tyrrell, and Mount (1972, Table 1).

functions of Figure 9.2. These shortages continued until effective price controls were lifted in 1974. In the meantime, gasoline had to be rationed by nonprice means, which included long waiting lines, limitation of sales to 10 gallons, closing stations nights and weekends, and so on. In terms of time cost to work and leisure, these devices were very costly to the economy.

An argument that always is heard against letting the market establish an equilibrium price is that higher prices would unduly hurt the poor. No one has bothered to see whether the poor in fact came out of the gasoline shortage better off than they would have been had prices been allowed to rise, but there are no *a priori* reasons for believing so. Some groups of well-to-do persons bought service stations (with their refinery quotas) for their private use.

Two sets of price controls over energy commodities remain in effect: the price ceilings on "old" domestic oil from wells in production prior to 1973, and the well-head prices for interstate natural gas. Both controls continue to distort both energy demands and energy supply potentials. Some gas supplies still sell for under $1 per 1000 cubic feet while prices in uncontrolled intrastate markets have gone over $2. The lack of enthusiasm for exploration and production for the interstate market is not hard to understand.

The unsatisfied demands that exist for energy commodities at these disequilibrium prices continue to spill over into the markets for higher-priced noncontrolled substitutes, especially imported oil and liquified natural gas. This creates balance of payments problems, increases our dependence on foreign supplies, and strengthens OPEC.

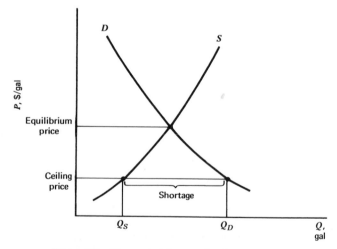

**Figure 9.2**  The market for gasoline in 1973–1974.

## 9.3. AFTERMATH OF THE ENERGY CRISIS

The United States in concert with the rest of the industrialized world suffered a major recession as a result of the oil crisis. This, in addition to the increased oil prices, slowed the growth of demand for oil, even reducing it from the 1973 level in 1974 and 1975. However, imports have continued to grow as domestic production continues to fall. Thus the basic problem of balance of payments and dependency on foreign supplies continues.

Many economists as well as the business community have advocated a return to the market as a major step toward a national energy policy. While the exact effects on supply and demand are extremely difficult to predict, there is good reason to expect longer-term reductions in demand and expansions of domestic supplies in response to higher prices. International comparisons (Section 9.5) will show that countries can attain per capita income levels as high as the United States using only one half to two thirds as much energy per capita.

Another effect of letting the prices of conventional energy resources rise would be to stimulate the development of new energy sources such as solar and geothermal. This process could be aided by programs of government aid to basic research, which is underfunded by the private sector because of the "public good" nature of technological knowledge.

What other policy tools might be used to advantage? Certainly there are roles for much-expanded programs of education and information. Homeowners are often unaware of the magnitudes of energy savings that can be achieved through insulation and through careful selection of more fuel-efficient furnaces and appliances. Programs of education are likely to be much more efficient than mandatory standards for all homes, since the latter cannot be adaptable to the infinite variation found in existing structures and in household energy use patterns.

In industry, the energy crisis has alerted many businesses to great opportunities for profitable energy-saving investments, many of which would have been profitable even at the old energy prices. Energy prices have been so low that management simply ignored energy technology in many industries. The sudden price increases and the threat of unreliable supplies have drawn management's attention to this area. A study by the Office of Emergency Preparedness in 1974 indicated that many firms were beginning to identify these opportunities, among them DuPont, Union Carbide, and Consolidated Natural Gas, while news stories reported fuel conservation programs by AT&T, Litton, TRW, Upjohn, General Electric, and others. One corporation found that requiring a daily report of energy use in each department of its plants resulted in a 15 percent reduction within a short time. A plant in New England saved

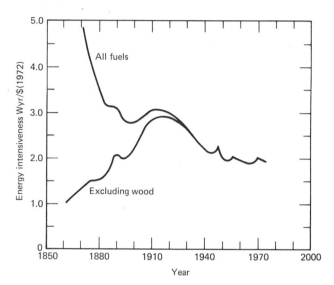

**Figure 9.3**    Energy intensiveness for the United States. Source: Krenz, 1977, p. 118. Reproduced by permission of Pergamon Press, Ltd.

large quantities of energy by changing its truck loading routine that had required the parking of trucks in open doors to the plant over the several-hour loading period.

Other industry steps have included the insulation of heat treating furnaces and heat recovery processes, on-line computer controls of thermal processes, and accelerated adoption of more efficient equipment. An example of the latter type of opportunity is found in the cement industry.[2] The average fuel consumption in U.S. cement kilns is $1.2 \times 10^6$ BTU per barrel of cement. The most efficient U.S. kiln uses 750,000 BTU per barrel. Modern European kilns use only 550,000 BTU. All of these steps would be encouraged by allowing energy prices to approach their equilibrium values.

A type of change that has been advocated to conserve energy (as it was earlier advocated to reduce pollution) is to change the composition of GNP toward the less energy intensive goods and services. People seem unaware that the energy intensiveness of the U.S. economy has been falling for over a century as shown in Figure 9.3., where energy intensiveness is measured in watt-years per (constant value) dollar of GNP. How different in energy intensiveness are the different sectors of

[2]Charles A. Berg, "Conservation in Industry," *Science*, Vol. 184, No. 4134, 19 April 1974, pp. 264–270.

the U.S. economy and how much would be gained by shifting the composition of GNP?

Krenz (1977) has shown that the average energy intensiveness of U.S. economic activity is about two watt-years (Wyr) per 1972 dollar of GNP. Approximately one third of the energy consumed represents direct consumer purchases, so that two thirds is used as intermediate input to the production of other goods. However, the measurement of

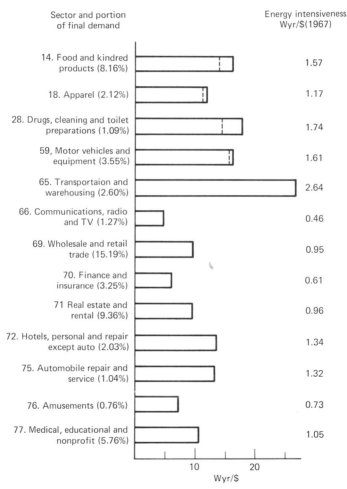

**Figure 9.4** The 1967 energy intensiveness of consumer goods and services. The dashed portion is the energy intensiveness based on consumer prices. A portion of sectors 65 and 69 is allotted to the sale of these goods. Source: Krenz, 1977, p. 122. Reproduced by permission of Pergamon Press, Ltd.

energy intensity must take into account not only that directly consumed in a given sector but that required as input for supplying sectors. Krenz has applied input-output analysis to this direct-plus-indirect energy content of the value added (the appropriate measure of output since the sum of value added across sectors equals GNP) of the different sectors of the U.S. economy. Figure 9.4 shown on page 179 presents his results (in terms of 1967 dollars) for the major two-digit consumer industries. The sectors shown account for 80 percent of consumption and 56 percent of GNP (the rest being investment, government, and net trade). If transportation and warehousing were omitted, all values would range between 0.46 and 1.74. Krenz also determined, using older I-O models and energy data, that the energy intensiveness of these sectors had changed very little over the 1958–1970 period.

It is clear from Krenz' data that a shift in final demands toward selected service sectors could have a noticeable impact on energy consumption, especially communications and amusements. While wholesale and retail trade appears rather low in total energy use (0.95), it

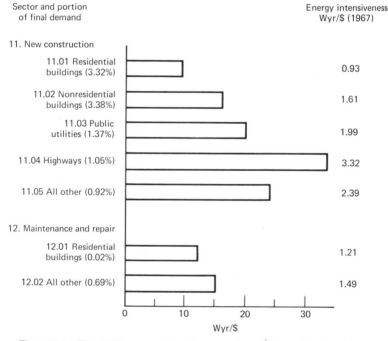

**Figure 9.5** The 1967 energy intensiveness of capital investments. Source: Krenz, 1977, p. 124. Reproduced by permission of Pergamon Press, Ltd.

must be recalled that the transportation inputs to that sector are, by I-O accounting convention, included in the transportation sector.

Krenz has also calculated the energy intensiveness of the capital goods sectors, as shown on the preceding page in Figure 9.5. These data make it clear that the composition of capital accumulation can also make a difference in natural energy consumption. For example, a reallocation of 1 percent of GNP from automobile manufacturing to residential construction would result in a 0.28 percent reduction in total energy consumption.

Given these data on the energy use patterns of different economic sectors, what can be said about the ability of the U.S. economy to approach the lower energy use patterns found in some other industrialized countries? First we must look at the data from other countries.

## 9.4.  INTERNATIONAL COMPARISON OF ENERGY USE

Very substantial differences are known to exist among countries in energy use per dollar of GNP. Figure 9.6 compares several countries over the postwar period. It has often been asserted that there exists a high correlation between energy use per capita and GNP per capita, and an international comparison shows this to be true (see Figure 9.7 on page 183). However, there remain striking differences in energy use per capita among countries with similar levels of GNP per capita, for example, the United States and Sweden, Canada and West Germany, and United Kingdom and Italy. Why should such differences exist?

In an accounting sense, total energy use in the economy can be stated as

$$(9.4.1) \qquad\qquad E = \sum_{j=1}^{n} e_j V_j$$

where $V_j$ is the value added in sector $j$ of the economy and $e_j$ is the energy directly consumed per dollar of value added. To compare countries of different sizes, it would be helpful to divide both sides of (9.4.1) by GNP to get

$$(9.4.2) \qquad\qquad E/\text{GNP} = \sum_{j=1}^{n} e_j \frac{V_j}{\text{GNP}}$$

showing that the overall energy/GNP ratio is a weighted average of the energy/value-added ratios of the various sectors. Two countries could thus differ in $E/\text{GNP}$ values because the $e_j$ coefficients differ, because

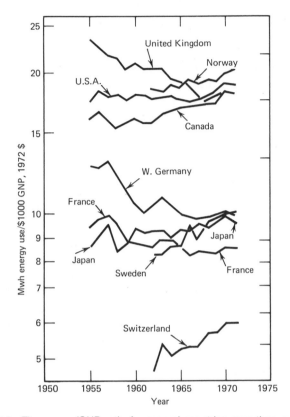

**Figure 9.6** The energy/GNP ratio for several countries over time, with hydroelectric power counted at 3kwht/kwhe. Source: Schipper and Lichtenberg, 1976, Fig. 1. Copyright 1976 by the American Association for the Advancement of Science.

the relative shares of the various sectors, $V_j$/GNP, differ, or for a combination of these reasons.

To get a better feeling for these structural differences, it will be interesting to compare the United States and Sweden, both of which had similar high GNP values per capita in 1973. Schipper and Lichtenberg have analyzed the two economies and their patterns of energy use (1976). Population densities are similar, but the United States has developed a more dispersed urban pattern than Sweden. Goods typically are transported farther in the United States, but climate is more severe in Sweden, the number of degree-days (weighted by population distribution) being 9200 for Sweden and 5500 for the United States. A summary comparison of energy consumption is given in Table 9.8 shown on page 184. The table shows that, overall, Sweden utilizes about 50 percent of the energy per capita used in the United States if the comparison counts hydroelectric power at a ratio of 1 kwh/kwhe or about 60 percent if hydroelectric is counted at a 3-kwh/kwhe ratio (as is the practice in the United States).

Sweden uses less energy per capita in each sector shown, the differences being most striking in transportation and industry. Swedish passenger transportation consists much more of rail and bus transport and less of air and automobile. Automobile vehicle miles per capita (1970) were 4160 for the United States and 2560 for Sweden, while better load factors, lower auto weight, and higher miles per gallon of fuel resulted in total kwh per capita in transportation of 3710 for Sweden and 11,200 for the U.S. In the three principal cities where more than 25 percent of the population resides, mass transit, motor bikes, and pedal bikes account for 75 percent of all commuting. Taxes strongly affect choice of modes in Sweden, the 1971 gasoline price of 70¢ per gallon containing a 50¢ tax. Excise and use taxes rise at least in proportion to

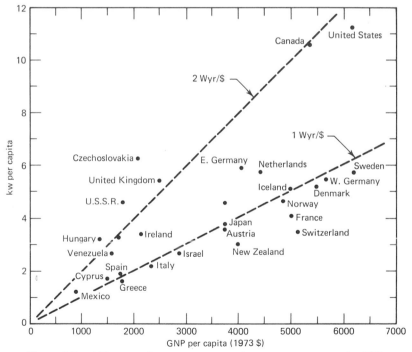

**Figure 9.7** 1973 per capita energy consumption rate versus per capita GNP. Source: Krenz, 1977, p. 117. Reproduced by permission of Pergamon Press, Ltd.

**Table 9.8.** Per Capita Energy Consumption in the U.S. and Sweden in 1971 [a]

| Consumption | United States | | | Sweden | | |
| --- | --- | --- | --- | --- | --- | --- |
| | kwh | kwhe | kwht | kwh | kwhe | kwht |
| Transportation | 24,025 | 25 | 24,075 | 7,350 | 200 | 7,775 |
| Commercial | 9,600 | 2,150 | 14,250 | 7,375 | 1,500 | 10,625 |
| Residential | 13,500 | 2,300 | 18,450 | 11,125 | 1,400 | 14,150 |
| Industry | 28,900 | 3,300 | 36,000 | 20,400 | 4,200 | 29,450 |
| Feedstocks | 5,600 | | 5,600 | 2,500 | | 2,500 |
| Utility losses | 14,200 | | | 3,700 | | |
| Actual consumption | 95,825 | 7,775 | 98,375 | 52,450 | 7,300 | 64,500 |
| Energy embodied in foreign trade | 1,800 | | 1,800 | −4,600 | | −4,600 |
| Net consumption | 97,625 | 7,775 | 100,175 | 48,150 | 7,300 | 59,900 |

[a]The totals in the kwh and kwht columns do not agree because of differences in counting hydropower. Hydropower was counted at 3413 Btu/kwhe in the kwh column. All kwht values were calculated by distributing utility losses to end consumers; consumption of electricity within electrical sectors was counted in "Industry." The kwht column for the United States includes hydropower at 10,460 Btu/kwhe; that for Sweden counts all electricity at 10,400 Btu/kwhe. The actual "heat rate" for thermal and back-pressure plants in Sweden is 8,870 Btu/kwhe, including distribution losses; the rate for production only is 7780 Btu/kwhe. Cogenerated electricity in the paper industry is excluded from the kwht columns.

Source: Schipper and Lichtenberg (1976), Table 2. Copyright 1976 by the American Association for the Advancement of Science.

vehicle weight. While long-haul freight trucks are more energy intensive in Sweden, short-haul tasks are typically carried out by small, light vehicles.

A larger fraction of Sweden's industry is found in the energy-intensive paper, chemicals, petroleum products, stone-clay-glass, and primary metals sectors, but the United States produces greater total industrial value added per capita than Sweden. Table 9.9 gives the energy (kwh) per dollar of value added for industry. It is certainly not obvious that Swedish industry is more efficient (in the physical sense) than that in the United States, so the differences in total energy per capita shown in Table 9.8 are attributable to greater industrial output per capita in the United States.

Space heating in Sweden is significantly more efficient than in the United States, in spite of the more severe climate, kwh/capita/year being 8200 in Sweden versus 9150 in the United States. This difference appears to be attributable to three things: (1) higher prices for fuels, (2) energy-saving building regulations, and (3) district heating systems in which central stations produce heat or cogenerate electricity and heat. In the

**Table 9.9.**   Energy Use per Dollar of Value Added
in Industry (kwh/$)

|  | United States | Sweden |
|---|---|---|
| Paper | 44 | 75 |
| Chemicals | 25 | 18 |
| Petroleum products | 143 | 82 |
| Stone, clay, glass | 36 | 33 |
| Primary metals | 52 | 38 |
| Total manufacturing | 13 | 15 |

Source: Schipper and Lichtenberg, 1976, Table 9. Copyright 1976 by the American Association for the Advancement of Science.

United States, total energy input into thermal-electric generation is accounted for by 32 percent electric power output and 68 percent waste
heat. In Sweden, the input is accounted for by 29 percent electric output,
24 percent heat utilized for space heating or industrial purposes, and 47
percent waste heat.

Energy prices are generally higher in Sweden, but less so than most
would expect. Table 9.10 compares energy prices in recent years. The
largest differences are in transport fuel, while electricity has been kept
low in price in Sweden because of the importance of hydropower. Very
little residential gas is used in Sweden.

In summary, in Sweden, good intracity public transport and the
high costs of auto transport have tended to concentrate urban populations. The resulting greater use of multifamily dwellings and central
heating plants have reduced energy for space heating. Shopping trips
are shorter and food storage costs are lower. In industry, while the
energy intensive industries comprise a larger fraction of industrial activity, energy efficiencies overall are not greatly different from the United
States where industry is more important in relation to the basic resources industries and the service sector.

Could the United States convert to the Swedish pattern and reduce
its per capita energy use by 40 to 50 percent? We've seen that much of
the difference is accounted for by different quantities and efficiencies of
transportation, different efficiencies of space heating, and a different
composition of GNP with the United States having a significantly higher
manufacturing output per capita. It seems clear from these observations
and Krenz' earlier data on the U.S. sectors' energy intensities that
modest shifts in GNP composition cannot result in large reductions in
energy use per capita. Changes in transportation and space heating

**Table 9.10.**   Energy Price Comparisons: United States and
Sweden (1974 unless otherwise indicated)

|  | United States | Sweden |
|---|---|---|
| Gasoline (¢/gal) | 45 | 116 |
| Diesel fuel | 35 | 90 |
| Heating oil | 35 | 41 |
| Residential gas (¢/10⁶ BTU) | 113 | 680 (1973) |
| Industrial coal ($/ton) 1970 | 13 | 18 |
| Electricity (¢/kwh) 1970 | 2.75 | 2.12 |

Source: Schipper and Lichtenberg, 1976, Table 12. Copyright 1976 by the
American Association for the Advancement of Science.

toward the Swedish pattern will require new patterns of urban living
with the related new investments, although no really new technologies
would be required. Shifting away from manufacturing in favor of the
service sector and agriculture will be limited by world if not domestic
market conditions, especially if other countries are similarly motivated.

It thus seems highly unlikely that the United States can significantly
change its energy use per capita unless it is willing to shift to policies
aimed at long-run changes in life-style of a significant nature.

## 9.5.   THE OUTLOOK FOR NEW SUPPLIES OF ENERGY COMMODITIES

In this section, we will summarize recent estimates of reserves of the
various energy commodities and, perhaps of greater importance, trends
in the success of exploration efforts.

**Petroleum.**   Over the years, many have tried to estimate the volumes of
oil and gas that might ultimately be recoverable worldwide. We already
know that such estimates are made on the basis of a large number of
assumptions that most frequently remain implicit. Table 9.11 lists some
of these estimates compiled by Seidl (Meyer, 1977) and the data are
plotted in Figure 9.8. The estimates have obviously increased over time
and some (e.g., Odell) have used the extrapolation shown in Figure 9.8
to estimate ultimately recoverable reserves of 4000 billion barrels. Others
have argued that, because of the burst of technology and information
during the time span of these estimates, it seems unlikely that future
increases of ultimate reserves should continue as in the past. Warman of
British Petroleum has estimated $1800 \times 10^9$ barrels.

Proven reserves have risen faster than production worldwide, as shown in Figure 9.9. However, discoveries have been quite unevenly distributed geographically, as the annual additions to proved reserves show (see Figure 9.10). As a result of high rates of discovery abroad and low rates in the United States, the ratio of proven reserves in the United States to world reserves has fallen from 32 percent in 1950 to about 5 percent in 1975.

This decrease has not been for lack of effort. The 30,000 wells drilled in the United States in 1974 constituted more than 80 percent of all wells drilled outside the socialist countries. While the average proved reserves per well have remained nearly constant at 95,000 barrels per well (including dry holes) in the postwar period, the average well in the rest of the world adds 30 to 60 times that quantity of reserves.

The 34 percent of crude actually recovered from a deposit has increased little since secondary recovery techniques (gas and water re-

**Table 9.11.** Estimates of World Ultimate Reserves of Crude Oil from Conventional Sources

| Year | Source | $\times 10^9$ bbl |
|------|--------|-------------------|
| 1942 | Pratt, Weeks, and Stebinger | 600 |
| 1946 | Duce | 400 |
|      | Pogue | 555 |
| 1948 | Weeks | 610 |
| 1949 | Levorsen | 1500 |
|      | Weeks | 1010 |
| 1953 | MacNaughton | 1000 |
| 1956 | Hubbert | 1250 |
| 1958 | Weeks | 1500 |
| 1959 | Weeks | 2000 |
| 1965 | Hendricks (USGS) | 2480 |
| 1967 | Ryman (Esso) | 2090 |
| 1968 | Shell | 1800 |
|      | Weeks | 2200 |
| 1969 | Hubbert | 1350–2100 |
| 1970 | Moody (Mobil) | 1800 |
| 1971 | Warman (BP) | 1200–2200 |
|      | Weeks | 2290 |
|      | U.S. National Petroleum Council | 2670 |
| 1972 | Linden | 2950 |
|      | Weeks | 3650 |

Source: Seidl, in R. F. Meyer (ed.), 1977 by permission of Pergamon Press, Ltd.

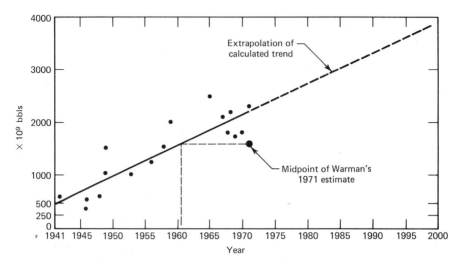

**Figure 9.8** Past estimates and future projections of world ultimate oil reserves. Source: Seidl in R. F. Meyer, ed., 1977, by permission of Pergamon
Press, Ltd.

charge) were introduced in the 1950s. Enhanced recovery techniques
costing from $3 to $20 per barrel are asserted to raise the recovery factor
to 45 percent or as high as 75 percent, but there has been little application or field proof to date.

The increase in oil prices has made it profitable to drill for smaller
pools and to keep marginal wells in production. In the United States,
wells producing 10 or less barrels per day (known as "strippers") have
been removed from price controls, allowing their output to be sold at
world prices of approximately $14 per barrel while "old oil" is held at $5
per barrel. Many submarginal wells that had been abandoned have been
brought back into production. Ironically, a government rule known as
"once a stripper, always a stripper" encourages investments to increase
stripper output beyond 10 barrels per day, while the absence of similar
treatment of old wells yielding far more than 10 barrels per day discour-
ages improvements in their productivity.

The intensity of past exploration and the extent of potential oil-
bearing areas are quite unevenly distributed around the globe as shown
in Figure 9.11. This figure was compiled by the U.S. Geological Survey.
The rectangular areas are proportional in size to the potential oil-bearing
areas of the indicated regions, while each dot represents 50,000 wells.
The United States has about 10 percent of the world's potential oil-

bearing area but has drilled 70 percent of the world's wells. The unexplored potentials for Africa and Latin America are striking.

From a worldwide viewpoint, the prospects for continued supplies of petroleum over the long term appear quite favorable from a technical point of view. While other regions of the world will someday repeat the pattern of exhausting resources now observed in the United States, that day is far off. The nontechnical issues of the availability of capital and

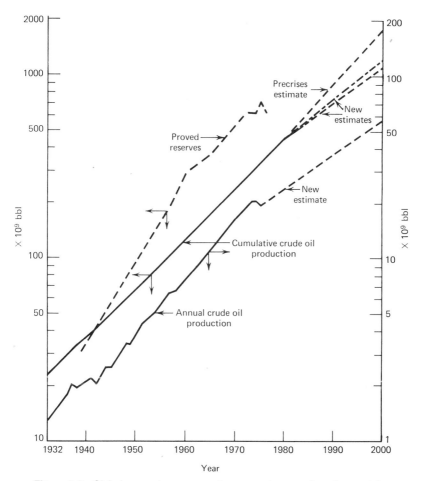

**Figure 9.9** Global proved reserves at year end—annual and cumulative crude oil production (MMbbls). Source: Seidl in R. F. Meyer, ed., 1977, by permission of Pergamon Press, Ltd.

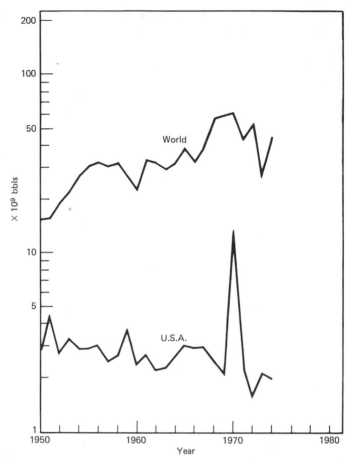

**Figure 9.10**   Reserves proved annually in the United States, world—MMbbls.
Source: Seidl in R. F. Meyer, ed., 1977, by permission of Pergamon Press, Ltd.

the existence of political conditions conducive to development of these
resources will be the major determinants of future supply.

**Heavy Oil.**   Leighton (in Meyer, 1977) has discussed the availability of
heavy oils in California which, as we have seen earlier, in company with
Venezuela, has vast quantities of high viscosity oils. The volume of such
oils now estimated to be in place is $47 \times 10^9$ barrels, a figure exceeding
the total U.S. proven reserves of the lighter oils. Leighton estimates that
$13 \times 10^9$ barrels can be recovered using 1975 technology and that anticipated improvements available by 1985 will make it technically possible
to recover $29 \times 10^9$ barrels.

**Deep Ocean Petroleum.** Petroleum has been produced from the continental shelves at depths up to 200 meters for several decades. It appears highly likely that large supplies of gas and oil occur in deeper waters beyond the shelf, for half the world volume of sediments are found there. However, no drilling data are available to permit estimates to be made. While great technological advances would be necessary to make recovery from these depths even technically feasible, the potential volume of reserves is huge.

**Oil Shale.** Oil shales are fine-grained sedimentary rock containing organic matter, mostly kerogen, that are capable of yielding oil when subjected to pyrolysis. A yield of 10 gallons of oil per ton of shale is usually considered the margin of potentially exploitable resources. Donnell (Meyer, 1977) gives the following estimates of the world's shale oil resources (Table 9.12). Oil shale was processed in Scotland and Sweden in the late 1930s and early 1940s and China and the U.S.S.R. are currently producing oil from these shales. The major deposits have been sampled, mapped, and assayed, and so are reliably known, but esti-

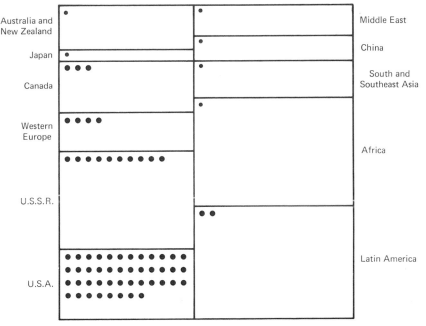

**Figure 9.11** Potential oil-bearing areas and worldwide concentration of oil drilling. Source: U.S. Geological Survey, news release, February 26, 1976.

**Table 9.12.**  Shale Oil Reserves of the World Land
Areas

| Continent | Recoverable Under Current Conditions | Economically or Technically Submarginal |
|-----------|--------------------------------------|------------------------------------------|
|           | ($10^9$ barrels)                     |                                          |
| Africa    | 10                                   | 90                                       |
| Asia      | 24                                   | 84                                       |
| Europe    | 30                                   | 46                                       |
| N. America | 80                                  | 2,120                                    |
| S. America | 50                                  | 750                                      |
| Total     | 190                                  | 3,090                                    |

Source: Donnell in R. F. Meyer (ed.), 1977, by permission
of Pergamon Press, Ltd.

mates have increased as knowledge has accumulated over time. For the
Piceance Creek Basin of Colorado, a 1923 estimate was $40 \times 10^9$ barrels.
Assays of oil and gas well cores and detailed geologic mapping of small
areas led to a $500 \times 10^9$ barrel estimate by 1948, and the most recent
(1964) estimate is $1.2 \times 10^{12}$ barrels. The major deposits by country are
given in Table 9.13. The Colorado deposits yield about 35 gallons of oil
per ton of shale, a high yield. Under these conditions, costs of produc-

**Table 9.13.**  Shale Oil Resources
by Country

| Country | $10^9$ Barrels |
|---------|----------------|
| Great Britain | 1.0 |
| W. Germany | 2.0 |
| Burma | 2.0 |
| Sweden | 2.5 |
| China (Mainland) | 27.9 |
| Sicily | 35.2 |
| Canada | 44.0 |
| Zaire | 100.6 |
| U.S.S.R. | 112.6 |
| Brazil | 800.8 |
| U.S.A. | 2,000.2 |

Source: Donnell, Table 2. In R. F. Meyer
(ed.), 1977 by permission of Pergamon
Press, Ltd.

tion are estimated to be in the $10 to $15 per barrel range, requiring a selling price of $20 or more.

Thus, the shale oil resources dwarf world petroleum reserves. If technology can reduce production costs, vast new supplies will become available. Potentially serious environmental impacts are associated with current surface retorting methods: air pollution from the retorting, water pollution from the powdered spent shale and from heavy brines raised with the shale, and shale disposal problems caused by the one-third expansion of shale volume in the retorting process. The big technological thrust is, therefore, toward *in situ* retorting.

While the economic and environmental future of the industry remain unclear, shale oil certainly represents a major *resource plateau* and a major challenge to technology.

**Tar Sands.**   Tar sand refers to consolidated or unconsolidated rocks with interstices that contain very viscous to solid bitumen that cannot be recovered by usual petroleum production techniques. Deposits in the United States are estimated to contain 23 to 30 billion barrels of oil, most of it in Utah. Efforts to recover oil date back 80 years, but have been ineffective to date. Some of the tar sands are sufficiently shallow that they could be stripmined as is being done at Athabasca, Canada, but most lie too deep. *In situ* recovery processes are now the major technological thrust. Again, we find a huge resource in comparison with current U.S. petroleum reserves, but substantial technological improvement is required to make it economically attractive.

**Natural Gas.**   Whiting has drawn together estimates of world gas reserves, given in Table 9.14. The total reserve is estimated to be 2,147 trillion cubic feet of which 1288 trillion or 60 percent is estimated to lie in conventional gas fields, the remainder being found in association with oil. Sixty-five percent of the gas in conventional fields is found in 119 large fields. During the last 10 years, total world reserves have increased from 868 to 2147 trillion ft.$^3$ The major portion of this increase was comprised of discoveries of a relatively small number of very large fields in newly explored areas. Most of these fields are in the U.S.S.R. and North Sea.

Whiting has estimated that half of the ultimate natural gas has already been discovered, implying 3400 trillion ft.$^3$ as an upper bound on future discoveries. Many of these discoveries will be in offshore areas, implying increasing costs of recovery since average inland production costs are about 18¢ per $10^3$ft$^3$ while average offshore costs are around 50¢ per $10^3$ft$^3$.

**Table 9.14.**  World Natural Gas Reserves (January 1, 1975)

|  | Natural Gas Trillion Cubic Feet |  | Natural Gas Trillion Cubic Feet |
|---|---|---|---|
| U.S.S.R. | 699.8 | Libya | 28.3 |
| Iran | 374.4 | Iraq | 27.5 |
| U.S.A. | 237.1 | Abudhabi | 24.9 |
| Algeria | 100.2 | Norway | 19.4 |
| Netherlands | 77.0 | Burnei-Malaysia | 18.2 |
| Saudi Arabia | 61.0 | Chica | 17.0 |
| Canada | 56.7 | Pakistan | 15.5 |
| Neutral Zone | 50.9 | Indonesia | 15.0 |
| Nigeria | 50.2 | West Germany | 12.5 |
| Venezuela | 42.9 | Mexico | 11.2 |
| Kuwait | 38.1 | Others | 139.1 |
| United Kingdom | 30.0 | Total | 2146.9 |

Source: Whiting. In R. F. Meyer (ed.), 1977, by permission of Pergamon Press, Ltd.

Not surprisingly, the picture of world gas reserves is similar to that of oil reserves, both because of the similarity of the processes by which they are formed and because 40 percent of the gas is found in association with oil. If we contemplate the remaining exploration potential for oil (see Petroleum above), especially in Latin America and Africa, it seems entirely possible that the above estimate of future discoveries may be low. The relevance of this to gas supply again depends on the exploration and investment climate found in the regions of great potential.

**Gas in Geopressure Zones.**   Geopressure simply means abnormal subsurface fluid pressure. In deep sedimentary basins, the conversion of kerogen to petroleum and petroleum to methane accelerates as temperatures and pressures increase. In formations that are tightly sealed, this methane supersaturates the waters in the formation. This gas in solution is extensively found and can produce usable supplies by separation from waters produced by large wells or by separation *in situ* as formation pressures are carefully reduced through control wells.

Estimates of quantities are sketchy, but the northern Gulf of Mexico basin is known to have large geopressure belts, underlying at least 150,000 mi$^2$ and extending downward 50,000 ft. Other areas of the world that are geologically similar to the northern Gulf of Mexico should contain similar zones, signaling another large hydrocarbon energy store requiring new technological approaches.

**Gas Hydrates.**   Gas hydrates are frozen natural gas and were discovered by Soviet petroleum geologists only 10 years ago. Subsequently, gas hydrates have been found in the Mackenzie Basin in Canada and in many offshore areas worldwide. Soviet experts have estimated as much as $35 \times 10^6$ trillion ft$^3$ of gas in this form worldwide. Even if subject to very large error, this is indicative of a large resource.

**Hot Dry Rock Geothermal Energy.**[3]   This refers to technologies for capturing the heat contained in hot rock strata far below the earth's surface. Currently, liquid and vapor geothermal resources provide energy for about 1590 megawatts of electric generating capacity, a very small quantity. Dry rock techniques are just being tried, principally at Los Alamos Scientific Laboratory in New Mexico. In this process, a pair of wells is drilled 2 to 10 kilometers below the earth's crust into impermeable granite. As depth increases, temperature increases by 20 to 60°C per kilometer. When sufficiently high temperatures are reached, the rock is cracked hydraulically so that water can flow from one well to the other, picking up heat as it flows. Heated water is then recovered from the second well and used for electric generation or other purposes.

The potential is large. Cummings et al. note that if 0.2 to 0.3 percent of the heat in known geothermal regions at depths less than 10 km and having temperatures above 15°C (60°F) could be recovered, this would amount to $60,000 \times 10^{15}$ BTU of heat which, converted to electricity at a (low) conversion efficiency of 10 percent would yield $6000 \times 10^{15}$ BTU. By comparison, ERDA estimates the heat content of all U.S. coal reserves to be about $13,000 \times 10^{15}$ BTU.

Cummings et al. estimate costs of electricity production ranging from 17.3 to 53.8 mills per kwh, depending on well flow rates and temperature gradients. In the lower end of this range, hot dry rock thermal electric power would be competitive with conventional sources which are expected to range up to 36 mills per kwh by 1985. While many technical problems remain to be worked out, this represents a large potential source of energy.

The data presented in this rather long section are not meant to cover all energy sources, nor are they intended to convey the impression that our energy future will necessarily be easy and comfortable. The data *are* intended to convey the fact that remaining energy resources are vast,

---

[3]For an excellent exposition of the economics of HDR energy production, see Ronald G. Cummings, James W. McFarland, and Susan C. Nunn, "An Economic Analysis of the Hot Dry Rock Geothermal Energy Resource," unpublished paper, Department of Economics, University of New Mexico, June 1977.

that the probability of discovering much more of the traditional oil and gas resources is quite high (given the appropriate economic and political motivation), and that there exist a number of major energy resource plateaus which technology may bring within economic grasp. Certainly, the technological challenges of tapping these new resources are just as exciting and even more important than was the development of our current coal and oil technologies.

## 9.6. NUCLEAR POWER: THE GREAT DILEMMA

The controversy over the comparative merits of fossil fuels and nuclear power is heated, confusing, and crucially important. While it will be impossible to review all of the issues here, we will present some materials that tie in with the rest of the natural resource picture: the availability of nuclear fuels, problems of waste disposal and the environment, and some problems associated with the major middle-term alternative to nuclear power—coal.

In October 1975, newspapers around the country carried a story about the problems Westinghouse Electric Corporation was having in connection with its nuclear program. They had contracts to build and supply fuel for more than 115 nuclear-powered plants. These contracts had been based upon Westinghouse' own contracts with uranium suppliers at prices around $7 per pound. By October 1975, prices had risen to the $25 to $30 range (1977 prices are over $40), and these suppliers were seeking to renegotiate the price. If Westinghouse could not renegotiate prices with its customers, it faced the unhappy choice of being 70 to 90 million pounds short of its uranium commitments or as much as $1 billion in the hole on these contracts.[4] What was happening?

The oil embargo and price increase had, naturally, increased the demand for alternative energy supplies, including nuclear, but what were the facts of uranium availability that permitted prices to rise from $7 to $30+ per pound, apparently on a long-term basis? Nearly all the high-grade uranium ore in the United States occurs in the sandstone and mudstone deposits of the Colorado Plateau, the Wyoming Basins, and the Gulf Coastal Plain in Texas (Lieberman, 1976). While small deposits have been discovered in Argentina, Gabon, and Niger, these sandstone deposits appear to be a unique geological occurrence.

An important characteristic of uranium in sandstone is the occurrence of many small deposits and a few large ones, the latter containing

---

[4]*Denver Post,* October 5, 1975, Section E, "Westinghouse Hurt by Uranium Prices."

most of the uranium. Of the 284 known deposits, three account for 23 percent of the reserves and ten account for 52 percent of the reserves. Lieberman's estimate of the ultimately recoverable volume of ore, $Q_\infty$, indicates that little high-grade ore remains to be discovered. To pursue this further, we must carefully define $Q_\infty$.

The uranium industry in the United States has traditionally defined proved reserves to be the quantity ultimately producible at a variable cost of $8 per pound or less. We know that the relevant reserve value is a function of price, so that at higher prices, larger quantities of ore would qualify as reserves. Lieberman first estimates $Q_\infty$ at $8 per pound, using estimating techniques similar to those used by Hubbert in estimating oil reserves, and then derives multipliers for increasing this quantity at higher prices. These multipliers were derived from careful studies of the grade distributions in well studied ore bodies.

The pattern of U.S. uranium exploration activity and gross additions to $8 reserves since 1948 are shown in Figure 9.12. If these data are expressed as pounds of $U_3O_8$ per foot drilled annually, they appear to fit an exponential curve as shown in Figure 9.13, in which cumulative drilling is measured on the $X$ axis. It is very clear that discovery rates

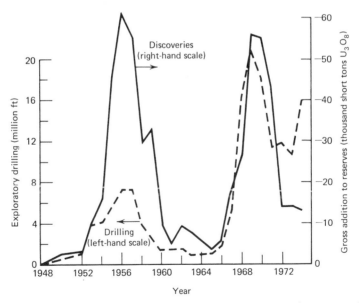

**Figure 9.12** History of exploratory drilling and discoveries of $8 per pound $U_3O_8$. Source: Lieberman, *Science*, April 30, 1976, Fig. 1. Copyright 1976 by the American Association for the Advancement of Science.

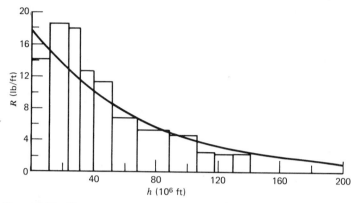

**Figure 9.13** Discovery rate compared to cumulative exploration. Source: Lieberman, *Science*, April 30, 1976, Fig. 3. Copyright 1976 by the American Association for the Advancement of Science.

have fallen significantly. Cumulative discoveries appear to fit a logistic curve quite well, which is given by the formula

$$(9.6.1) \qquad\qquad Q(t) = \frac{Q_\infty}{1 + ae^{-b(t - t_0)}}$$

This fit is shown in Figure 9.14. The derivative of this cumulative discovery curve has a form similar to the well-known normal density function (bell-shaped curve), the area of which represents cumulative discovery. If annual discoveries to 1975 are plotted and if the density function corresponding to the logistic curve of Figure 9.14 is plotted, one arrives at the estimate of total ultimate reserves of 630,000 tons as shown in Figure 9.15. Lieberman uses ratios of 1.2, 1.5, and 1.8 as multipliers to estimate the ultimate reserves that would be available if price were sufficient to justify variable costs of $10, $15, and $30 per ton. Using ERDA estimates of rates of use and allowing for plutonium recycling, he estimates the following ultimate reserves and years of exhaustion of U.S. uranium resources (Table 9.15). ERDA estimates of ultimate $30 reserves in 1976 were 3,450,000 short tons, three times greater than the figure above, but there appears to be little basis for the ERDA figure.

The preceding data serve two purposes: they illustrate a method that has been widely used to estimate ultimate reserves of various minerals, and they point up the relatively small supply of uranium that appears likely yet to be discovered. The latter fact makes clear the reason for pressures to develop the so-called "breeder" reactor which, by producing plutonium as a by-product, will greatly expand the effective nuclear fuel supply.

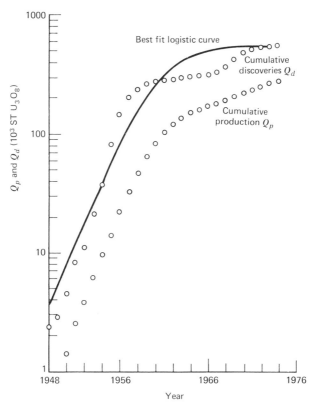

**Figure 9.14** Cumulative production and cumulative discoveries. Source: Lieberman, *Science*, April 30, 1976, Fig. 4. Copyright 1976 by the American Association for the Advancement of Science.

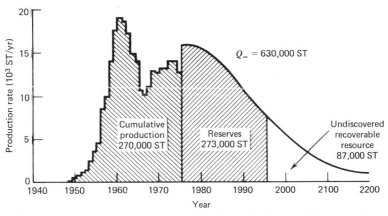

**Figure 9.15** Possible cycle of production for $U_3O_8$. Source: Lieberman, *Science*, April 30, 1976, Fig. 5. Copyright 1976 by the American Association for the Advancement of Science.

**Table 9.15.**  Ultimate U.S. Uranium Reserves and
Projected Year of Exhaustion

| Variable Cost | $Q_\infty$ (Short Tons) | Year of Exhaustion |
|---|---|---|
| Up to $ 8 | 630,000 | 1986 |
| Up to $10 | 756,000 | 1988 |
| Up to $15 | 945,000 | 1990 |
| Up to $30 | 1,134,000 | 1992 |

Source: Lieberman, 1976, Table 6. Copyright 1976 by the
American Association for the Advancement of Science.

The breeder reactor both produces and consumes plutonium and
requires the shipment and processing of this highly toxic material. While
it is argued that the probability of a significant accident such as core
meltdown at a power plant is negligible, this has not been proved to the
satisfaction of many members of the scientific community. The prospects of sabotage of power plants and the possible theft of plutonium for
weapons purposes emphasize the large risks that human society runs in
opting for this avenue of energy development.

A major problem with all nuclear technologies is the ultimate disposal of the final radioactive waste products. These materials will have
to be immobilized, stored, and monitored indefinitely. Several technical
and social uncertainties surround this process. First, the reprocessed
wastes generate large quantities of heat, which precludes large-scale
underground disposal for at least 50 years after removal from the reactor. Second, the long-term stability of the glass or ceramic materials in
which the wastes are captured is not guaranteed. Radioactive elements
also migrate toward the surfaces of containing glass blocks, so that they
can eventually be leached from the surface. The major hazard is contact
of the confining blocks with groundwater, a condition that cannot totally
be prevented over the long term because of the activity of the earth's
surface. The time periods involved in storage are indicated by the half-
lives of the principal waste products: iodine-129, 16 million years;
neptunium-237, 2 million years; and plutonium-239, 24,000 years.[5]

In light of these uncertainties and possible irreversibilities, Kneese
(1973) has recommended a strategy of relying on fossil fuels (primarily
coal) while alternative clean technologies (solar, fusion, geothermal) are
pursued. His argument is that, while fossil fuels produce definite dam-

---

[5]Regarding storage problems, see Marsily et al., "Nuclear Waste Disposal: Can the
Geologist Guarantee Isolation?" *Science*, Vol. 197, No. 4303, August 5, 1977, pp. 519–526.

ages, both human and material, these damages are reversible and we do know how to contain them even if at considerable expense. If, at some future date, it becomes clear that these technologies will not work, then nuclear technologies can still be used.

But the issue is not totally clear, for the use of coal has very substantial costs associated with it. Resistance to large coal-fired electric plants was most dramatically illustrated by the demise of the huge 6000-megawatt Kaiparowitz plant in Utah that would have consumed 60,000 tons of coal per day, provided power equivalent to the needs of a city of six million persons, and would have degraded air quality around some of the most dramatic scenic attractions in North America: Lake Powell, Grand Canyon, Zion and Bryce Canyon National Parks, and so on. Internationally, the transboundary transport of sulphur dioxide with resultant "acid rains" has become a major issue. An OECD study[6] summarizes the $SO_2$ export-import budget for most European countries and shows that, while many countries show a rough balance, Austria, Finland, Norway, Sweden, and Switzerland involuntarily import more than twice what they export. Denmark and the United Kingdom export much more than they import. Norway receives about a quarter of the total airborne sulphur wastes produced by British sources. These wastes build up in the winter snowpack, resulting in high acid spring runoff that kills many fish.

Lave and Seskin, in a sequence of studies, have produced overwhelming evidence that human morbidity and mortality are strongly associated with particulate and $SO_2$ air pollution, both products of coal and oil combustion.[7] They estimate that a 50 percent reduction in current urban U.S. levels of these pollutants would result in a 5 percent reduction in mortality rates, equivalent to an increase in life expectancy of about one year. Lave also made the following comparison between the quantifiable health effects of coal and nuclear power generation (Table 9.16). There seems to be little doubt that the day-to-day noncatastrophic impacts of coal-fired electric generation are more damaging than those of nuclear.

A serious new complication from the use of fossil fuels has recently been called to the public's attention: a continuing buildup of carbon dioxide in the earth's atmosphere. An eminent National Academy of Science panel reported in July, 1977, that by the end of this century, the

[6]See *Nature*, Vol. 268, July 14, 1977.

[7]For example, see "Acute Relationships Among Daily Mortality, Air Pollution, and Climate" in E. S. Mills (ed.), *Economic Analysis of Environmental Problems*, New York: Columbia University Press, 1975.

**Table 9.16.** Dollar Estimates of Health Effects

|  | *Coal* | *Uranium* |
|---|---|---|
| Mine accidents | 8¢/10³kwhe | 0.6¢/10³kwhe |
| Mine chronic disease | 24¢/10³kwhe | 1.8¢/10³kwhe |
| Public | 10 to 500¢/10³kwhe | 0.0003 to 0.03¢/10³kwhe |
| Total | 40 to 530¢/10³kwhe | 2.4¢/10³kwhe |

Source: Lave, "Coal or Nuclear: the Unintended Consequences of Electricity Generation," American Economic Association, *Proceedings,* May 1976.

$CO_2$ content of the atmosphere will have risen 25 percent above its level before the Industrial Revolution, and by the end of the next century it will have doubled.[8] This $CO_2$ buildup can act like a greenhouse, blocking the escape of infrared radiation into space and raising the earth's surface temperatures. It appears possible that there will be a global warming of 10°F with three times that rise at high latitudes. The buildup is attributable to the oxidation of fossil fuels, cement manufacture, and the clearing of forests.

The effects of such a warming would be catastrophic to the world system as we know it. Agriculture would be forced out of currently temperate regions into northern latitudes where soils are much poorer. The arid margins where so much of the world's population now lives would become desert, fish life likely would be severely reduced because of changes in circulation patterns that distribute nutrients, and ocean levels might rise as much as 20 feet, flooding all coastal regions and cities.

The panel stated that early research must be started because it will take decades to reduce the great uncertainties surrounding this phenomenon. Then, if it is found that fossil fuel burning must be stopped, it will require a generation or more to shift to other fuels.

Thus, the major intermediate term alternative to the breeder reactor appears to have global dangers associated with it that are just as profound as the problems of nuclear waste storage and nuclear catastrophy. The tradeoffs are difficult to comprehend and compare and the answer is not obvious. Caution, alertness to research results, a willingness to reduce all energy uses, and a willingness to change life-styles profoundly if need be all seem called for.

[8] *The New York Times,* 25 July 1971, p. 1.

# Chapter 10

# MINERAL AVAILABILITY AND EXPLORATION

This chapter presents information on what is known about the occurrence of minerals such as iron, aluminum, copper, nickel, and cobalt in the earth's crust and discusses recent developments in geological theory regarding availability of different groups of minerals. The possibility of additions to stocks through planned exploration activities is then introduced into the natural resources commodity sector model developed in Chapter 5 to determine the effects on *in situ* rents and natural resource commodity prices. The great uncertainties faced in exploration and development by the firm are then discussed and Baysean exploration strategies are explained. Finally, possible deviations between privately and socially desirable levels of exploration are analyzed.

## 10.1. PHYSICAL CHARACTERISTICS OF MINERAL RESOURCE AVAILABILITY

While mineral resources are widely diffused through the earth's crust and oceans, deposits sufficiently rich to be economically exploitable are quite rare. This can be seen by comparing average "crustal abundance" with the concentration necessary for commercial exploitation under current technological and economic conditions. Table 10.1 relates the minimum concentration for commercial exploitation to crustal abundance in parts per million.

The cutoff grades represent the margin of exploitation with respect to concentration, but other conditions relating to the size and location of the deposit must also be met. Thus we can conclude that exploitable

**Table 10.1.** Cutoff Grade and Crustal Abundance
for Selected Minerals

| Element | Crustal Abundance (ppm) | Cutoff Grade (ppm) | Ratio |
|---|---|---|---|
| Mercury | 0.089 | 1,000 | 11,200 |
| Tungsten | 1.1 | 4,500 | 4,000 |
| Lead | 12 | 40,000 | 3,300 |
| Chromium | 110 | 230,000 | 2,100 |
| Tin | 1.7 | 3,500 | 2,000 |
| Silver | 0.075 | 100 | 1,330 |
| Gold | 0.0035 | 3.5 | 1,000 |
| Molybdenum | 1.3 | 1,000 | 770 |
| Zinc | 94 | 35,000 | 370 |
| Uranium | 1.7 | 700 | 350 |
| Carbon | 320 | 100,000 | 310 |
| Lithium | 21 | 5,000 | 240 |
| Manganese | 1,300 | 250,000 | 190 |
| Nickel | 89 | 9,000 | 100 |
| Cobalt | 25 | 2,000 | 80 |
| Phosphorus | 1,200 | 88,000 | 70 |
| Copper | 63 | 3,500 | 56 |
| Titanium | 6,400 | 100,000 | 16 |
| Iron | 58,000 | 200,000 | 3.4 |
| Aluminum | 83,000 | 185,000 | 2.2 |

Source: Cook, 1976, Table 1. Copyright 1976 by the
American Association for the Advancement of Science.

deposits ("mines") are really quite rare. This physical infrequency of occurrence is also emphasized by a statistical summary of the production of 23 minerals in 1975[1] showing that 90 percent of total production (except Peoples' Republic of China and U.S.S.R.) was accounted for by 1100 mines.

The characteristics of these rare concentrations and the ease with which they can be identified are crucial to future availability. Economic geologists have frequently pictured the occurrence of minerals as a pyramid with relatively small quantities at the top representing the high concentration and the widening base as the increasing quantities to be found in deposits of lower concentration (and higher cost). This picture

[1]*Mining Journal* (London), International Mining Survey, September 1975, pp. 185–221. The minerals were asbestos, bauxite, boron, diamonds, fluorspar, phosphate, potash, iron, manganese, chromium, nickel, molybdenum, tungsten, titanium, copper, lead, zinc, tin, mercury, silver, gold, platinum, and uranium.

has been challenged, however, and further analysis has shown it not to be representative of many important minerals.

One should distinguish between the features of a specific deposit and the distribution of deposits by mineral concentration and size. Some individual deposits exhibit sharp boundaries and relatively small internal variation of concentration. An example would be porphyry copper deposits. Other deposits exhibit a gradual reduction in concentration. Examples are found in the history of the depletion of iron ore in the Lake Superior district (Figure 3.1 Chapter 3) and in the production history of the Comstock Lode shown in Figure 10.1.

The aggregate supply curve for a mineral then depends on the distribution of deposits by size, location, and average concentration. There is an active controversy over the nature of this curve. Brobst (1976) has nicely summarized the present understanding of these phenomena by defining three concentration thresholds: the potential economic threshold, the mineralogical threshold, and the average crustal abundance. The potential economic threshold corresponds to the lower boundary of Figure 2.1 (Chapter 2), that is, the lowest concentration of subeconomic resources for which there is some chance of commercial exploitation through technological and price changes. The mineralogical

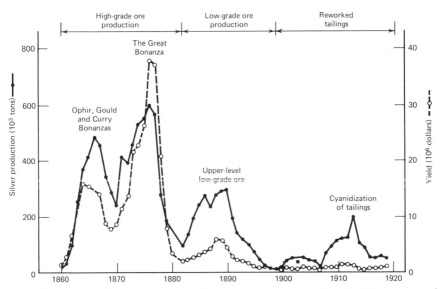

**Figure 10.1**   Production history of the Comstock Lode in Nevada. Source: Cook, 1976, Fig. 2. Copyright 1976 by the American Association for the Advancement of Science.

**Table 10.2.**  Percentage Distribution by Weight
and Value of the U.S. Use of the
Nonfossil Nonrenewable Resources,
1975

|                                     | % Total Weight | % Total Value |
|-------------------------------------|:--------------:|:-------------:|
| Sand, gravel, rock, clay, etc.      | 90             | 12            |
| Iron, aluminum, and magnesium       | 4              | 52            |
| Other nonmetals                     | 5              | 13            |
| All other                           | 1              | 23            |

Source: H. E. Goeller, "The Age of Substitutability: A
Scientific Appraisal of Natural Resource Adequacy," in
V. Kerry Smith (ed.), 1979.

threshold represents the minimal set of natural conditions that permitted the formation of a recoverable mineral among the other ordinary
rocks. Below this threshold, the element is dispersed in the crystal
structures of the ordinary rocks according to laws of crystal chemistry
that allow substitution of some elements for others; that is, the elements
are bound together in the crystal structure and cannot be separated
by physical means. This is particularly true of metals dispersed in
silicate materials which make up most of the earth's crust.

Materials that are bounded by the mineralogical threshold and the
average level of crustal abundance have very different physical (and as a
consequence, economic) characteristics than those above the threshold.
With concentrations down to the mineralogical threshold, the minerals
can continue to be separated and concentrated and using conventional
technology. Of course, costs increase, even more than in inverse proportion to the concentration, but there are no large discontinuities in costs.
At the mineralogical threshold, however, the process of separation
changes entirely, in such a way that the required technology and energy
inputs are radically changed. Depending on the type of host silicate
mineral, the necessary energy input will jump by factors of 100 to 1000.

Among the 10 elements that account for 99 percent of the earth's
crust are found four metals: aluminum (8 percent of the crust); iron (5
percent); magnesium (2 percent); and titanium (0.4 percent). Magnesium is recovered primarily from seawater, so has reached an essentially infinite resource plateau. The mineralological thresholds of the
other three "abundant" metals occur at very low concentrations, so
for them it is possible to continue recovering the metal from increasingly
diffuse ores at smoothly increasing costs.

The remaining metals that account for much less than 1 percent of the earth's crust exhibit such thresholds at much higher concentrations. The significance of these observations can be seen by comparing the values of the different groups of resources shown in Table 10.2. Many important metals fall in the "all other" category that exhibits mineralogical thresholds could increase their cost incredibly.

Figure 10.2 pictures the required energy inputs for the abundant and scarce minerals. The existence of a mineralogical barrier would not pose difficulty if large quantities of a resource existed at concentrations in excess of the threshold. However, current knowledge indicates that the scarce minerals probably have a bimodal distribution by concentration, in contrast to the unimodal distribution of the abundant minerals. The two possible distributions are exhibited in Figure 10.3. Note that the division between the two humps of the bimodal distribution represents the mineralogical threshold for the scarce minerals. In such a case, one could expect an early period during which larger tonnages become available as concentrations fall, only to be followed by diminishing tonnages of ore. This appears to be the case with mercury, gold, and silver. Beyond the threshold, vast quantities may be available, but only at extreme energy costs.

These geological theories, partly confirmed to date, have important implications for future resource availability. The analogy of the resource "pyramid" will not hold for many important minerals unless we are able

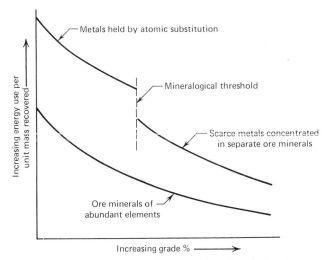

**Figure 10.2** Energy requirements for recovering abundant and scarce elements. Source: Brobst, 1979, Fig. 5.

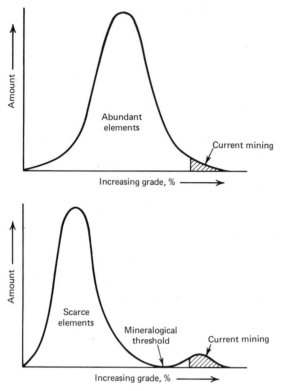

**Figure 10.3**   Possible distributions of scarce and abundant minerals. Source: Brobst, 1979, Fig. 4.

to command huge quantities of cheap energy. Without such energy and major advances in technology, it appears that there is little probability of pushing mineral exploitation beyond the mineralogical threshold and even less hope that we will be able to use the average crust of the earth to obtain our minerals.

## 10.2.   THE EFFECTS OF EXPLORATION ON THE SOCIALLY OPTIMAL PATHS OF NATURAL RESOURCE USE, PRICE, AND *IN SITU* RENTS

A model of the socially optimum use of nonrenewable resources over time was developed in Chapter 5. Review the basic model and related text from Equations 5.1.1 through 5.1.7. A model of likely competitive market behavior was developed by omitting from the first model the environmental costs. To simplify exposition in this section, we use the latter model. The discussion of Chapter 5 was based on the assumption of a fixed stock of natural resources, but the objective of this section is to introduce the possibility of exploration and discovery.

As Fisher has stated (1978), once exploration and discovery are introduced, optimal depletion is no longer simply a matter of running down the stock but involves the allocation of resources to finding new stocks. This makes the so-called "nonrenewable resource problem" much more like a renewable resource problem, except that the conditions of "renewal" will change according to the conditions of the "exploration production function."

The idea of an exploration production function that yields new additions to stocks was introduced in Chapter 2 [see (2.1.4)]. We now insert it into our basic model in slightly changed form:

$$(10.2.1) \qquad H(t) = h[L_2(t), M(t), t]$$

where $L_2(t)$ represents the capital-labor input into exploration and $M(t)$ represents cumulative discoveries as *a surrogate for the information* that has been generated and accumulated from past exploration and that conditions the effectiveness of further exploration. That is,

$$(10.2.2) \qquad M(t) = \int_0^t H(\tau)\, d\tau$$

Given the possibility of discovery, the basic stock accounting identity becomes

$$(10.2.3) \qquad S(t) = S(0) + \int_0^t [H(\tau) - R_0(\tau)]\, d\tau$$

Two "state variables" thus exist, $S(t)$ and $M(t)$, and their time rates of change are:

$$(10.2.4) \qquad \begin{aligned} \dot{S}(t) &= H(t) - R_0(t) \\ \dot{M}(t) &= H(t) \end{aligned}$$

The optimization problem of deriving the time paths of resource use and exploration activity can be stated as:

$$(10.2.5) \quad \underset{L_1(t),\, L_2(t)}{\text{maximize}} \int_0^\infty \left[ \int_0^{R_0(t)} D(\eta, t)\, d\eta - w_1 L_1(t) - w_2 L_2(t) \right] e^{-rt}\, dt$$

subject to: $S(t) = S(0) + \int_0^t [H(\tau) - R_0(\tau)] \, d\tau$

$$M(t) = \int_0^t H(\tau) \, d\tau$$

$$S(t) \geq 0$$

The Hamiltonian corresponding to this control theory problem is:

(10.2.6)   $\phi = \int_0^{R_d(t)} D(\eta, t) d\eta - w_1 L_1(t) - w_2 L_2(t) + q_1(t)[H(t) - R_0(t)]$
$$+ q_2(t)H(t)$$

where $q_1(t)$ and $q_2(t)$ are now the Lagrangean multipliers or costate variables corresponding to the two time rates of change of the state variables as given in (10.2.4). The Hamiltonian $\phi$ represents the rate of net benefits being generated by the natural resources sector at time $t$, where $q_1(t)$ is the now familiar user cost or scarcity rent and $q_2(t)$ is the marginal value of additional information generated by discovery. The optimum programs of resource use and exploration can be characterized by differentiating the Hamiltonian $\phi$ first with respect to $L_1(t)$ and then with respect to $L_2(t)$.

(10.2.7)   $\dfrac{\partial \phi}{\partial L_1(t)} = D[R_0(t), t] \cdot \dfrac{\partial R_0(t)}{\partial L_1(t)} - w_1 - q_1(t) \dfrac{\partial R_0(t)}{\partial L_1(t)}$

Setting this equal to zero and rearranging terms, we get, once again,

(10.2.8)        Basic Condition 1a: $p(t) = \dfrac{w_1}{\dfrac{\partial R_0(t)}{\partial L_1(t)}} + q_1(t)$

$$= MC_R(t) + q_1(t)$$

The partial derivative with respect to $L_2(t)$ is

(10.2.9)   $\dfrac{\partial \phi}{\partial L_2(t)} = -w_2 + q_1(t) \dfrac{\partial H(t)}{\partial L_2(t)} + q_2(t) \dfrac{\partial H(t)}{\partial L_2(t)}$

implying

(10.2.10)        Basic Condition 1b: $q_1(t) = \dfrac{w_2}{\dfrac{\partial H}{\partial L_2(t)}} - q_2(t)$

$$= MC_H(t) - q_2(t)$$

Basic Condition 1a is precisely the same as in Chapter 5: stating that under an optimum program of production and exploration the natural resource commodity price, $p(t)$, will equal marginal extraction cost, $MC_R(t)$ plus the scarcity rent, $q(t)$. Basic Condition 1b, however, introduces quite a different result regarding the behavior of scarcity rent. It tells us that *when stocks can reliably be supplemented through a costly process of exploration and discovery, the scarcity rent on* in situ *resources will equal the marginal replacement costs of stocks*, $MC_H(t)$, *adjusted for the value of information that is generated in the process.*

Exploration and discovery thus transform the finite, exhaustible resources problem into one of optimum restocking or optimum exploration. But our treatment of exploration has overlooked the uncertainty involved in exploration. The exploration production function (10.2.1) must really be treated as stochastic (probabilistic). The level of uncertainty or, in more technical terms, the distribution of the stochastic error term which should be represented in (10.2.1) will depend on the geology of the resources being tapped and the amount of "risk pooling" that takes place.

The geological uncertainty relates to the issues raised in the preceding section. If the idea of the "resources triangle" with ever more resources available at lesser concentrations is applicable, then there may be little uncertainty and finding more is just a matter of exploring until you've found what is needed. However, for those resources that are theorized to occur in randomly located infrequent locations, the element of risk may be quite substantial.

The pooling of exploration risks becomes relevant here. An oil "wildcatting" operation is very risky, since only one search operation is carried on at one time. The probability of finding exploitable oil is low and the capitalization of the enterprise is also typically low. The probability that the money runs out before a profitable well is brought in is thus quite high. If many such ventures can be undertaken by one enterprise, the probability of financial failure can be greatly reduced. This is the reason why even the largest oil companies form consortia to finance the extremely costly exploratory ventures on the outer continental shelf.

Looking back at the Basic Conditions 1(a) and (b), we should again raise the question of whether or not the institutional framework within which production and exploration decisions are made will permit and motivate the attainment of these conditions. The issue of scarcity rents $q_1(t)$, was fully investigated in Chapter 5 where the problems of common property resources were discussed as they relate to the establishment of markets for *in situ* resources. The nature of the value of information from exploration, $q_2(t)$, is a new issue, however, and will be discussed in Section 10.4. First, however, we pursue the important issue of the risks involved in exploration by looking more carefully at the exploration decision problem of the individual firm. A type of decision procedure often followed in exploration operations—known as Baysean decision making—is explained.

## 10.3.  DEALING WITH THE RISKS OF EXPLORATION AND DEVELOPMENT FROM THE MINING FIRM'S VIEWPOINT: BAYSEAN DECISION STRATEGIES

The process of identifying and quantifying new reserves to replace those used up through production is a vital part of the activities of any natural resources firm. An optimal size for reserves will always exist for the firm as was demonstrated for a simple static case in Chapter 2. This optimum is always finite, however, since it is costly to discover and carry reserves which will benefit only future operations.

The firm, unless it is quite small, typically will have several stages of exploration activity going on simultaneously: final refinement of data on reserves soon to be developed and various stages of exploratory activity ranging from geological mapping prior to land acquisition to the study of remote sensing satellite data. The process is sequential, starting with very general data on large areas thought to be good prospects because of their geological characteristics or because of prior experience there, and narrowing the locations to be further investigated by gaining additional geological and economic information about the sites. An example will be useful.

Consider exploration for copper-zinc deposits in the Canadian Shield region. The area has long been known as a copper-producing region. A first step in seeking new deposits might be the analysis of computer-processed images from the National Aeronautical and Space Administration's LANDSAT earth resources survey satellites. Each of these images covers 115 by 115 miles, an area that could require more than 1000 aerial photographs for coverage. From such images, large scale linear or curvilinear features can be identified, suggesting possible areas for mineral deposits.

When these areas have been identified, a second step might be to fly electromagnetic surveys along the fault line to detect magnetic anomalies suggestive of sizable deposits. At this point, lands may have to be leased or government permission obtained for follow-up ground exploration. Further investigation of individual anomalies by on-site investigation may then follow for those sites that are legally, physically, and economically accessible.

Exploration is thus a sequential process of investment in information, succeeding steps being taken only if the information gathered to date indicates acceptable probability of success. The parameters that will influence this sequence of decisions include: (1) the probability distributions over deposits of the various sizes and grades, given the information gathered to date; (2) the value of the ore at points of sale or refining; (3) the costs associated with developing and producing a deposit of known size and grade in the particular location; (4) the costs of the various exploratory activities. However far the process may be carried, the information generated hopefully will not be lost, so that exploration that is currently terminated either because the conditions of a deposit make it appear uneconomic or because the probability of an adequate deposit appears too low may still have elevated certain deposits from the speculative to the hypothetical category (see Figure 2.1, Chapter 2) or from the submarginal to the paramarginal category.

Let's take a more careful look at the nature of this decision process since it will help us understand the basic features of rational decision making under uncertainty, which is critical to all facets of natural resources management. We imagine a mineral firm engaged in an exploration process like the one described above. We assume that certain strategic decisions have been made, such as the minerals to be sought and the region or regions where potential operations are to be located. Thus, the basic activity of studying large-scale satellite survey data can be assumed to be a continuing process. However, following up features identified from satellite images and gaining information on potential extensions of deposits currently known or developed are decisions that must repeatedly be made.

The decision process to be described here is generally referred to as a *Baysean* decision process because it involves revising estimated probabilities of deposits in the light of additional information, using the procedure of Bayes theorem.[2] It is assumed that the firm is willing to base its sequence of exploration and development decisions relating to one deposit on the expected value of the relevant payoffs. This would be reasonable for a large firm for which the consequences of any one venture would be small relative to total capital. If the venture is large relative to the firm's capital (i.e., if the maximum loss that might result would significantly impair the firm's ability to continue business as usual), then we assume that the firm has specified an appropriate utility index, the expected value of which reflects its attitudes toward risk.[3]

---

[2]For an excellent elementary treatment of this topic, see Robert Schlaifer, *Probability and Statistics for Business Decisions,* New York: McGraw-Hill Book Co., 1959.

[3]See Schlaifer, Chapter 2, ibid. Such an index is called a "von Neumann-Morgenstern" utility index after the men who developed the concept for simplifying decision making under uncertainty.

To simplify presentation, we assume that the firm, having identified certain features in a subregion that may warrant further investigation, must decide whether or not to proceed with only one remaining stage of the exploration process, say on-site evaluation. If that investigation reveals a sufficiently large and rich deposit, development can proceed. The following notation is used:

$\theta_i$ ≡ a summary of various size and grade characteristics of the deposit. In particular, $\theta_1$ signifies a large, rich deposit; $\theta_2$ a medium size, medium value deposit; and $\theta_3$ a small, low-value deposit.

$d_0$ ≡ the decision not to develop the deposit.

$d_1$ ≡ the decision to develop.

$\Pi(\theta_i, d_j)$ ≡ the net payoff, not deducting exploration costs, of undertaking $d_j$ when $\theta_i$ characterizes the features of the deposit. We assume that $\Pi(\theta_i, d_0) = 0$ for all $\theta_i$, while $\Pi(\theta_1, d_1) = 100$ (say a million dollars), $\Pi(\theta_2, d_1) = 10$, and $\Pi(\theta_3, d_1) = -50$.

$p(\theta_i)$ ≡ the probability of $\theta_i$ derived from geological mapping and general geological information, that is, the probabilities before on-site evaluation.

$Z_j$ ≡ a summary of the outcome of on-site evaluation, assumed to be $Z_1 = $ "favorable" on-site data and $Z_2 = $ "unfavorable" on-site data.

$p(Z_j|\theta_i)$ ≡ the conditional probability that $Z_j$ occurs as the outcome of on-site evaluation, given that $\theta_i$ is the true state of the deposit, that is, the conditional probability of $Z_j$ given $\theta_i$.

$p(\theta_i|Z_j)$ ≡ the conditional probability of $\theta_i$ given that $Z_j$ is observed.

$p(\theta_i, Z_j)$ ≡ the joint probability that both $\theta_i$ and $Z_j$ occur.

$K$ ≡ the cost of carrying out the on-site evaluation.

Suppose, for some reason, a decision on developing the deposit had to be made without on-site evaluation (patently unrealistic for mining since the locational characteristics of the deposit are not even known in sufficient detail to permit the siting of the mine). The expected payoff of not developing would be zero, while the expected payoff of developing would be

(10.3.1)        $E_1(\pi) = 100\, p(\theta_1) + 10\, p(\theta_2) - 50\, p(\theta_3)$

For example, if the three probabilities are .4, .3, and .3, respectively, then $E_1(\pi) = 28$. If on-site evaluation were impossible, then the expected payoff indicates that development would be attractive.

Since proceeding in such an uninformed manner would not even be possible, it is reasonable to ask first of all whether any further investigation appears worthwhile. An *upper bound* on the value of additional information is provided by what is called the *value of perfect information.* We picture this value in the following way: while the exploration for and development of a particular deposit is a one-time event, we think of the firm as engaging in many such decisions over time, permitting an interpretation of the probabilities as relative frequencies. Then, if we had perfect information, that is, a perfect predictor of $\theta_i$ for each deposit, $p(\theta_1)$ percent of the time we would develop large deposits, $p(\theta_2)$ percent of the time we would develop medium deposits, and $p(\theta_3)$ percent of the time we would *not proceed* with development because of the correctly predicted loss incurred in developing small deposits. Using the numbers above, the average value of perfect information would be $100(0.4) + 10(0.3) + 0(0.3) = 43$. Since we can expect a payoff of 28 on the average without further investigation, any further investigation costing more than $43 - 28 = 15$ should be ruled out.

The next step is to derive a *decision rule* that will indicate which action to take ($d_0$ or $d_1$) contingent on the outcome of the site evaluation. *Bayes' theorem* states that

$$(10.3.2) \qquad p(\theta_i | Z_j) = \frac{p(\theta_i, Z_j)}{p(Z_j)}$$

or, symmetrically, that

$$(10.3.3) \qquad p(Z_j | \theta_i) = \frac{p(\theta_i, Z_j)}{p(\theta_i)}$$

Geologists can estimate the values of $p(Z_j | \theta_i)$, that is, the probabilities of the various on-site outcomes, given the real nature of the deposit. Multiplying (10.3.3) through by $p(\theta_i)$ produces a computable expression for the joint probability of $\theta_i$ and $Z_j$:

$$(10.3.4) \qquad p(\theta_i, Z_j) = p(Z_j | \theta_i)\, p(\theta_i)$$

Since the $p(\theta_i)$ have been estimated from general geological exploration data and the geologists have estimated the $p(Z_j | \theta_i)$, (10.3.4) permits the construction of the joint probability distribution of $\theta$ and $Z$. For illustra-

**Table 10.3.** Joint Probability Distribution of Mine Characteristics and Drilling Results

|  | Favorable Outcome, $Z_1$ | Unfavorable Outcome, $Z_2$ | $p(\theta_i)$ |
|---|---|---|---|
| Large deposit, $\theta_1$ | .280 | .120 | .4 |
| Medium deposit, $\theta_2$ | .060 | .240 | .3 |
| Small deposit, $\theta_3$ | .009 | .291 | .3 |
| $p(Z_j)$ | .349 | .651 |  |

tion, assume the following conditional probabilities: $p(Z_1|\theta_1) = .7$, $p(Z_1|\theta_2) = .2$, $p(Z_1|\theta_3) = .03$, $p(Z_2|\theta_1) = .3$, $p(Z_2|\theta_2) = .8$, $p(Z_2|\theta_3) = .97$. The values in Table 10.3 can then be computed. The unconditional or marginal probabilities of $Z_1$ and $Z_2$ are gotten by adding down the columns, while the unconditional probabilities of $\theta_1$, $\theta_2$, and $\theta_3$ are gotten by summing the rows. Bayes' theorem (10.3.2) now indicates how to compute the revised or posterior probabilities of the $\theta_i$, given the on-site outcomes: $p(\theta_1|Z_1) = 0.280/0.349 = 0.802$; $p(\theta_2|Z_1) = 0.060/0.349 = 0.172$; $p(\theta_3|Z_1) = 0.009/0.349 = 0.026$, and so on. These numbers are exhibited in Table 10.4. The revised or *posterior* expected payoffs of development can now be computed and compared with the zero payoff of nondevelopment.

$$E_2(\Pi|Z_1) = 100\ (.802) + 10(.172) - 50(.026) = 80.62$$
$$E_2(\Pi|Z_2) = 100\ (.184) + 10(.369) - 50(.447) = -.26$$

If the firm observes $Z_1$, it presumably finds development attractive because of its large (revised) expected payoff but will decide not to develop if $Z_2$ is observed. A clearer picture of the entire process is seen in Figure 10.4.

**Preposterior Analysis.**   The firm has now developed a strategy of what it should do contingent on the outcome of the on-site evaluation, but

**Table 10.4.**   Posterior Probabilities of Mine Characteristics, Given On-Site Drilling Results, $P(\theta_i|Z_j)$

|  | $Z_1$ | $Z_2$ |
|---|---|---|
| $\theta_1$ | .802 | .184 |
| $\theta_2$ | .172 | .369 |
| $\theta_3$ | .026 | .447 |

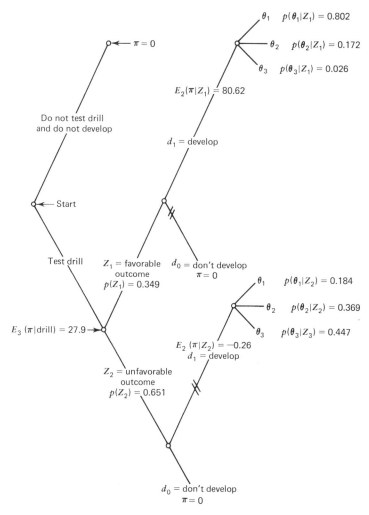

**Figure 10.4** Decision tree for the test drilling and development decisions.

should it proceed? Table 10.3 gave the unconditional probabilities that $Z_1$ and $Z_2$ would be observed, so it is possible to compute the expected payoff, given that on-site evaluation takes place.

$$E_3 \text{ (II|drill)} = 80(.349) + 0(.651) = 27.92$$

Since on-site evaluation is necessary for developing, it will be attractive provided its cost does not exceed 27.92, that is, if $K < 27.92$. Thus the firm has developed the basis for a decision of whether or not to proceed with on-site evaluation.

This set of steps closely approximates the exploration process that is followed formally or informally by mining firms.[4]

## 10.4. EXPLORATION AND DISCOVERY FROM SOCIETY'S VIEWPOINT

To what extent can the privately rational processes followed by firms in deciding on exploration and development lead to the socially optimal levels of exploratory activity and additions to reserves? Several factors appear to be capable of causing deviations of private exploratory behavior from socially desirable patterns.

First, if exploration is carried on in a competitive setting, each firm is likely to guard the information generated to prevent its falling into competitors' hands. If firms had exclusive rights to explore and develop fixed parcels of land, this might not be important. Under such circumstances, information generated by one firm would benefit others by indicating conditions that might continue across property boundaries, but the transmission of information to others would not be likely to injure the firm which developed the information since secure tenure to *in situ* resources has been assumed.[5]

In real-life situations, however, tenures are not fixed and information generated through exploration may have a very high value if it is obtained before other firms get it. Lands potentially containing resources may be subject to lease from public and private agents. Superior information may permit leasing under very favorable conditions or the buying up of leases from competitors. In the *extreme* case of common property *in situ* resources that are subject to leasing or other claim arrangements, guarding exploration information may be the *only* way of appropriating the resource.

Thus, we have at least three motivational factors at work in exploration that pull the private operator in opposite directions, each away from the socially desirable level of exploratory activity: (1) exploration infor-

---

[4]For an interesting application of probabilistic methods to the issues of preliminary exploration over very large areas, see M. Allais, "Methods of Appraising Economic Prospects of Mining Exploration Over Large Territories: The Algerian Sahara Case Study," *Management Science*, Vol. 3, pp. 285–375, 1957.

[5]If more effective exploration by other firms meant more production and the depression of prices, firms might still be reluctant to release information.

mation would have value to other firms but generally cannot be sold to them causing the firm to *under invest* in exploration; (2) information may be the only way of securing tenure over *in situ* resources, motivating firms to guard their information, leading to duplication of exploratory effort, that is, too much exploration; and (3), in the true common property case [an extreme case of (2)], firms will be motivated not only to duplicate exploration activities and guard their information, but to accelerate exploration far too much so as to establish their claims before others do so. On balance, it appears likely that *too much effort* is put into exploration, but that much of this effort is duplicative, generating the same information many times over. Whether the total effort be too small or too great, the pattern of exploration activities is clearly highly inefficient from an economic viewpoint.

To relate these observations to our earlier model in Section 10.2., the costate variable $q_2(t)$ represented the marginal value of information when *that information was optimally used* to facilitate further exploration. The discussion above has now noted that there are many practical reasons why private exploratory behavior will not follow the socially optimum pattern. The *social* value of information generated is likely in practice to be considerably less than it could be.


## 10.5. SUMMARY AND OUTLOOK

We have seen that the crustal occurrence of resources can follow either the traditional "resource triangle" model of ever-increasing resources at lower concentrations or qualities or a model of rare high concentration deposits beyond which the resource occurs in totally different molecular forms. While iron and aluminum follow the first pattern, the more exotic metals that play increasingly important roles in evolving technologies appear to follow the second. The policy implications of the two patterns may be quite different.

When the possibility of additions to stocks through exploration is introduced, the exhaustible resources case becomes much more like a renewable resources case or the older Ricardian model, for the extension of stocks becomes simply a matter of incurring the costs of exploration. We have seen that the scarcity rent on *in situ* resources would be determined by the effective costs of augmenting stocks through exploration. When the informational value of exploration activity was analyzed, it appeared that private parties would be unlikely to undertake the socially optimum amounts and patterns of exploration.

Risk to the firm engaged in exploration cannot be ignored, even though the pooling of exploration risks can sometimes be accomplished. We have seen how exploration firms can combine geologic and economic information in a rational, probabilistic framework for stepwise decision making, including evaluating from an *ex-ante* viewpoint the value of information to be obtained from exploration.

Regarding the future outlook, we have seen in Chapter 9 that returns to exploration activity in the developed Western countries seem to be falling for all minerals. In Canada in 1950, 1 in 100 preliminary mineral prospects led to mine development; in 1970, only 1 in 1000. Yet large parts of the earth's surface remain largely unexplored because of remoteness and political conditions.

Large strides are being made in exploration technology. Remote sensing from satellites has begun to play a key role in the world search for both minerals and fuels, opening up for preliminary investigation at low-cost vast remote areas of the earth's surface. It is interesting to recall that when Allais wrote of exploring the Algerian Sahara in 1957[6], surveys by jeep or helicopter constituted the initial stage of exploration. Remote sensing has reduced these initial exploration costs by 20 to 50 percent and has already led to major discoveries—for example, copper mines in Pakistan. Substantial improvements in these techniques appear possible simply through adapting existing technologies such as higher resolution cameras, thermal sensors, and multispectral line scanners. While these steps probably cannot overcome the diminishing returns to exploration in intensively explored regions, they promise the likely discovery of new resources in many parts of the world.

[6]M. Allais, ibid.

# Chapter 11

# THE ECONOMICS OF FOREST MANAGEMENT

Forestry provides a fascinating array of economic issues for several reasons: it is an important industry in the United States and many parts of the world; timber management was probably the earliest case of the formal application of economic principles to the management of natural resources; it represents the case of multiple-objective management of a multiple-purpose (or output) system; and, in terms of this book, it represents our introduction to renewable resource systems.

## 11.1. BACKGROUND OF U.S. FORESTRY

In earlier chapters we have seen that forestry, or at least forest output, was of great concern in medieval times, in England during the early Industrial Revolution, and in nineteenth-century America. Indeed, concern with the cutting of forests was one of the earliest causes of environmental concern in the United States, leading to the establishment of the national forests in 1891. Under the influence of Gifford Pinchot, forestry became an early U.S. example of the application of science to natural resources management as it had become much earlier in Western Europe.

Forest lands in the United States are arbitrarily defined as "lands at least 10% occupied by forest trees or formerly so occupied and not presently in non-forest use." Such lands comprise one-third of the land area of the country. These lands fall into three major ownership categories: public, forest industry, and other private holdings. Public

**Table 11.1.** Data on Productive Forest Lands[a] in the U.S., 1970 by Ownership

| | Units | Total | National Forests | Other Public | Forest Industry | Other Private |
|---|---|---|---|---|---|---|
| Forest area | | | | | | |
| North | $10^6$ acres | 178 | 10 | 21 | 18 | 128 |
| South | $10^6$ acres | 193 | 11 | 7 | 35 | 140 |
| West | $10^6$ acres | 129 | 71 | 16 | 14 | 28 |
| Total | | 500 | 92 | 44 | 67 | 296 |
| Percentage | | 100 | 18 | 9 | 13 | 60 |
| Volume of standing timber | $10^9$ cu ft | 649 | 218 | 68 | 100 | 263 |
| | % | 100 | 33 | 10 | 15 | 41 |
| Annual growth | $10^9$ cu ft | 18.6 | 2.6 | 1.8 | 3.5 | 10.8 |
| | % | 100 | 14 | 10 | 19 | 58 |
| Annual harvest | $10^9$ cu ft | 14.0 | 2.2 | 0.9 | 3.7 | 7.2 |
| | % | 100 | 16 | 6 | 26 | 51 |
| Annual growth as % of productive capacity | % | 48 | 37 | 54 | 59 | 46 |

[a]"Productive" forest land as the term is used here is called "commercial" forest land in forestry terminology, meaning lands falling into site classes I–V (i.e., having a potential growth above 20 cubic feet per acre per year).

Source: Clawson (June, 1974), Tables 3 and 10. Resources for the Future, Inc. Reprinted with permission.

forest lands consist primarily of the national forests administered by the U.S. Forest Service (Department of Agriculture), plus national park forest lands administered by the National Park Service (Department of Interior), forest lands administered by the Bureau of Land Management (Department of Interior), and state forest lands. Forest industry refers to lands owned or leased by businesses engaged in the production of forest products for a profit, while "other private" holdings are those associated with activities that are primarily nonforest product related, especially farm and residential lands. Attention in this chapter will be focused primarily on forest industry and public forest lands since they represent the lands for which management objectives are most clearly defined.

Table 11.1 presents general data on the more productive forest lands of the United States comprising 500 million acres. The rows of Table 11.1 presenting percentages will perhaps give the clearest picture of the forest sector. Note the following points:

1.  National forests, forest industry lands, and other private holdings constitute the major classes of productive forest lands, with "other private" holding 60 percent of the total.

2.  The volume of standing timber found on the national forest lands is greatly in excess of the proportion of forest area, indicating dense stands of mature timber on the average.

3.  Annual growth in the national forests is significantly less than the proportion of forest area (another sign of the old age of these forests), while forest industry lands exhibit a disproportionately high growth.

4.  Annual harvests from the national forests are disproportionately low, as are harvests from "other private" lands, while harvests from forest industry lands are high.

5.  National forests typically display low growth in relation to their ideal productive capacity, while forest industry lands exhibit a significantly higher percentage of their ideal capacity.

If all forest lands were managed exclusively for timber production, these observations would clearly indicate some real problems in the way our forests are being used; that the national forests and, to a lesser degree, the "other private" lands are producing far less than their share of national timber output. Another dimension of that problem is the huge volume of standing timber in the national forests. One must ask whether the national forests are being managed properly and whether or not the huge stock of capital represented by the standing timber is warranted. As later discussion will show, there is a great deal of evidence that the national forests could be managed more efficiently without sacrificing nontimber outputs. The same may be true of the "other private" holdings that loom so large.

National forest lands and, in many cases, the "other private" forest lands are managed partly for nontimber purposes. The national forests are expressly directed by the Multiple Use-Sustained Yield Act:[1]

> to develop and administer the renewable surface resources of the national forests for multiple use and sustained yield of the several products and services obtained therefrom.

While the Act is vague concerning what these multiple uses are to be, tradition has established recreation, wilderness, wildlife, watershed, and

[1]Act of June 12, 1960 (74 Stat. 215; 16 U.S.C. 528–531).

**Table 11.2.** Degree of Compatability among Various Forest Uses

| Primary Use | Maintain Attractive Environment | Provide Recreation Opportunity | Wilderness | Wildlife | Natural Watershed | General Conservation | Wood Production and Harvest |
|---|---|---|---|---|---|---|---|
| Maintain attractive environment | | Moderately compatible; may limit intensity of use | Not inimical to wilderness but does not insure | Compatible to most wildlife, less so to a few | Fully compatible | Fully compatible | Limited compatibility; often affects amount of harvest |
| Provide recreation opportunity | Moderately compatible unless use intensity excessive | | Incompatible; would destroy wilderness character | Incompatible for some kinds; others can tolerate | Moderately compatible; depends on intensity of recreation use | Moderately compatible; incompatible if use too heavy | Limited compatibility depends on harvest timing and intensity; roads provide access |
| Wilderness | Fully compatible | Completely incompatible, can't tolerate heavy use | | Highly compatible to much wildlife, less so to others | Fully compatible | Fully compatible | Completely incompatible, precludes all harvest |
| Wildlife | Generally compatible | Limited compatibility; use intensity must be limited | Mostly compatible though some wildlife require vegetative manipulation | | Generally fully compatible | Generally fully compatible | Generally limits volume or conditions of harvest |
| Natural watershed | Fully compatible | Moderate compatibility; may require limitation on intensity | Not inimical to wilderness but does not insure | Generally compatible | | Fully compatible | Moderate compatibility; restricts harvest methods but does not prevent timber harvest |
| General conservation | Fully compatible | Moderately compatible; if use not excessive | Not inimical to wilderness but does not insure | Generally compatible | Fully compatible | | Compatible but requires modifications in methods of timber harvest |
| Wood production and harvest | Compatible if harvest methods strictly controlled | Moderately compatible | Completely incompatible; would destroy wilderness | Compatible if harvest methods fully controlled | Compatible if harvest methods fully controlled | Compatible if harvest methods fully controlled | |

Source: Clawson, June 1974, Table 1, p. 115. Resources for the Future, Inc. Reprinted with permission.

timber production as purposes of the national forests. This does not imply that all uses be established in all forest areas, and even the Act quoted above states that

> ... due consideration shall be given to the relative values of the various resources in particular areas... latitude for periodic adjustments in use to conform to changing needs and conditions; that some land will be used for less than all the resources...

Clawson has compiled a useful comparison of the compatibility of the various uses of forest lands as exhibited in Table 11.2. This qualitative information suggests that the optimum pattern of forest management for the production of multiple outputs may involve patterns of specialization of use rather than attempting all uses everywhere.

These observations suggest the following major policy issues for U.S. forestry:

1.  How best to accommodate the multiple uses of the public forest lands, including the extent of specialized uses.
2.  When and how to harvest timber from the lands that are sufficiently productive to warrant harvesting.
3.  To what extent improved management of the extensive "other private" forest lands could and should be achieved.

A review of legislative debates and the professional literature of forestry of the last two decades will also reveal significant national or special interest concern with: (1) the impacts of national forest policy on communities dependent on forest product production; (2) the impact of foreign trade in logs and lumber on the economy; and (3) the lack of responsiveness of national forest timber management to short-term changes in the lumber market. These issues will be touched on at the close of the chapter.

## 11.2.  TIMBER HARVESTING PRACTICES: THE OPTIMUM ROTATION

The simplest problem a forest manager could face would be the following classic problem: a cleared area (say one acre) is being considered for timber growing. If trees are planted, the trees will be allowed to grow to an age $t$ when they will be cut and the useful timber sold. The area will then be replanted (or allowed to grow again from natural reseeding), the trees again being allowed to grow to age $t$, and so on. No multiple uses or nontimber outputs are to be considered. If the price of a unit of cut timber is constant over time, what is the optimum cutting age of trees, $t^*$, and what would be the value of this acre if committed to timber growing with cutting taking place at intervals of $t^*$ years? The interval from planting to cutting is known as the "rotation," so $t^*$ is referred to as the optimum rotation.

What considerations would be relevant to the determination of $t^*$? The following factors would surely have to play a role:

1. The costs of planting.
2. The price of cut timber.
3. The rate of discount applicable to future costs and receipts.
4. The pattern of growth of useful timber with the age of a tree.

By price here we mean the proceeds from selling a unit volume of useful timber less the costs of harvesting the timber and transporting it to the point of sale. In forestry jargon, this is called "stumpage value." It should be relatively simple to formulate the problem as one of maximizing the *present value* of the stream of receipts minus expenditures forthcoming from the continued use of the land in timber growing.

Before setting up the problem, however, let us consider a few of the issues involved. Trees' percentage growth rates vary over their lifetime, being high when the trees are young and lower or even negative (due to rot, disease, or blowdown) when the trees are old. Thus, as long as keeping a tree involves costs, a point in the tree's life is likely to be reached when keeping it longer adds more to costs than to receipts. But what are the costs of holding a tree? We're going to abstract from management costs such as cutting away deadwood, thinning stands of trees, spraying, and so on, but just *keeping* the tree another year involves two significant costs:

1. The proceeds from cutting the tree are deferred and interest (earnings in alternative uses of those funds) on those proceeds is lost.
2. The land occupied by the tree is foreclosed to any alternative use and the income from that alternative use is foregone.

The first item seems obvious to an economist, for it is simply the opportunity cost of the capital now tied up in the tree. The standing tree is capital just as any inventory of productive assets would be, capital created by the act of planting and subsequent growth. No business manager is willing to keep capital in a particular use unless it is producing a satisfactory rate of return. The same principle applies to the capital represented by a stock of trees.

The second item is less intuitive, especially when the alternative use is simply the growing of more trees. If a developer of resorts stood ready to pay the owner for the land to build a hotel, the site opportunity cost would be more obvious, but it still exists when the alternative use is simply starting a new generation of trees—the usual case for forest lands. The market value a newly cut, newly planted piece of land would have would be approximately the present value of the anticipated stream of receipts minus expenditures when kept in timber production. This is called the "site expectation value" in the forestry literature. Its role in the determination of the optimal rotation was correctly described by the innovative German forester Faustmann in 1849. It is the annual rent that such a piece of land could command that is foregone by letting the trees grow another year.

A quick assessment of the benefits and costs associated with allowing the trees to grow another year then suggests the following rule for determining the optimal rotation:

> allow the trees to continue growing as long as the annual *increase* in the stumpage value exceeds the interest foregone on the stumpage value plus the rental value of newly planted land.

The following notation will be used for further analysis:

$S(t)$ ≡ stumpage value of timber on an acre of land when the trees have a uniform age of $t$ years.

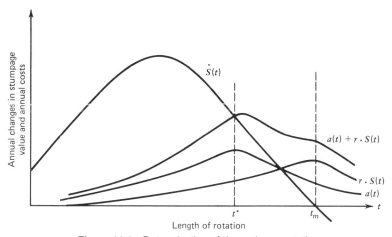

**Figure 11.1** Determination of the optimum rotation.

$\dot{S}(t)$ ≡ the time rate of change of stumpage value.

$k$ ≡ the cost of replanting an acre.

$a(t)$ ≡ the annual rental value of a newly planted acre of forest land when planned future rotations are $t$ years in length.

Figure 11.1 shows the nature of the optimum rotation. $t_m$ is the length of rotation that would result in the greatest value of harvested timber *at each cutting* (where $\dot{S}(t) = 0$) but $t_m$ would not be optimum for, at that point, the annual costs of carrying the timber exceed the annual increases in its value. The optimum rotation, $t^*$, occurs at that point where total annual costs, $a(t) + r \cdot S(t)$, equal the annual increase in stumpage value. Professional foresters and biologists have at times argued that $t_m$ represents the optimum, but this overlooks the costs involved.

## 11.3.    THE OPTIMUM ROTATION: MATHEMATICAL DERIVATION

The problem can be stated as a very straightforward maximization problem, especially if we use continuous discounting rather than discrete annual discounting. If we consider the present value of the stream of costs and receipts as a function of the rotation, we have

$$(11.3.1) \quad
\begin{aligned}
PV(t) &= -k + S(t)e^{-\rho t} - ke^{-\rho t} + S(t)e^{-2\rho t} - \ldots \\
&= [S(t)e^{-\rho t} - k](1 + e^{-\rho t} + e^{-2\rho t} + \ldots) \\
&= [S(t)e^{-\rho t} - k]/(1 - e^{-\rho t})
\end{aligned}$$

The replanting cost, $k$, is considered to be incurred right now, while the first receipt of the stumpage value is delayed $t$ years. The continuous discount factors, $e^{-\rho t}$, $e^{-2\rho t}$, and so on, are very simply related to the more usual discrete time discount factors, $1/(1 + r)^t$, by selecting $\rho$ so that, at integer values of $t$,

$$(11.3.2) \qquad\qquad\qquad \frac{1}{(1 + r)^t} = e^{-\rho t}$$

Taking natural logs of each side and solving for $\rho$ gives:

$$(11.3.3) \qquad\qquad\qquad \rho = \log_e(1 + r)$$

Up to about 10 percent, $\rho$ and $r$ are quite close, but they diverge increasingly at higher values.[2]

| [2] $r$ | 0.0300 | 0.0500 | 0.0600 | 0.1000 | 0.2000 | 0.5000 |
|---|---|---|---|---|---|---|
| $\rho$ | 0.0296 | 0.0488 | 0.0583 | 0.0953 | 0.1823 | 0.4055 |

Differentiating (11.3.1) with respect to $t$ yields

(11.3.4) $PV'(t) = \dfrac{e^{-\rho t}\{[S'(t) - \rho S(t)](1 - e^{-\rho t}) - \rho[S(t)e^{-\rho t} - k]\}}{(1 - e^{-\rho t})^2}$

Setting this equal to zero and simplifying in turn yields

(11.3.5) $\qquad \dot{S}(t^*) = \rho S(t^*) + \rho \dfrac{[S(t^*)e^{-\rho t^*} - k]}{(1 - e^{-\rho t^*})}$

The optimum rotation is thus characterized by the marginal stumpage value equaling interest on the value of the standing timber plus interest on the capitalized value of an infinite sequence of deferred receipts minus immediate planting costs, $S(t^*)e^{-\rho t^*} - k$. A case that approximates the growth of Douglas fir in British Columbia (from Pearse, 1967) is given in Table 11.3.

While the data underlying Table 11.3 are not accurate, they permit four important observations:

1. The site expectation value, $PV(t)$, does not play a very important role in determining the optimum rotation when discount rates are as high as 0.06.
2. The site expectation value, $PV(t)$, drops off rather sharply as the permitted rotation is allowed to exceed the optimum derived here.
3. Increasing the discount rate from 0.06 to 0.10 significantly reduces the optimum rotation.
4. For either discount rate, the optimum rotation based on the timber management factors considered in this analysis is much shorter than the average age of mature Douglas fir found in the Northwest of the United States and in British Columbia.

Observation 4 appears to be consistent with the observations made from Table 11.1 regarding the unusually mature timber found on U.S. national forest lands. Since the average age of fir stands in national forests in the Northwest is well in excess of the 140 years covered in Table 11.3, the management policy currently in effect is closer to that of cutting timber only when $\dot{S}(t)$ has fallen to zero or less. Naturally, some of those lands still contain virgin timber. For such lands, there is the question of the rate at which the forest should be converted to "fully regulated" forest under explicit rotation management. Certainly, efficient multiple-use management under some conditions will imply an optimum rotation different from that based purely on optimum timber management.

**Table 11.3.** Determination of the Optimum Rotation for Douglas Fir [a] with Discount Rates of 0.06 and 0.10

|   |   |   | $\rho S(t)$ | | $PV(t)$ | | $\rho PV(t)$ | | $\rho S(t)+\rho PV(t)$ | |
|---|---|---|---|---|---|---|---|---|---|---|
| $t$ | $S(t)$ | $\dot S(t)$ | 0.06 | 0.10 | 0.06 | 0.10 | 0.06 | 0.10 | 0.06 | 0.10 |
| 30 | 0 | 45 | 0 | 0 | −12 | −11 | | | | |
| 40 | 668 | 86 | 40 | 67 | 56 | 2 | 3 | 0 | 43 | 67 |
| 42 | 848 | 94 | 51 | 85 | 63 | 3 | 4 | | 55 | 85 |
| 44 | 1043 | 101 | 63 | 104 | 69 | 3 | 4 | | 67 | 104 |
| 46 | 1250 | 107 | 75 | 125 | 74 | 3 | 4 | | 79 | 125 |
| 48 | 1470 | 113 | 88 | 147 | 78 | 2 | 5 | | 93 | 147 |
| 50 | 1701 | 118 | 102 | 170 | 79 | 2 | 5 | | 107 | 170 |
| 52 | 1943 | 124 | 117 | 194 | 80 | 1 | 5 | | 122 | 194 |
| 54 | 2195 | 128 | 132 | 220 | 79 | 0 | 5 | | 137 | 220 |
| 56 | 2456 | 133 | 147 | 246 | 78 | −1 | 5 | | 152 | 246 |
| 58 | 2725 | 137 | 164 | 273 | 76 | | 5 | | 169 | 273 |
| 60 | 3002 | 140 | 180 | 300 | 64 | | 4 | | 184 | 300 |
| 70 | 4500 | 152 | 270 | 450 | 60 | | 4 | | 274 | 450 |
| 80 | 6000 | 153 | 360 | 600 | 39 | | 2 | | 362 | 600 |
| 90 | 7500 | 145 | 450 | 750 | 24 | | 1 | | 451 | 750 |
| —  | | | | | | | | | | |
| 140 | 11,000 | −47 | 660 | 1100 | −8 | | | | | |

[a] $S(t) = 1200 - 140t + 3.834t^2 - 0.01667t^3$ and $k = \$10$.

## 11.4. SENSITIVITY ANALYSIS OF THE OPTIMUM ROTATION

The effects that changes in the parameters of (11.3.5) would have on $t^*$ could be most easily studied if it were possible to solve explicitly for $t^*$ rather than just approximating the conditions numerically. Unfortunately, the functions involved are sufficiently complicated that this is not possible even for very simple forms of $S(t)$. Our analysis will have to take the informal format of a discussion of what seems likely.

**Discount Rate.** Considering the plot of the left- and right-hand sides of (11.3.5) as shown in Figure 11.1, can one make definite statements about shifts in the point of intersection as $\rho$ changes? Unfortunately, the shape of the curve of the right-hand side as well as its level will change as $\rho$ changes, so the point of intersection *could* shift either to the left or the right. However, it seems likely that the $\rho S(t)$ term will dominate movements of the right-hand side as it did in Table 11.3, so that an increase in $\rho$ will decrease the optimum rotation under most circumstances.

**Increasing Price of Timber.** Substitute $S(t) = p \cdot f(t)$ into (11.3.5) where $f(t)$ is the salable volume of timber and $p$ its unit price. As $p$ rises, the value of additional growth increases but so do the carrying costs of the timber. As the discount rate rises, the site expectation value rapidly approaches zero so that (11.3.5) can be approximated by $pf(t) = \rho p f(t)$. Even so, it is not possible to make general statements about the effect of changing prices on the optimum rotation since the point of intersection depends on the precise shape of $f(t)$. It seems *likely* that, at very high discount rates, the optimum rotation would be shortened by a rise in prices and lengthened when discount rates are low.

**Severance Tax.** Suppose an *ad valorem* tax is imposed at each cutting. This is simply equivalent to redefining the private manager's stumpage value function to be $\hat{S}(t) \equiv (1 - \tau) S(t)$, so that $\hat{S}'(t) = (1 - \tau) S'(t)$. A quick look at (11.3.5) tells us that in the absence of planting costs, $k$, the $(1 - \tau)$ terms would cancel from both sides of the equation, leaving $t^*$ unchanged. With $k > 0$, the right-hand side of (11.3.5) experiences a larger percentage reduction than the left-hand side, implying an increased rotation since it is necessary to reduce $S'(t)$ to reestablish equality. A severance tax per cubic foot of timber cut will have the same effect, provided price is not affected by changes in the rotation. This can be seen by letting $S(t) = p \cdot f(t)$.

**Increases in Planting and Management Costs.** If we assume that such cost increases can be treated as increases in $k$, the effect clearly is to shift the right-hand size of (11.3.5) downward, increasing the rotation. If, at the same time, the management activities (such as clearing, pesticides spraying, fertilizing) shift $S(t)$ upward, the net effect may be in either direction.

**Annual Property Taxes.** Private forestry firms may have an annual property tax levied against them, which is an increasing function of the value of the standing timber inventory. Since reducing the average value of standing timber over the rotation period will reduce property taxes, timber will be cut younger, that is, the privately optimum rotation will be shortened.

**Variation in the Distance to the Sawmill.** When trees are cut, they are topped, stripped of branches, and the log is hauled to a market center or a sawmill. Thus there are various costs that are a function of this distance, among them the transportation of the logs and the costs of transporting or maintaining workers in the forest. These can be represented by a downward shift in the stumpage value function, without a change in $S'(t)$. It will be necessary to increase the rotation to reestablish the equality of (11.3.5). Thus, the optimal rotation will be longer, the greater the distance to the mill.

## 11.5.  MULTIPLE-USE FOREST MANAGEMENT

The multiple-use philosophy of the U.S. Forest Service has already been introduced and the compatibility of the various potential uses of forest land were qualitatively analyzed in Table 4.4. When dealing with the management of such disparate uses as wilderness, mining, recreation, and timber, it would be presumptuous indeed to attempt to capture all relevant aspects of the problem in a formal quantitative model. There are many more management issues than just the timber rotation. For example, if the forest is not of uniform age, what method of cutting should be used: selective cutting of mature trees of clear-cutting of all trees? Each method has advantages. What method of restocking should be used: natural reseeding from seed trees left standing, from trees along the clear-cut edge, artificial seed spreading, or the planting of seedlings? Again, each method has certain advantages, including differences in cost, in survival rates, and in the appearance of the resulting forest.

Several forest uses other than timbering represent benefits to society generated by the forest but difficult for a private forest owner to capture from the beneficiaries. All forests act as valuable watersheds, catching heavy rainfalls and allowing them to soak into the soil and return to streams in a much more even pattern. In the mountains, winter snow accumulates in the forests and evaporates and melts much more slowly than in exposed positions. The benefits from this natural regulating capability take the forms of reduced downstream flooding, reduced soil erosion, reduced need for reservoirs, and reduced silting of existing reservoirs. If these downstream benefits are taken into account, the rotation and methods of harvesting and replanting would probably differ from those based solely on on-site timber management.

Similarly, recreational and esthetic values are affected by timber age, methods of cutting, and replanting. Clear-cutting may be visually damaging to a vast area and may, if inappropriately used, lead to soil erosion and impairment of regrowth. The "slash" left from clear-cutting (branches, stumps, and other wastes) may impair recreational values. On the other hand, clear-cutting will lead to the regrowth of grasses for wildlife grazing and browsing, the young trees and bushes will provide better bird protection, and the forest "edge" along the cut areas will provide the best terrain for most types of game. Thus, multiple-use management decisions are complex.

However, multiple-use management can be overdone. Not all areas are physically well suited to all uses. Similarly, the structure of demands for the products and services of forest areas may differ widely among regions, implying certain patterns of specialization. Specialization of function is not uncommon in economics. Regions specialize in the production and services to which they are well suited, and nations similarly specialize according to the principle of *comparative advantage,* depending on their technological, economic, and physical characteristics.

Specific forest areas will be best suited to some subset (perhaps one) of the various possible uses. "Best suited" means that if we carried out comparative benefit-cost analyses of alternative patterns of management, making the best possible allowances for difficult-to-quantify outputs such as esthetics and scientific values, certain combinations of uses would be found most valuable for the various regions. It is clear that the demands for various services would be just as important determinants of optimal use patterns as the physical supply characteristics of the land. For example, an area that by soil, elevation, and rainfall might be ideally suited for timber growing might nonetheless be left uncut for recreational purposes if located close to densely populated areas having few recreation alternatives.

Some forests areas are, ironically enough, poorly suited to growing trees. This doesn't imply that existing trees should be destroyed, but it may mean that the area should not be managed for timber production since timber management involves costs and may imply tradeoffs against other uses. Clawson (1975, 1976) has very convincingly shown that some U.S. national forest areas should abandon timber production as a purpose. Figure 11.2 exhibits his data on the costs and receipts per 1000 board feet for various national forests in 1972 and 1973.

The costs in Figure 11.2 which appears on the following page do not include general administrative costs, firefighting, insect and disease control, and several other categories partly attributable to timber management. Nonetheless, the data indicate that timber management expenditures tend to be higher per 1000 board feet in regions where values are low than where they are high. In general, if the costs of timber management exceed the value of the timber produced, timbering should be dropped. There may well be some positive external effects on other forest activities (e.g., stand-improvement measures like thinning may improve recreational values), but usually there will be more efficient ways of improving the setting for those other activities. If the resources now used in timber management in low productivity areas were applied to high productivity areas, a much higher return would be enjoyed.

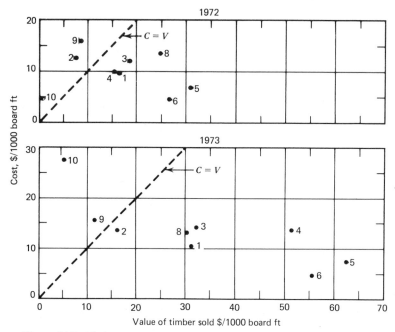

**Figure 11.2** Timber management costs and values per thousand board feet of timber sold: U.S. national forests, 1972 and 1973. Source: Clawson, "The National Forests," *Science*, Vol. 191, No. 4228, February 20, 1976, Fig. 3. Copyright 1976 by the American Association for the Advancement of Science.

A significant part of timber management costs in the national forests are for *timber appraisal* prior to timber sales. Private sawmills cut the timber after bidding successfully for a lease that specifies the time span and other conditions of cutting. While some of these sales are highly competitive, others involve locations in remote areas where possibly only one mill has the capacity for processing the stumpage. To guard against noncompetitive low bids, the Forest Service carries out appraisals to estimate the value—a costly procedure. Clawson (1975) has suggested that the procedure should be changed so that parties paid by the Forest Service would do the cutting and hauling to market where competitive auctioning of the logs would take place.

Timber sales relate to a final dimension of the multiple-use management practiced on the national forests. Some communities whose economies are based on sawmills and other wood products plants are very dependent on continued sales of stumpage from particular national forest areas. The federal government has assumed certain responsibilities toward these communities and their states, making payments to the counties and states in lieu of taxes (since federal lands cannot be taxed). The Forest Service in turn feels a responsibility toward these communities and may modify timber management practices to avoid large fluctuations in activity levels. This may involve noncompetitive timber sales or decisions to sell timber that otherwise would not be sold or would be sold later. In such cases, real conflicts between national and local interests exist.

## 11.6. SOME TRADITIONAL CONCEPTS IN FOREST MANAGEMENT

A classical forestry concept is that of the "fully regulated" forest as the goal of forest management. In concept, a fully regulated forest is one of equal areal distribution of age classes, the oldest of which is at rotation age. Such a forest would be capable of producing a uniformly sustainable flow of timber and can be most easily pictured by looking at Figure 11.3 (a) and (b).

This concept originated with German foresters a century ago and led to the commonly accepted planning goal of converting natural forests to the regulated condition, usually during the first rotation after management begins. Note from Figure 11.3a that the distribution of tree numbers by age class depends on the rotation selected. With the total area of the forest fixed, the longer the rotation, the fewer trees and the smaller the timber volume occurring in each age class. That is, if a rotation of length $t_2$ were substituted for $t_1$, the curve in Figure 11.3b showing the distribution of timber volume by age class would shift downward and be extended to the right.

A fully mature or virgin forest would have all trees at the same age and the total volume of standing timber would be the total rectangle of Figure 11.3b, considerably in excess of the timber volume of the regulated forest. The mature forest would have no net growth, losses from disease, rot, and blowdown equaling the slow growth of the old trees. With the rotation of $t_1$ decided on by some criterion, conversion to the fully regulated condition could proceed with the annual harvesting of a $1/t_1$ fraction of the standing volume each year. At the end of $t_1$ years, the forest would be under full regulation and capable of sustaining the same offtake indefinitely.

Similarly, an initially immature forest having no rotation-aged trees would not be cut until some trees reached rotation age, with the total harvest in any one year not exceeding the annual fully regulated harvest. This would lead to the fully regulated condition in $t_1$ years or less, depending on the initial age distribution.

There is no economic rationale for the "fully regulated forest." The

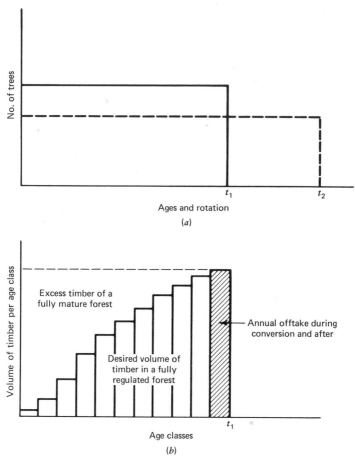

**Figure 11.3** Distributions of numbers of trees and volumes of timber by age classes in a fully regulated forest.

process of moving very gradually from the mature forest to the fully regulated condition (e.g., over one rotation of 50 to 100 years) can be quite costly in terms of interest on the large inventory of timber and in terms of the foregone rapid growth of the new plantings. The desirability of the fairly even flow of stumpage produced by the transition to regulated status would depend on timber market conditions and on other objectives of forest management such as sawmill community stability. If the stumpage harvested from the forest area in question constituted a large part of total supply, a rapid cutting of the mature forest might glut the market, greatly reducing the value of the timber and possibly disrupting other supply sources. On the other hand, if the volumes involved are relatively small, cutting more rapidly would be advantageous.

A formula frequently used in forest management for determining the "allowable cut" in the transition to fully regulated forest is the following:

$$(11.6.1) \qquad AC = \min\left( \frac{V - V^*}{C} + G,\, V \right)$$

where $V$ is the actual volume of rotation-aged timber, $V^*$ is the volume of rotation-aged timber desired under fully regulated conditions, $G$ is the existing annual growth, and $C$ is the conversion period (usually one rotation). For a mature, no-growth forest, the allowable cut is determined by $(V - V^*)/C$, say $(2.5 \times 10^6 \text{ bd ft} - 25{,}000 \text{ bd ft})/100 = 24{,}750$ bd ft per year. An immature forest with $V^* = 50{,}000$ bd ft per year would have sufficient growth but no salable timber ($V = 0$), so no cut would be taken. If, however, the two forests were merged for management purposes, the formula would indicate an allowable cut of $(2.5 \times 10^6 - 75{,}000)/100 + 25{,}000 = 49{,}250$ bd ft per year.

This formula, like the concept of the fully regulated forest, has no basis in economics nor in silviculture. It can lead to seemingly inconsistent results, as with the combining of forests above, and in U.S. national forest management practice is largely displaced by "nondeclining, even flow" requirements that have become the embodiment of "conservation and stability" in national forest timber management.

## 11.7.  UNANSWERED QUESTIONS AND FUTURE DEVELOPMENTS

There has been concern that timber harvesting practices are not more responsive to national and international wood products market conditions. Lumber prices and stumpage prices are notoriously unstable as illustrated in Figure 11.4. These fluctuations are largely due to very unstable markets for wood products, especially lumber for residential construction. Whenever prices shoot upward, there are public outcries to increase the timber harvest from the public lands and to prohibit exports of lumber and logs. Indeed, current legislation prohibits the export of logs cut from the national forests. The effect of this legislation has been to divert foreign demands for logs from the United States to Canada, taking up supplies that had formerly flowed to the United States. The net result at best is a negligible increase in supplies and a loss of foreign earnings.

To what extent should public forest management, especially in light

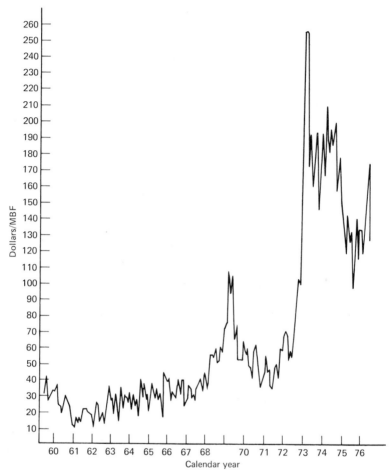

**Figure 11.4** Average stumpage prices for all timber sold by Department of Natural Resources, State of Washington, July 1959 to April 1976. Source: M. Clawson unpublished manuscript on forest management, October, 1976.

of its large inventories of mature timber, attempt to respond to or anticipate market price fluctuations? If one looks at national forest timber sales in relation to lumber price movements, there appears to be little relationship. However, timber sales contracts allow the buyer a span of several years to cut the timber. It has been shown[3] that the private firms do correlate their actual logging and sawmill operations with market conditions.

[3]Ronald Johnston, University of Washington Ph.D. dissertation, unpublished, 1976.

Regarding the long-term trends in timber prices, Barnett and Morse (1963) found a distinct upward trend in the relative price of forestry products as noted in Chapter 6. It is shown quite clearly in a recent Forest Service report[4] that the price of lumber has been increasing relative to the general price level at a trend rate of 1.5 percent per annum over the period 1800 to 1965. What does this imply for timber management—in particular for the optimum rotation? Without having to "do" any mathematics, we can reformulate the optimum rotation problem (11.3.1) and simply observe the results.

First, we bring price explicitly into the stumpage value function by letting $S(t) = pf(t)$ where $p$ is the net price per unit of timber and $f(t)$ is the physical yield function. If there is a continuous increase in stumpage prices at a continuous rate $\alpha$, one can write:

$$(11.7.1) \qquad p_k = p_0 e^{\alpha(t_1 + t_2 + \cdots + t_k)}$$

where $p_k$ is the price obtaining at the end of the $k$th rotation. Ignoring planting costs, the present value of an acre of forest can then be written:

$$(11.7.2) \quad PV(t_1, \ldots t_k, \ldots )$$
$$= p_1 f(t_1)e^{-\rho t_1} + \ldots + p_k f(t_k)e^{-\rho(t_1 + \cdots + t_k)} + \ldots$$
$$= p_0 f(t_1)e^{-(\rho - \alpha)t_1} + \ldots + p_0 f(t_k)e^{-(\rho - \alpha)(t_1 + \cdots t_k)} + \ldots$$

If we compare (11.7.2) to (11.3.1), we can see that the two problems would be identical if the rotations were required to be the same length, except that in (11.7.2) the "discount" rate is $(\rho - \alpha)$, the difference between the actual discount rate and the rate of stumpage price increase. Since it is already known that reducing the discount rate will increase the optimum rotation under most conditions, it can immediately be concluded that *a trend of increasing relative prices has the effect of progressively lengthening the optimum rotation.*

What is the relative price outlook for forest products and services in the future? On the supply side, it is clear from the earlier discussion of national forest management that a reallocation of management resources and a revision of harvest policies could substantially increase the sustainable output of timber on those lands. Spurr and Vaux[5] estimate the

[4]Forest Service, U.S. Dept. of Agriculture, *The Outlook for Timber in the United States*, Forest Resource Report No. 20, October 1973.
[5]Stephen H. Spurr and Henry J. Vaux, "Timber: Biological and Economic Potential," *Science*, February 20, 1976, Vol. 191, No. 4228, pp. 752–756.

biological potential from fully stocked productive[6] forest lands to be 29.1 × 10⁹ cu ft per year, and, with more intensive rational management, 34.6 × 10⁹ cu ft per year. They estimate the *economic* potential to be 29.4 × 10⁹ cu ft per year, but under existing institutional constraints and practices only 19.0 × 10⁹ cu ft per year could be harvested. These figures can be contrasted to the current harvest rate of about 14.0 × 10⁹ cu ft per year shown in Table 11.1.

Genetic improvements, in addition to steps mentioned earlier, promise substantial increases in productivity. The large forest products companies are investing large sums in "high-yield forestry," tree improvement programs aimed at speeding up growth and uniformity of trees. In the U.S. Northwest, seed orchards and grafting, practices begun only within the last decade, are replacing traditional cone gathering expeditions. The Weyerhaeuser Company expects to be producing seed for all their Douglas fir needs by 1984 instead of simply "growing wild trees."[7] They hope to double the growth rate, a task requiring at least four generations of firs, but which would imply an average rotation of 20 years instead of today's 80 years. Irrigation and fertilization are complementing these efforts.

On the demand side, total domestic demand has been projected to lie in the 19.0 to 29.4 × 10⁹ cu ft per year range, depending on timber prices, the prices of substitutes, and technological developments.[8] There is great current interest in *reversing* the trend of the past 100 years by substituting renewable resources for nonrenewables. Cellulose would be the base for many such substitutions, as in building materials, insulation, hydrocarbon stocks, and fuels. "Energy farms" where rapidly growing softwoods would be grown, quickly harvested, pulverized, and burned have been discussed.

A very important factor on the demand side is the demand for the nontimber forest services, especially recreation and esthetics, and the ways in which they are accommodated. Environmental constraints instigated by recreational activities and demands for wilderness preservation have already reduced harvests from public lands. The studies noted above conclude that improved policies to stimulate timber growth and to more rationally manage both the public forests and those private lands now being poorly managed would imply no acceleration in the rates of relative price change historically observed and only a modest tradeoff against recreational and esthetic values. A failure to change existing practices could double the rate of relative price change and exacerbate the conflicts between timbering and other forest uses.

[6]That is, "commercial" forests, those in Site Classes I–V.
[7]"Douglas Firs Grown in 'Orchards,'" *Vancouver Sun,* July 12, 1975, p. 26.
[8]Spurr and Vaux, op. cit.

# Chapter 12

# COMMON PROPERTY RESOURCES: THEORY AND EXAMPLES

The expression "common property resource" has already been used in the earlier parts of this book with only intuitive suggestions of the technical meaning of the term. Chapter 5 noted the difficulties of establishing markets for *in situ* resources when the *in situ* resources were of the common property type. The inability of a resource user to retain the cost savings from carrying *in situ* resources forward in a common pool situation was mentioned as one reason why private resource management decisions might not be socially efficient. The environmental effects of resource use often occur through the use of air or water bodies as waste sinks, and the capacities of those bodies to assimilate wastes have been referred to as common property resources.

Careful thought about these systems will uncover two conditions that create the "common property resource": (1) unrestricted access to the resource system by all those who care to use it, and (2) some type of adverse interaction among the users of the system (i.e., the creation of "externalities" among the users). If free access can be denied, then appropriate management of the resource can be exercised by the party denying access. If there is no adverse interaction among users, there is no reason to deny access. In either case, there would be no "common property resource problem."

The feature of unfettered access is shared to a significant degree by a wide spectrum of natural resource systems: the American bison on the open plains, minerals on the public lands, most international fisheries, underground oil pools and groundwater deposits not protected by specific laws, ambient air and water systems, the occurrence of congestion in unmanaged wilderness areas, and crowding on summer beaches. The problems associated with these resource systems have led to commonly heard phrases such as, "Everyone's property is no one's property"; "Get it (the resource) while the getting's good"; "Why should I save it, if my neighbors will just use it up?" The examples all evoke an image of the helplessness of the individual to achieve rational management of the resource and all involve a tendency to overuse the resource, to use it up too fast, or even to destroy a normally self-renewing system.

The nature of the externalities created by mutual use of a resource system can be thought of either in terms of the "direct interactions" occurring among the users, or as a situation of the common use of a fixed asset that produces diminishing returns to the variable inputs applied by the various users, that is, the "asset utilization approach."[1]

While these systems all share the characteristics of unlimited access and undefined or unassigned property rights, each also has some unique attributes that make the problem and likely remedies different for each system. These differences will be noted in the theory and examples to follow. These systems may also suffer from problems not stemming from the common property nature of the resource. A fishery, for example, may be overexploited or even destroyed because of its common property attributes. However, a fishery managed by a (privately) rational monopolist may also be targeted for destruction through overfishing by the monopolist for reasons having nothing to do with the potential common property attributes of the resource.

This use of the term "common property resources" has become traditional in economics, but it is at variance with legal terminology and its meaning in several other disciplines. Common property (*res communes*) as developed in the English common law, the German land law, and Roman law refers to a distribution of property rights in a resource system where a well-defined set of users has a well-defined (not necessarily equal) rights to use the resource, while all potential users not belonging to that set are excluded. Under such systems of property rights, many natural resource systems have been well managed on a sustainable yield basis for hundreds of years, for example, the hunting resources of various primitive peoples, the still existing English and Welsh commons, the Alpine meadows of Bavaria, Switzerland, and Au-

---

[1]Mohring and Boyd have developed these two approaches to the conceptualization of externalities in "Analyzing 'Externalities': 'Direct Interaction' *versus* 'Asset Utilization' Frameworks," *Economica*, November 1971, pp. 347–361.

stria, and the many high-quality streams under strict English and German riparian doctrine.[2]

Ciriacy-Wantrup and Bishop (1975) provide a very clear differentiation between the usual economic use of the term (*res nullius* or unowned resources) and the *res communes* concept, presenting a valuable discussion of historically successful management institutions under *res communes*. Our further discussions will be concerned with the open access or *res nullius* type of resource system.

## 12.1  THE ANALYTICS OF THE STATIC COMMON PROPERTY PROBLEM[3]

Consider an open access resource the exploitation of which proves beneficial to independent entrepreneurs who find themselves in a competitive industry setting, both in terms of extraction of the resource and in terms of its later sale to customers. We propose to look at the operation of such a system in terms of its likely equilibrium tendencies compared to its socially optimum management. The analysis will be in terms of comparative statics, that is, snapshots of the system as it would exist in equilibrium and at its social optimum without consideration of the time paths of the system when displaced from these points. Figure 12.1 exhibits the important features of such a system. The periodic rate of output (per season, per day, etc.) is $X$, $TC(X)$ represents the total cost as a function of $X$, $TWP(X)$ the total willingness of customers to pay for the output, and $TR_i(X)$ the total revenue accruing to all firms at a particular product price level. $TC(X)$ is shown with increasing steepness, indicating increasing marginal costs of expanding the periodic output rate, possibly because of crowding at the resource site (crowding externalities) or because the resource stock is (temporarily) drawn down to a lower level, increasing the marginal recovery effort. All firms operate at the same marginal cost level since they are assumed to be profit maximizers facing the same product price. $TWP(X)$ is shown increasing at a decreasing rate, measuring the total area under the demand curve for $X$.

[2]Riparian doctrine refers to a system of water law guaranteeing access to use of water to owners of land bordering water bodies, while restricting consumptive use and pollution to levels not having adverse impacts on other such landowners.

[3]The first three sections are based on Haveman's fine exposition of the common property resources problem (1973). We have chosen to include congestion and pollution in the set of common property problems.

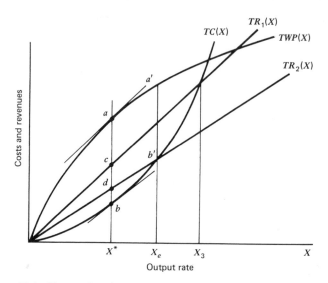

**Figure 12.1** The static common property model. Source: Adapted from Haveman (1973), Fig. 1.

The socially optimum rate of output, $X^*$, is characterized by the equal slopes of the $TC$ and $TWP$ functions or, in more familiar words, as the output rate at which marginal cost, $TC'(X)$, equals price, $TWP'(X)$. For this rate of output to be purchased by customers and to induce this rate of production from the firms, price must be set at $TWP'(X^*)$. Total revenues that would accrue from the various $X$ values if this price obtained are shown by $TR_1(X)$. If $X^*$ could be induced or enforced, society would gain the amount $ab$ from the utilization of the resource, $ac$ accruing as consumers' surplus and $cb$ as producers' (economic) profit. Since $TC(X)$ includes the going rate of return on invested capital, $cb$ is pure, or excess, profit.

Will the market move the various firms to an aggregate output of $X^*$? Since price has been equated to the firm's marginal cost, each *existing* firm is maximizing its profit. $X^*$ appears to be a stable competitive equilibrium, except that a pure economic profit is being generated. Price theory tells us that competitive equilibrium is characterized by zero pure profit. What is the difference between the usual competitive equilibrium and the situation at $X^*$?

The explanation lies in $TC(X)$ and the nature of the property rights in the resource. The early units of $X$ recovered each period are recovered at relatively low cost. They earn a "rent" or excess profit, while the last units produced earn their firms no profit because marginal cost has risen to equal price. If the firms constituting the industry at $X^*$ shared among themselves the *exclusive right of access* to the resource, they would, indeed, protect this rent on the early units of production by refusing to expand output and by either refusing admission to any more firms or by selling out to new firms only at a price equal to the capitalized value of the rents being earned. Any firm buying into the industry at this price would experience only the going rate of return on its total investment, so there would be no motivation for an expansion of the number of firms. Under the usual private property situation, this is exactly what would happen.

However, the firms that would exist at $X^*$ cannot keep other firms out, simply because of open access to the resource. Other firms, observing the excess profits being made in this particular resource, are attracted to enter the industry, expanding the rate of output beyond $X^*$. While each new entrant would very much like to become a member of the club and prevent further entry, they cannot block other firms from getting in. As output expands, price must fall to induce customers to take more. As long as $TR$ exceeds $TC$, entry of new capacity will continue. Equilibrium will finally be established at $X_e$.

If we compare $X_e$ with $X^*$, three things stand out: (1) producers' profits, $cb$, have been eliminated; (2) consumers' surplus has expanded; (3) the total surplus of $TWP$ over $TC$ has shrunk. Net benefits to society from exploiting the resource have not been eliminated if the picture is that of Figure 12.1. However, if the resources in question were only a small part of a larger resource system (as a regional ocean fishery in relation to oceanic catches) so that the relevant $TWP$ curve was, in fact, $TR_1(X)$, then equilibrium would be established at $X_3$ where *all* net benefits to society from the regional resource have been eliminated.

To summarize, the absence of the usual property rights in the common property resource system prevents the establishment of the usual competitive equilibrium and permits the profits that would exist at the optimum rate of output to attract excess capital to the industry. This inflow of excess capital continues until costs have risen sufficiently and prices have fallen sufficiently that all pure profits are eliminated. The remaining net benefits to society may be positive or zero, depending on the demand curve for the product, but will surely be less than at $X^*$.

Policy prescriptions to rectify such divergences will be discussed later in the chapter.

## 12.2. CONGESTION OF FACILITIES AS A CASE OF COMMON PROPERTY RESOURCE MANAGEMENT

Congestion occurs in many forms, from rush hour traffic to crowding at the beach. In the natural resources field, congestion is of greatest importance in connection with outdoor recreation, a problem that will be discussed in detail in a later chapter. At this point, we want to analyze the structural differences between congestion and the archetypal common property resource problem analyzed in the previous section.

Congestion can be thought of as mutual interference among units using a common facility. The interference can be of a physical type where units physically obstruct each other, making their production functions interdependent, as with vehicles on a highway, airplanes at an airport, or ships in a harbor. The interference can also take the form of negative psychological effects from proximity of units even when physical movements are in no way interdependent. The prime example would be the degradation of the perceived quality of a wilderness recreation experience caused by the sighting or passing of other persons.

The common facility being used is frequently provided by the public sector, although this is not at all necessary. Common examples would be highways, harbors, airports, beaches, parks, sidewalks, and wilderness areas. A necessary condition is that the "capacity" of the common facility not be expandable in the short run in response to changing user demands.

Suppose congestion in the form of frequent encounters, near misses, and crowded landings is occurring on a stream used by recreational canoers. The negative impact is primarily on the utilities of the users, on their enjoyment, and (in quantitative terms) on their willingness to pay for such recreation. The actual money costs of the canoers are little affected if at all. Another contrasting example is found on the Upper Mississippi River, which is used almost exclusively by commercial barge tows carrying bulk commodities long distances. They must travel the navigable channels of the river and pass through the locks at each dam. At surprisingly low levels of traffic, they begin to interfere with one another, especially through crowding or queueing at the locks where long waits can occur while other barge tows are being served. While this congestion may involve some psychic costs for the tow captains as they slip their flotillas past one another, its primary effect is directly on operating costs.

Thus, the costs of congestion can best be pictured as a reduction in willingness to pay for use of the facility if the negative effects impact primarily consumers' utility functions, but as an increase in system costs if the service being generated is an intermediate good. Our attention is now briefly directed to the latter case.

Figure 12.2 shows the total willingness to pay for the use of the facility *in its uncongested state*, $TWP(X)$. $TC_1(X)$ shows the total variable operating cost of the facility as a function of the rate of use (traffic flow),

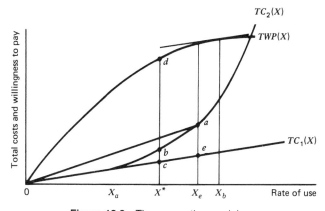

**Figure 12.2** The congestion model.

$X$. These costs are initially borne by the public operators of the facility, but may be passed on to the users through a user charge. $TC_2(X)$ shows that, beyond the threshold level $X_a$, costs in addition to system operating costs begin to develop—congestion costs in the form of greater times of transit and possibly higher accident rates. The congestion costs accrue to the individual user units. In the absence of congestion, $X_b$ would be the optimum level of use, where marginal system operating costs equal the marginal willingness to pay.

It is quickly seen that the socially optimum level of use of the facility is $X^*$, where the slopes of $TWP$ and $TC_2$ are equal, that is, where marginal willingness to pay equals marginal cost. If we assume that a user charge equal to marginal operating cost of the facility is assessed against each user, then users pay $cX^*$ to the facility, mutually incur $bc$ in congestion costs, and enjoy net benefits of $db$.

Will users be motivated to stop expanding use of the system at $X^*$? If we assume that congestion equally affects all users and that the same user charge is assessed against all users, each user experiences the *average variable costs* of using the system rather than the marginal cost. Graphically, average variable cost is shown by the slope of the chord drawn from the origin, $O$, to any point on $TC_2(X)$. It can be seen that for all $X$ greater than $X_a$, this slope is *less* than the slope of $TC_2$. Thus users will continue to expand use of the system until the marginal willingness to pay, $TWP'$, equals average variable cost. Such a point is reached at $X_e$ where total net benefits are less and congestion costs more than at $X^*$.

Thus, the uniqueness of the congestion type common property resource problem is not excessive use, but that this excessive use is caused by the failure of the user to take cognizance of the full marginal costs their use imposes on the system, that is, the excess of marginal cost over average variable costs.

## 12.3.   ENVIRONMENTAL POLLUTION AS A CASE OF COMMON PROPERTY RESOURCE MANAGEMENT

The ambient environment, especially the ambient air and water bodies but also the broad visual field, constitutes a common property resource for waste disposal under most (but not all) legal systems. Historically, all parties have been free to put smoke and fumes into the air, wastes of all types into water bodies, and to disrupt the scenery with road cuts, spoils piles, forest clear-cuts, and view-blocking structures. These uses of the environment have been limited by legal liabilities for directly caused probable damages, but the common law concept of liability was both very narrow and required very direct causation. With hundreds of polluters and hundreds of parties sustaining damages from pollution, what damage could be attributed to any one polluter? If users of the environment are in direct conflict (e.g., the air for disposal of smoke and for breathing), which use takes precedence?

The pollution-type common property problem differs from the two types analyzed earlier in that conflict of interest exists between two usually distinct sets of parties: the pollutors and the damaged parties (receptors of the diffused pollution). In the archetypal excess entry problem of Section 12.1, the basic conflict is between producers who are already exploiting the common property resource and those who want to enter to share in the excess profits. In the congestion case, the conflict is among users of the common facility. In both, some information, albeit inadequate, concerning the effects of their decisions is fed back through the market or the physical system to the users of the system. This feedback tends to limit the overuse of the system, usually to a level at which some net benefits continue to accrue to society. In the pollution case, the dominant unidirectional movements of the environmental media frequently make significant feedback unlikely. While interesting exceptions exist, polluters tend to be upstream or upwind and receptors downstream. They are largely nonoverlapping groups. In Figure 12.3, $X$ represents a product the production of which causes pollution damaging to third parties. $TC_1$ represents privately born production costs, while $TC_2$ incorporates damage from pollution. The optimum rate of production would be at some point, $X^*$, where $TWP' = TC_2'$. In a competitive market system not having constraints on waste disposal in the environ-

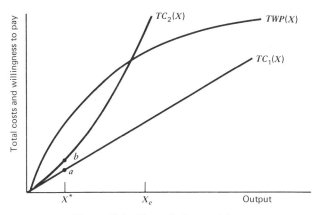

**Figure 12.3**   The pollution model.

ment, the private firms will equate marginal production costs to price, that is, $TC'_1 (X) = TWP'(X)$ at $X_e$.

While optimum management of pollution usually calls for some pollution to occur (as at $X^*$), the unconstrained market equilibrium may involve such a great level of pollution that net benefits to society from the activity are actually negative, as they are at $X_e$. The pollution-type common property problem can thus lead to a net social loss from use of the resource.

## 12.4.   POLICY TOOLS FOR IMPROVING THE MANAGEMENT OF COMMON PROPERTY RESOURCES

All the common property resource problems involve an overuse or excessive exploitation of the resource that is traceable to the existence of some type of negative externality, that is, a cost neither born nor taken into account by the decision maker. When such externalities occur within the setting of a market economy that relies primarily on prices to motivate appropriate patterns of resource allocation, taxes naturally suggest themselves as tools for correcting these inefficiencies. Taxes become private costs to the producer but, of course, do not represent real resource costs to the economy. They will affect producers' behavior and, insofar as they are passed on to the customer, will affect customers' behavior, too. Since externalities and costs incurred to reduce externalities are real costs of production, it is desirable that they be reflected in the prices of goods.

A prime example of the archetypal common property problem of Section 12.1 is the fishery. The fishery in fact combines the problem of excessive entry of resources seeking to capture the excess profits with two types of congestion—physical congestion in the fishing area and the so-called stock externality. The first is self-explanatory and is frequently read about in the press: trawlers cutting each others' nets on the Newfoundland Banks, collisions in the fog, confusion over the ownership of nets and lobster pots, and the like. These problems are perfectly analogous to highway congestion: each vessel knows it will add to the congestion but will have to bear only a small part of the costs it creates. The stock externality results from the fact that harvesting costs increase as the stock of fish is reduced. The time and effort required to capture a certain poundage of fish increase as the stock becomes smaller and more dispersed.

Referring to Figure 12.1, appropriate behavior could be motivated by levying a unit tax on the quantity of fish harvested, so that increases in output beyond $X^*$ would become unattractive. This tax would be set so that the total tax bill on the production of $X^*$ units of fish would amount to $cb$. $TC(X)$ would be shifted upward at each point by $tX$. The tax would siphon off the excess profits and avoid the excessive investment of resources. Note that the real costs of harvesting $X^*$ are not affected by the tax.

Fisheries management practices have not included taxes on the harvest, possibly because of administrative problems with assessing and collecting the tax. Three tools have been used to push the harvest toward $X^*$: limitations on the fishing season, restrictions on the types of equipment permitted, and, more recently, licensing all fishing vessels with a strict limit on the number permitted.

Let us compare the effects of each of these controls with the effects of a tax. The effect of a limited season is to induce fishermen to get their catch while they can. To do so, physically more efficient equipment is put to work: more powerful boats, power-assisted net handling, bigger nets, and possibly more boats. The attempt is to sustain the previous catch within the shorter season. If the limited season *is* effective in reducing the catch to $X^*$, the net result has been to produce the lower catch at a higher cost with more equipment now standing idle a larger part of the year.

The results of restricting permissible equipment are much the same. We have all looked with admiration on the little sailboats called "skipjacks" that are used in harvesting oysters in Chesapeake Bay. They are powered only by sail, are limited to their traditional size, and are permitted only a limited crew. The same annual catch could be taken by many fewer men and boats if modern technology were permitted. Its prohibi-tion is used as a tool to restrict the catch by driving $TC(X)$ up, so that catches will fall towards $X^*$. *These cost increases are real, in contrast to the tax,* again resulting in a lower catch at higher cost. Fishermens' incomes are driven toward poverty levels.

The control of congestion through taxes or appropriate (time of day) pricing is seldom observed in practice. Figure 12.2 shows that a unit tax $t$, imposed on the users of the facility whenever the rate of use exceeds $X_a$, could be designed to reflect the excess of marginal over average cost at $X^*$. By this device, users would perceive the correct marginal costs at $X^*$ and would adjust their decisions accordingly. In practice, congestion is permitted to choke off further use at $X_e$, so that total congestion costs become $ae$ rather than the smaller, optimal amount $bc$. Administrative difficulties are often cited as reasons for not imposing appropriate prices or taxes, but parking taxes, toll road fees, and tunnel and bridge fees are widely used for other purposes. They could be used to reflect and con-trol congestion.

Finally, in the control of pollution, economists have long recom-mended effluent taxes. Recently, several countries in Europe have im-posed such taxes, but practice in the United States remains tied to quan-titative limitations on effluent loads, the imposition of certain abatement technologies (e.g., the "best practicable" practices imposed on industry for 1978 and the "best available" to be required by 1983), and subsidizing traditional collective treatment facilities. With reference to Figure 12.3, an appropriate effluent tax structure would make the marginal cost born by producers correspond to $TC'(X^*)$.

The utilization of effluent taxes has some administrative com-plexities. Contrary to many assertions, it would be necessary to monitor polluters just as much as under current effluent standard systems, un-less the Dutch system is adopted. The Dutch government has a standard "model" of each type of polluter: municipal, industrial, and agricultural. The model specifies a particular technology and specific relationship between product output and pollution. Given knowledge of the firm's output, a charge is levied on the basis of the standard model's indicated waste discharge. If the firm claims that its waste discharge performance is better than the standard model, it must prove it, including the installa-tion of appropriate monitoring systems. If a firm discharges more waste than predicted, it probably would not admit it to the pollution authority, but the continuing charges give it an incentive to find ways of abating its pollution load, especially if the charges are high.

Although effluent taxes may present administrative difficulties, it can be persuasively argued that their long-term results would be a much more effective, lower-cost program of environmental protection than under current practices. Effluent *standards* that are usually uniform for all polluters of a given class (e.g., paper firms, canning plants, etc.) fail on at least two grounds: (1) they will not achieve a given reduction in pollution at minimum cost since the costs of cleanup will be different for different polluters; (2) they provide no continuing incentive to pursue further abatement once the original standard has been reached. Requiring the adoption of particular abatement technologies will also result in a more costly abatement program since it fails to utilize internal process changes that frequently are the least-cost abatement method.

For a more detailed treatment of the economics of environmental management, consult one of the many good elementary books such as Freeman, Haveman, and Kneese (1973) or an advanced theoretical work such as Baumol and Oats (1975). Kneese and Schultze (1975) provide a splendid critique of U.S. policy.

## 12.5. MORE ON CONGESTION IN NATURAL RESOURCE SYSTEMS

Subsequent chapters are devoted to further study of the archetypal common property problem exemplified by fisheries and water resources systems. This section presents further consideration of congestion-type problems in natural resource systems: congestion in recreation areas and in river transportation systems.

As noted in Section 12.2, congestion in recreation areas is an increasing problem, especially in wilderness areas where much of the pleasure from the experience comes from a sense of isolation. One frequently hears the term "carrying capacity" applied to recreation areas in a way similar to the use of that term in wildlife or range management: a continuing or periodic rate of use that is consistent with the maintenance of the long-term productivity of the resource. In wilderness applications, the term refers to an intensity and pattern of use that will not seriously diminish the quality of the recreational experience and that is consistent with the preservation of the ecological integrity of the area. We suggest a more precise, formal definition of "recreational carrying capacity."[4]

Let *WP* represent the typical individual willingness to pay for recreational use of an area such as a standard backpacking trip. Let *E* be the

---

[4]This presentation is similar to that of Cicchetti and Smith in "Congestion, Quality Deterioration, and Optimal Use: Wilderness Recreation in the Spanish Peaks Primitive Area," *Social Science Research,* Vol. 2, No. 1, March 1973, pp. 15–30.

number of encounters with other parties—assumed to reduce the quality of the experience.[5] If $N$ represents the number of parties actually in the area, the following relationships can be empirically estimated:

(12.5.1) $\qquad WP = f(E)$ such that $f'(E) < 0$

(12.5.2) $\qquad E = g(N)$ such that $g'(N) > 0$

Assume also the existence of some ecological constraints that it seems wise to observe and that relate to the intensity of use of the area, for example,

(12.5.3) $\qquad\qquad\qquad h_1(N) \leq b_1$
$$h_2(N) \leq b_2$$

The problem of managing the area for recreation in a socially optimum manner can then be formalized as maximizing the total willingness to pay for use of the area, subject to these ecological constraints, that is,

(12.5.4) $\qquad \max_{N} \{\theta(N) \equiv WP \cdot N = f[g(N)] \cdot N\}$

$\qquad$ subject to: $h_1(N) \leq b_1$
$$\qquad\qquad\qquad h_2(N) \leq b_2$$

The solution to this problem, $N^*$, can be called the optimal carrying capacity and is derived not simply from ecological considerations (as some insist should be done) but also from human use considerations.

A relationship like (12.5.1) can be derived from user surveys, and (12.5.2) can be derived from simulations of paths of movement at different intensities of use. The U.S. Forest Service has developed computer simulation models of several forest recreation areas to study these issues.

Our second example is drawn from the various uses of the interior rivers of the country. Rivers are natural resource systems of many uses: irrigation, municipal and industrial water supply, hydroelectric power, recreation, waste disposal, and transportation. Chapter 14 discusses the fascinating policy problems and analytical methods relating to water resources generally but here we treat just the problem of waterway transport congestion.

The rivers of the world carry vast quantities of goods and comprise

---

[5]Survey studies show this definitely to be true.

**Table 12.1.** Inputs, Outputs, and Delay Costs of a Three-Dam River System

| Expected Arrival Rates per Day Up | Down | Total Tows into System in 31 Days (Actual) | Total System Delay Cost over 31 Days | Average Delay Cost per Tow into System | Marginal Delay Cost per Tow |
|---|---|---|---|---|---|
| 10 | 10 | 598 | $22,900 | $38 | — |
| 12 | 12 | 736 | 36,800 | 50 | $101 |
| 14 | 14 | 854 | 68,000 | 80 | 265 |
| 16 | 16 | 987 | 118,000 | 120 | 382 |
| 18 | 18 | 1092 | 217,400 | 199 | 938 |
| 20 | 20 | 1214 | 587,600 | 484 | 3035 |

Source: Howe *et al.*, 1969, Table 17, p. 90. Resources for the Future, Inc. Reprinted with permission.

perhaps the most picturesque transport systems ever developed. Who cannot spend days watching the ebb and flow of commerce on such wonders as the Rhine, the Danube, the Chao Phraya, the Ganges, the Mekong, or the Mississippi? In the United States and increasingly on the Rhine and Danube, modern pusher-type towboat technology is replacing colorful diversity and river transport is becoming an efficient, highly capital intensive system requiring careful planning both by the government agencies that design and operate the waterways and by the transport firms whose barge flotillas and towboats use them. Congestion at the dams where the tows must pass through locks is a major management issue.

A river transportation simulation model created by Howe, Carroll, and Steinberg[6] has been used to study system performance as the basis for estimating the benefits from undertaking waterway improvements. A major benefit stemming from improvements to channels, locks, dams, and navigation systems on heavily used waterways is the reduction in delay costs to the tows using the system. That these delay costs are not trivial is demonstrated by Table 12.1, which presents results of a realistic simulation of a section of the Ohio River under 1966 conditions. Note also the increasing divergence between average delay cost per tow coming into the system and the marginal delay cost per tow. The relationship of these costs to the determination of equilibrium and optimum traffic flows is best illustrated by Figure 12.4, an alternative to Figure 12.2. The $ADC_1$ function is given numerically by column 5 of Table 12.1,

[6]Charles W. Howe, Joseph L. Carroll, et al., *Inland Waterway Transportation*, Baltimore: Johns Hopkins Press, 1969.

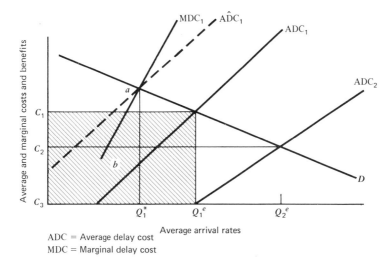

**Figure 12.4** Determination of optimum and equilibrium traffic flows. Source: Howe et al., Fig. 16, p. 87. Resources for the Future, Inc. Reprinted with permission.

while $MDC_1$ is given by column 6. The likely equilibrium level is greater than the optimum, $Q_1^*$, and the costs of exceeding $Q_1^*$ by relatively small numbers can be very large, as we have seen in Table 12.1.

The introduction of a user charge per tow equal to $ab$ would shift the users' perceived average cost curve to $A\hat{D}C_1$, discouraging use beyond $Q_1^*$. Again, appropriate pricing could greatly improve the efficient use of our waterways by reducing excessive delays, saving the waterways' transport capacities for those carriers to whom it has greatest value, and delaying the need for investments in new capacity.

Chapter 13

# THE MANAGEMENT OF FISHERIES: A CASE OF RENEWABLE BUT DESTRUCTIBLE COMMON PROPERTY RESOURCES

The fisheries of the world have received a lot of popular attention in recent years as concern about permanent destruction of fish stocks and related marine mammals (especially the whales and porpoises) has mounted. Another major concern has been the distribution of the benefits from exploitation of marine fisheries: who should have access to the fisheries? The extended attempts of the United Nations to deal with these issues and the failure of the Law of the Sea Conferences to arrive at internationally acceptable arrangements have led many nations unilaterally to declare extended offshore boundaries for exclusive control of economic activities, usually out to 200 miles.

These steps are only the latest in a long history of attempts to manage both internal and international fisheries. The situation in the United States is nowhere better described than in Christy's foreward to Crutchfield and Pontecorvo's well-known study of the Pacific salmon fisheries:[1]

[1]James A. Crutchfield and Giulio Pontecorvo (1969), p. v. with permission of the Johns Hopkins University Press, publisher.

Fisheries in the United States are beset by senseless restrictions and marked by obsolescence, waste, and poverty. The contribution of fishermen to the national economy is negligible. Their total catch of all species is lower now than it was before the Second World War. And there is little hope for change—unless dramatically new institutions and new forms of management can be developed and adopted.

The fundamental cause of waste is open access to the stocks. Where resources are unowned or the common property of a community, there are no controls over access; no means for allocating or restricting inputs of capital and labor; and no way of preventing declining yields and the disappearance of net revenues to the industry.

Crutchfield and Pontecorvo characterized natural resources management and fisheries in particular as an aspect of what economists call capital theory:[2]

> ... Clearly, optimal time rates of use involve both efficient conversion of part of the existing stock to current economic output, and the appropriate reservation of part of the stock for production of future supplies.

Our central theme is that rational fishery management must evolve from the objective of maximizing the net economic yield of the resource. One reason for this approach is that the traditional definition of regulatory objectives in purely physical terms has left conservation authorities vulnerable to political pressures by denying them a vital basis for choice. The vulnerability comes about in the following way: a fishery shows biological evidence of "overfishing," i.e., aggregate yields may fall, the amplitude of annual oscillations in yield may increase, or—more probably—both phenomena are observed. At the same time, generally in response to an improvement in earnings as a result of a positive income elasticity of demand, fishing effort is increased. In order to protect the resource, the administrative body created to deal with the problem of "overfishing" must reduce fishing mortality. Since the fishery is an open access resource, it is impossible under current conditions to reduce effort by restricting the inputs. The regulators cannot stop more people using more equipment from going fishing. In this situation, the obvious alternative is to reduce progressively the efficiency of the individual inputs and thereby reduce the pressure exerted on the resource by a growing number of fishing units. ... It is important to realize that the need for regulation of open access fisheries arises from economic reactions of profit-seeking units.

---

[2]Ibid., pp. 4–8 with editorial additions and deletions as noted.

If this fact is realized, a simple, consistent, and readily enforceable program can be developed.

The setting for any management of salmon resources is both physical and institutional. On one side is a set of complex biological problems: How is it possible to manage the population dynamics of an organism that lives in an environment over which the biologist has little control in order to approximate a chosen level of physical yield from the resource? On the other side, the question arises: How can this be accomplished within the constraints of a given set of legal and social institutions, which lead in the absence of intervention, to gross inefficiency and waste in the use of both human and physical capital? Clearly, any meaningful solution for the problems of a commercial fishery must account for both these facets of its structure.

In keeping with this admonition, we will develop several relatively simple models of the biological and economic dimensions of the fishery that help us understand the nature of the problems faced and the efficacy of various proposals for improved policy.

## 13.1.  BASIC BIOLOGICAL RELATIONSHIPS

In an undeveloped (unfished) fishery, the distribution of fish numbers by age would be like that shown in Figure 13.1. Mortality from predation and disease continually cut away at the population. If fishing is introduced using a technique that would capture only fish of a specific size or larger, the distribution of Figure 13.1 would be truncated at $A_1$. As age increases, average size also increases, but some age is reached for a given year-class (those fish spawned in a given year) at which the predations of age more than offset the increase in individual size. The year-class achieves its maximum biomass at this point, as shown in Figure 13.2. If fish of a given year-class were of identical sizes, net mesh size could be adjusted to catch only fish of age $A_2$ or greater. After initial

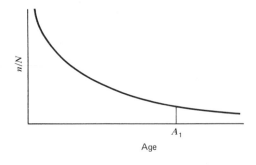

**Figure 13.1**  Age distribution of a fish population.

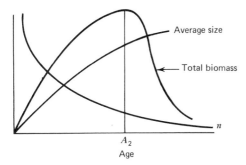

**Figure 13.2** Size, biomass, and number as functions of year-class age.

development of the fishery, this would mean that a sustainable annual catch equaling the maximum biomass could be approached as the annual fishing effort is expanded to screen the entire region containing the population. If we let the capital-labor input, $L(t)$, stand for the input of boats, human inputs, the fuel, this idealized catch-effort relationship would appear as the top curve in Figure 13.3. That is, as $L(t)$ is expanded without limit, sweeping the entire region containing the fish population, a catch approaching the maximal biomass of the $A_2$ year-class would be approached.

Of course, it may not be economically efficient to allow each year-class to attain its maximum biomass, just as it was shown to be uneconomic to allow a stand of trees to grow to maximum volume.

In fact, increasing effort may tend to disperse the fish and interfere with reproduction. Smaller, younger fish, perhaps including those upon whom reproduction depends, are increasingly caught or injured. Thus, a realistic catch-effort curve would look like the lower ones of Figure 13.3. A larger fish stock generally makes a given catch level easier, so if $S_1 > S_2$ the $R_0[L, S_1]$ curve will lie above $R_0[L, S_2]$.

The next important relation is the growth law of the population or

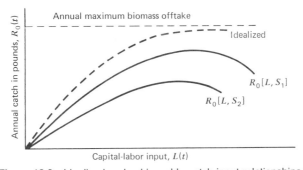

**Figure 13.3** Idealized and achieveable catch-input relationships.

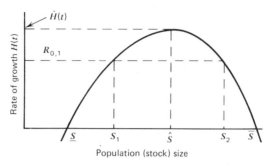

**Figure 13.4**   The stock-growth relation.

stock, which can generally be written $H(t) = h[S(t), \ldots]$, indicating that growth is a function of the stock and certain other variables, in a way analogous to the "exploration production function" of Chapter 10. In all cases, the general shape of the growth curve is like that of Figure 13.4. There are two levels of stocks at which the unfished population reaches zero growth, $\underline{S}$ and $\overline{S}$. A fish population in equilibrium with its natural environment would reach $\overline{S}$, a point where competition for nutrients reduces the aggregate growth in numbers and size to equality with losses from natural mortality and predation. It should be noted that $\overline{S}$ is a *stable* equilibrium point in that any displacement of $S$ to the left or right of $\overline{S}$ sets up forces to return $S$ to its $\overline{S}$ value. To the right of $\overline{S}$, overcrowding causes $H(t)$ to become negative, while $H(t)$ becomes positive for $S$ less than $\overline{S}$.

Interestingly, $\underline{S}$ is an *unstable* equilibrium point. If $S$ precisely equals $\underline{S}$, the population will remain at that size, but a slight perturbation to the right starts positive growth, while a leftward perturbation sends the population toward zero, usually because the reproductive capacity of a small dispersed population is insufficient to offset natural losses.

$\hat{S}$ is the stock associated with the maximum natural growth rate, $\hat{H}(t)$. This growth rate represents the greatest rate of catch which could be sustained indefinitely, that is, without reducing the population. Fisheries biologists refer to $\hat{H}(t)$ as the "maximum sustainable yield" of the fishery and have historically espoused the achievement of $\hat{H}(t)$ as the goal of good fisheries' management. We will investigate this matter later.

Assume that a catch rate of $R_0, [0 < R_0 < \hat{H}(t)]$, has been established. Figure 13.4 shows us that this rate of offtake is consistent with two population sizes, $S_1$ and $S_2$. $S_2$ is economically superior to $S_1$ because the effort (and thus the cost) of catch rate $R_0$ will be less with the larger population (see Figure 13.3).

## 13.2.  AN EXAMPLE OF A STATIC FISHERIES MANAGEMENT MODEL

Crutchfield and Pontecorvo (1969) present a model of the Pacific salmon fishery which, while somewhat specialized to the conditions of that anadromous fishery, is very similar to other widely used fisheries models. While the model is static (as contrasted with our basic resources model in Chapters 5 and 10), it permits us to illustrate many of the important insights gained through many decades of fisheries study. The first relation is the stock-growth relation:

$$(13.2.1) \qquad\qquad H(t) = k_1 S(\bar{S} - S)$$

If we plot this relation as in Figure 13.4, we find that $\underline{S} = 0$ and $\hat{S} = \bar{S}/2$. Furthermore, $\hat{H}(t) = k_1 \, \bar{S}^2/4$ [found by substituting $\hat{S}$ for $S$ in (13.2.1)].

The second relation is the production function for fishing operations, often called the "catch-effort" relation:

$$(13.2.2) \qquad\qquad R_0(t) = k_2 L(t) \cdot S(t)$$

If we interpret $L(t)$ as an index of total inputs, this relation implies that *cost* increases linearly with catch and inversely with stock size, an obvious simplification of the more general relation illustrated in Figure 13.3.

This static model permits an analysis of management schemes in which the stock, $S$, is maintained at a constant level. Such management schemes are often called "steady state" schemes because of the constant stock. In such cases the natural rate of growth, $H(t)$, must just offset the catch, $R_0(t)$. If we set (13.2.1) equal to (13.2.2), we can quickly determine that there are two stock levels at which this condition holds:

$$(13.2.3) \qquad\qquad S_e = \begin{cases} 0 \\ \bar{S} - \dfrac{k_2}{k_1} L(t) \end{cases}$$

Obviously, $S_e = 0$ is not a desirable steady state, so the second value is the relevant one. The steady-state production function, that is, the constant stock catch-effort relation, is gotten by substituting $S_e$ into (13.2.2), which yields

$$(13.2.4) \qquad\qquad R_0(t) = k_2 L(t) \bar{S} - \dfrac{k_2^2}{k_1} L(t)^2$$

This quadratic function is plotted in Figure 13.5.

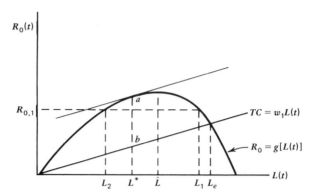

**Figure 13.5** Constant stock catch-effort relation.

What is the optimum level of fishing activity under steady-state conditions? In terms of Figure 13.4, what is the optimum stock level? In terms of Figure 13.5, what is the optimum level of capital-labor input? Note that if we fix the value of $S_e(t)$, the corresponding level of $L(t)$ is thereby determined [see (13.2.3)]. If we set the level of $L(t)$, the corresponding steady-state stock is determined. Looking at Figure 13.4, we see that *two* stock levels are consistent with each feasible level of catch, for example, $S_1$ and $S_2$ each are consistent with catch level $R_{0,1}$. However, as we can see by looking at Figure 13.5, it takes different quantities of capital-labor, $L(t)$, to produce $R_{0,1}$ with different stocks. It is clearly cheaper to produce $R_{0,1}$ with $L_2$ (which is the input requirement corresponding to $S_2$) than with $L_1$ (which corresponds to the smaller stock, $S_1$). Thus, we see that:

> *Steady-State Result 1:*
> from the point of view of minimizing current fishing cost for a given level of output, stocks greater than $\hat{S}$ are preferred to stocks less than $\hat{S}$.

Consider Figure 13.5 once again. The marginal productivity of the capital-labor input, $L(t)$, clearly falls as $L(t)$ increases. Since $L(t)$ is not free, the marginal cost of the catch rises without limit as the marginal product drops to zero at $\hat{L}(t)$. Since $\hat{L}(t)$ is the input level required to obtain the "maximum sustainable yield," we can thus draw the following important conclusion for steady-state fisheries management:

> *Steady-state Result 2:*
> as long as the inputs used in fishing are scarce (cost > zero), it does not pay to extend the catch rate to the maximum sustainable yield.

Figure 13.5 can be used to illustrate an additional important result, at least for a special case. Assume the price of fish to be fixed and equal to 1. Let $w$ be the cost of a unit of $L(t)$, measured in the same value units as the price of fish. Then the curve in the figure represents the total value of the fish or the total revenue derived by the fisherman from the sale of the catch. The straight line, $TC = w \cdot L(t)$, represents total cost. The distance between the two represents (in this simple case) the value of this fishery to society and the profits being experienced by the fisherman. These net benefits will be maximized at a point where this distance is greatest (also the point where the slopes of the two curves are equal), $L^*(t)$. At this point, a net benefit or profit is being created by the fishing operations: $ab$.

Will competitive conditions establish the input level $L^*(t)$ for the fishery? It must be remembered that the unit cost of inputs, $w$, includes the competitive rate of return on capital. The profit $ab$ is, therefore, pure profit in the economic sense—a return beyond what is required to keep capital-labor in the industry. The only way an outsider can share in these profits is to buy a boat and start fishing. If entry is not controlled, say by limited licensing, more labor-capital will be attracted to the fishery since, presumably, only the competitive rate of return is available in other industries. Thus, inputs will continue to expand toward the value $L_e$ where the net benefits (and net profits) of the industry disappear. Thus we have:

> Steady-state Result 3:
> if the fishery is a common property resource, that is, if there is free access, then there will be a tendency towards excessive inflow of labor-capital (toward the point $L_e$) and excessive reduction of the stock, $S$.

We now turn to considerations of managing the fishery over time without assuming steady-state management, for we don't know under what conditions management of the fishery in a steady-state would be economically efficient.

## 13.3. OPTIMUM FISHERIES MANAGEMENT OVER TIME

Once again we turn to the basic natural resources management model developed in Chapter 5 and elaborated in Chapter 10. The model fits the fisheries case very well, as we see below. The production function for caught fish is written as:

(13.3.1) $$R_0(t) = g[L(t), S(t), t]$$

The growth of the stock is assumed to be a function of the stock and is written as before:

(13.3.2) $$H(t) = h[S(t)]$$

The stock accounting identity is identical with that used in the case of exploration and discovery:

(13.3.3) $$S(t) = S(0) + \int_0^t [H(\tau) - R_0(\tau)] \, d\tau$$

The problem of optimum fisheries management over time can now be stated as

(13.3.4) $$\underset{L(t)}{\text{maximize}} \int_0^\infty \left[ \int_0^{R_0(t)} D[\eta, t] d\eta - w \cdot L(t) \right] e^{-rt} \, dt$$

Since the rate of change of the stock is simply $\dot{S}(t) = H(t) - R_0(t)$, the Hamiltonian of the problem is

(13.3.5) $$\phi = \int_0^{R_0(t)} D[\eta, t] \, d\eta - w \cdot L(t) + q(t)[H(t) - R_0(t)]$$

If we maximize $\phi$ with respect to $L(t)$, we once again get Basic Condition 1:

(13.3.6) $$p(t) = \frac{w}{\dfrac{\partial R_0}{\partial L(t)}} + q(t)$$

$$= MC_R(t) + q(t)$$

Here, $p(t)$ is the dockside price of fish, $MC_R$ is the marginal cost of catching fish, and $q(t)$ is the marginal scarcity rent per unit of the fish stock. Once again the scarcity rent represents the optimized intertemporal opportunity cost of reducing the fish stock by one unit, future costs that would take the form of increased fishing costs and reduced growth of the stock. Optimum fisheries management requires not simply that any old value of $q(t)$ exist, but that $q(t)$ accurately reflect this intertemporal opportunity cost.

   An idealized social manager exploiting this fishery would recognize this intertemporal opportunity cost and would adjust the catch rate at each point of time so that the last unit caught generated an *apparent* pure profit of $q(t)$—apparent in the sense that it is, in fact, offset by the present value of the future opportunity costs. However, an outsider observing the fishery would see pure profits being made on the last unit caught and even higher average profits (because of increasing marginal cost). Note the total profits, *ab*, being generated under optimal management in the static case of Figure 13.5. If there is open access to the fishery, outside fishermen are likely to be induced to come in, pushing catch rates and capital investment beyond their desirable levels and reducing the fish stock below its desired level. An equilibrium level of fishing effort like $L_e$ of Figure 13.5 is likely to be established. In the special case where fish price is assumed constant, all of the social net benefits of the fishery are wiped out by increased costs and reduced catches. In technical jargon, this process is referred to as "dissipation of the rent of the fishery," in the sense that the inflow of inputs and the catch rate will be extended until marginal catch cost equals price, reflecting the newcomers' willingness to act as if $q(t) = 0$.

   Under optimum management, what happens to $q(t)$ over time? In a way similar to the derivation of $\dot{q}(t)$ in Chapter 5, control theory permits us to derive the following relation:

$$(13.3.7) \qquad \dot{q}(t) = r \cdot q(t) - [p(t) - q(t)] \frac{\partial R_0}{\partial S(t)} - q(t) \cdot \frac{\partial H}{\partial S(t)}$$

$$= \left[ r - \frac{\partial H}{\partial S(t)} \right] q(t) - MC_R \cdot \frac{\partial R_0}{\partial S(t)}$$

This points out that, under optimum management, society would get its rewards from maintaining a (not necessarily constant) stock of fish in the forms of *in situ* rent increases, $\dot{q}(t)$, increased growth, $\partial H/\partial S(t)$, and reduced fishing costs, $MC_R \cdot [\partial R_0/\partial S(t)]$. In the absence of "stock effects" like the effect on growth, $\partial H/\partial S(t)$, and the effect on catch costs, $MC_R \cdot [\partial R_0/\partial S(t)]$, (13.3.7) simply says that the stock should always be adjusted to a level at which carrying forward one more unit will yield an increase in *in situ* rents, $\dot{q}(t)$, equal to the return that could be gotten in other investments outside the fishers, $r \cdot q(t)$. Equation 13.3.7 reminds us that, with stock effects, the increase of *in situ* rents need not be that high and can even become negative.

   Intuitively interpreted, (13.3.7) tells us that, when the discount rate is high relative to stock effects, $q(t)$ should rise as stocks are progressively drawn down. It is even possible that extinction of the fish species through reduction of the stock below $\underline{S}$ is the economically most efficient path to follow. On the other hand, if the discount rate is low relative to stock effects, then $\dot{q}(t)$ should fall as stocks are increased. When the potential dynamic behavior of the system is analyzed, it is found that the initial level of stocks is quite important in determining the optimum management program. Lee and Pannu[3], using a variant of the preceding model, have proved the following characteristics of the optimum management program:

1.  The larger the initial stock, $S(0)$, the less likely that extinction will be part of the optimum solution.
2.  If $r < h'[\underline{S}(t)]$ extinction will *never* be the economically optimum policy.
3.  If $r = h'[\underline{S}(t)]$ extinction is either never optimal (depending on some complex relations between marginal profitability conditions and stock equilibrium conditions) or there will be some interval of $S$ values above $\underline{S}$ such that if the initial stock, $S(0)$, falls in that interval, it will be optimal to reduce the stock to $\underline{S}$, but otherwise $S^* > \underline{S}$.
4.  If $r > h'[\underline{S}(t)]$, there will always be some initial interval above $\underline{S}$ for which extinction provides the optimum policy, but above which $S^* > \underline{S}$.

These results tell us that the maximization of the present value of the fishery by employing an optimum dynamic strategy need not but can imply extinctions of the fishery. Under fairly general conditions, if the initial stock is large enough, the optimum economic strategy will not call for extinction.

Does this mean that economists would recommend the extinction of fish species under appropriate market conditions? Social decisions take place in a multiple-objective or multiple-criterion framework of which economic net benefits are but one criterion. The responsible economist would generate information on the present values of the fishery under different schemes of management. If the highest present value of net benefits appears to be generated by a pattern of fishing that eventually would exterminate the fish stock, this would be stated, along with the information on other schemes that would preserve a viable fish stock. The decision makers then would understand the tradeoffs involved and could proceed to their decision.

[3]Dwight R. Lee and Sukhraj Singh Pannu, "The Optimal Extinction of a Renewable Natural Resource," Department of Economics Discussion Paper, University of Colorado, 1975.

## 13.4. THE DYNAMIC BEHAVIOR OF A COMPETITIVELY EXPLOITED FISHERY

An unregulated fishery such as those oceanic fisheries lying outside the economic boundaries of the various nations or even domestic coastal and lake fisheries in times prior to public regulation are examples of common property resource systems. This means that stock externalities, both interfirm and intertemporal, will be only partially taken into account or ignored altogether by the fishermen. While the interfirm stock externality takes the form of increased harvesting costs for all firms resulting from one firm's catch, the intertemporal stock externality takes the form of reductions in future catches and profits resulting from today's catch. When no defensible property rights exist in the fishery and there is no regulation, the individual firm cannot take a very long view. It is likely to assume a very short time horizon, seeking to maximize its profits while it can.

Thus, when we attempt to describe the likely competitive, unregulated behavior of fishing firms exploiting a fishery, it seems reasonable to assume year-by-year attempts at profit maximization by each firm. Smith (1969) has analyzed this situation by assuming $K$ identical firms each catching at a rate $y$, so that the total catch is $Y \equiv Ky$. He introduces a linear demand function, $p = \alpha - \beta Y$ and a quadratic growth function, $(a - bS)S$. In this case, $\underline{S} = 0$, $\overline{S} = a/b$ and $\hat{S} = a/2b$. Costs for the firm are assumed to be $c = (\gamma y^2/S) + \hat{\pi}$ where $\hat{\pi}$ is the minimum net return required to keep the firm in the industry. While the industry faces a downward sloping demand curve, the individual firm perceives the price of fish to be unaffected by its own actions and equal to $\alpha - \beta Y = \alpha - \beta Ky$. The profit experienced by a firm is, by definition, total revenue less total cost:

$$(13.4.1) \qquad \pi \equiv py - C = (\alpha - \beta Ky)y - \frac{\gamma y^2}{S} - \hat{\pi}$$

Since cost is defined to include the minimum net return required to keep the firm in the industry, whenever $\pi > 0$ additional firms will be attracted to the industry. When $\pi < 0$, firms will leave the industry. Smith assumes this entry-exit relation to be

$$(13.4.2) \qquad \dot{K} = \begin{cases} \delta_1 \pi & \text{for } \pi \geq 0 \\ \delta_2 \pi & \text{for } \pi < 0 \end{cases}$$

The firm, in its shortsighted attempts to maximize profits, adjusts its catch rate, $y$, to equate its marginal cost to price, that is,

(13.4.3)                        $2 y \gamma / S = \alpha - \beta K y$      or

$$y_e = \frac{\alpha S}{2 \gamma + S \beta K}$$

With this catch rate established for each firm, the rate of change of the stock of fish will be

(13.4.4)                        $\dot{S} = (a - bS)S - K y_e$

The competitive fishery's dynamic behavior is now fully described by Equations 13.4.1 to 13.4.4. The system would be in equilibrium whenever $\dot{K} = \dot{S} = 0$. If $y_e$ is substituted into the $\dot{K}$ and $\dot{S}$ functions, the loci of points for which $\dot{K} = 0$ and $\dot{S} = 0$ can be determined. Two special cases are exhibited in Figure 13.6 where the two curves representing $K$ and $S$ combinations for which $\dot{K} = 0$ and $\dot{S} = 0$ are graphed. Diagrams of this type are known as *phase diagrams* and provide a graphical way of indicating the possible time paths of $K$ and $S$ and possible steady-state solutions to the two differential equations for $\dot{K}$ and $\dot{S}$ given by (13.4.2) and (13.4.4).

Figure 13.6a typifies a fishery for which commercial exploitation is not possible. The smallest stock that would induce even one firm to enter is larger than the maximum physical stock.

Figure 13.6b illustrates a more general case in which there are two stable equilibrium points toward which the variables $K$ and $S$ might converge, points $R$ and $P$; and one unstable equilibrium point $Q$. The curve $\dot{K} = 0$ divides the space into two regions: that above the curve in which the number of firms is excessive relative to the stock so that $\pi < 0$ and $\dot{K} < 0$; and that on or below the curve for which $\pi \geq 0$ and $\dot{K} \geq 0$. Similarly, the curve $\dot{S} = 0$ defines two regions: that above the curve in which the stock is insufficient to provide growth to offset the total catch of the $K$ firms, so that $\dot{S} < 0$; and that on or below the curve representing points for which the stock is large enough to generate growth in excess of catch. Any point in the plane thus has two forces acting on it, one in the $K$ direction and one in the $S$ direction, the length of each vector indicating the magnitude of the force. Thus a point like $A$ would induce large forces to increase both $K$ and $S$, while a point like $B$, close to the equilibrium point $P$, would have only very weak forces pushing it toward $P$.

The two curves of Figure 13.6b divide the plane into six regions according to the net forces acting on the points in each region as indicated by the force arrows. These force arrows illustrate why $P$ and $R$ are stable equilibria while $Q$ is not.

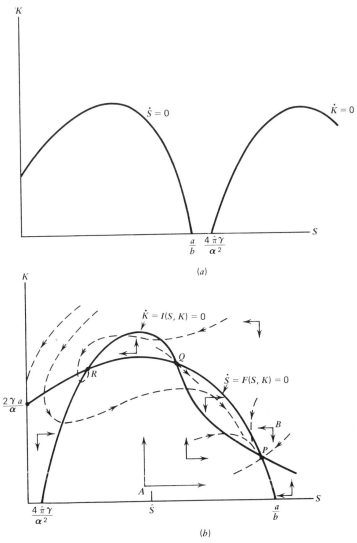

**Figure 13.6** Possible time paths and equilibrium points for the number of firms ($K$) and the fish stock ($S$) in a competitive fishery. Source: Smith, 1969, Figs. 6 and 4.

The magnitudes of the entry and exit coefficients, $\delta_1$ and $\delta_2$, plan an important role in determining the likelihood of extinction in this system. If firms are easily induced into the fishery but slow to leave when it becomes unprofitable, that is, $\delta_1 > \delta_2 > 0$, then it is much more likely that whenever the stock approaches its critical level, the level of fishing effort will not abate in sufficient time to save the resource.

Another interesting result of this model which was also true of the Lee-Pannu model of the preceding section is that the equilibrium stock, either competitive or optimal, can exist at a point on either side of $\hat{S}$, the point of maximum sustainable yield. This illustrates the further insights provided by a dynamic model, since our original static model of Section 13.2 indicated that $S^* > \hat{S}$. Given the dynamics of a competitive fishery or the time path of $K$ and $S$ associated with truly dynamic economic optimization of the fishery, the optimum steady-state stock, $S^*$, can be greater than, equal to, or less than the stock corresponding to the maximum sustainable yield, $\hat{S}$.

## 13.5.  REGULATION ALTERNATIVES FOR FISHERIES MANAGEMENT

Analysis of fisheries management using the foregoing models has identified a number of problems. The initial static model exposed the nature of the common property problem of open access fisheries: dissipation of the potential net benefits through excessive inflow of manpower and capital. Our dynamic optimization model (13.3.4) and Lee and Pannu's results showed that present-value maximization could lead to extinction as an economically rational objective quite independent of common property access, provided private discount rates are high enough. Finally Smith's analysis of the dynamic features of competitive fisheries management showed that the dynamics of entry and exit (of firms) from the industry, combined with the biological responses of the fish stock can lead to an unprofitable, unstable industry characterized by undue depletion of the fish stock and the possibility of unintended extinction.

As quantitative examples of the resultant wastes, Crutchfield and Pontecorvo (1969) estimated that the United States and Canada could maintain the same catch of Pacific salmon at an annual cost of $50 million less than the costs under existing industry practices. Christy (1973), in summarizing other studies, noted that Peru's Pacific fishery (the largest catch in the world) was so overcapitalized with excess vessels that the same catch could be maintained at savings of $50 million per year. Christy also noted that the North Atlantic cod fishery was so overexploited in the mid-1960s that the same catch could be taken with a savings of $50 to $100 million per year through coordinated, rational management.

There are three main classes of management techniques: (1) regulations relating directly to the fishery itself, such as closed seasons, closed areas, and limits on total catch; (2) regulations relating to the *kind* of effort or fishing technology, such as constraints on net mesh and trawling techniques; and (3) regulations concerning the amount of fishing effort, exemplified by limited licensing of trawlers or the imposition of taxes and fees to affect the incentives for investment in the industry.

It seems probable that some mixture of these management techniques would be optimum for most fisheries since we must deal simultaneously with common property aspects, the dynamics of the industry, long-term protection against species extermination, and maintenance of a program that is administratively feasible. It is interesting that in the Northwest Atlantic fisheries, the management systems include an ad hoc mixture of closed areas, closed seasons, restrictions on gear, and national quotas without any imposition of user taxes or other financial incentives. Canada, however, has developed a management system for the Pacific salmon fishery that incorporates a limit on the number of vessels, license fees that will increase along with the value of the fishery, and compensation to fishermen whose licenses cannot be renewed.

If limitations on the season and types of gear are used alone, they will fail to modify the common property nature of the fishery. In the absence of restraints on the inflow of capital and manpower, an inflow of additional efforts to capture the fish within the shorter period or smaller area will be induced. If the value of fish keeps rising to support these excess inputs, the result is likely to be a set of progressively tighter regulations. In the Pacific halibut fishery, the season was reduced from nine months to four weeks in one major management area and to less than two months in another. In the eastern tropical Pacific yellowfin tuna fishery, the season has been progressively reduced from nine to three months.[4] Red salmon fishing in Bristol Bay, Alaska, has long been restricted to four weeks, but there was talk of closing fishing altogether in 1973 and 1974 because of small runs. Runs estimated at more than 50 million fish had dwindled to a little over 2 million by 1973. The reasons are not fully understood, but factors at work include two successive extreme winters that killed young fish, increased predation of the weakened fish, and perhaps excessive high seas fishing by American and foreign groups. The fishermen surely knew, whatever the cause,

[4]Christy, pp. 30–31.

that the years when one boat could gross $20,000 to $50,000 had passed and that no one was able to break even. The native Alaskan fishermen who had no alternatives were especially hard hit.[5]

The Bristol Bay situation produced a classic quota that boldly illustrates the common property syndrome. Said one fisherman when faced with complete closing of the season, "Why should they close it if the Japanese are going to be out there? I'd just as soon wreck it ourselves as have them wreck it."

Shortening of the season not only raises the direct cost per unit catch but it places pressure on prices and processing, storage, and distribution facilities. It also tends to put pressure on other fish stocks as the unoccupied boats seek other catches.

A limit on total catch, complemented by restrictions on fishing techniques to avoid impairment of reproductive capabilities of younger stock and externalities on intermingled species, probably is the most desirable measure, provided the appropriate incentives exist to avoid overcapitalization. These incentives could be provided by awarding exclusive rights to the fishery to one firm that would then have the motivation to take the limited catch at minimum cost. If the fishery were large or of a unique, desirable species, it might be necessary to guard against monopolistic exploitation by requiring a minimum catch.

A way of achieving the limit on total catch while retaining free entry conditions would be to place a tax on the fish caught, the tax being that which would cause the common property equilibrium to correspond to the economically efficient catch. This is illustrated in Figure 13.7. The optimum unit tax on catch is not directly observable in Figure 13.7, but it would be that value that reduced the net price to the fishing firm enough to produce total revenue curve $R_2$. Industry profits would then be exhausted at $L^*(t)$. The unit cost, $c$, is meant to represent the most efficient way of catching the volume $L^*(t)$, for only firms using such technologies would be able to cover their costs.

Figure 13.7 suggests another form of tax that might be capable of inducing the optimum effort—a unit tax on inputs, $L(t)$—which would raise total cost to $\hat{c} \cdot L(t)$. Again, $L^*(t)$ and $L_e(t)$ would coincide. Raising costs to the firm through a tax is greatly preferred to the imposition of obsolete, costly technologies as is done in the Chesapeake Bay oyster fishery, for the tax is merely a transfer to the public sector, not a real resource cost. The problem with a tax on effort is to *define* "effort" in such a way that the tax will not distort the selection of technology from

[5]Associated Press story by C. Barough, published in the *Boulder Daily Camera*, Sept. 22, 1973, p. 11.

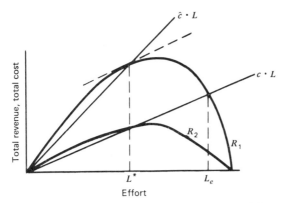

**Figure 13.7** The effects of optimum taxes on catch.

the real minimum cost technology and so the tax cannot be escaped through tricky adaptations of technology.

This problem would be shared by any management program that relied on a direct control over "effort." Total effort has (at a bare minimum) three dimensions: (1) the size or power of the "typical" boat, (2) the number of boats, and (3) the amount of time spent fishing per boat. All three must be controlled. The incentive system used must equally affect all three or the tax (or quantitative constraint) will be evaded. If the tax is per boat, boats will grow larger or more powerful. If it is some function of horsepower and size, more days will be fished. Attempts have been made to define "standardized vessel days" for management purposes, but the difficulties are almost unsolvable in settings where boat types and gear are varied. For example, what are the comparative catching capacities of an old 1000-ton stern trawler and a new 300-ton side trawler? Not only is the matter of defining effort in an operational way difficult, but useful innovation may be stifled for fear that innovative gear may be more heavily taxed.

The advantages of a tax on catch, in addition to allowing free choice regarding entry, include the continuing inducement to minimize costs, to innovate, and the generation of revenues that may be useful to the management agencies in funding enforcement and in compensating fishermen who may be forced from the industry. However, such taxes have seldom been used. Political resistance arises largely from the anticipated negative impacts on employment provided by the fishery and the hardships of the transition period while resources are being withdrawn and technologies updated, although these problems would be common to all efficient management programs. The tax on catch naturally requires monitoring of the catch, which administratively may be more difficult than licensing vessels and monitoring types of gear.

A device quite similar to the tax on catch is the auctioning of licenses or permits tied to the desired total catch. If this process can be kept competitive, that is, if the annual catch is large relative to the efficient size of the fishing firm, it can limit the total catch while transferring the net benefits to the public sector.

Fisheries regulation, like forest management, may have social objectives other than economic efficiency. It may be desired to share the resource among more fishermen than would be efficient, that is, to maintain a higher level of employment. When fisheries span international boundaries, it may be extremely difficult to exploit the fishery efficiently while dividing net benefits equitably. There has been discussion of international fishing agencies, perhaps under U.N. direction, which could exploit all economies of scale while harvesting the optimum catch. Their net revenues could then be shared among the countries whose territorial waters are involved and, of course, among others if desired.


## 13.6.   SUMMARY

This chapter introduced us to the management of a dynamic renewable resource system, the fishery. The basic biological relationships were introduced in simplified form, permitting us to combine the economic and biological aspects. We have seen that fishing effort is generally subject to diminishing returns, and that it is possible to drive a fishery to extinction through overfishing.

Under steady-state fisheries management, the management objective of "maximum sustainable yield" was seen to be inefficient. Furthermore, the optimum steady-state stock of fish was found to exceed that corresponding to maximum sustained yield. It was further demonstrated that open access tends to attract excessive fishing effort, driving the social net benefits from fishing toward zero and keeping stocks below the optimum level.

Consideration of non-steady-state management showed that Basic Condition 1 relating price, marginal extraction cost, and *in situ* scarcity rents was also applicable to fisheries management. Open access was again seen to lead to "dissipation of the rent" on the fishery, that is, the ignoring of intertemporal opportunity costs and externalities on other fishermen. The likely result appears to be that social net benefits are greatly reduced or even driven to zero.

Several studies have shown that extinction could be the economically most efficient management scheme, and that extinction could also result from free, competitive ingress to the fishery.

Finally, the chapter pointed to the gross inefficiencies induced by current attempts to regulate fisheries. The desirability of licensing and tax schemes was then demonstrated.

# Chapter 14

# WATER RESOURCE SYSTEMS

This chapter briefly describes one of our most vital, most misunderstood, and most highly politicized natural resource systems—water. The development and management of water is now largely a public sector function. Several factors account for this: the interdependence of water users, scale economies and large capital requirements, and the common property nature of many water systems in both quantity and quality dimensions. As public sector projects, water systems are easily adapted to the system known in political science as "distributive politics," that is, the spreading of costs over the taxpayers at large and the concentration of benefits within a localized group of beneficiaries. For this reason, special interest groups tend to dominate the logrolling process by which resources are allocated to water projects. This process continues in spite of the inefficiency of much current U.S. water investment from economic and environmental viewpoints. Water policy is, therefore, an intriguing case study of the integration of a natural resource system, technology, economics, and politics.

## 14.1. CHARACTERISTICS OF WATER RESOURCE SYSTEMS

Water occurs both as a stock and as a flow. Streams or overland runoff from precipitation find their ways into lakes, reservoirs, or the oceans. Groundwater exists as a stock, usually subject to flows of recharge. An important characteristic of water flows is that they are stochastic, that is, they are governed by physical processes that are best described as probabilistic. All naturally occurring water flows are therefore described by probability distributions and not simply by one number such as the average rate of flow.

The stochastic nature of flows is directly attributable to the nature of the physical systems generating them such as the accumulation and melting of mountain snows, the occurrence of precipitation and its infiltration into the soil and subsoil, and so on. These processes are subject to many influences that cannot be predicted with the current state of meteorology and related sciences, but it is often possible to quantify the resultant probability distribution of flows. Decisions on system development and related water-using activities are then based on these probability distributions. Water projects are intended to modify or transform the probability distribution of stream flows into patterns more useful (or less harmful) to man. Reservoirs and flood control works are the prime examples.

If a river has a uniform natural flow over time, then it provides a highly reliable supply for withdrawal or consumptive uses. If withdrawals are largely nonconsumptive and are returned to the stream, the waters can be used repeatedly. Total withdrawals could exceed the flow rate of the river. Consumptive uses are, of course, bounded by the flow of the river. The *hydrograph* of a large river in a high rainfall region is shown in Figure 14.1 and is seen to be relatively uniform throughout the year.

The hydrograph of a snow-fed stream is much more seasonal in

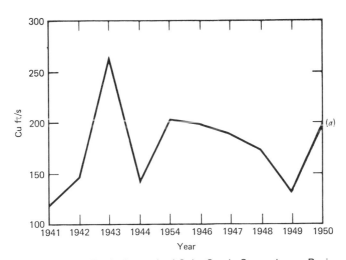

**Figure 14.1**   The hydrograph of Oaks Creek, Susquehanna Basin.

nature and much more predictable one year at a time since the snowpack is measurable and the timing of the melt is fairly predictable. The hydrograph of the snow-fed Upper Colorado River is contrasted in Figure 14.2 with the totally erratic hydrograph of a desert stream that is fed only by random downpours. These hydrographs exhibit the short-term fluctuations in flow rates of streams typical of various climatic zones. There are also longer-term fluctuations, as exhibited in Figure 14.3 below for the Colorado River, the long-term average flow of which has varied

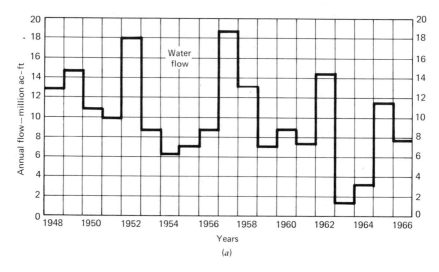

(a)

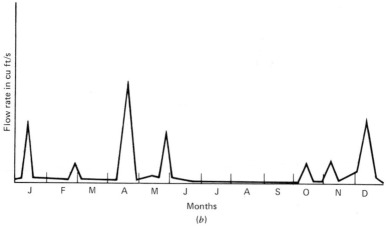

(b)

**Figure 14.2** (a) Annual flow of the Colorado River at Lees Ferry and (b) monthly flows of a desert stream.

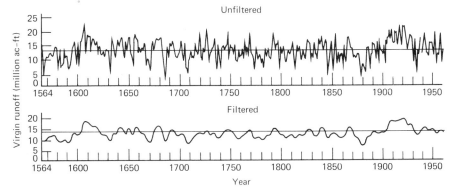

**Figure 14.3** Tentative 400-year reconstruction of annual runoff at Lees Ferry, Arizona. This reconstruction is based on tree-ring chronologies within the Upper Colorado River Basin collected as part of the Lake Powell Research Project and on chronologies that were in the files of the Laboratory of Tree-Ring Research. Source: Lake Powell Research Project Bulletin Number 14, November 1975 by Gordon C. Jacoby, Jr., Fig. 4.

significantly over the period of record. When flows are compared over time, the attempt is usually made to convert the measured flow back to the "virgin flow," which is the natural flow rate in the absence of human withdrawals and other modifications.

Groundwater and the *aquifers* that contain it are large and valuable components of the natural water system. It has been estimated that there is 30 times more fresh water in the ground than in all the world's streams and lakes. Aquifers provide natural regulation and efficient storage of water, capturing surface runoff through infiltration and then, in many cases, returning the water to adjacent streams. The dry-season flows of many rivers are composed entirely of groundwater.

Groundwater is often pumped for municipal, industrial, and agricultural purposes, and the aquifers provide natural evaporation-free water storage. Some aquifers are intimately connected with surface streams or lakes, especially in gravel-filled river valleys. The streams help recharge the groundwater during high flows and, in turn, are fed by the aquifers during periods of low flow. Such systems are best managed *conjunctively* to take greatest advantage of these features.

Not all aquifers receive recharge. In such cases, the groundwater constitutes a finite nonrenewable stock that should be managed as such. A striking example is the great Ogallala aquifer, which reaches from southern Nebraska to northwestern Texas and eastern New Mexico, holding waters deposited in ancient times but, because of sparse rainfall and soil structures, receiving essentially no recharge.

Floods are an important feature of surface water systems, for they bring both great benefits and losses to us all. In economically and technically primitive areas, river floods often serve to irrigate large acreages and to fertilize the land with organically rich sediment. This used to be true of the entire Nile River before the new Aswan High Dam, and remains the case in the Upper Nile Valley. More frequently, however, as human activities encroach on the flood plain, river floods cause extensive damage. The design of optimal flood control systems is an interesting economic problem for it involves a balance of structural and nonstructural measures, ranging from dams and the elevation of buildings to zoning and evacuation systems. Human perception of flood dangers plays a major and sometimes perverse role in determining the results of flooding and the kinds of programs undertaken to combat floods. The classic studies of White (1958) and Kates (1965) illuminate commonly observed modes of behavior and the needs for education and public sector intervention.

Drought is, superficially, the opposite of flood, but such events are much more extended over time and generally relate primarily to precipitation. As with floods, it is possible to delimit certain physical conditions, beyond which drought or flood is said to occur. However, the *policy relevant* definition of drought and flood must include the effects of human presence, preparedness, and reaction. Thus, an appropriate definition of drought might be "a shortage of precipitation of seasonal or longer duration relative to the expectations of water users." A sugarcane-growing area, which normally receives 60 inches of rain per year and which requires 50 for a normal cane crop, can be said to experience drought when it receives only 40 inches, while a wheat-growing region requiring 15 inches annually suffers no drought when receiving only 20 inches. This is why one hears no reference to drought in the Sahara Desert, while shortfalls of rain in the bordering regions to the south can create tragedy.

A survey of water resources must include atmospheric water resources, not simply because of natural precipitation patterns but because of our ability to modify weather patterns, both intentionally and unintentionally. Unintentional weather modification has occurred in the rainfall patterns over metropolitan areas where rainfall has increased significantly as a result of temperature changes and airborne particulate matter. Intentional weather modification has involved fog dissipation, precipitation modification, hail suppression, and hurricane modification. The dispersal of supercooled fog at airports is a successful and widely used technique. Precipitation modification has meant "cloud seeding," usually with silver iodide vapors from aircraft or ground generators, to increase precipitation. It appears that efforts to seed orographic clouds (those formed by air masses rising over mountain ranges) whose upper level temperatures fall within a critical, narrow range have been successful in increasing mountain snowfall by 10 to 20 percent.[1] The results of attempts to seed other cloud types are still indeterminate. Hurricane modification is still in the early experimental stages (Project Stormfury of the National Oceanic and Atmospheric Administration), utilizing storm seeding from aircraft.

Overall, it appears that snowpack augmentation in catchment basins where a water storage system is already well developed will be a valuable source of added water at low marginal cost. An estimated increment of around 2 million acre-feet per year in the Upper Colorado Basin would be of great help in resolving the water conflicts arising in that Basin. Possible downwind externalities in the forms of deposition of silver iodide or decreases in precipitation appear not to have been significant.

The quality of water is an increasingly important dimension of water systems. Pollution has increased from population, industry, and agriculture to the point where esthetics, recreational values, and even human health are endangered. The largest program of public expenditure aside from defense in U.S. history is now in progress to improve and protect water quality.[2] Water quality has many dimensions, among which are dissolved oxygen that is critical to marine life, suspended solids that cause turbidity, dissolved solids (salts) that cause hardness and damage crops and piping systems, and many natural and artificial chemical agents, some of which (like PCBs, mercury, and DDT) are concentrated in the water-based food chains and cause toxic effects in fish and humans.

Human health is directly linked to the availability of water in sufficient quantity and quality. While most industrialized nations find it easy to provide adequate water for human needs in urban areas, small towns still have problems of shortage and contamination of supply. The dramatic impacts of water shortage and contamination in the developing countries of Africa are described by the Whites and David Bradley in *Drawers of Water*. Persons subsist on as little as 2 liters per day and suffer from many water-borne diseases, while large parts of each day must be spent by women and children in carrying water from distant sources.

---

[1]The interested reader can consult a vast literature that includes several reports by the U.S. National Academy of Science and the annual reports of the Bureau of Reclamation's Project Skywater.

[2]See Kneese and Schultze (1975) for an excellent review and critique.

While many of the developing countries face problems of providing sufficient water for drinking, cooking, and minimal cleanliness and reductions in widespread typhoid, typhus, bilharzia, malaria, and other diseases, the advanced countries face primarily problems of contamination of water by the complicated chemical by-products of modern industry and agriculture.

All of the aspects of water resources systems surveyed above are related to patterns of land use. Some of our drought problems occur because crops are being grown in areas that probably should be left as rangeland. The exhaustion of groundwater in several regions is occurring because of overdevelopment of agriculture and population relative to long-term carrying capacities. Water "shortage" is frequently thought to exist while grossly inefficient irrigation practices continue. For many decades, the prevailing philosophy in the United States (and much of the rest of the world) has been to bring the water to the people and their activities. At present, however, the marginal cost of expanding or even sustaining water supplies in arid regions has become so high in economic and environmental terms, that serious thought must be given to a national land-use policy.

## 14.2.  THE NATURE OF WATER SYSTEM DEVELOPMENTS

Water tends to be quite unevenly distributed in space and time. The distribution of average annual runoff in the United States is shown in Figure 14.4. Runoff represents the quantity or flow rate of water that actually reaches streams or other water bodies. It therefore measures the maximum amount of water available for capture and control, although it does not include precipitation that percolates into the surface to be evaporated or transpired by plants.

Regions that have very little precipitation or runoff may still have large water supplies, either in the form of groundwater or from rivers flowing in from other regions of origin. Thus, the Lower Colorado River Basin (especially Arizona and Southern California) has very low rainfall but generally plentiful water supplies from the aquifers of Central Arizona, from the now highly controlled Colorado River, and from supplies developed in Northern California.

Regions of sparse rainfall also experience highly variable rainfall and runoff. This can be seen in Figure 14.5 which presents the ninety-fifth percentile runoff rates as a percentage of mean runoff for the major water resource regions. Thus in 19 years out of 20, the North Atlantic region's runoff will equal or exceed 68 percent of its mean runoff of 163

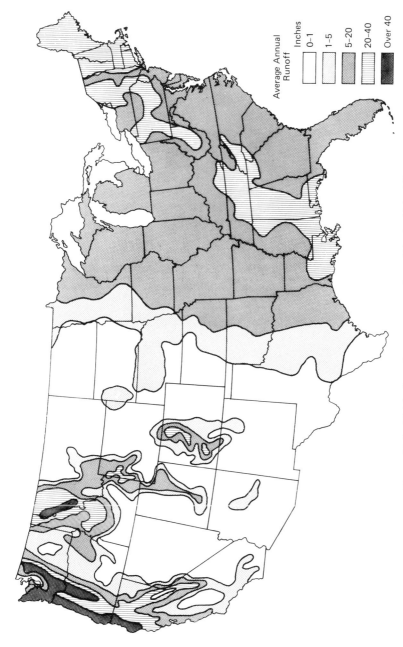

**Figure 14.4**  Distribution of average annual runoff in the United States.

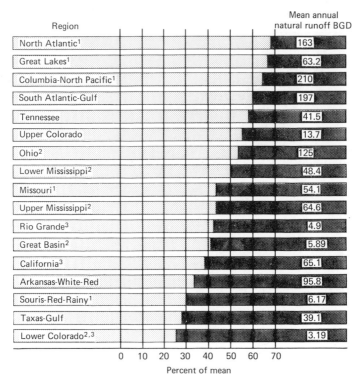

| Region | Mean annual natural runoff BGD |
|---|---|
| North Atlantic[1] | 163 |
| Great Lakes[1] | 63.2 |
| Columbia-North Pacific[1] | 210 |
| South Atlantic-Gulf | 197 |
| Tennessee | 41.5 |
| Upper Colorado | 13.7 |
| Ohio[2] | 125 |
| Lower Mississippi[2] | 48.4 |
| Missouri[1] | 54.1 |
| Upper Mississippi[2] | 64.6 |
| Rio Grande[3] | 4.9 |
| Great Basin[2] | 5.89 |
| California[3] | 65.1 |
| Arkansas-White-Red | 95.8 |
| Souris-Red-Rainy[1] | 6.17 |
| Taxas-Gulf | 39.1 |
| Lower Colorado[2,3] | 3.19 |

0    10   20   30   40   50   60   70
Percent of mean

[1] Does not include runoff from Canada
[2] Does not include runoff derived from upstream regions
[3] Does not include runoff from Mexico

**Figure 14.5**   Percentage of mean annual runoff equalled or exceeded in 19 of 20 years.

billion gallons per day while the lower Colorado's runoff will equal or exceed only 25 percent of its already low mean runoff in 19 years out of 20.

Water development consists of controlling these natural flows so that the supply pattern more nearly coincides with the demand pattern over space and time. For example, water is captured in reservoirs on the Feather River in Northern California and sent via canals to the arid Central Valley and beyond to Los Angeles, a process of redistribution spatially and in time since the waters would otherwise run to the ocean as the snows of the Sierras melted. Naturally, the systems used to accomplish this control are costly and need to be designed and evaluated according to economic as well as technical criteria.

As with all public sector programs, water development and management are meant to serve several national objectives: economic efficiency (sometimes called national economic development in the water resources literature); protection or enhancement of environmental quality; the distribution of economic well-being among regions; and perhaps others that assume significance in specific cases, such as saving lives, serving particular groups of people, or facilitating national independence in the provision of certain commodities. For federal water development projects, these objectives are set forth in detail in the U.S. Water Resources Council's "Principles and Standards for Planning Water and Related Land Resources" (1973). The *weights* given to these objectives are implicitly determined in the decision-making process, although various procedures for *multiple objective planning* have been suggested.[3]

The most natural geographical area for the planning and management of water resources is, for fairly obvious reasons, the river basin. The water resource regions listed in Figure 14.5 represent, in most cases, collections of basins of rivers that are tributary to some major river, such as the Missouri, the Mississippi, the Columbia, the Ohio, and the Rio Grande. The water resource region or smaller basin areas are hydrologically connected areas, not only in terms of surface flows but often in terms of groundwater. The structural and nonstructural measures used to control water are best planned on a river basinwide basis because projects and procedures used for water control in smaller subareas will exert impacts (either beneficial or detrimental) on the rest of the basin. Whenever important externalities exist, it is simplest and most efficient to "internalize" them by incorporating the entire basin under one management. Some prominent examples of detrimental externalities resulting from failure to plan on a river basin basis will be examined later.

The most prominent artificial components of water resource systems are usually dams and reservoirs that regulate surface water flows. In most cases, these dams and reservoirs will be *multipurpose* in nature, providing perhaps municipal water supply, agricultural water supply, electric power generation, flood control (by reserving reservoir capacity to capture flood water), water-born transportation, and perhaps water quality enhancement (by releasing water during periods of natural low flow). This means that the design of a river basin system and even the design of individual projects involves trading one purpose off against another to find the balance providing the highest net benefits.[4]

---

[3]For example, see Douglas A. Haith and Daniel P. Loucks, "Multiobjective Water Resources Planning" in Asit K. Biswas (ed.), *Systems Approach to Water Management*, New York: McGraw-Hill, 1976.

[4]See Biswas, ibid., or Charles W. Howe, *Benefit-Cost Analysis for Water System Planning*, Washington, D.C.: American Geophysical Union, 1971.

Planning the development of the water resources of a river basin can, in theory, involve inspection of a huge number of different combinations of structures, operating procedures, and nonstructural measures. For example, suppose an undeveloped river basin has 20 potential reservoir sites each capable of supporting two sizes of dam. Since each site has three alternatives (including no dam), there would be $3^{20} = 3.5 \times 10^9$ possible combinations of sites and dam sizes, quite aside from different times of construction and operating rules for the individual dams. If professional judgment could eliminate 99.9 percent of these combinations, and analysis of the remaining $3.5 \times 10^6$ combinations required one minute of computer time per combination, it would take 6.6 years of computer time! Thus, river basin planning is indeed complex and the difference between the net benefits of a carefully planned program of development and a piecemeal approach (unhappily the more common) can be huge.

Reservoirs perform the regulating function of transforming uneven river flows into a more uniform pattern of withdrawals. To get a feeling for the process, imagine a perfectly regular, deterministic flow pattern for an unregulated river as shown in Figure 14.6. Superimposed on the diagram is a desired uniform rate of water withdrawal, $w$. What volume of storage (say in acre-feet) will be required to permit this rate of withdrawal? Naturally, if the flow curve $f$ is always above the desired rate of withdrawal, $w$, then no storage would be required. Water could simply be diverted directly from the river. As shown in the figure, however, there is a season each year when desired withdrawal rates exceed flow,

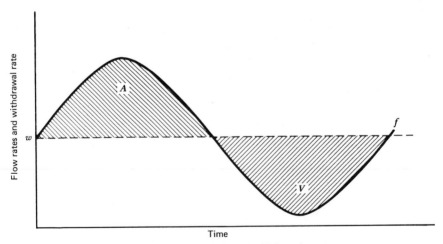

**Figure 14.6**   River flows and withdrawal rates.

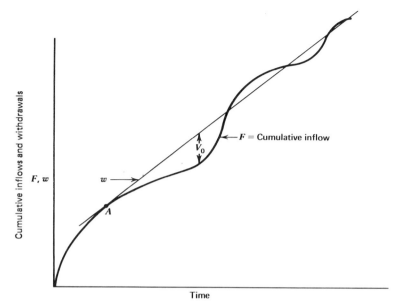

**Figure 14.7** A Rippl diagram.

requiring the storage of water during high flows for release during low flows. The total required storage volume would be $V$, provided that $V \leq A$.

Another way of looking at this is to draw the *cumulative* inflow and withdrawal curves (i.e., the areas under the curves above) as shown in Figure 14.7. Such a diagram is known as a Rippl diagram after the engineer who first used it in reservoir design in 1882. One uses the diagram in the following way: pick a high point like $A$ on the cumulative inflow curve, $F$, where the slope of $F$ (the inflow rate) equals the desired withdrawal rate, $w$. To the immediate right of this point, the inflow rate is less than the withdrawal rate (by construction). Extend the tangent line, $W$, to the northeast. The required storage volume $V$ is then estimated to be the largest observed deviation of $F$ below $W$, $V_0$ in this case.

To call $V_0$ the "required" storage makes it clear that no economic evaluation of benefits and costs has been employed. Even the physical analysis is somewhat arbitrary, because the choice of starting point will affect the answer. The point $A$ is usually chosen as the beginning of a low flow period so that the design will be "conservative" in the sense of keeping the probability of shortage low. Since the data for such an analysis come from the historical record of streamflow, there is, of course, no guarantee that the record will be repeated. The modern science of hydrology has grown out of the study of the probability characteristics of water flows to permit more adequate handling of problems of this type.

The Rippl diagram provides several key insights into the design and cost features of reservoirs. Clearly, the more variable the inflow rate, the more storage will be required, especially when the inflows show strong positive serial correlations over time. It is also clear from the diagram that any river will, for practical purposes, have a maximum uniform withdrawal rate. Should the tangent withdrawal line deviate increasingly above $F$, the withdrawal rate would not be feasible. Stretching our intuitions a little, we can at least find plausible that the maximum uniform withdrawal rate (ignoring evaporation losses) would be the mean flow rate of the stream. To achieve this rate would require huge volumes of storage, since some water might have to be carried over many years from some rare incident of extremely high flow to an interval of unusually low flow. In practice, because of evaporation losses, it is

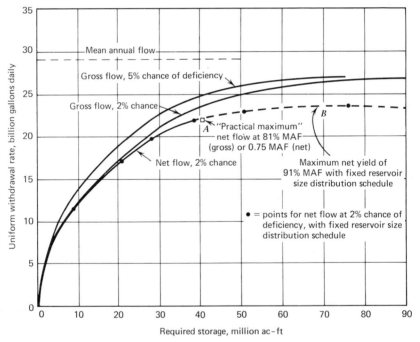

**Figure 14.8** Storage required in the Upper Missouri Basin. Source: George O. G. Löf and Clayton H. Hardison, "Storage Requirements for Water in the United States," *Water Resources Research*, Vol. 2, No. 3, 1966. Reproduced by permission of the American Geophysical Union.

not physically possible to achieve a "yield" equalling the mean flow. As higher reliable yields are desired, the required volume of storage rises disproportionately. This is best seen in so-called "storage-yield curves" for particular rivers such as the Upper Missouri—see Figure 14.8. Note that, while the theoretical yield can approach the mean flow, the practical net yield reaches a maximum of about 23 billion gallons per day with storage of 70 million acre-feet. If storage exceeds this volume, evaporation losses exceed the amount of any added carryover.

Also note that several curves are shown, each with a specified chance of deficiency, that is, a probability that the system really will not permit the indicated level of withdrawal in any year. These probabilities are not zero because there is no theoretical upper bound to the length of low flow periods. These probabilities are, in practice, estimated by computer simulations of river flows with varying volumes of storage.

Given the storage-yield curves for a particular river, knowledge of potential dam sites permits estimating the costs of providing varying volumes of storage. The costs are partly for dam construction and partly for land and other resources that will be lost to the reservoir. If these costs are expressed on an annual basis the average and marginal costs of water supply at the storage site (with a specified level of reliability) can be computed. Such cost curves are shown for the Upper Missouri Basin in Figure 14.9.

Once surface water is provided at the storage site, it must be transported to the areas of use. In speaking of use, we must distinguish withdrawal rates and consumptive rates. Water diverted for once-through cooling of a thermal-electric plant may be returned totally to the stream (although at an elevated temperature that will increase evaporation), while water diverted for city use may be one third consumed, the rest possibly being returned to the water source (usually degraded in quality). Water diverted for the irrigation of crops may be almost fully consumed, being lost through evaporation, transpiration from plants, and perhaps being caught in aquifers that do not return it to the stream.

Where the diversions are not fully consumed, the *return flows* can be very important to subsequent users, making it possible to withdraw far more from a river than its actual flow. Suppose a quantity $W$ is withdrawn and that the initial user consumes a fraction $r$, returning $(1 - r)$ $W$ to the stream. As subsequent users withdraw that quantity in turn, consuming a fraction $r$, and so on, the following total quantity of withdrawals is generated:

(14.2.1) $TW = W + (1 - r)W + (1 - r)^2W + \ldots + (1 - r)^{n-1}W$

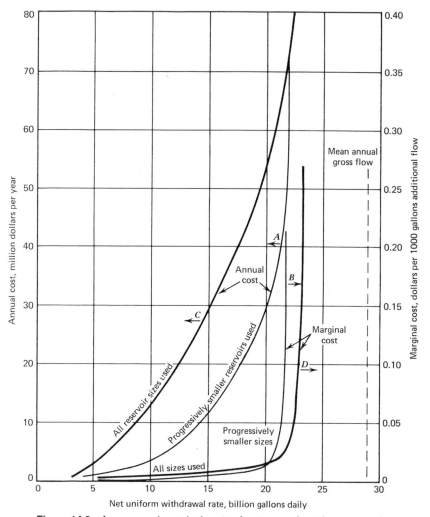

**Figure 14.9** Average and marginal costs of water supply at the storage site, Upper Missouri Basin. Source: Löf and Hardison, ibid. Reproduced by permission of the American Geophysical Union.

As the number of sequential users becomes large, this can be approximated by

(14.2.2) $$TW = \frac{W}{r}$$

This is referred to as the "return flow multiplier."

## 14.3. THE COLORADO RIVER: A BRIEF CASE STUDY

The Colorado River Basin has an area of approximately 300,000 square miles, located in southwestern Wyoming, western Colorado, eastern Utah, northwestern New Mexico, Arizona, Southern California, and a corner of Nevada. Figure 14.10 shows the Basin, of which the Green, Upper Main Stem, and San Juan comprise what is called the Upper Basin.

The climate ranges from continuous snow cover and heavy precipitation on the western slopes of the Rocky Mountains to desert conditions in the south. Most of the moisture falls as winter snow, with spring and summer rainfall being localized infrequent storm activity. Water supply in the Basin thus is highly dependent upon construction of dams, ground water, and transfers of water among the various subbasins.

The major economic activities of the Upper Basin have been agriculture, cattle and sheep raising, and the mining of metallic minerals. In the post-World War II period, recreational use of all parts of the Basin has expanded tremendously, ranging from exclusive international skiing resorts like Aspen and Vail to mountain hiking, fishing, open river and reservoir boating, and desert area exploration. This broad recreational use is facilitated by the extensive federal government land holdings, which constitute 70 percent of the Basin's area.

Most recently, the huge coal and oil shale deposits that underlie much of the Basin have attracted intensive development pressure. The federal government is intent on expanding the use of these energy resources. The state governments of the area are less certain about the desirability of large-scale strip mining of coal with associated power plants and the development of oil shale refining. Environmental problems could be critical, water requirements would be large, and interference with the swift growth of recreation and tourism is imminent.

The availability of water for further economic expansion of the Basin is a major issue. At the time of the original agreement concerning the divisions of the waters of the Colorado River (the Colorado River Compact ratified in 1929), the average annual water available was thought to be 15 million acre-feet per year (maf/yr) and 7.5 maf/yr was allotted to the Lower Basin. Since that time, long-term average flows have been decreasing, until it is now felt that the average annual flow may be as low as 12.5 maf. In addition, a United States-Mexican treaty of 1944 calls for a guaranteed delivery of 1.5 maf/yr to Mexico, and it is not clear how this obligation is to be divided between Upper and Lower Basins, although it has been declared a "national obligation" by recent legislation. It is

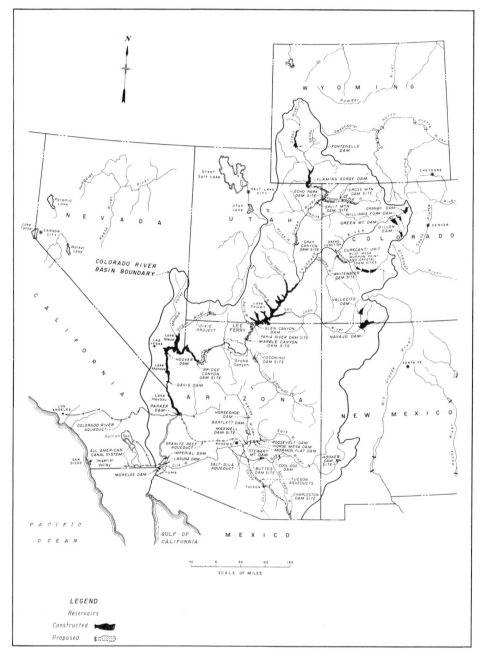

**Figure 14.10**  The Colorado River Basin. Reprinted from *Hearings Before the Subcommittee on Irrigation and Reclamation of the House Committee on Interior and Insular Affairs,* 89th Cong., 1st Sess., ser. 17, pt. 1, at 516 (1965).

probable that about 5.0 million acre-feet per year is legally available for consumptive use in the Upper Basin, with 2.5 to 3.0 maf currently being consumptively used.

The fact that the Upper Basin is not fully consuming the water available to it does not mean that the water is going unused. Table 14.1 gives the annual rates of use in the Lower Basin. Adding this total to the 2.5 to 3.0 maf/yr of Upper Basin consumptive use makes it clear that the river's flow is now fully utilized and, indeed, in a typical year no flow whatsoever reaches the river's original terminus, the Gulf of California.

As further development takes place in the Upper Basin, some of the current uses of water will have to be foregone. Southern California is a prime candidate to give up water use, since that state has a legal right to only 4.4 maf/yr while currently using 5.2 maf/yr. It has been calculated that the opportunity cost of marginal withdrawals of water from agriculture in Southern California ranges from $10 to $100 per acre-foot, depending on the availability of substitute commodities as inputs into the agricultural and food processing industries and the mobility of resources out of agriculture (Howe and Easter, 1971, Table 30).

Certainly Upper Basin demands will grow. Large expansions of thermal-electric power are planned, based on the extensive coal deposits, and even larger expansions will be necessitated if shale oil development proceeds. A shale oil capacity of $1.5 \times 10^6$ bbls/day would require directly about 210,000 af/yr, plus the very sizable indirect consumptive uses related to the necessary electric power and population. Coal gasification plants in the San Juan subbasin may consume over 200,000 af/yr.

It is clear, therefore, that water is a scarce commodity with an increasing opportunity cost to all emerging uses. Patterns of regional development will be constrained by water availability, so it is important to investigate the economic, environmental, and equity implications of alternative patterns of growth and what the tradeoffs are.

**Table 14.1.** Current Annual Consumptive Rates of Use of Colorado River Water in the Lower Basin (maf/yr)

| | |
|---|---|
| California (current use) | 5.2 |
| Arizona (allotment) | 2.8 |
| Nevada (allotment) | 0.3 |
| Mexico (treaty) | 1.5 |
| Evaporative losses | 1.0 |
| | 10.8 |

Accompanying the growth of water use in the Upper Basin, there has been a deterioration of water quality in the form of a rising trend of total dissolved solids (TDS). Current TDS levels at Imperial Dam in the Lower Basin average 850 ppm and are predicted to rise to 1100 ppm by the year 2000, and perhaps higher if the consumptive uses and likely TDS additions of the shale oil industry occur. Current levels are 50 percent attributable to natural point and diffuse sources, 40 percent to agricultural return flows, and 10 percent to municipal-industrial uses and out-of-basin transfers. There are agricultural areas in the Upper Basin that are shallowly underlain by salt deposits. When these lands are irrigated, percolating water dissolves large quantities of salt that then is added to the stream by the return flow. Additions of dissolved salts of as much as 10 tons per year per acre irrigated are found in the Grand Valley of western Colorado.

The United States and Mexico have had extensive conflicts over the quality of the Colorado River as it passes into Mexico. While an upward trend in TDS had been observed for years, in 1960 the TDS content at the Mexican border leaped to 6000 or more ppm as a result of the Wellton-Mohawk Irrigation Project. Agricultural production in the Mexicali Valley was severely damaged, and farming remains impaired even at the lower levels (1500 ppm) which have been achieved at substantial cost. The United States has agreed to improve the water quality for Mexico even more through the construction of a large desalting plant to treat the return flows from the Wellton-Mohawk Project.

Thus it is quite clear that the external effects of any developments that increase TDS in the Colorado River are no longer negligible and must be taken into account in any socially responsible and economically efficient regional planning.

A few observations on the institutional setting are vital at this point. The Upper Colorado River Basin represents part of five states: Wyoming, Colorado, Utah, New Mexico, and Arizona. Each state has its own system of water law governing the establishment of legal title to surface and ground waters, although all laws are "appropriation doctrine," which permits claims to water by individual parties in priority according to date of first use. While the waters of the entire river were distributed between Upper and Lower Basins by the 1929 Colorado River Treaty, an Upper Basin Compact of 1954 has allocated the Upper Basin waters among the States. A United States Supreme Court decree in 1964, resulting from a long-standing lawsuit among the Lower Basin States, allocated the Lower Basin's 7.5 maf/yr among California (4.4 maf), Arizona (2.8 maf), and Nevada (0.3 maf). Each state seeks to protect its share of the water. In addition, the federal government has asserted some rather nebulous but potentially sizable claims because of its vast land holdings.

Thus there is no river basin authority that has management responsibility for the entire basin. This institutional setting has the following effects:

1.  States that have claims to water in excess of their current uses are eager to put their water to use regardless of efficiency considerations, for fear that some change of law may deprive them of their unused water.
2.  Water cannot be reallocated among states or between upper and lower basins without very substantial changes in existing laws and compacts.
3.  States are not concerned with the downstream effects of their actions, either in terms of reducing existing downstream water uses or the damages from increased salinity.

The same failures to acknowledge the opportunity costs of water and external salinity damages hold within a given state among water users. For reasons too complex to raise here, the water rights established by different users are difficult to buy and sell if any change in type and location of use is involved. Markets for water rights are thus quite imperfect, transactions costs are high, and opportunity costs are very poorly reflected. Individual users (90 percent agricultural) have little incentive to maintain high physical efficiency in use. In like manner, there are no penalties for increasing the TDS levels of streams through return flows, so there is no private incentive to avoid those irrigated agricultural lands that add so much to the salinity loads.

Overall, the institutional setting provides little incentive for increasing the economic efficiency of water use or for economically managing the TDS level of the waters of the Basin.

## 14.4.  ECONOMIC ASPECTS OF GROUNDWATER MANAGEMENT

Groundwater is a valuable resource. In some situations it is subject to renewal or recharge from natural or artificial sources, but in others it is a stock resource subject to exhaustion. In situations where ground and surface water are intimately interconnected as in an alluvial river valley, the *conjunctive* management of surface and groundwater can greatly improve the productivity of the system since the aquifer is a natural reservoir without the disadvantages of evaporation losses.

Groundwater specialists often prescribe "safe yield" for groundwater basins; that is, they seek to constrain pumping to patterns that extract from the aquifer only the average amount being recharged. In this way, the stock is never permanently drawn down (mined) and a "sustained yield" is achieved, subject to the random variations in the recharge pattern. Some of the advantages of abiding by the safe yield rule are that pumping costs will not increase over time, surface subsidence is avoided, and other undesirable impacts such as salt water intrusion into coastal aquifers may be avoided.

On the other hand, it is not at all clear that abiding by "safe yield" is a socially desirable policy. The values gained through use of the water may be changing over time, and, as usual, the discount rate should affect the optimum use over time. The principles involved are illustrated in the following application of the basin natural resource management model, which is then followed by the analysis of some real-life examples.

To draw together the elements of the groundwater management problem, we slightly modify the basin model of Chapters 5 and 10. One unique feature of the groundwater problem is that pumping costs per unit of water produced are a function of the depth of the water table that depends on the volume of groundwater in stock.[5] Thus we write unit pumping cost as $w[S(t)]$. The other unique feature is the stock-recharge relationship. If the aquifer has a regular source of recharge, for example, a large drainage basin or a river, drawing down the stock can induce a greater rate of recharge. Of course, one must either be sure that this induced recharge has a zero opportunity cost or one must assign a unit cost to it. The stock-recharge relation can be written as:

$$(14.4.1) \qquad\qquad H(t) = h[S(t)]$$

The management problem can now be stated as the following maximization problem:

$$(14.4.2) \quad \underset{R_0(t)}{\text{maximize}} \int_0^\infty \left[ \int_0^{R_0(t)} D(\eta, t)\, d\eta - w\,(S(t)) \cdot R_0(t) \right] e^{-rt}\, dt$$

$$\text{subject to: } S(t) = S(0) + \int_0^t [H(\tau) - R_0(\tau)]\, d\tau$$

$$S(t) \geqslant 0$$

where $R_0(t)$ is the pumping rate and $D(R_0, t)$ is the demand function for water. The rate of change of the stock is simply $\dot{S}(t) = H(t) - R_0(t)$, so

[5] The effective depth from which water must be pumped is related also to short-term pumping patterns, for a "cone of depression" forms around the well casing. We assume an average relationship between stock and depth.

the associated Hamiltonian is simply:

(14.4.3)   $\phi = \int_0^{R_0(t)} D(\eta, t)\, d\eta - w(S(t)) \cdot R_0(t) + q(t)[H(S(t)) - R_0(t)]$

For this groundwater case, we can again derive the two basic conditions:

(14.4.4)   Basic Condition 1: $p(t) = w[S(t)] + q(t)$

(14.4.5)   Basic Condition 2: $\dot{q}(t) = r \cdot q(t) - \dfrac{\partial \phi}{\partial S(t)}$

$$= \left( r - \frac{dH}{dS(t)} \right) q(t) + \frac{dw}{dS(t)} R_0$$

Basic Condition 1 states that the marginal value of water, determined by the demand function $D(R_0, t)$, should be equated to the sum of unit pumping cost plus the scarcity rent on the water *in situ*. The intertemporal opportunity costs in this case take the forms of changes in induced recharge rates and changes in unit pumping costs. Basic Condition 2 states that the rate of change of scarcity rent, $\dot{q}$, is related to the discount rate and the stock effects, $dH/dS$ and $dw/dS$. It should be noted that both of these terms are *negative*. The optimized value of $\dot{q}(t)$ is raised by $dH/dS$ because carrying larger stocks *decreases* induced recharge. $\dot{q}(t)$ is lowered by $dw/dS$ because part of the reward for carrying stocks forward is in the form of reduced future pumping costs.

## Optimizing Groundwater Management: A Case of Groundwater Mining in La Costa de Hermosillo, Mexico.

The rich agricultural region surrounding Ciudad Hermosillo, La Costa de Hermosillo, has developed a rich agricultural base by pumping irrigation water from the large coastal aquifer. Farms of the area are large, competently managed, and heavily capitalized. Total groundwater use in the area has been running about 1.2 billion cubic meters per year, while natural recharge from inland mountain streams is no more than 350 million m³. The large "overdraft" has meant a steady reduction in the stock of water, resulting in increasing pumping costs and the intrusion of salt water into the aquifer from the ocean. As the salt water has progressed, pumps must be taken out of commission, crop yields are reduced, and some acreage must be taken out of production.

Cummings[6] modeled the large aquifer so that its behavior under

[6]Ronald G. Cummings, *Interbasin Water Transfers: A Case Study in Mexico*, Baltimore: Johns Hopkins Press, 1974.

different pumping rates could be calculated. The water-using agricultural activities were modeled in a linear programming format and related urban business activities were related to agriculture using some simple economic base relationships. The optimal program of groundwater use from the aquifer was derived from the model by maximizing the present value of regional income, subject to the physical constraints of the aquifer. The results are given in Table 14.2.

The study predicts that it will take 36 years before the optimal rate of pumping falls to the rate of recharge. That is, even with the salt water intrusion, it pays to mine the aquifer for 36 years and only then to manage the aquifer at its "safe or sustainable" yield. The implicit value (shadow price) of water in storage (not discounted) rises gradually. In year 29, it finally rises to 2.24 cents per $m^3$, a figure close to the cost of replacement water from more distant sources. At that point in time it may pay to provide that replacement water. Deferral of the replacement project's cost for more than 30 years results in a huge cost saving from a present value viewpoint.

**Intertemporal and Conjunctive Groundwater Management.** Bredehoeft and Young (1970) have combined an investigation of the importance of location of pumping activity over the aquifer with that of intertemporal water allocation. Earlier studies [e.g., Burt's classic study (1964)], assumed very simple representations of the hydrologic behavior of the aquifer being pumped. Burt showed that under a wide range of physical and economic circumstances, the optimal policy consisted of mining the groundwater at a decreasing rate, converging to an equilibrium wherein the withdrawal rate equals recharge, as was demonstrated empirically in the preceding Mexico study. Burt's results left undetermined the possible importance of the location of pumping out of the aquifer and the importance of detailed aquifer modeling. Bredehoeft constructed a detailed model of a large aquifer typical of Central Arizona, while Young constructed a detailed linear programming model of agricultural activity to represent the year-by-year optimization of cropping patterns and rates of water application.[7] Study 1 assumed (1) that pumping areas were placed in two pairs of townships widely spaced over the aquifer, (2) an initial saturated thickness of the aquifer of 1000 feet, and (3) a pumping tax ranging from zero to $25 per acre-foot, interpreted as a regulatory device to overcome the common property tendencies to ignore externalities on other pumpers and to use the water

[7]Year-by-year optimization is justified as a description of irrigator behavior within the common property context.

**Table 14.2.** Solution for the Optimum Rate of Groundwater Use in La Costa de Hermosillo

| Year | Annual Rate of Pumping (Million m³) | Groundwater Storage at the Beginning of Year (Million m³) | Increase in Storage Attributable to Pump Relocation (Million m³) | $q(t)e^{rt}$ Shadow Value of Water (Not Discounted) (Dollars/m³) | Increase in Saltwater Intrusion (km) |
|---|---|---|---|---|---|
| 1 | 1,219.1 | 22,253.0 | 1,989.6 | 0.0008 | 0.96 |
| 2 | 1,219.1 | 23,023.6 | 795.3 | 0.0035 | 0.96 |
| 3 | 1,219.1 | 22,234.0 | 828.1 | 0.0038 | 0.96 |
| 4 | 1,219.1 | 21,412.0 | 829.4 | 0.0042 | 0.96 |
| 5 | 1,219.1 | 20,588.7 | 829.5 | 0.0046 | 0.96 |
| 6 | 1,219.1 | 19.765.3 | 829.5 | 0.0051 | 0.96 |
| 7 | 1,219.1 | 18,941.9 | 829.5 | 0.0054 | 0.96 |
| 8 | 1,219.1 | 18,118.5 | 829.5 | 0.0060 | 0.96 |
| 9 | 1,206.3 | 17,295.1 | 143.3 | 0.0067 | 0.95 |
| 10 | 1,206.3 | 17,834.8 | | 0.0074 | 0.95 |
| 11 | 1,206.3 | 16,941.7 | | 0.0080 | 0.95 |
| 12 | 1,206.3 | 16,048.6 | | 0.0089 | 1.7 |
| 13 | 1,206.3 | 15,091.2 | | 0.0096 | 1.7 |
| 14 | 1,218.6 | 13,976.3 | | 0.0109 | 1.7 |
| 15 | 1,202.2 | 12,806.5 | | 0.0118 | 1.7 |
| 16 | 1,126.5 | 11,638.3 | | 0.0122 | 1.4 |
| 17 | 1,048.7 | 10,546.3 | | 0.0124 | 1.4 |
| 18 | 978.5 | 9,552.7 | | 0.0134 | 1.3 |
| 19 | 915.3 | 8,656.0 | | 0.0138 | 1.3 |
| 20 | 865.1 | 7,848.5 | | 0.0141 | 1.0 |
| 21 | 796.5 | 7,115.5 | | 0.0156 | 0.9 |
| 22 | 756.7 | 6,471.1 | | 0.0173 | 0.9 |
| 23 | 603.5 | 5,890.4 | | 0.0175 | 0.5 |
| 24 | 555.3 | 5,480.2 | | 0.0178 | 0.4 |
| 25 | 552.5 | 5,164.1 | | 0.0184 | 0.4 |
| 26 | 527.0 | 4,876.2 | | 0.0188 | 0.4 |
| 27 | 524.6 | 4,621.5 | | 0.0192 | 0.4 |
| 28 | 512.5 | 4,378.2 | | 0.0203 | 0.3 |
| 29 | 510.3 | 4,150.0 | | 0.0224 | 0.3 |
| 30 | 508.1 | 3,928.0 | | 0.0246 | 0.3 |
| 31 | 506.0 | 3,709.9 | | 0.0272 | 0.3 |
| 32 | 503.9 | 3,495.1 | | 0.0296 | 0.3 |
| 33 | 501.8 | 3,283.1 | | 0.0320 | 0.3 |
| 34 | 500.0 | 3,074.1 | | 0.0360 | 0.3 |
| 35 | 497.7 | 2,868.0 | | 0.0360 | 0.3 |
| 36 | 350.0 | 2,644.5 | | 0.0400 | 0.3 |

Source: Cummings, 1974, Table 29, p. 98. Resources for the Future, Inc. Reprinted with permission.

too rapidly. Study 2 assumed (1) that pumping areas were uniformly spaced over four centrally located townships on the aquifer, (2) an initial saturated thickness of 1000 feet, and (3) a pumping tax ranging from zero to $25 per acre-foot. The pumping tax proceeds were assumed to be returned to the farmers as a reduction in their overhead costs so that the tax could influence short-run water use decisions without affecting the long-run decision to stay in business.

The study found that (1) the tax that maximized the present value of net farm income fell in the $20 to $22 range, indicating that the unregulated or untaxed rate of water use was substantially in excess of the socially optimum rate; (2) in Study 1 with a $22 per acre-foot tax, no well goes dry over the 50-year horizon and no farm area suffers economic failure, while in the absence of a tax some wells start going dry shortly after year 30 and all areas fail economically by year 45; (3) in Study 2 with a $20 tax, some wells go dry by year 25 and one area fails at year 40, while with a zero tax areas start failing economically at year 15 and all have failed by year 40; (4) the wide spacing of withdrawal areas used in Study 1 increased the optimal present value of net farm income to $60 million from approximately $52 million in Study 2.

In alluvial (gravel and sand filled) valleys, where transmissibility is high, the aquifers and streams can be intimately related. This is best illustrated by data from the South Platte River in Figure 14.11 that shows the percentage of the daily rate being pumped during a 120-day growing season that is actually being diverted from the South Platte at different

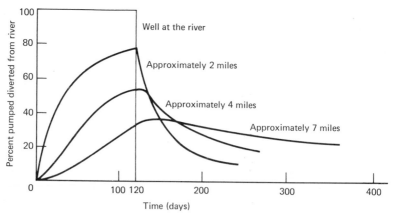

**Figure 14.11**  Percent of water pumped actually diverted from the river at different times during the irrigation season and at different distances from the river. Source: Young and Bredehoeft, 1972, Fig. 8. Reproduced by permission of the American Geophysical Union.

times after the start of pumping. In the 1972 study, Young and Brede-hoeft again combined detailed physical models of the river's hydrology and the valley aquifer with economic linear programming models of irrigated agriculture in the area of investigate the economic and physical consequences of different combinations of surface (ditch) diversions and pumping. The study found that (1) if properly managed, the alluvial aquifer can act as a valuable seasonal reservoir for efficient water storage, taking its recharge both from precipitation and from river high flows; (2) unregulated pumping can lead to highly inefficient and inequitable allocations of water among users, as waters are drawn from one use to another, often away from senior surface rights holders; and (3) if sur-face diversions and ground-water pumping are carefully planned in a coordinated fashion, the economic results of the system can be much superior to historical patterns of use.

**Instruments for Public Groundwater Management.**   We briefly con-sider two illustrations of attempts to manage groundwater use. The first, located in the High Plains of Texas around Lubbock, illustrates steps taken when the imposition of pumping taxes was not permitted by the state's constitution. The second represents one of the few situations in which a pumping tax has been used.

The Ogallala formation (aquifer) extends from Nebraska nearly to the border of Mexico, underlying Eastern Colorado, Eastern New Mex-ico, and Northwestern Texas. It underlies these vast areas at depths from 150 to 350 feet and is comprised of porous sandstone and sand ranging in thickness from inches to 400 feet, but water movement through the aquifer is slow and recharge is negligible. The High Plains Underground Water Conservation District No. 1 was established by election in 1951 to deal with the problem of the rapidly falling water table.

To assist in understanding the factors affecting the depth to water and the changes in pump capacities, a digital management model of the aquifer has been developed in cooperation with Texas Tech University. The main regulatory device has been well spacing according to size of well. For example, a 4-inch or smaller well must be 200 yards from the nearest well, while a 10-inch or larger must be 440 yards away. The stimulation of reuse of tailwater and provision of information regarding when and how much to irrigate are the primary educational devices used. In 1965, the Internal Revenue Service recognized groundwater depletion as a deductible expense. While of obvious financial advantage to the farmer, this requires an accurate determination of the change in the stock of water under the farmer's land each year, thus letting the farmer see the impact of his actions on his stock of water and better plan for the future. Naturally, this is not sufficient to eliminate suspected overuse of water because of the remaining common-property characteristics of the resource.

Various abuses typical of a common property resource have continued and have led to pressure for further controls. In particular, the drilling of very large capacity wells on very small tracts of land for purposes of exporting the water for municipal or industrial uses has been a continuing problem. In the 1950s, one city bought 17 widely spaced one-acre plots for the development of a network of municipal wells. More recently, a city purchased a one-acre plot and sank a well of sufficient capacity to extract within 22 days a volume equal to the entire stock under that acre of surface area. It is obvious to the least informed observer that this pump will quickly be taking the neighbors' water. The District is now trying to get member approval of minimum acreage requirements and minimum setbacks from property boundaries.

From today's vantagepoint, it seems likely that the High Plain's groundwater has been used too fast and wastefully, although no study similar to Cummings' has been done. If a start *de novo* could be made, the water probably would be used more slowly and the size of the regional economy would be kept smaller to prolong its life and to avoid the shocks of the exhaustion of a limiting resource base. Such a policy would certainly have reduced current pressures on the federal government to undertake horribly costly "rescue operations" in the form of long distance water transfers.

Along the Texas Gulf Coast in an area where serious land surface subsidence problems were resulting from extensive rice irrigation groundwater pumping, the Harris-Galveston Coastal Subsidence District was established in 1975. The District initially imposed a pumping tax (called a "permit fee") of 1.2 cents per 1000 gallons pumped, later reduced to 0.69 cents per 1000 gallons or $2.25 per acre-foot. While not very high in absolute terms, the effect has been to slow pumping significantly below initial projections.


## 14.5. WATER QUALITY MANAGEMENT

This section can give only a brief survey of the water quality field. For more extensive treatment, refer to Kneese and Bower (1968), Kneese and Schultze (1975), and the articles referenced below. The subject is sufficiently important, however, that the major economic issues need to be emphasized.

The major constituents of water quality (or its obverse, water pollution) are the level of dissolved oxygen (vital to marine life of all kinds), the quantity of suspended particulate matter that affects the penetration of sunlight and visual appearance, the concentration of dissolved solids that affects hardness and the usefulness of the water for irrigation and municipal uses, nutrients that affect algae growth and trace elements that can be harmful. The early scientific work on water quality concentrated on dissolved oxygen, both because oxygen deficiencies were major problems and because the physical processes of oxygen depletion and replacement in streams were well understood and subject to mathematical modeling. Since the mid-1960s, our understanding of the importance of nutrients, dissolved solids (especially salt), and toxic materials has grown. The earliest federal attack on water pollution involved promoting the construction of sewage treatment plants for municipalities to reduce the organic waste loads that were seriously depleting oxygen with resulting fish kills and odors. While reducing the gross pollution load, these plants released large quantities of nitrogen and phosphorous generated by the biological processes and by detergents. These nutrients often promoted the rapid growth of algae that died and decomposed, again causing serious oxygen deficits and esthetic problems. Many cities and industries are now being required to use higher levels of treatment that can remove the nutrients.

Imagine a water body along the shores of which are located identifiable sources of pollution (boxes in Figure 14.12) and identifiable *receptors* or parties damaged by pollution (circles). In the most general case, the water body is like a lake in which all pollutors affect all receptors, but if the water body is a river without tidal effects, particular pollutors affect only receptors downstream. We consider the system shown in Figure 14.12 in its "steady state," that is, under the assumption that pollution

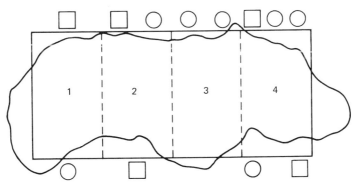

**Figure 14.12** A water body surrounded by pollutors and receptors.

loads, water flows (and other processes like reaeration), and the damage proneness of receptors remain constant over time.[8] We now want to model the main elements of the system relevant to a socially optimum program of pollution control, where optimality means minimizing the sum of abatement costs and the residual damages from pollution.

First, however, let us use our economic intuition to anticipate the general nature of the optimality conditions. In general, we will seek a solution in which the marginal benefits from additional abatement will just fall to equality with the marginal abatement costs. It is now our job to give some real-world content to this obvious condition. We should be especially interested in reducing the concentration of pollutants in those zones (1 to 4 in Figure 14.12) having highly damage-prone receptors, concentrating the pollution reductions among those pollutors exhibiting low abatement costs or especially damaging effects because of proximity to receptors.

Now we will construct a simple model that would give us the capability of computing the solution for an actual case. Let

$\overline{X}_i \equiv$ the initial rate of pollution from source $i$ (e.g., in pounds of oxygen demanding wastes per day)

$X_i \equiv$ source $i$'s new pollution rate

$A_i \equiv (\overline{X}_i - X_i) \equiv$ the rate of abatement of pollution per period by source $i$

$C_i(A_i) \equiv$ the cost per period of abatement by source $i$

$Z_j \equiv$ the concentration of the pollutant in zone $j$ (e.g., in milligrams per liter)

$D_j(Z_j) \equiv$ the monetary value of damage to all receptors in zone $j$ per period resulting from the ambient concentration $Z_j$

It is assumed that $C_i(A_i)$ is the minimum achievable cost of attaining $A_i$, possibly including the loss of net benefits from product output should reduction of production be a part of this minimum cost program. It is also assumed that $D_j(Z_j)$ is the minimum damage level possible under $Z_j$, that is, that all steps by receptors that reduce damage by more than their cost have been taken.

A water quality model must have an explicit representation of the *physical process* by which pollution rates at sources are transformed into ambient concentrations in the various zones. We symbolize this part of

---

[8]The existence of such a steady state is assumed, eliminating the possibility of a continuing buildup of pollutants.

the model by a set of functional relationships relating the pollution rates at all sources to the concentration in zone $j$:

(14.5.1)        $Z_j = f_j(X_1, X_2, \ldots, X_m), j = 1, \ldots, n$

In the special case of a river, this set of relations would be "triangular" in form such that only upstream pollution would affect the concentration in a given zone.

The problem of water quality management can now be posed as an optimization problem:

(14.5.2) minimize $\left[ \phi(A_1, \ldots, A_m; Z_1, \ldots, Z_n) = \sum_{i=1}^{m} C_i(A_i) + \sum_{j=1}^{n} D_j(Z_j) \right]$

subject to: $Z_1 = f_1(X_1, \ldots, X_m) = f_1(\bar{X}_1 - A_1, \ldots, \bar{X}_m - A_m)$

.

.

.

$Z_n = f_n(X_1, \ldots, X_m) = f_m(\bar{X}_1 - A_1, \ldots, \bar{X}_m - A_m)$

Substituting directly for the $Z_j$ in the damage function, one can proceed to differentiate the cost function with respect to the $A_i$'s, arriving at the following conditions for the optimum levels of abatement, $A_1^*, \ldots, A_n^*$:

(14.5.3)        $\dfrac{dC_1}{dA_1} = \sum_{j=1}^{n} \dfrac{dD_j(Z_j)}{dZ_j} \cdot \dfrac{\partial Z_j}{\partial X_1}$

. . . .

$\dfrac{dC_m}{dA_m} = \sum_{j=1}^{n} \dfrac{dD_j(Z_j)}{dZ_j} \cdot \dfrac{\partial Z_j}{\partial X_m}$

The interpretation of these conditions is quite simple—that abatement at each source should be carried to a level where marginal abatement costs rise to equality with the sum of marginal damage costs to all receptors that are attributable to that source.

If effluent taxes were to be used to motivate the pollutors to take account of the damages being caused the receptors, the optimum effluent tax per unit of pollution per period for pollution $i$ would be given by the right-hand side of line $i$ in (14.5.3). In general, this tax would differ pollutor by pollutor.

Scientific capabilities for estimating the components of the model

above differ from part to part. Costs of abatement can be accurately
estimated for new plants, while older plants pose unique problems,
partly because the best ways of reducing pollution often lie in modifying
their production processes rather than simply adding some kind of
"end-of-pipe" treatment. Damage functions probably can never be estimated in such a way as to capture total damages, but some excellent
studies of particular types of damage have been carried out, such as
Anderson, Kleinman, et al. (1977) on salinity damages to irrigated agriculture and municipal users, Lave and Seskin (1977) on the effects of
air pollution on human mortality, and Ridker (1967) on the general economic costs of air pollution. The ability to model the diffusion processes
represented by the functions $f_j$ is well developed for rivers and moder-
ately well developed for estuaries and bays, although abilities to model
the biological processes such as eutrophication and the water-based
food chains are still quite limited.

The fact that damages cannot be fully estimated and that many
would be skeptical of monetary values for health and esthetics imply
that water quality management (and, indeed, environmental quality
management generally) must proceed without the damage functions of
(14.5.2). This leaves (at least) two approaches: to determine what programs of abatement can be justified on the basis of partial damages or to
establish somewhat arbitrary standards for ambient water quality. An
example of the former would be to show that the reductions in agricultural damages that would result from a reduction of salinity in a river
used for irrigation would more than offset the costs of an upstream
salinity abatement project, such as sealing off some salt springs. In the
case of standards, various kinds of expert opinion are combined to set
maximum levels for pollution concentration. The optimum water quality
problem is then restated as an abatement cost minimization problem:

$$(14.5.4) \qquad \text{minimize} \left[ \phi(A_1, \dots, A_m) = \sum_{i=1}^{m} C_i(A_i) \right]$$

$$\text{subject to } f_1(\bar{X}_1 - A_1, \dots, \bar{X}_m - A_m) \le \hat{Z}_1$$

$$\cdots \cdots$$

$$f_n(\bar{X}_1 - A_1, \dots, \bar{X}_m - A_m) \le \hat{Z}_n$$

where the $\hat{Z}_j$ are the standards for each zone. This problem can be
solved by applying the Kuhn-Tucker conditions to the Lagrangian function of this problem, as shown in Section 14.6, but the results indicate
again that there is no simple rule of thumb such as "all polluters cut back
by equal percentages." The minimum cost solution is achieved by

abatement levels unique to each polluter, based on comparative costs of abatement and the comparative effectiveness in meeting the standards of reducing pollution at different points.

## 14.6.  MINIMUM COST OF MEETING STANDARDS

Starting with (14.5.4), the Lagrangian function is formulated as

(14.6.1)  $L(A_1, \ldots , A_m); \lambda_1, \ldots , \lambda_n) =$

$$\sum_{i=1}^{m} C_i(A_i) + \sum_{j=1}^{n} \lambda_j [f_j(\bar{X}_1 - A_1, \bar{X}_2 - A_2, \ldots , \bar{X}_m - A_m) - \hat{Z}_j]$$

The necessary conditions for a minimum cost program of abatement are:

(14.6.2)                $$\frac{dC_1(A_1)}{dA_1} \geqslant \sum_{j=1}^{n} \lambda_j \frac{\partial f_j}{\partial X_1}$$

$\cdots\cdots$

$$\frac{dC_m(A_m)}{dA_m} \geqslant \sum_{j=1}^{n} \lambda_j \frac{\partial f_j}{\partial X_m}$$

and if $>$ holds in row $i$, $A_i^* = 0$

$$f_1(\bar{X}_1 - A_1, \ldots , \bar{X}_m - A_m) < \hat{Z}_1$$

$\cdots\cdots$

$$f_n(\bar{X}_1 - A_1, \ldots , \bar{X}_m - A_m) < \hat{Z}_n$$

and if $<$ holds in row $j$, $\lambda_j^* = 0$

$\lambda_j$ represents the implicit marginal value of reducing the concentration of pollution in zone $j$ by one unit. If the standard had not quite been met, the value of a unit reduction in $Z_j$ would be the costs that could be avoided under cost-efficient assignment of the $A_i$'s. If the standard had been met, any further improvement has no value, as stated by the last condition above. The first $m$ conditions thus tell us that abatement at each source should be carried to a level where marginal cost just equals the sum of the implicit marginal values times the incremental effects of a unit reduction of the pollutant from source $i$ on the concentrations in all zones. Furthermore, no abatement should be carried out for sources whose marginal costs exceed the minimum feasible marginal cost of achieving the standards.

If a water-quality authority wanted to achieve the optimum levels of abatement through the imposition of effluent taxes, the appropriate taxes would be given by the right-hand sides of the first $m$ inequalities above.

## 14.7.   TWO CASE STUDIES OF WATER QUALITY MANAGEMENT

Two excellent case studies of river basin water quality management are mentioned here, both because they illustrate the nature of excellent applied studies and because they provide practical insights into the efficacy of using effluent charges to effect water quality standards.

Johnson (1967) studied the establishment of dissolved oxygen (DO) standards for the Delaware River and estuary. A computerized dissolved oxygen model that divided the river and estuary into 30 zones was the physical basis for the analysis. The major sources of pollution were identified and their waste loads estimated. The objectives of the study were to calculate the least-cost program of abatement that would permit predetermined standards to be met, and then to compare that program to the estimated results of alternative strategies for meeting the standards—uniform percentage reductions by all sources, a uniform effluent charge imposed on all pollutors, and a system of effluent charges that could differ by zone.

The study required estimation of the real economic cost of different levels of abatement at the various sources. "End-of-pipe" treatment techniques were assumed and engineering cost estimates were made. The analysis of the impact of effluent charges, however, required estimates of the after-tax-and-grant costs to industries and municipalities of the various levels of abatement. Such cost functions are referred to as "reaction functions" since they determine how a firm will react to a given effluent charge, based on the behavioral assumption that a firm or municipality will increase abatement to the point where their after-tax-and-grant marginal costs rise to equality with the effluent charge.

A typical set of results is exhibited in Table 14.3, which compares the annual costs of achieving various DO goals using the four strategies. Two results stand out: (1) the rapidly increasing costs of maintaining higher standards and (2) the large cost differences among the various strategies. The uniform percentage cutback, which has frequently been used in the past, is the least efficient by a wide margin. This strategy has been advocated on grounds of equity, but the equity is deceptive; equal percentage cutbacks by different firms will have vastly different costs. The single effluent charge represents an improvement over UT, and

**Table 14.3.**  Annual Systemwide Treatment Costs of Specified DO Goals Under Alternative Strategies: The Delaware River (millions of dollars per year)

| $DO^a$ | $UT^b$ | SECH | ZECH | LC |
|-----|-----|-----|-----|-----|
| 2 | 5.0 | 2.4 | 2.4 | 1.6 |
| 2-3 | 8.4 | 7.7 | 6.3 | 5.8 |
| 3 | 11.2 | 7.7 | 7.4 | 6.9 |
| 3-4 | 20.0 | 12.0 | 8.6 | 7.0 |
| 4 | 23.0 | 23.0 | 23.0 | 16.0 |

[a] The goals represent a uniform minimum of 2 ppm of DO, a mixed goal of 2 ppm in the lower zones and 3 in the upper zones, etc.
[b] UT means uniform percentage cutbacks on oxygen demanding wastes by all pollutors, SECH means single level of effluent charge on all pollutors, ZECH the zoned effluent charge, and LC the least cost program.

ZECH in turn an improvement over SECH, especially for the higher standards. By making the zones finer and more numerous, ZECH can be made to approach LC. Note, however, that these costs do not include administrative costs that are likely to increase somewhat from UT to LC. It seems unlikely that these administrative cost differences would offset the treatment cost differences.

Fox, Dorcey, and others (see Dorcey, 1973) undertook a similar but much more extensive study of the Wisconsin River, which was heavily polluted by paper mill and municipal wastes. The administrative, behavioral, and political aspects of water quality management were investigated in detail. Part of the results are presented in Table 14.4. Again, substantial cost differences were found, and adopting different risk levels was shown to affect cost strongly.

A very interesting aspect of the Wisconsin River study was its investigation of the feasibility and efficiency of effluent charges. When the "reaction functions" (effective marginal financial cost functions) typical of paper mills and municipalities were estimated, they were found to look like the curves in Figure 14.13. Remember that the data for this study came from a later period than those for the Delaware study and that the applicable tax and subsidy arrangements for the financing of treatment plants had changed since the Delaware study was completed. Nonetheless, these reaction curves are startling for they are totally different from the usually assumed upward sloping marginal cost curves on which recommendations for effluent taxes are based. What are the implications of these curves?

**Table 14.4.** Costs of Alternative Water Quality Management Systems: The Wisconsin River

| Type of System | Risk Level, %[a] | DO Goal | Annual Costs (Millions of Dollars) |
|---|---|---|---|
| Secondary treatment for all pollutors | NA | NA | 7.0 |
| Cost minimization subject to 50% municipal abatement | 1 | 2–5[b] | 5.3 |
| Same | 10 | 2–5 | 4.5 |
| Same | 20 | 2–5 | 3.9 |
| Minimum cost | 10 | 2–5 | 3.7 |

[a]Risk level is the probability of one or more failures annually to meet the DO goals.
[b]The goals represent 2 ppm for some zones and 5 ppm for others as actually adopted for the Wisconsin River.

For the paper mills, if the effluent charge is set below $c$, they won't clean up at all, while if the charge is above $c$, they will go to the highest level possible. For the municipalities, if the charge is below the minimum point on the reaction function, there will be no abatement, while charges above that level will induce high levels of abatement along the right-hand tail of the function. Under these conditions, effluent charges will induce discontinuous responses from pollutors and no charge has the capability of inducing only 20 percent or 30 percent removal if that were called for. The use of an effluent charge scheme individualized to each pollutor to approximate the least cost solution displayed in Table 14.3 had, as a result, a total cost of $4.8 million annually, while a zoned effluent charge resulted in costs of $5.5 million,

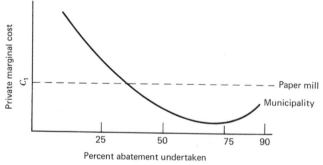

**Figure 14.13** Reaction functions for various levels of abatement: Wisconsin River. Source: Dorcey, 1973, Figs. 1 and 2.

and a single charge led to total costs of $6.4 million. Thus the effluent charges appear to be significantly less efficient than theory would suggest.

However, the calculated inefficiencies stem in part from the limited number of end-of-pipe technologies for abatement incorporated in the model. In addition to end-of-pipe treatments, industries typically can make internal process changes that will reduce their pollution loads, often at quite low cost. In the longer run as plants are replaced, specially designed manufacturing processes can result in quite clean plants. Thus there really are many more response options over time. One of the advantages of the effluent charge approach is that it provides a *continuing stimulus* to seek ways of abating pollution and will stimulate better design of new plants.

## 14.8. SOME CHARACTERISTICS OF THE DEMAND FOR WATER

One often hears assertions regarding the vital nature of water, that this resource is different from others, that we can't get along without it, and so on. It's interesting that Adam Smith used water and diamonds in his *Wealth of Nations* to pose an apparent value paradox: that water was absolutely vital to human existence and yet sold for a pittance while diamonds were absolutely inessential and sold at very high prices! Economists soon unraveled the distinction between the marginal utility of a commodity to a user and the average utility. The marginal utility of water for the first few gallons per day will be very high, but the marginal utility falls quickly as consumption and sanitation needs are satisfied. For diamonds, scarcity created by high mining costs and international cartelization of supply keeps marginal utilities of the affluent high. Since willingness to pay is determined by marginal utility and not total or average utility, prices in competitive markets reflect that marginal value.

This simple principle is frequently overlooked when people consider the value of water. While they may see its reasonableness for personal water uses, they fail to extend the principle to agriculture and industry where it is, in fact, equally applicable. Every farm enterprise and industry has numerous uses of water: irrigation of hay crops and fruit crops, process water, cooling water, sanitation water, and water for human use. Depending on the cost of water to the user, these enterprises will use large or small quantities, applying it first to the vital or high value uses and progressively extending its use to less important things. We can therefore expect water demands to be responsive to price, both in the short and the long runs.

**Table 14.5.**    Patterns of Household Water Use from the Johns Hopkins Residential
Water Use Research Project

| Period of Demand | Gallons per Day per Dwelling Unit | | |
|---|---|---|---|
| | FHA Standards[a] | Metered National Ave. | Nonmetered National Ave. |
| Average daily | 400 | 398 | 692 |
| Maximum daily | 800 | 870 | 2354 |
| Peak hour rate[b] | 2000 | 2115 | 5170 |

[a]Federal Housing Administration.
[b]Peak hour rate of demand expressed on a daily basis.

Source: F. P. Linaweaver, Jr., John C. Geyer, and Jerome B. Wolff, "Summary Report on the Residential Water Use Research Project," *Journal of the American Water Works Association,* Vol. 59, No. 3, March 1967, p. 278.

Illogical comparisons of rates of use often lead to popular misperceptions of the price responsiveness of demands, especially for water and energy. Following a price increase and an initial reduction in demand, quantities used may rise again to former levels or beyond, leading people to say that price has only a temporary effect. The appropriate comparison is with what demand *would have been without the price increase.* There is convincing evidence that water demands are price elastic and that price effects are permanent.

Howe and Linaweaver (1967 and 1968) analyzed an excellent data set collected by the Johns Hopkins University Residential Water Use Research Project.[9] The Project had already demonstrated very significant differences in water use patterns between households that were metered (thereby putting a price on each gallon used) and those that were not, as shown in Table 14.5. In the areas where households were not metered (a fixed monthly fee usually being charged), not only were average daily rates much higher than in metered households, but maximum day rates and peak hour rates were *much* higher. The latter two rates of demand are critical to the design of urban supply systems, requiring much higher system capacities than if peak rates were low. These data are convincing evidence in themselves of a significant and permanent price impact.

When demand functions were fitted to the underlying data, the following functions were found to conform to theoretical expectations

[9]Carried out at Johns Hopkins from 1962 to 1967.

**Table 14.6.**  Residential Water Use Before and After Metering: Boulder, Colorado

| Year | Consumption PDU Northern Routes (1000 Gal per Month) | Consumption PDU Southern Routes (1000 Gal per Month) | Consumption PDU Total (1000 Gal per Month) |
|---|---|---|---|
| 1955 | 8.6 | 8.6 | 8.6 |
| 1956 | 8.7 | 8.7 | 8.7 |
| 1957 | 9.2 | 9.2 | 9.2 |
| 1958 | 10.9 | 10.9 | 10.9 |
| 1959 | 9.9 | 9.9 | 9.9 |
| 1960 | 9.2 | 9.2 | 9.2 |
| 1961 | 9.3 | 9.3 | 9.3 |
| 1962 | 9.5 | 7.4 | 8.1 |
| 1963 | 4.4 | 6.1 | 5.4 |
| 1964 | 4.9 | 5.7 | 5.5 |
| 1965 | 4.9 | 6.3 | 5.9 |
| 1966 | 4.9 | 6.5 | 6.0 |
| 1967 | 4.9 | 6.5 | 6.0 |
| 1968 | 4.2 | 6.0 | 5.5 |
| Ave. flat rate | 9.4 | 9.1 | 9.2 |
| Ave. metered rate | 4.7 | 6.2 | 5.9 |

Source: Steve H. Hanke, "Demand for Water Under Dynamic Conditions," *Water Resources Research*, Vol. 6, No. 5, October 1970, Table 3, p. 1260.

and to have statistically significant parameter values:

(14.8.1)  average daily inhouse use: $q_1 = 206 + 3.6V - 1.3p_w$
average summer outside use (East): $q_2 = 3657E^{0.3}\, p_s^{-0.9}$
average summer outside use (West): $q_2 = 1130V^{0.4}\, p_s^{-0.7}$

These demand functions exhibit very significant responses of daily rates of demand to price, where $p_w$ and $p_s$ represent the approximate prices applicable at the margin during the winter and summer seasons. Since the data were cross-sectional data, the functions are interpreted to be estimates of long-term equilibrium relationships, not simply ephemeral effects.

To investigate further the permanence of price effects, Hanke[10] gathered and analyzed data from two major meter routes in Boulder, Colorado, prior to and after the installation of meters. The data of Table 14.6 show a dramatic, permanent drop.

[10]S. H. Hanke, "Demand for Water Under Dynamic Conditions," *Water Resources Research*, Vol. 6, October 1970, pp. 1253–1261.

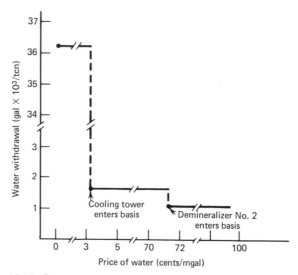

**Figure 14.14**   Demand function for water withdrawals: 1000 tons per day ammonia plant. Source: Calloway, et al., 1974, Fig. 6. Reproduced by permission of the American Geophysical Union.

Industrial demands for water have been studied to a limited extent. To illustrate the kinds of results and the responsiveness of these demands to price, we reproduce the demand curve for water withdrawals by a 1000 ton per day ammonia plant as modeled by Calloway, Thompson, and Schwartz (see Figure 14.14).[11]

Finally, to illustrate the price responsiveness of agricultural irrigation demands to price, we exhibit the value-of-marginal-product curves for farms of several sizes typical of Tulare County, California, as modeled by Moore and Hedges (Table 14.7). The marginal net returns per acre-foot show what a profit-maximizing farmer would pay for various quantities of water. As water grows more scarce or its price to the farmer rises, more efficient methods of applying the irrigation water are used, water applications are reduced on crops not too sensitive to water availability, and the acreages of low-valued crops are reduced. While irrigated agriculture of necessity is a large consumer of water, current rates of consumption result from the uneconomically low prices that are charged for irrigation water by state and federal water projects.

[11]James A. Callaway, Andrew K. Schwartz, Jr., and Russell G. Thompson, "Industrial Economic Model of Water Use and Waste Treatment for Ammonia", *Water Resources Research*, Vol. 10, No. 4, August 1974.

**Table 14.7.** Marginal Value of Water as a Function of Water Applied, by Farm Size, Tulare County, California

| 80 Acres | | 160 Acres | | 320 Acres | | 640 Acres | | 1280 Acres | |
|---|---|---|---|---|---|---|---|---|---|
| Acre-Feet | Net Returns per Additional Acre-Foot | Acre-Feet | Net Returns per Additional Acre-Foot | Acre-Feet | Net Returns per Additional Acre-Foot | Acre-Feet | Net Returns per Additional Acre-Foot | Acre-Feet | Net Returns per Additional Acre-Foot |
| 0 | $— | 0 | $— | 0 | $— | 0 | $— | 0 | $— |
| 28 | 77 | 56 | 77 | 115 | 80 | 229 | 83 | 459 | 82 |
| 32 | 54 | 280 | 50 | 505 | 53 | 1,009 | 56 | 2,019 | 56 |
| 144 | 43 | 289 | 48 | 562 | 52 | 1,125 | 51 | 2,250 | 51 |
| 176 | 36 | 351 | 40 | 580 | 49 | 1,160 | 50 | 2,320 | 50 |
| 181 | 24 | 369 | 17 | 703 | 38 | 1,408 | 42 | 2,817 | 38 |
| 187 | 21 | 609 | 13 | 720 | 27 | 1,443 | 29 | 2,886 | 27 |
| 309 | 14 | 636 | 10 | 759 | 19 | 1,517 | 19 | 3,337 | 22 |
| 320 | 12 | 637 | 9 | 963 | 14 | 1,926 | 17 | 3,853 | 19 |
| 347 | 9 | 694 | 8 | 1,210 | 13 | 1,950 | 14 | 4,866 | 18 |
| 348 | 8 | 728 | 2 | 1,330 | 10 | 2,457 | 13 | 5,180 | 17 |
| 351 | 3 | | | 1,377 | 10 | 2,650 | 9 | 5,615 | 16 |
| 380 | 2 | | | 1,400 | 9 | 2,807 | 8 | 6,017 | 8 |
| | | | | 1,465 | 2 | | | 6,100 | 7 |
| | | | | 1,519 | 1 | | | | |

Source: Charles V. Moore, and Trimble R. Hedges, "Economics of On-Farm Irrigation Water Availability and Costs...," Giannini Foundation Research Report No. 263, University of California, Berkeley, 1963.

# Chapter 15

# NATURAL AREAS AND ECOSYSTEMS AS NATURAL RESOURCES

Concern for the future has been the pervasive theme of the preceding chapters. The adequacy of natural resource stocks has been discussed as well as the dynamics of technological innovation and resource exploration. Concepts of intergenerational equity and discounting processes have been described and critiqued. We must now explicitly recognize that "provision for the future" can take many forms and that, even after we have decided how much present sacrifice (saving) will be made, the composition of the legacy we leave for future generations is a complex matter, indeed. This legacy consists not merely of man-made capital, but of human capital, knowledge and technology, the conditions of the air and water-environments, *in situ* stocks of known and suspected natural resources, and areas of undisturbed natural environments or ecosystems. The natural area component deserves special attention for two reasons: the conversion of natural areas is, in many cases, an irreversible process, and the demand for the use of undisturbed natural areas for recreational purposes (broadly interpreted) is growing strongly worldwide.

Processes of economic growth and technological change involve important irreversibilities and asymmetries (see Figure 15.1). Not only can natural areas and their ecosystems frequently *not* be recreated once disturbed by development, but the processes of technological change that have accounted for such an important part of the growth of output are generally incapable of supplementing our stocks of natural areas.

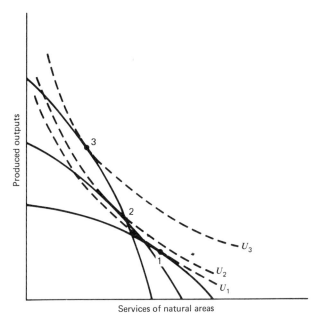

**Figure 15.1**  Irreversibility of development of natural areas and the asymmetry of technological change.

These factors can be represented by the shifts in the aggregate production frontier as shown by Krutilla in his classic "Conservation Reconsidered" (1967). The progression of the production frontier from (1) to (2) to (3) represents the effects of the reductions in undeveloped natural areas (X intercept shifting left) and the effects of better technology in increasing the output potential for manufactured goods. If we imagine a family of social indifference curves to reflect society's values, the optimum points shift upward and to the left. Since the slope at the points of tangency represents the (negative of) the ratio of the price of natural area services to that of produced output, we can see that this relative price would rise over time, even with no shift in tastes. These observations on the likely trend of relative prices or values of natural area services imply that benefit-cost analyses and other planning procedures must take this trend into account.

In some situations, these irreversibilities and asymmetries may not be as absolute as depicted here. Parts of West Virginia that were laid waste by mining 75 years ago have reforested and present excellent hunting, fishing, and camping experiences. Other areas, however, were so eroded that they remain bare and their streams dead, filled with silt and acid mine drainage. Also, certain types of technological improvement effectively expand our natural areas. Transportation, making more remote areas accessible, is the most obvious example, but improved mining and forest harvesting techniques have reduced the disruption caused by these activities. It might be possible, if we worked at it, to design and manage dams and reservoirs in ways that would facilitate returning the reservoir site to other uses at the end of the dam's life.

## 15.1. ECONOMIC ASPECTS OF UNIQUE NATURAL AREAS

A unique natural area has, by definition, very limited substitutes. The demand for the use of such an area is therefore likely to exhibit certain important features: a steeply sloped demand function and a significant *option demand*.

As an extreme example, consider Yosemite Park's potential for aesthetic and recreational uses as contrasted with its potential for producing gravel. The area is certainly unique and highly valued for the former use, and the demand for its recreational services would look something like the demand curve in Figure 15.2a. On the other hand, the demand for gravel from Yosemite (a very common commodity) would look something like the curve in 15.2b, but the costs of producing gravel might be quite low. While the price and quantity scales of these figures are not the same, the figures suggest that if the area were left open for private development, it might prove privately more profitable to mine gravel than to preserve the area for recreation. That is, $\Pi_G$ might exceed $\Pi_R$, even if the total social net benefits [the entire shaded area in (a)] greatly exceeded $\Pi_G$. This occurs because the private recreational

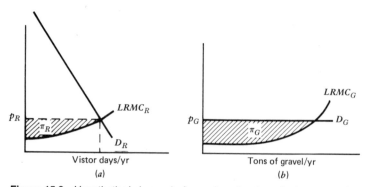

**Figure 15.2** Hypothetical demands for and costs of producing recreational services and gravel in Yosemite Park.

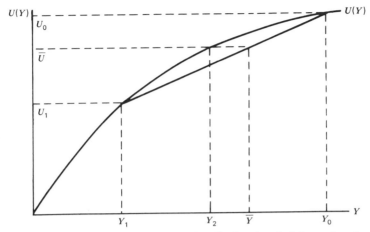

**Figure 15.3** A segment of a consumer's utility function depicting option demand.

developer, even if possessing some monopoly power, cannot capture all the consumer surplus generated by recreational uses.

This suggests that, if the depiction of demand curves is correct, the public sector may have to play an active role in the development and management of unique natural areas. It may well be that the existence of the large consumer surplus is more a manifestation of the author's personal value biases than of any general economic principle, but the argument still seems reasonable.

In addition, there may be a substantial *option demand* for the preservation of unique natural areas that would not be taken into account by private developers. Option demand is defined as a willingness to pay for the preservation of an area by an uncertain user, that is, someone who is not sure that he or she will have the opportunity to use the area. This willingness to pay is in excess of the *expected value* of any consumer's surplus that would be generated for the user when he or she chanced to visit the area.

The argument for the existence of significant option demand for unique natural areas is as follows[1]: (see Figure 15.3) assume an individual to be a risk averter faced with uncertainty regarding whether or not his or her future circumstances (schedule, travel plans, free time, health, etc.) will permit him or her actively to demand use of the area. When circumstances are such that the visit is not feasible, the individual

[1]For a detailed exposition of the argument, see Charles J. Cicchetti and A. Myrick Freeman III, "Option Demand and Consumer Surplus," *Quarterly Journal of Economics*, August 1971.

experiences a utility level of $U_0$ corresponding to income, $Y_0$. When circumstances are such that the individual's rationally selected market basket of goods and services includes a visit to the area, utility is assumed once again to be $U_0$.

When it happens, however, that circumstances lead the individual to demand use of the area but he or she finds the area no longer available, the utility level is substantially reduced, say to level $U_1$ along a concave segment of the utility function. The corresponding level of money income would be $Y_1$, the difference $Y_0 - Y_1$ being the monetary measure of the consumer surplus lost because of the unavailability of the area.

If we let $P_0$ be the relative frequency (probability) of circumstances leading to no demand and $P_1$ be the relative frequency of circumstances leading to active demand, the individual's expected (average) utility level will be $\bar{U}$ if the area is not available:

$$(15.1.1) \qquad \bar{U} = P_0 U_0 + P_1 U_1$$

The monetary measure of the individual's expected (average) income in this situation would be:

$$(15.1.2) \qquad \bar{Y} = P_0 Y_0 + P_1 Y_1$$

The monetary measure of the expected (average) loss of consumer surplus to this individual would be $P_1 (Y_0 + Y_1)$ which, in the figure, equals $Y_0 - \bar{Y}$.[2] A very sophisticated benefit-cost analyst might include this to be an element of cost for any development project that would radically change the area, making it unavailable. *Is this a sufficient measure of the individual's loss?* The answer is *no*, since the individual would be willing to pay more than this to *guarantee* the availability of the area.

To see this, we note that if the individual had a monetary income of $Y_2$, his or her utility level would be $\bar{U}$, the same as average utility with the natural area unavailable. He or she should, therefore, be willing to pay any sum up to $Y_0 - Y_2$ to guarantee the availability of the area, that is, they would pay this much for an option guaranteeing its availability. We note that $Y_0 - Y_2$ exceeds $Y_0 - \bar{Y}$ by the amount $\bar{Y} - Y_2$, which measures the individual's option demand.

The existence of such an excess of willingness to pay over expected loss of consumer surplus obviously depends on the three assumptions built into the analysis: (1) that the individual is risk averse, that is, the

[2] $Y_0 - \bar{Y} = Y_0 - (P_0 Y_0 + P_1 Y_1) = Y_0 - [(1 - P_1)Y_0 + P_1 Y_1] = P_1 (Y_0 - Y_1)$

utility function is strictly concave; (2) that the loss of consumer surplus $Y_0 - Y_1$ is large enough to be "significant" to the individual; (3) that the individual's utility level when he or she demands use of the area and finds it available is the same as on "no demand" days. The first two assumptions seem reasonable enough, but the third seems a bit far-fetched. If the individual cherishes a visit to the area, the utility function with respect to money incomes should shift *upward* on those days when he or she is fortunate enough to be able to make such a visit. The opportunity set has been significantly expanded.[3] It can be shown, however, that any uniform upward shift of the utility function will maintain the excess of the willingness to pay for an option over the expected loss of consumer surplus. Thus, the case for the existence of significant individual and aggregate option values for truly unique areas seems to rest on firm ground.

Both the likelihood of significant consumer surplus and the existence of option demand dictate caution or conservatism in proceeding with the conversion of unique natural areas to traditional patterns of development. Another reason for being slow to develop such areas is that information is likely to be gained regarding the trends in the benefits from development and from preservation. Arrow and Fisher[4] have demonstrated that the optimal decision rule concerning when to develop becomes more conservative when information can be gained through waiting. This additional (unquantified) value is sometimes referred to as "quasi-option value."

## 15.2. MEASURING THE DEMAND FOR OUTDOOR RECREATION

One of the major uses of the natural environment is for recreation: backpacking, fishing, canoeing, skiing, and the like. Outdoor recreation participation has burgeoned in recent years, causing many popular areas to become crowded and pushing the recreation frontier into more remote areas. At the same time, large new areas have been set aside for wilderness preservation, and attempts have been made to *manage* recreation, especially on the federal lands. This management often takes the form of planning for multiple-purpose use of public lands as noted in

---

[3]Other analogies suggest the utility functions must shift. One does not typically use ambulance services, but on the unfortunate day when one is needed, the utilities associated with various income levels must surely be different.

[4]Kenneth J. Arrow and A. C. Fisher, "Environmental Preservation, Uncertainty, and Irreversibility," *Quarterly Journal of Economics*, Vol. LXXXVIII, No. 2, 1974.

the chapter on forestry, for example, combined timber, range, watershed, and recreation management. It may involve separating incompatible activities such as backpacking and jeeping or cross-country skiing and snowmobiling. It may also involve limiting access to some areas to avoid exceeding their "carrying capacities" as was suggested in Section 12.5.

It should be obvious that projections of "demand" for the recreational use of land are crucial inputs into recreation and land use management. "Demand" means not only projections of the numbers of persons likely to show up at recreation sites but also the values or net benefits associated with those recreational experiences.

Recreation participation studies have taken many forms: site specific studies (who uses a site or how many will use a site); activity specific studies (how many recreation-days will be generated in a particular region for a specified activity like hunting, fishing, or boating); projections of total expenditures on recreational activities, related equipment sales; and so on. While such studies are essential for planning, very few of them have estimated the benefits associated with existing or prospective recreation sites or areas. Benefit measures are needed whenever recreation appears as a project purpose or when alternative design or management strategies imply tradeoffs between recreation and other outputs. To illustrate, suppose that there are two strategies for the design and management of a reservoir: one that would provide $5 \times 10^{12}$ kwh of electric power and 100,000 boater recreation days, and another that would provide $8 \times 10^{12}$ kwh of power but only 50,000 recreation days (presumably because of greater fluctuations in water level, mud flat exposure, etc.). To judge which strategy is superior, we need to know the unit values of both a kilowatt-hour of power and a recreation day.

Market prices provide handy value measures for recreational services when they exist, as they do for downhill ski resorts, holiday beach hotels, tennis courts, and swimming pools. In many cases, however, market prices do not exist for recreation, either because the facilities are publicly provided and entrance fees have been kept at nominal levels for equity reasons or because the nature of the activity makes it impractical for private enterpreneurs to make users pay. Even if the development of recreational facilities can be turned over to private enterprise, planners both public and private must estimate participation rates and willingness to pay *ex ante*, that is, before a project is in place. Thus, methods for recreation demand estimation are essential.

**The Survey Method of Recreation Demand Estimation.** Perhaps the most direct way of estimating demand for recreation is through survey techniques. These could take many forms, from general population surveys to site specific estimates of use rates and users' willingness to pay. An excellent example of the latter is Davis' study of the value of big-game hunting in a 500,000 acre private forest in Maine (1964). Potential uses for the study results would be to optimize the mix of recreational and timbering operations. Big-game hunting seems ideally suited to willingness-to-pay studies, for it is usually a carefully planned activity with no significant externalities.

Willingness to pay for a hunting outing in the area was determined by Davis through on-site interviews with a sample of hunters. The interview process included, among other things, a bidding game in which the hunters could react to (hypothetical) increases in admission prices to the area. Bids were systematically raised or lowered until the hunter switched his or her decision from using the area to not using the area (or vice versa), a good reflection of actual behavior since most hunters were nonresidents who came to the area only once per season. A household demand curve was derived from these data by regression analysis. The result is given by the following equation:

(15.2.1) $$W = 0.74L^{0.76}E^{0.20}Y^{0.60}$$

where $W$ is the willingness to pay of a household unit for admission to the recreation area, $L$ is the length of visit in days, $E$ is years of acquaintance with the area, and $Y$ is annual household income in thousands of dollars.

Following the determination of this equation from the sample data, the hunter population was further sampled to determine the distribution of the $L$, $E$, and $Y$ characteristics. For various $(L,E,Y)$ intervals, the average $W$ value was computed and plotted against the estimated number of household visits falling in that interval, to yield the demand curve given in Figure 15.4.

Demand is shown to be sensitive to price in the $5 to $20 range, while total revenue (price times quantity) is almost constant and near its maximum over the $6 to $12 range. A timber company wanting to manage its land jointly for timber and recreation might therefore choose to charge $12 and thereby achieve approximately maximum revenues with minimal interference with timbering operations. Alternatively, a social manager wanting to calculate the total value of recreation under unre-

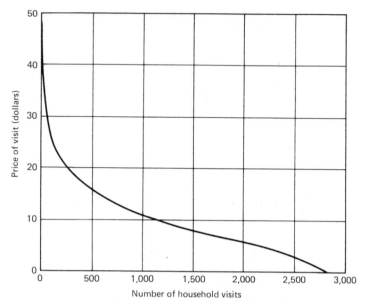

**Figure 15.4** Simulated demand function for big-game hunting. Source: Davis, 1964, Fig. 1, p. 398.

stricted access to the area could calculate the area under the curve to be approximately $29,000 per year.

**The Travel Cost Method.** Clawson and Knetsch (1966), generalizing on earlier work by Hotelling, developed a method by which travel costs could be used as surrogates for recreationists' willingness to pay for the use of recreation areas. Cesario and Knetsch have generalized this method to include travel time as a further differentiating surrogate for willingness to pay. The basic idea is to assume that people who live $X$ miles from a recreation site and who face time and travel costs in getting to the site would use the site just as frequently as people $X + h$ miles from the site when faced with an admission fee to the site equal to the additional time and travel costs associated with the distance $h$. From this assumption and observations regarding the frequency of use of different groups, one can deduce a demand function for the site. In the procedure, allowances are made for differences in income of the groups of users and for differences in alternative recreational opportunities. Insofar as new sites are located in areas similar to those from which the estimating data were taken, these estimated demand functions can be

used to estimate both the rates of use of prospective sites and the value
of a new site as a recreational asset.

The Texas Water Development Board used this technique to evaluate the recreational values of reservoir sites that were being considered
for inclusion in the Texas Water Plan. To illustrate, their analysis started
with the following participation rate function (Grubb and Goodwin,
1968):[5]

$$\log_e (Y + 0.8) = -5.60 + 0.57 \log_e X_1 - 1.19 \log_e X_2 \\ +0.75 \log_e X_3 - 0.33 \log_e X_4 + 0.21 \log_e X_5$$

where

$Z$ = the number of visitor days per year from a particular county to a
particular reservoir

$X_1$ = population of the county of origin

$X_2$ = the round trip cost from the county of origin

$X_3$ = per capita income in the county of origin

$X_4$ = a "gravity" variable to reflect the offsetting attractions of other
available lakes

$X_5$ = size of the surface area of the conservation pool of the lake

The above function was statistically fitted from actual observations on
the uses of Texas lakes. This participation function was then used to
estimate the demand function for new sites by inserting values of the
variables for the counties surrounding the new sites and by a sequence
of additions to the travel cost variable that represents a sequence of
increasing admission charges. Adding the participation rates over all
counties for each hypothetical admission rate ($0, 1, . . .) will yield points
on the demand function, illustrated in Figure 15.5. The approximate area
under the curve up to the rate of visitation consistent with the intended
admission charge is the measure of recreation benefits yielded annually
by the lake.

The effect of water quality on the demand for water-based recreation is an increasingly important factor about which little is known.

[5]H. W. Grubb and J. T. Goodwin, "Economic Evaluation of Water Oriented Recreation in
the Preliminary Texas Water Plan," Report 84, Texas Water Development Board, Austin,
1968. The dependent variable is stated as $(Y + 0.8)$ so that $Y$ values close to zero will not
unduly influence the estimated parameter values.

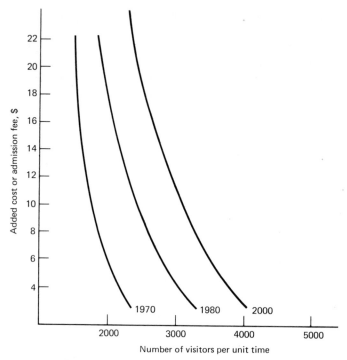

**Figure 15.5** Shifting recreation demand curves.

Frankel[6] demonstrated that water-quality improvement programs usually cannot be justified in terms of savings in downstream intake treatment costs. This finding has been reinforced by studies that show that industrial cooling water users often benefit from the lower corrosive powers of oxygen-deficient water. Irrigators downstream from cities benefit from the nutrients introduced into the stream in sewage plant effluent. Thus recreational and aesthetic values must be the prime justification for programs of water quality improvement.

Further survey work relating water quality to recreational willingness to pay is badly needed. An example of interesting pioneering work is found in the study "Option Values, Preservation Values, and Recreational Benefits of Improved Water Quality: A Case Study of the South Platte River Basin, Colorado" by Walsh et al.[7] where a bidding technique

[6]Richard Frankel, "Water Quality Management: Engineering-Economic Factors in Municipal Waste Disposal," *Water Resources Research,* Vol. 1, Second Quarter, 1965.
[7]Richard G. Walsh et al., Colorado State University Experiment Station Project 15-1771-277, Department of Economics, Fort Collins, September 30, 1977.

based on photographs of streams of different qualities was used to elicit three types of willingness to pay: (1) the willingness to pay for improved water quality by stream users, (2) an option value of users for preserving recreational quality water, and (3) a willingness to pay for preservation of water quality and natural ecosystems for future generations by nonstream users. The values per household were fairly high: about $57 annually for (1), $23 for (2), and about $42 annually for (3). Very similar techniques have been used experimentally by the Resource and Environmental Economics Laboratory at the University of Wyoming to value the aesthetic manifestations of air quality in southeastern Utah.

## 15.3.  A SUGGESTED BENEFIT-COST EXERCISE IN COMPARING DEVELOPMENT WITH PRESERVATION

To fix some of the foregoing concepts for measuring recreation benefits and to place them in a benefit-cost analysis context, it is suggested that the reader work through the following problem scenario in which the preservation of a river site is being compared to the advantages of power development. Write a two-page report summarizing and justifying quantitatively your recommendations.

**Problem Scenario.**  You are hired as a consultant to the Office of Management and Budget to analyze the benefits and costs of building a dam on the Yellowstone River in comparison with the preservation of the area. Your analysis is to be backed by explicitly stated quantitative data that are a product of your analysis.

The site being considered for development would have *no* recreational value if the dam is built. It is felt that there would be growing use of the area for recreation if the dam is not constructed. The analysis is restricted to three "periods." Current period benefits and costs are not to be discounted, but those of Period 2 are to be discounted by a discount *factor* [i.e., $1/(1 + r)$] of 0.8 and those of Period 3 by a factor of 0.6.

The following data are given:

1.  Cost of dam construction: $5,000,000.
2.  Power benefits per "period" from having the dam: $3,000,000.
3.  Recreational use of the area is known to come from the populations of two nearby counties. The following data, present and projected, are available on those counties:

|                | County 1 | | County 2 | |
|                | Population | Ave. Hsd. Inc. | Population | Ave. Hsd. Inc. |
| --- | --- | --- | --- | --- |
| Present period | 3000 | 10,000 | 5000 | 15,000 |
| Period 2       | 4000 | 12,000 | 6000 | 17,000 |
| Period 3       | 5000 | 15,000 | 7000 | 18,000 |

4. Travel cost to the area is $2 per trip from County 1 and $4 per trip from County 2.

5. Careful earlier analyses of recreation participation rates in very similar areas have produced the following "participation rate function," giving annual recreation days generated per county as a function of population ($P$), average household income ($I$), surface acreage of water recreation sites at other locations ($A$), and travel costs per trip ($TC$):

$$y_i = 2.0P_i + 0.001\,(P_i \times I_i) \\ - 50A - 5000\,TC_i.$$

6. It is known that a 500-acre lake available for recreation purposes already exists in the area.

## 15.4. CLOSING OBSERVATIONS ON THE NATURAL ENVIRONMENT AS AMENITY AND CONSTRAINT

The maintenance of environmental quality has become a major national objective (e.g., as manifested in the *Principles and Standards* of the U.S. Water Resources Council). This environmental objective can be thought of as having three dimensions: (1) maintenance of a high quality ambient environment, (2) prevention of further deterioration in the global environmental systems such as the upper atmosphere and the ocean depths, and (3) the provision of socially appropriate quantities of natural environmental systems for recreational and scientific purposes.

It now appears that adequate ambient environmental quality levels are attainable (although expensive), even in the face of continuing economic and population growth. Evidence is found in the reports of the Council on Environmental Quality (e.g., 1976). Pollution abatement technology is still relatively young, and it seems quite likely that significant advances will continue in those technologies. This is not to assert that ambient environmental quality will not constrain economic activity, for its costs have risen to a significant fraction of the gross national product and have caused a slowing in the growth of output available for consumption and other types of investment. Nonetheless, these costs are predictable and will rise smoothly with the standards we impose and levels of output, rather than standing as an absolute barrier to further growth.

It is not clear that some of the larger-scale environmental changes can be prevented through technological change or even reversed as a result of future decisions. The buildup of carbon dioxide and fluorocarbons in the upper atmosphere, the accumulation of radioactive wastes in the earth's crust and oceans, and other forms of oceanic pollution are examples. While the implications of these conditions are not clearly known at present, it is conceivable that future generations may face the need to restrict economic activity severely to avoid catastrophic global consequences such as the flooding of coastal areas or severe genetic damage. It is not clear that the common property nature of the global environment will make globally concerted actions possible, even if needed. What is clear is that the risks faced by future generations are being substantially increased as a result of our past and current resource use patterns.

A final facet of the relationship between environmental conditions and future production possibilities is found in the uncertainty of our understanding of the factors to which our past growth can be attributed. Smith and Krutilla[8] have suggested that omission of use of the environment as a factor of production for waste disposal may have biased our estimates of the causes of economic growth. Since the waste assimilative capacities of the environment have been common property resources, they have been freely used, and one would expect that technological innovation would have been strongly biased toward the use of that factor. If this has been true, Smith and Krutilla argue, much of the growth of output that has been imputed to technological change, education, and other qualitative factors should have been attributed to increasing use of the environment. Increased use of this factor may not be available in the future. Furthermore, if technological change has in fact been less productive than we have thought, future technological change must be more heavily discounted as a partial solution to our resource problems.

[8]V. Kerry Smith and John V. Krutilla, "Resource and Environmental Constraints to Growth," Discussion Paper D-17, Resources for the Future, Inc., Washington, D.C., November 1977.

# Chapter 16

# ELEMENTS OF A RESPONSIBLE NATURAL RESOURCES POLICY

We have now completed a wide-ranging review of economic, technical, and social issues related to our use of natural resources. The concepts of natural resource stocks and rates of use have been explained. Processes of exploration and the market motivation for expanding and holding stocks of natural resources *in situ* have been investigated. We have seen that concern over natural resource adequacy is certainly not new but has been felt in one form or another for centuries.

We have learned to conceptualize various stages of the economic growth process in terms of the roles of natural resources and the ways these resources might constrain economic growth. Since serious constraints appear to have been avoided, we have investigated in some detail the major factors that have been at work mitigating natural resource shortage, overcoming short-term stringencies by finding more or alternative resources and increasing the efficiency of their use.

The role of markets and their likely functioning under contemporary conditions has been discussed at length, along with questions of what criteria should be used to judge market performance or used as the basis for social planning. Problems that are poorly handled by unrestricted markets and that are still not adequately addressed by public sector actions or rules—such as the many manifestations of the common property problem—have been analyzed.

Finally, the major issues associated with particular natural resource commodities or industries and the economic tools needed for understanding these issues have been analyzed: energy, nonfuel minerals, forestry, fisheries, water resources, and natural environments.

As we consider natural resource problems on a commodity by commodity basis, we gain confidence in our ability to comprehend the issues and to recommend alternative courses of action that appear to be capable of solving the problems as we currently perceive them. The issues are so numerous and so pervasive, however, that we can rightfully wonder whether or not any general policy guidelines are possible— guidelines that can direct the efforts of individual legislative committees, management agencies, and state and federal executives to formulate and execute a coherent and *responsible* natural resources policy.

This final chapter seeks to review the major factors on which our future natural resource situation depends, ultimately arriving at policy guidelines that appear to follow logically from our study of these factors and that seem to be economically and morally defensible.

## 16.1.  DEFINITION OF A RESPONSIBLE NATURAL RESOURCES POLICY

The underlying issue to which we implicitly refer when we speak of "a responsible natural resources policy" is the sustainability of aggregate production and a livable environment over the very long-term future. This suggests the following definition:

> A responsible natural resources policy on the part of the present generation of society consists of a set of rules, inducements, and actions relating to natural resource use that are sufficient to move the economy to an efficient, indefinitely sustainable, nondeclining pattern of aggregate consumption, with no irreversible deterioration of the physical environment, and without the imposition of significantly greater risks on future generations.

Individual elements in this definition may seem infeasible at the present time, but this is a *goal,* not a requirement for immediate execution. We probably cannot stop some types of further deterioration of the environment for some time, especially oceanic systems, but the time may arrive when such deterioration will have to be stopped of human survival is to be assured. No set of policies not having this as a goal could be called *responsible.*

The definition not only imposes stringent conditions but it fails to clarify important issues such as the following that national governments and international agencies alike will face. Can we treat only part of the world system in light of the distributions of natural resources and population among the various countries? Whose aggregate consumption are we referring to? Does such a set of policies exist?

Since the possibility of worldwide determination and coordination of policies seems remote, practical policy guidelines must be addressed to the national policy stance. This need not and cannot mean ignoring the rest of the world. Increasing international *interdependence* through natural resources and investment patterns must be recognized. Nationally felt obligations to the rest of the world like the avoidance of transboundary pollution or a readiness to supply materials support during natural calamities must influence the formulation of our natural resources policies.

The definition above obviously relates to the Rawlsian criterion and Page's concept of maintaining a "constant effective resource base," which were discussed in Chapter 8. It also relates to Daly's work in which he has urged greater attention to the ends of economic activity, a primary concern for survival of human and other life systems, and greater emphasis on intergenerational equity. Alarmingly little attention has been paid to these fundamental issues by policy makers or economists.

## 16.2. A REVIEW OF CRUCIAL FACTORS CONDITIONING FUTURE NATURAL RESOURCE AVAILABILITY

The work of Barnett and Morse, its updating by V. K. Smith and others, Ridker's investigations for the U.S. Commission on Population Growth and the American Future, and an apparent easing of world energy supplies in recent times all indicate that the future looks favorable for the industrialized countries for the next 15 or 20 years, barring international conflicts that could shut off trade. Can we say anything about the longer-term future?

Among the many technological and institutional factors discussed so far that will condition long-term natural resource availability, 12 appear to be particularly crucial. We review these factors below under the headings of technological factors, demand and life-style factors, and institutional and equity factors.

*Technological Factors*

1. Physical conditions of mineral resource availability. This factor was discussed at length in Chapter 10. It appears that many of the rarer metals of increasing importance to new technology are found in the

earth's crust in a bimodal distribution, that is, in a few, widely scattered rich deposits and then occurring in low concentrations in ordinary rock or silicate. The latter require extraordinary quantities of energy for recovery that may rule out their exploitation.

2. The ability to substitute man-made or renewable inputs for exhaustible natural resource inputs. We have found evidence of quite significant elasticities of substitution of capital for natural resources in manufacturing (Chapter 6). It has also been noted that past technological change has frequently led to the substitution of nonrenewable for renewable resources. With proper price incentives, it seems likely that these trends can be reversed over long time periods. Greater durability of manufactures and more recycling are possible.

3. Exploitation of scale economies. Past technological change has frequently led to more efficient production at larger scales of operation. It appears that most of these opportunities have been exhausted. However, the revolutionary advances in microelectronic control systems may open new economies of miniaturization of systems, including residential energy, water, and waste systems.

4. The nature of anticipated future technological changes. It was noted in Chapter 7 that many past innovations stemmed from large numbers of small experiments being carried out until some breakthrough was made, frequently by chance. Even with some major technologies that were the object of large-scale industrial research and development programs (such as thermal-electric generation), progress consisted of many small improvements over time. Now we hear of the need for fusion power, direct solar-electric conversion, pollution-free energy systems, and other technologies for which massive research and development programs seem required. Even then, success is far from assured. The whole environment for such research is quite different from that within which most past successes occurred. Will the public and private sectors sort out their respective roles and will the efforts succeed?

5. Environment as amenity and constraint. The value of a high-quality environment increases, while the detrimental impacts of exploiting more diffuse resources with increasingly energy-intensive methods become increasingly serious. While pollution abatement technologies seem capable of protecing the ambient systems at reasonable cost, abilities to control degradation of global systems such as the upper atmosphere and the oceans are much less certain. Environmental conditions may pose the ultimate limits to human activity. Not only may the waste assimilative capacities of

the environment no longer be available as before, but it seems likely that continued extinction of plant and animal species will lead to less resilient, less varied, less interesting environments.

### Consumption and Life-style Factors

6. There are major possibilities for substitution of less resource-intensive goods and services in consumption. The increasing importance of services is one manifestation of this. There is increasing evidence that consumers *are* sensitive to changes in relative prices, as exhibited in energy and water demand studies.

7. Changes in life-style. This is frequently mentioned in popular writing but very infrequently in the professional literature. Certainly economists know very little about the process of changes in individual and group value systems. Are there possibilities for major, discrete changes in the ways we live as opposed to marginal adjustments to relative price changes? Very little is known scientifically about such possibilities and how they might be accomplished.

### Institutional and Equity Factors

8. The environment for innovative activity. The United States shows a continuing ambivalence toward what it expects from the private sector. Government constraints have increased costs and reduced the attractiveness of change by increasing its risks. Natural resource commodity prices are not permitted to reflect real scarcities, so the private production sector does not respond and private consumers fail to adapt.

9. Market processes for allocating natural resources over time have some inevitable biases that call for public sector intervention. Among these are the failure to give appropriate weight to environmental externalities, the apparent difficulties in establishing efficient markets for *in situ* resources (partly because of common property problems of all types), and the use of discount rates that appear to be much higher than political expressions of social time preference. Can these biases be corrected by appropriate regulations, taxes, or subsidies? It is not at all clear that the public sector would, in fact, have fewer biases were it to take increasing responsibility for natural resource allocation.

10. Intertemporal risk bearing. We have seen that facing risk is like incurring a cost. Many current-resource-use patterns appear to be increasing the risk faced by future generations, for example,

whether or not the carbon dioxide buildup will be important, whether or not ocean pollution may affect the oxygen content of the atmosphere, whether or not new technologies we have come to count on will, in fact, occur. Furthermore, these risks are not subject to pooling or spreading. Are we pushing unfair risks onto future generations?

11. Future international trade. In Chapters 2 and 9, we have seen that vast quantities of most raw materials still exist in the world and that large discoveries continue to be made. However, these are occurring primarily in the unexplored regions of the world, not in the heavy resource-using industrialized world. Will world political conditions permit the continued discovery, development, and distribution of these resources? The world becomes continually more interdependent but not necessarily more stable.

12. Natural resources data base. The data base for resources management is much less well developed than for other problem areas such as population, health, social programs, manufacturing, and the like. Present reserve information is still dependent on the private sector in the cases of major energy commodities. Good research and policy making requires a solid data base.

## 16.3. GUIDELINES FOR A RESPONSIBLE NATURAL RESOURCES POLICY

The preceding technological, social, and institutional factors that will condition future natural resource availability might be classified, in terms of our current state of knowledge, into two sets: those that clearly lend optimism to the future outlook, and those that raise major uncertainties. An attempt to do this would be likely to result in a larger number of pessimistic factors than optimistic. This strongly suggests that the United States needs to adopt new policies that will help to reduce the uncertainties noted above and that will motivate both public and private actions aimed at mitigating natural resource scarcity. The following general principles are suggested as guidelines for more detailed action programs.

As with the several objectives recognized in multiple-objective planning (economic efficiency, environment, etc.), there may be conflicts or tradeoffs among these principles and between this set and the level of economic activity.

1. *The avoidance of irreversibilities in all renewable resource systems.* This represents Professor Wantrup's (1952) call for observance of "safe

minimum standards" for all renewable systems, that is, the avoidance of those physical conditions that would make it uneconomical to halt and reverse depletion. Krutilla and Fisher have emphasized the same need from a broader environmental point of view. The rationale was that, in nearly all cases, the maintenance of a safe minimum standard costs very little in relation to the possible losses that might follow from extinction of the resource system. The safe minimum standard thus acts as a base level of preservation, above which economic optimization is free to determine practices. By this practice, the narrowing of potential genetic and physical development over time is avoided.

The concept of the safe minimum standard must be defined specifically for each renewable resource system. For unique ecosystems of scientific and esthetic value, the standard might be defined in terms of minimum contiguous areas needed to permit natural perpetuation of the system. For wild animal species, the standard might consist of densities of population sufficient to guarantee reproduction. Such a standard would imply various policies for hunting, the setting aside of wildlife refuges, and so on. For soil and range systems, the standards could be set in terms of maximum permissible erosion rates, and minimum soil and turf conditions. For water systems, the standard would involve minimum quality conditions, maximum sedimentation rates, and limits on the exploitation of groundwater to assure reversibility of conditions.

2. *The avoidance of irreversibilities in local ambient environmental conditions,* for example, the buildup of nitrates in groundwater, pesticides in groundwater, pesticides in soils, or persistent chemicals in lakes.

3. *The avoidance of irreversibilities in the condition of global environmental systems.* Further changes in these systems cannot be totally avoided. Even if the high-income nations decided to take the necessary steps, the common property nature of the global environmental systems would result in some continued change. Yet, these changes are the major source of the increasing risk being imposed on future generations. These issues should be actively debated in the national and international policy arenas with the objective of international consensus on the assignment of specific national goals for protecting these systems.

4. *A clear determination of the role of free markets and prices.* Current practice consists of a bad mixture of attempts at public control and partial reliance on private markets. The market can be much more effectively enlisted as a part of resources policy, while undesired side effects from market processes can be mitigated through appropriate

taxation and redistribution. The demonstrated responsiveness of technical change to changes in factor prices emphasizes the importance of letting prices reflect the actual conditions of scarcity.

5. *Undertaking a program of resource planning at the federal level for nonrenewable resources, aimed at the perpetuation of a "constant effective natural resource base."* The natural resource information base in the United States is very poor in comparison with, say, agricultural, transportation, or health statistics. The absence of futures markets leaves little opportunity for consensus on future supply-and-demand conditions. This indicates a more active data and forecasting role for appropriate agencies of the federal government.

Once these objectives have been achieved, other activities should be considered that would be aimed at maintaining over time a "constant effective natural resource base." This concept was proposed by Page (1977) and implies not an unchanging resource base but a set of resource reserves, technologies, and policy controls that maintain or expand the production possibilities of future generations.

6. *Increased long-term support of social and technological research and development.* The past importance of technological improvement and human adaptation in the mitigation of resource scarcity has been elaborately demonstrated. Recent years have seen a slackening in private sector research and a decrease in the level of national government support. Given the nature of emerging problems and the "public good" nature of knowledge generated through research, higher levels of research and development support, some directed at specific technologies and social changes, are called for.

Calling for research and development support still fails to define an efficient strategy for allocating that support. How government agencies are to decide on efficient extramural allocations of funds and efficient in-house research programs is not totally clear. The history of success of agricultural research within public sector laboratories and experiment stations should be studied in this regard. The decentralized nature of that program made it responsive to regional problems and the needs of the user of applied research results. The effectiveness of other research and development support programs such as those supported by the Office of Water Research and Technology might also provide valuable insights.

## 16.4. NECESSARY CONDITIONS FOR A RESPONSIBLE DECISION-MAKING PROCESS

Regions in early stages of economic development tend to place primary emphasis on the maximization of net economic benefits (i.e., benefits minus costs) as a criterion for the development and management of resources. As regional incomes are raised, other criteria assume increasing importance: protection of the physical environment, health and safety, special benefits for poorer areas, and so on. The application of multiple criteria to policy and project design and evaluation is called "multiple objective planning" and is a practice of increasing importance and attention in nearly all countries. The application of multiple criteria raises many conceptual problems: What weights should be given to the various criteria? How are some criteria to be quantified? When there is no longer a single criterion for the goodness of a project, who should make the decisions about project selection and financing?[1]

Generally, the persons involved in designing and evaluating policy alternatives are *not* the decision makers but are technical specialists who generate information to be used by the decision makers in making the final policy selection. The reason for emphasizing this is that decision making is a political process involving the weighting of the various national or regional criteria that are served by resources policy. The assignment of these weights is a political step for it involves balancing the interests of different groups in society. Furthermore, natural resource development and management decisions are not economically, politically, or technologically independent of decisions being made in other sectors: transportation, agriculture, industry, and so on. For example, the decision to develop a resource in one region may not be based primarily on maximum national economic advantage but on considerations of equity among regions or because of environmental considerations.

This picture of the decision-making process emphasizes the importance of a *continuing dialogue* between policy analysts and decision makers. The decision makers want information on the performance and impacts of alternative resource policies. At the same time, since the number of alternatives that can be designed and evaluated is limited, the policy analysts require an understanding of the weights that decision makers are likely to place on the various national and regional criteria so they can define a range of policy alternatives that provides meaningful variation and yet remains relevant. The flow of unbiased information in both directions is crucial to responsible decision making.

When certain levels of decisions are left to the policy analyst or

---

[1]As an example of emerging procedures for multiple-objective planning, see the summary of the Principles and Standards for Planning Water and Related Land Resources, U.S. Water Resources Council, published in the Federal Register, Vol. 38, No. 174, Sept. 10, 1973.

technical expert (e.g., the economist or the mining geologist), politicians may disagree with the decisions being made or may be unhappy with the information being presented to them. This disagreement can occur because the technical expert does not understand the criteria and weights being used by the politician, or because the technical expert is being asked to make conflict-ridden decisions that are political in nature.

At times, dissatisfaction with technical results has led to political interference with the *methods of technical analysis*. For example, dissatisfaction with the lack of approval of inland waterway projects under the benefit/cost analysis procedures correctly developed by the U.S. Army Corps of Engineers led Congress to legislate incorrect methods of water transportation benefit measurement in the Transportation Act of 1965. Similar dissatifaction with the failure of irrigation projects to pass the benefit/cost test led Congress to dictate the use of inappropriate discount rates for many federal water projects.

Clearly, technical personnel must be allowed to use the best scientific methods in providing multiobjective evaluations of alternative policies or projects. On the other hand, technical agencies (e.g., the Bureau of Mines, Bureau of Reclamation, Corps of Engineers, State Departments of Natural Resources, etc.) must be required to provide unbiased analyses of the impacts of a policy or project on all national objectives. Agencies often become self-serving by catering to special interest groups and presenting heavily biased economic, environmental, and social analyses to the decision makers. Then benefit-cost analyses and environmental impact statements become ways of obfuscating the facts and keeping the project implications hidden. Unless agencies are allowed and required to use the most appropriate scientific methods and politicians are willing to make decisions on the basis of unbiased, publically available data, the applications of benefit-cost analysis, social impact analysis, and environmental impact statements will be a sham.

# BIBLIOGRAPHY

Anderson, Jay C., Alan P. Kleinman, and others, *Salinity Management Options for the Colorado River: Damage Estimates and Control Program Impacts*, Completion Report PRWG 149-1, Utah Water Research Laboratory, Utah State University, Logan, Utah, October 1977.

Arrow, K. J. and A. C. Fisher, "Environmental Preservation, Uncertainty, and Irreversibility," *Quarterly Journal of Economics*, Vol. 88, May 1974.

Barnett, Harold J., "Scarcity and Growth Revisited" in V. Kerry Smith (ed.), *Scarcity and Growth Reconsidered*, Baltimore: The Johns Hopkins Press, 1979.

Barnett, Harold J. and Chandler Morse, *Scarcity and Growth: The Economics of Natural Resource Availability*, Baltimore: The Johns Hopkins Press, 1963.

Baumol, William J. and Wallace E. Oates, *The Theory of Environmental Policy*, Englewood Cliffs, N.J.: Prentice-Hall, Inc., 1975.

Berndt, Ernst R. and David O. Wood, "Technology, Prices, and the Derived Demand for Energy," *Review of Economics and Statistics*, Vol. LVII, No. 3, August 1975, pp. 259–268.

Binswanger, Hans P. "The Measurement of Technical Change Biases with Many Factors of Production," *American Economic Review*, December 1974, pp. 964–976.

Bradford, David F., "Constraints on Government Investment Opportunities and the Choice of Discount Rate," *American Economic Review*, December 1975, pp. 887–899.

Bredehoeft, John D. and Robert A. Young, "The Temporal Allocation of Groundwater—A Simulation Approach," *Water Resources Research*, Vol. 6, No. 1, February 1970.

Brobst, Donald A., "Fundamental Concepts for the Analysis of Natural Resource Availability" in V. Kerry Smith (ed.), *Scarcity and Growth Reconsidered*, Baltimore: The Johns Hopkins Press, 1979.

Brown, Gardner, Jr. and Barry Field, "The Adequacy of Measures for Signalling the Scarcity of Natural Resources" in V. Kerry Smith (ed.), *Scarcity and Growth Reconsidered*, Baltimore: The Johns Hopkins Press, 1979.

Burt, O. R., "Optimal Resource Use Over Time with An Application to Groundwater," *Management Science*, Vol. 11, 1964, pp. 80–93.

Caudill, Harry M., *Night Comes to the Cumberlands*, Boston: Little, Brown and Co., 1963.

Chapman, D., T. Tyrrell, and T. Mount, "Electricity Demand Growth and the Energy Crisis," *Science*, Vol. 178, No. 4062, November 17, 1972, pp. 703–707.

Christensen, Laurits K. and William H. Greene, "Economies of Scale in U.S. Electric Power Generation," *Journal Political Economy*, August 1976, pp. 655–676.

Christy, Francis T., Jr., *Alternative Arrangements for Marine Fisheries: An Overview*, RfF/PISF-A Paper 1, Washington: Resources for the Future, Inc., May 1973.

Ciriacy-Wantrup, S. V., *Resource Conservation: Economics and Policies*, Berkeley: University of California Division of Agricultural Sciences, 1963.

Ciriacy-Wantrup, S. V. and Richard C. Bishop, "Common Property as a Concept in Natural Resource Policy," *Natural Resources Journal*, Vol. 15, No. 4, October 1975, pp. 713–728.

Clawson, Marion (ed.), *Forest Policy for the Future*, Resources for the Future, Inc., Working Paper LW-1, June 1974.

Clawson, Marion, *Forests: For Whom and For What?* Baltimore: The Johns Hopkins Press, 1975.

Clawson, Marion, "The National Forests: A Great National Asset Is Poorly Managed and Unproductive," *Science*, Vol. 191, No. 4228, February 20, 1976, pp. 762–767.

Clawson, Marion and Jack L. Knetsch, *Economics of Outdoor Recreation*, Baltimore: the Johns Hopkins Press, 1966.

Cole, H. S. D., Christopher Freeman, et al., *Models of Doom: A Critique of the Limits to Growth*: New York: Universe Books, 1973.

Cook, Earl, "Limits to Exploitation of Nonrenewable Resources," *Science*, 191(4228), February 20, 1976, pp. 677–682.

Crutchfield, James A. and Giulio Pontecorvo, *The Pacific Salmon Fisheries: A Study of Irrational Conservation*, Baltimore: The Johns Hopkins Press, 1969.

Daly, Herman E., "Entropy, Growth, and the Political Economy of Scarcity" in V. Kerry Smith (ed.), *Scarcity and Growth Reconsidered*, Baltimore: The Johns Hopkins Press, 1979.

Darmstadter, Joel and Hans H. Landsberg, "The Economic Background of the Oil Crisis," *Daedalus*, Journal of the American Academy of Arts and Sciences, Vol. 104, No. 4, Fall 1975.

Dasgupta, Partha and Geoffrey Heal, "The Optimal Depletion of Exhaustible Resources," *The Review of Economic Studies: Symposium on the Economics of Exhaustible Resources*, 1974, pp. 3–28.

Davis, Robert K., "The Value of Big Game Hunting in a Private Forest," Transactions of the 29th North American Wildlife and Natural Resources Conference, Washington, D.C.: The Wildlife Management Institute, 1964.

Dorcey, Anthony, H. J., "Effluent Charges, Information Generation, and Bargaining Behavior," *Natural Resources Journal*, Vol. 13, January 1973, pp. 118–133.

Eckstein, Otto, *Water-Resource Development: The Economics of Project Evaluation*, Cambridge, Mass.: Harvard University Press, 1961.

Fisher, Anthony C. and John V. Krutilla, "Valuing Long Run Ecological Consequences and Irreversibilities," *Journal of Environmental Economics and Management*, Vol. 1, No. 2, 1974, pp. 96–108.

Fisher, Anthony C., "On Measures of Natural Resource Scarcity" in V. Kerry Smith (ed.), *Scarcity and Growth Reconsidered*, Baltimore: The Johns Hopkins Press, 1979.

Freeman, A. Myrick III, Robert H. Haveman, and Allen V. Kneese. *The Economics of Environmental Policy*, New York: John Wiley and Sons, 1973.

Gramm, W. Philip, "The Energy Crisis in Perspective," *Wall Street Journal*, November 30, 1973.

Griffin, James M. and Paul R. Gregory, "An Intercountry Translog Model of Energy Substitution Responses," *American Economic Review*, Vol. 66, No. 5, December 1976, pp. 845–857.

Haveman, Robert H., "The Opportunity Cost of Displaced Private Spending and the Social Discount Rate," *Water Resources Research*, Vol. 5, No. 5, October 1969.

Haveman, Robert H., "Common Property, Congestion and Environmental Pollution," *Quarterly Journal of Economics*, Vol. LXXXVII, No. 2, May 1973, pp. 278–287.

Hayami, Yujiro and Vernon W. Ruttan, *Agricultural Development: An International Perspective*, Baltimore: The Johns Hopkins Press, 1971.

Hays, Samuel P., *Conservation and the Gospel of Efficiency: The Progressive Conservation Movement, 1890–1920*, Cambridge, Mass.: Harvard University Press, 1959.

Herfindahl, Orris C., *Copper Costs and Prices: 1870–1957*, Baltimore: The Johns Hopkins Press, 1959.

Herfindahl, Orris C., *Natural Resource Information for Economic Development*, Baltimore: The Johns Hopkins Press, 1969.

Hotelling, Harold, "The Economics of Exhaustible Resources," *Journal of Political Economy*, Vol. 39, No. 2, April 1931, pp. 137–175.

Howe, Charles W. and K. William Easter, *Interbasin Transfers of Water: Economic Issues and Impacts*, Baltimore: The Johns Hopkins Press, 1971.

Howe, Charles W. and F. P. Linaweaver, Jr., "The Impact of Price on Residential Water Demand and Its Relation to System Design and Price Structure," *Water Resources Research*, Vol. 3, First Quarter 1967 pp. 12–32.

Howe, C. W., "Municipal Water Demands" in W. R. Sewell and B. T. Bower, (eds.), *Forecasting the Demands for Water*, Ottawa: Queen's Printer, 1968.

Humphrey, David B. and J. R. Moroney, "Substitution Among Capital, Labor, and Natural Resource Products in American Manufacturing," *Journal of Political Economy*, February 1975, pp. 57–82.

James, Estelle, "A Note on Uncertainty and the Evaluation of Public Investment Decisions," *American Economic Review*, Vol. LXV, No. 1, March 1975.

Johnson, Edwin L., "A Study in the Economics of Water Quality Management," *Water Resources Research*, Vol. 3, No. 2, Second Quarter 1967, pp. 291–305.

Kates, Robert, *Industrial Flood Losses: Damage Estimation in the Lehigh Valley*, Department of Geography Research Paper No. 98, University of Chicago, 1965.

Kneese, Allen V., "The Faustian Bargain" in *Resources Newsletter*, No. 44, Sept. 1973, Resources for the Future, Inc., Washington, D.C.

Kneese, Allen V. and Charles L. Schultze, *Pollution, Prices, and Public Policy*, Washington, D.C.: The Brookings Institution, 1975.

Krenz, Jerrold H., "Energy and the Economy: An Interrelated Perspective," *Energy*, Vol. 2, 1977, pp. 115–130.

Krutilla, John V., "Conservation Reconsidered," *American Economic Review*, Vol. 57, No. 4, June 1967.

Krutilla, John V. and Anthony C. Fisher, *The Economics of Natural Environments*, Baltimore: The Johns Hopkins Press, 1975.

Krutilla, John V. and Otto Eckstein, *Multiple Purpose River Development*, Baltimore: The Johns Hopkins Press, 1958.

Landes, D. S., *The Unbound Prometheus: Technological Change and Industrial Development in Western Europe from 1750 to Present*, Cambridge: Cambridge University Press, 1969.

Landsberg, Hans H., Leonard L. Fischman, and Joseph L. Fisher, *Resources in America's Future: Patterns of Requirements and Availabilities, 1960–2000*, Baltimore: The Johns Hopkins Press, 1963.

Lave, Lester B. and Eugene P. Seskin, *Air Pollution and Human Health*, Baltimore: The Johns Hopkins University Press, 1977.

Lee, Dwight R., "Price Controls, Binding Constraints, and Intertemporal Economic Decision Making," *Journal of Political Economy*, Vol. 86, No. 2, Part 1, April 1978, pp. 293-302.

Lieberman, M. A., "United States' Uranium Resources—An Analysis of Historical Data," *Science*, Vol. 192, No. 4238, April 30, 1976, pp. 431-436.

Malthus, Thomas, *An Essay on Population*, reprint of 6th edition, London: Ward, Lock, and Company, 1826.

Marsh, George Perkins, *Man and Nature: or Physical Geography as Modified by Human Action*, New York: Charles Scribner, 1865.

Meadows, Donella H., Dennis L. Meadows, et al., *The Limits to Growth*, New York: Universe Books, 1972.

Meyer, R. F. (ed.), *The Future Supply of Nature-Made Petroleum and Gas*, Elmsford, N.Y.: Pergamon Press, 1977.

Nef, J. U., "The Progress of Technology and the Growth of Large-Scale Industry in Great Britain, 1540-1640," in E. M. Carus-Wilson (ed.), *Essays in Economic History, Vol. 1*, New York: St. Martin's Press, 1966.

Newell, Louis, "Lucius Nunn, AC Electricity Saved Colo. Mining in 1890's," *Denver Post*, October 5, 1975.

Nordhaus, W. D., "Resources as a Constraint on Growth," *American Economic Review Papers and Proceedings*, May 1974, pp. 22-26.

Page, Talbot, *Conservation and Economic Efficiency: An Approach to Materials Policy*, Baltimore: The Johns Hopkins University Press, 1977.

Pearse, P. H., "The Optimum Forest Rotation," *Forestry Chronicle*, June 1967.

Potter, Neal and Francis T. Christy, Jr., *Trends in Natural Resource Commodities: Statistics of Prices, Output, Consumption, Foreign Trade, and Employment in the United States, 1870-1957*, Baltimore: The Johns Hopkins Press, 1962.

President's Materials Policy Commission, *Resources for Freedom* (5 vols.), Washington: USGPO, June 1952.

Rawls, John, *A Theory of Justice*, Cambridge, Mass.: Belknap Press, 1971.

Ricardo, David, *Principles of Political Economy and Taxation*, London: Everyman edition, 1926.

Ridker, Ronald, *Economic Costs of Air Pollution*, New York: Praeger Publishers, 1967.

Rosenberg, Nathan, *Technology and American Economic Growth*, New York: Harper Torchbooks, 1972.

Rosenberg, Nathan, "Innovative Responses to Materials Shortages," Papers and Proceedings of the 85th Annual Meeting of the Amer. Econ. Association, May 1973, pp. 111-118.

Russell, Clifford S., David G. Arey, and Robert W. Kates, *Drought and Water Supply: Implications of the Massachusetts Experience for Municipal Planning*, Baltimore: The Johns Hopkins Press, 1970.

Schipper, Lee and Allan J. Lichtenberg, "Efficient Energy Use and Well-Being: The Swedish Example", *Science*, Vol. 194, No. 4269, December 3, 1976, pp. 1001-1013.

Scott, Anthony, *Natural Resources: The Economics of Conservation*, Ottawa: McClelland and Stewart Limited, Carleton Library No. 68, 1973.

Sheerin, John C., "The Dynamics of Resource Exhaustion Under Price Controls," Ph.D. Dissertation (unpublished), Dept. of Economics, University of Colorado, July 1977.

Smith, V. Kerry, "A Re-evaluation of the Natural Resource Scarcity Hypothesis," (mimeo) Resources for the Future, Inc., Washington, D.C., 1976.

Smith, V. Kerry (ed.), *Scarcity and Growth Reconsidered*, Baltimore: Johns Hopkins University Press, 1979.

Smith, Vernon L., "On Models of Commercial Fishing," *Journal of Political Economy*, Vol. 77, No. 2, March/April 1969, pp. 181–198.

Solow, R. M., "The Economics of Resources or the Resources of Economics," Papers and Proceedings of the 86th Annual Meeting of the American Economic Association, May 1974.

Solow, R. M., "Intergenerational Equity and Exhaustible Resources," *Review of Economic Studies: Symposium on the Economics of Exhaustible Resources*, 1974.

Spencer, Vivian Eberle, *Raw Materials in the United States Economy: 1900–1969*, U.S. Bureau of the Census and U.S. Bureau of Mines, Working Paper 35, U.S. Government Printing Office, 1972.

Spiegel, Henry William, *The Development of Economic Thought*, New York: John Wiley and Sons, 1952.

U.S. Bureau of Mines, "Availability of Uranium at Various Prices from Resources in the United States", Information Circular 8501, Washington: USGPO, 1971.

U.S. Commission on Population Growth and The American Future, Vol. 3, *Population, Resources, and the Environment*, Ronald G. Ridker (ed.), USGPO, 1972.

U.S. Water Resources Council, *The Nation's Water Resources*, Washington, D.C.: USGPO, 1968.

U.S. Water Resources Council, "Principles and Standards for Planning Water and Related Land Resources," *Federal Register*, Vol. 38, No. 174, part III, September 10, 1973.

White, Gilbert F., Anne U. White, and David J. Bradley, *Drawers of Water: Domestic Water Use in East Africa*, Chicago: University of Chicago Press, 1972.

White, Gilbert F. et al., *Changes in Urban Occupancy in Flood Plains in the United States*, Department of Geography Research Paper No. 57, University of Chicago, 1958.

Whitney, J. W., *Economic Geology*, 70(527), 1975.

Young, R. A. and John D. Bredehoeft, "Digital Computer Simulation for Solving Management Problems of Conjunctive Groundwater and Surface Water Systems," *Water Resources Research*, Vol. 8, No. 3, June 1972.

Zwartendyk, J., *What Is "Mineral Endowment" and How Should We Measure It?*, Mineral Bulletin MR126, Mineral Resources Branch, Dept. of Energy, Mines and Resources, Ottawa, Canada, 1972.

# Index

Abramovitz, Moses, 69
Acquifers, 279
Agriculture, irrigated, 136
Air pollution, 201
Allowable cut, 237
Anderson, Jay C., 306
Appropriation doctrine, 294
Arey, David G., 145
Army Corps of Engineers, U. S., 58
Arrow, K. J., 80n, 161, 321

Barnett, Harold J., 5, 10, 61, 117, 120, 239, 332
Baumol, William J., 252
Bayesean decision strategies, 212
Bayes theorem, 213, 215
Bell, Frederick H., 121n
Benefit-cost analysis, 237, 339
  biases in, 339
Berndt, Ernst R., 126, 175
Binswanger, Hans P., 124, 131n
Bishop, Richard C., 243
Biswas, Asit K., 285
Bower, Blair T., 142, 302
Bradley, David, 281
Bredehoeft, John D., 298
Brobst, Donald A., 205
Brown, Gardner M., Jr., 111, 112, 117, 125
Bureau of Land Management, U.S., 59, 222
Bureau of Mines, U.S., 9, 60
Bureau of Reclamation, U.S., 59
Burt, O. R., 298

Callaway, James A., 314
Carroll, Joseph L., 254
Carrying capacities, 322
Caudill, Harry M., 4
Chapman, D., 175

Charcoal, 45
Chesapeake Bay, 251
Christenson, Laurits K., 13, 125, 126, 138
Cicchetti, Charles J., 252, 319
Ciriacy-Wantrup, S. V., 166, 243, 335
Clawson, Marion, 55, 225, 324
Club of Rome, 3
Coal, 45, 169
  gasification of, 6
Colorado River, 278, 279, 291, 293
Colorado River Compact, 291
Commission on Population Growth and the American Future, U.S., 127, 332
Common property, 111, 245, 248, 249
  res communes, 243
  res nullius, 244
Common property resources, 218, 241, 263, 302
Comparative advantage, 233
Competitive equilibrium, 245
Comstock Lode, 205
Congestion, 245, 246
Conjunctive management, 279, 295
Conservation, 52, 53, 54
Conservation movement, 52
Constant effective natural resource base, 336
Constant elasticity of substitution production function, 85, 86
Consumer surplus, 321
Control theory, 80, 91, 210
Cook, Earl, 204, 205
Costs, 108
Council on Environmental Quality, U.S., 59
Crustal abundance of minerals, 23, 203, 205
Crutchfield, James A., 256, 257, 261

Cummings, Ronald G., 195, 297, 299
Cut off grades of minerals, 203

Daly, Herman E., 165, 167
Darmstadter, Joel, 171
Dasgupta, Partha, 83, 84, 85, 121
Data base, 335
Decision making process, 337
Delaware River, 308
Demand, oil, 177
Department of Energy, U.S., 59
Discount factors, 228
Discounting, 149, 152, 158
Discovery, 12, 132, 211, 219
Dorcey, Anthony H. J., 309
Drought, 288

Ecological constraints, 253
Economic Development Administration,
    U.S., 60
Economics, normative, 15
    policy formation, 14
    positive, 15
Economic threshold, 205
Ecosystems, 316
Efficiency, 149
    Pareto, 151
Effluent standards, 252
Effluent taxes, 251
Electric power generation, 139
Electronics, 137
Employment, 33
    in resource industries, 32
Energy, 169
    demand for, 170
    new supplies, 186
    price of, 185
Energy consumption, 169
    U.S., 172
    world, 171, 172
Energy crisis, 170, 173, 177
Energy intensiveness, 178, 179, 180
Energy use, international comparison,
    181, 183
    per dollar of value added, 185
English common law, 242
Environment, 18, 248
    as amenity and constraint, 328
    conditions, 5
    services of, 4
Environmental amenities, 109

Environmental constraint, 241
Environmental effects, 94, 110
Environmental impact statements, 339
Environmental Protection Agency, U.S.,
    59
Environmental standards, 110
Environmental systems, 336
Equity, 149
Esthetic values, 232
Exploration, 9, 18, 19, 203, 208, 211, 212,
    219
Exploration production function, 209, 260
Externalities, 241, 249, 285
Extinction, 264

Field, Barry, 111, 112, 117, 125
Fisher, Anthony C., 108, 161, 166, 209, 321
Fisheries, 250, 256, 259
    competitive conditions, 263, 269
    dynamic behavior, 267
    open access, 270
    regulation of, 271, 274
Fisheries management, 261
    optimum over time, 264
Fish and Wildlife Service, U.S., 60
Floods, 280
Foreign trade, 225
Forest lands, 221, 222
Forest management, 221
    multiple use, 232
    fully regulated forest, 235
Forestry, high yield, 240
Forest Service, U.S., 29, 222, 253
Frankel, Richard, 326
Freeman, A. Myrick III, 252, 319
Frontier economy, 62, 63, 65, 67, 87
Futures markets, 102, 103

Gas, see Natural gas
Gas hydrates, 195
General equilibrium, 62
General Mining Act of 1871, 59
Geological Survey, U.S., 9, 58, 188
Geothermal energy, hot dry rock, 195
Godwin, William, 50
Goodwin, J. T., 325
Government agencies, U.S., 58
Government regulations, 114
Gramm, W. Philip, 6
Greene, William H., 13, 125, 126, 138
Gregory, Paul R., 126, 175

Griffin, James M., 126, 175
Griliches, Zvi, 132
Groundwater, 276, 279
  management of, 295, 297, 301
Growth, regional, 15
Growth potential, economic, 83
Grubb, H. W., 325

Hamiltonian function, 92
Hanke, S. H., 313
Haveman, Robert H., 252
Hayami, Yujiro, 131
Heal, Geoffrey, 83, 84, 85, 121
Health effects of air pollution, coal mining,
  202
Heavy oil, 190
Hedgers, 102
Hedges, Trimble R., 315
Helium storage program, 152
Herfindahl, Orris C., 54, 112, 140
Historical episodes, 44
Hotelling, Harold, 94, 324
Howe, Charles W., 254, 285, 312
Humphrey, David B., 124
Hydrograph, 277

Income taxation, effects on resource
  production, 103
Industrial revolution, 3
Information, from exploration, 219
  value of, 211, 215
*In situ* resources, 18, 63
  markets for, 103
  prices of, 110, 118
  rents on, 75, 119, 208
  stock of, 16
Intertemporal comparisons of well-being,
  149
Intertemporal decisions, 151
Intriligator, Michael C., 80n
Inventories, optimum, 24
Iron making, 44
Iron ore, 47
Irreversibilities, 317, 336
Irrigation practices, 282

Jevons, William Stanley, 6, 46
Johnson, Edwin L., 308
Johnson, Manuel H., 121

Kates, Robert W., 145, 280

Kelvin, Lord, 56
Kleinman, Alan P., 306
Kneese, Allen V., 252, 302
Knetsch, Jack L., 55, 324
Kraynick, Roger, 148n
Krenz, Jerrold H., 179, 180, 183
Krutilla, John V., 161, 167, 317, 329
Kuhn-Tucker conditions, 306
Kurz, M., 80n

Lagrange technique, 75
Landsberg, Hans H., 171
Lave, Lester B., 201, 306
Leasing policies, 104
Lee, Dwight R., 105, 266
Leopold, Luna, 55
Licensing, 271
Lichtenberg, Allan J., 182, 184, 185, 186
Lieberman, M. A., 197, 198, 199, 200
Lifestyle, 334
*Limits to Growth*, 3
Linaweaver, F. P., Jr., 312

Maass, Arthur, 158
McFarland, James W., 195
Major, David B., 158
Malthus, Thomas Robert, 49
Malthusian Model, 68
Manthy, Robert, 115
Marglin, Stephen, 157
Market, 177, 336
  failure of, 103
  role of, 5
Market adjustment processes, 89, 98
Market structure, competitive, 94
  monopolistic, 97
Marsh, George Perkins, 7, 54
Marshall, Alfred, 52, 151
Maximin criterion, 167
Maximum sustainable yield, 260, 262
Mercury, production and prices, 114
Meyer, R. F., 187, 188, 189, 190, 192, 193
Mill, John Stuart, 51
Mineral availability, 203
Mineralogical threshold, 205, 206, 207
Mitigating factors for scarcity, 129
  future, 147
Moore, Charles V., 315
Moroney, J. R., 124
Morse, Chandler, 5, 10, 61, 120, 239, 332
Mount, T., 175

Multiple objective planning, 285, 338
Multiple Use-Sustained Yield Act of
    1960, 59, 223

National forests, 223
National Oceanic and Atmospheric
    Administration, U.S., 60
National Park Service, U.S., 222
Natural areas, 316
  economic aspects of, 318
Natural gas, 169, 193
  in pressure zones, 194
  U.S., 173
Natural resource commodities, 18
Natural resources policy, elements of
    responsible policy, 338
Nondeclining even flow forest policy, 237
Nordhaus, W. D., 116, 117n
Nuclear power, 196
Nunn, Susan C., 195

Oats, Wallace E., 252
Ogallala acquifer, 134, 279
Oil, *see* Petroleum
Oil shale, 191
Open access resource, 243
Opportunity cost, 155
  intertemporal, 75
Optimum resource use over time, 89, 90,
    208
Optimum rotation, forest, 225, 227, 228,
    229
Option demand, 318
Ore minerals, 207
Organization of Petroleum Exporting
    Countries, 127, 169, 174
Outdoor recreation, demand for, 321
Overfishing, 257

Page, Talbot, 332, 337
Paley Commission, *see* President's
    Materials Policy Commission
Pannu, Sikhraj Singh, 266
Petroleum, 169, 173, 186
  deep ocean, 191
  imports of, 171
Pigou, A. C., 156
Pinchot, Gifford, 7, 53, 56, 221
Policy formation, 15
Policy guidelines, 335
Pollution, 248

  air, 201
Pontecorvo, Giulio, 256, 257, 261
Powell, John Wesley, 58
President's Materials Policy Commission,
    7, 48
Price, 35, 108, 109, 110, 146, 336
  energy, 185
  as indicators of scarcity, 111
  of *in situ* resources, 110, 114
  lumber, 238
  oil, 170, 173
  raw materials, 35
  relative, 11, 114, 115
  timber, 239
  water, 312
Price controls, 105
Price and income elasticities, electricity
    demand, 175
Price movements, 111
Price regulations, 104
Principles and Standards for Planning
    Water and Related Land Resources,
    285, 338
Property rights, 245
Public goods, 177

Quasi-option value, 321
Quimby, Thomas, H. E., 142

Ramsey, Frank, 156
Rawls, John, 167
Reaction function, 310
Recreation, 31
  carrying capacity, 252
  demand estimation, 323
  participation studies, 322
  values, 232
Recycling, 12, 140
Rent, 108, 110, 224
  on *in situ* natural resources, 75, 108, 119,
    208
  land, 50
  Ricardian, 76, 77, 78, 119
  scarcity, 78, 79, 88, 109, 110, 119, 211
Research and development, 14, 148, 337
Reserves, 3, 4, 7, 9, 10, 19, 21, 24
  natural gas, 37
  non fuel minerals, 38-41
  oil, 36, 37
  proved, 21
Reserves-to-use ratios, 17, 25, 26

Reservoirs, 277
Resources, 8, 20, 21
  common property, 9
  identified, 22
  *in situ*, 18
  non renewable, 136
  renewable, 3, 136, 256, 335
  undiscovered, 22
Resource base, 8, 20
Resource consumption, 28, 29, 30
Resource pyramid, 207
Resource recovery, 134
Resource triangle, 211, 219
Return flows, 289
  multiplier, 290
Ricardian economy, 62, 64, 65, 67, 87
  with technical change, 69
Ricardo, David, 7, 50
Ridker, Ronald, 127, 306, 332
Ripp diagram, 287
Risk, 149, 160, 164
  attitude towards, 213
  bearing, 334
  of exploration, 212
  pooling, 163
  spreading, 163
Roosevelt, Theodore, 59
Rosenberg, Nathan, 130, 135
Runoff, 282
Russell, Clifford S., 145
Ruttan, Vernon W., 131, 137

Safe yield, 295
Scale economies, 137
Scarcity, 10, 61, 62, 108, 129
  empirical indicators of, 108
  increasing, 112
  index of, 10
Scarcity rents, 78, 79, 88, 109, 110, 119, 211
Schipper, Lee, 182, 184, 185, 186
Schmookler, Jacob, 132
Schultze, Charles L., 252, 302
Schumacher, E. F., 151
Schwartz, Andrew K., Jr., 314
Scott, Anthony, 54
Seskin, Eugene P., 201, 306
Severance tax, 231
Sheerin, John C., 105
Shipbuilding, 45
Simple Ricardian economy, *see* Ricardian
  economy

Smith, Vernon L., 267, 269
Smith, V. Kerry, 115, 117, 252, 329, 332
Social discount rate, 162
Social time preference, 154, 155, 156, 157
Soil Conservation Service, U.S., 59
Solow, Robert M., 13, 85, 86, 121, 167
South Platte River, 326
Special interest groups, 339
Speculator, 101, 102
Spofford, Walter O., Jr., 140n, 141
Stability of resource markets, 101
Steady state, 261, 303
Stock, 19
  *in situ*, 16
  natural resources, 18
Stock effects, 71, 72, 73, 75, 78, 88, 94, 149
Stock-growth relation, 260
Storage-yield curves, 289
Stripper oil wells, 119
Stumpage, Douglas Fir, 112
Stumpage value, 226
Substitution, 12, 112
  in consumption, 139, 334
  elasticity of, 112, 121, 122
  partial elasticities of, 123
  in production, 135
Supreme Court decree of 1964, 294
Survey method, 323
Sweden, 181, 182, 183

Taconite, 48
Tar sands, 193
Taxes, 271
Technological change, 11, 69, 87, 130, 132,
  134, 135, 148
  asymmetry of, 137
Telluride, Colorado, 12, 129
Texas Water Development Board, 325
Thompson, Russell G., 314
Timber, 44, 45
  appraisal of, 235
  management of, 221
  production of, 223
Trade, 12, 15, 139
  agricultural, 42
  extractive, 42
  fuels, 42
  international, 37, 335
  minerals, 42
Transportation, 139
Travel cost method, 324

Tyrrell, T., 175

Uncertainty, 160
Unit production cost, 109, 110
Upper Basin Compact of 1954, 294
Uranium, 196, 197, 199, 200
  oxide, 22
User cost, 71, 75, 78, 79, 88, 119

Walsh, Richard G., 326
Waste, 144, 145
  radioactive, 200
Water-born diseases, 281
Water consumptive uses, 277
  demand for, 311
  marginal value of in agriculture, 315
  withdrawal, 277
Water demand functions, 312
Water quality, 281, 294, 302

minimum cost, 307
  two case studies, 308
Water resource systems, 276, 312
  development of, 282
Water supply, cost of, 290
Water systems developments, 282
Water use, household, 312
Weather modification, 280
Whale oil, 6
White, Anne U., 281
White, Gilbert F., 280
Willingness to pay, 323
Wisconsin River, 309
Wood, David O., 126, 175
Wood-using technologies, 135

Young, Robert A., 298

Zoned effluent charge, 310, 311